Building English Skills

Purple Level
Revised Edition

Building English Skills

PURPLE LEVEL

Yellow Level

Blue Level

Orange Level

Green Level

Red Level

Gold Level

Silver Level

Aqua Level

Brown Level

Plum Level

Pink Level

Cherry Level (K)

THE McDOUGAL, LITTELL ENGLISH PROGRAM

Building English Skills

Purple Level
Revised Edition

Joy Littell, EDITORIAL DIRECTOR

McDougal, Littell & Company
Evanston, Illinois
Sacramento, California

Prepared by the Staff of
THE WRITING IMPROVEMENT PROJECT

Joy Littell, Editorial Director, McDougal, Littell & Company

Sylvia Z. Brodkin, formerly, West Hempstead High School,
West Hempstead, New York

Eric Kraft, Writer and Editor, Stow, Massachusetts

Robert J. Lumsden, Evanston Township High School, Evanston, Illinois

Elizabeth J. Pearson, formerly, West Hempstead High School,
West Hempstead, New York

Agnes Stein, English Department, Bloomfield College, Bloomfield, New Jersey

Marcia Baldwin Whipps, East High School, Salt Lake City, Utah

The Staff wishes to thank the more than 1500 students who contributed samples of their writing for analysis.

Acknowledgments: See page 536.

ISBN: 0–88343–926–3

Contents

Handbook

1.0 The Classification of Words 335

2.0 The Parts of a Sentence 383

3.0 Sentence and Clause 414

4.0 Complete Sentences 435

5.0 Agreement of Subject and Verb 446

6.0 Pronoun Usage 460

7.0 Adjective and Adverb Usage 483

8.0 Verb Usage 492

9.0 The Right Word 512

10.0 Capitalization 522

11.0 End Marks and Commas 535

12.0 The Semicolon, the Colon, the Dash, and Parentheses 550

13.0 The Apostrophe 559

14.0 Quotations 566

15.0 Spelling 573

16.0 The Plurals of Nouns 583

17.0 The Forms of Letters 588

18.0 Good Manuscript Form 596

The Composition Chapters (First half of text)

Vocabulary Development. Chapter 1 emphasizes *word distinctions, development of a critical vocabulary,* and *context clues.* An adequate vocabulary, and the ability to use synonyms precisely, are prerequisites to good writing.

Sentence Combining. Chapter 2 presents a basic course in sentence combining. Its purpose is to help students create mature sentences, and to help them become aware of the options open to them in combining ideas.

Sentence Improvement. Chapters 3–6 provide an intensive program for sentence improvement based on a study of over 3000 student themes. The chapters deal with those sentences which, though grammatically correct, are nonetheless unsatisfactory. For example, Chapter 3 deals with empty sentences, the circular sentences that say nothing (pages 46–48); it also deals with overloaded sentences, the sentences that contain too many ideas (pages 48–50).

The Process of Writing. Chapter 7 analyzes the three major steps in writing: *pre-writing, writing the first draft;* and *rewriting, or revising,* which includes proofreading.

The Paragraph. Chapters 8–10 provide an intensive study of the paragraph. All three chapters provide a wealth of first-rate models, along with helpful analysis.

The Composition. Chapter 11 provides a clear, workable blueprint for all expository writing longer than a paragraph.

The Paraphrase and the Summary. Chapter 11 involves students in writing the paraphrase and the summary, invaluable tools in research and writing.

Writing about Literature. Chapter 13 analyzes a short story and three poems as a basis for writing a critical analysis.

The Research Paper. Chapter 14 provides a step-by-step method for writing a research paper. A sample research paper is included.

The Handbook (Second half of text)

The Handbook is arranged in 18 numbered sections, as follows:

Grammar. Sections 1–4 provide a thorough treatment of grammar in a contemporary setting.

Usage. Sections 5–9 deal with problems of usage.

Capitalization, Punctuation, Spelling, and Manuscript Form. Sections 10–18 deal with the mechanics of writing.

Special Features of the Handbook. The Handbook has distinct advantages over other available handbooks:

1. The typographic arrangement is clear and attractive. Type and open space have been used to set off definitions and examples so as to make them easy to find and easy to read.

2. Within each topic, there is a full explanation of each concept, followed by examples, and where appropriate, by the definition or generalization printed in boldface type.

Chapter 1

Vocabulary Development

Everything you read affects you in some way. What you read may bring you pleasure or displeasure, even when it was primarily meant to inform, persuade, or amuse you. No matter what you read, you react. Part of your reaction is your criticism of the work. *Criticism* in this case means analysis and judgment.

What you feel about a work may be difficult to express. You may be able to say that you like or dislike a short story, for example, or that you think it is good or bad. However, if you must support and elaborate your opinion with specific reasoning, you may be at a loss for words.

Whether you continue your education or enter the business world, the situations that require precise criticism will increase. The purpose of this chapter is to help you equip yourself with a vocabulary to use in evaluating people and things and in analyzing literature and events.

Part 1 Studying Distinctions Among Words

Words that have similar meanings are called **synonyms.** Most synonyms do not have exactly the same meaning. They are not interchangeable. Synonyms share the same general meaning, but have different shades of that meaning.

Why study synonyms? There are two good reasons. First, a knowledge of synonyms will make your reading more exact. A good writer chooses words with care. If you know the distinctions among words, you will get more out of your reading. If you do not, you will miss much of what a good writer has to say. Second, if you know the distinctions among words, you can state your own meaning more precisely. Your speech and writing will be more vivid and more persuasive. They will achieve your purpose more surely and more effectively.

Study the following **synonymy** (comparison of synonyms) for *naive.** Note how all the words are related, and also how they differ in specific meanings.

naive implies simplicity and innocent trust, but sometimes suggests an almost foolish lack of worldly wisdom [his *naive* belief that all advertising is honest].

ingenuous suggests a childlike frankness or straightforwardness [his *ingenuous* delight in any kind of flattery].

artless implies the appealing open and natural quality of one who is indifferent to the effect he or she has on others [a simple, *artless* style of folk singing].

unsophisticated implies a lack of poise, worldliness, subtlety, etc. resulting from a limited experience of life [an *unsophisticated* farm boy].

* These distinctions are based on those found in *Webster's New World Dictionary*, Students Edition.

You can see that these four words are similar in meaning, yet distinct in the exact shade of meaning each conveys. If you are looking for a word with the general meaning that these four words share, you can search among the synonyms for the exact shade of that general meaning that best expresses your idea.

How can you learn the synonyms of words in common use? You can learn some of them by reading and attentive listening, but this is a slow process. A more effective method is to go to a dictionary. Among the standard dictionaries, you can find a full treatment of synonyms in *Webster's New World Dictionary*, Students Edition. *Webster's Dictionary of Synonyms* is also useful.

If you are interested in expanding your vocabulary, you will find the following procedure helpful.

1. Study a synonymy in a dictionary.
2. Write down the distinctions among the synonyms.
3. Compose sentences that illustrate these distinctions.
4. Try substituting one synonym for another in your sentences so that you will get a feeling for the distinctions among words.

Exercises Distinctions Among Words

A. The word *suave* and its synonyms demonstrate the different implications carried by words of similar meaning.

suave implies the smoothly gracious social manner of one who deals with people easily and tactfully, sometimes suggesting a surface politeness too smooth to be convincing [his *suave* manner with waiters].

urbane suggests the social ease of a highly cultured person with much worldly experience [an *urbane* conversation on European theater].

diplomatic implies skill and tact in dealing with people and handling delicate situations, sometimes in such a way as to gain one's own ends [a *diplomatic* answer].

politic also expresses this idea, often emphasizing the immediate practical reasons for doing a thing [a *politic* move].

Use correctly in an original sentence each of the four synonyms above. Be sure that each sentence carries the precise meaning that the word implies.

B. Look up the distinctions among the following groups of synonyms. Use each synonym correctly in an original sentence.

1. likeness, similarity, resemblance
2. think, reason, cogitate, reflect, speculate, deliberate
3. aversion, antipathy, repugnance, abhorrence, loathing
4. brave, courageous, bold, audacious, valiant, intrepid, plucky
5. bear, suffer, endure, tolerate, stand, brook

C. Consult your dictionary to answer the following questions.

1. You go to a play that someone has told you is *funny*. One scene makes you laugh until you ache. Would you describe the scene as *amusing* or *comical?*

2. You can *criticize* a color-blind friend for the color combinations he wears, but can you *blame* him?

3. If you are reading a *copy* of the Declaration of Independence, are you looking at a *duplicate* or a *facsimile?*

4. If you ran three miles you would undoubtedly be *tired*. Would you describe yourself more accurately as *weary* or *exhausted?*

5. When a candidate hears he has lost the election, he tries to face his supporters with *equanimity*. Would you describe his bearing as one of *composure* or of *nonchalance?*

6. Is an *intelligent* person necessarily *intellectual?* Explain.

7. There are *many* stars in the sky. Would you say the stars are *numerous* or *innumerable?*

8. What makes a *plot* a *conspiracy?*

9. Would you be more comfortable with someone who is *frank* or with someone who is *open?* How does an *outspoken* individual make you feel?

10. If all people are *equal*, are they the *same?* Are they *equivalent?* Are they *identical?*

D. Shakespeare was a master of the use of the exact word. Study the following passage:

> Good name in man, and woman, dear my lord,
> Is the immediate jewel of their souls:
> Who *steals* my purse *steals* trash: 'tis something, nothing;
> 'Twas mine, 'tis his, and has been slave to thousands;
> But he that *filches* from me my good name
> *Robs* me of that which not enriches him,
> And makes me poor indeed.
>
> —*Othello*

Look up the three verbs *steal, filch,* and *rob* in the dictionary. Be prepared to explain what you think Shakespeare's reasons were for using each of these three words in its particular context.

E. Study the synonymy for the word *make* in *Webster's New World Dictionary,* Students Edition. Substitute a more precise synonym for *make* in the sentences below.

1. General Electric *makes* many kinds of appliances.
2. Mr. Jaspers was *making* a bird house for his backyard.
3. Marty *made* the bread dough into several long, thin loaves.
4. Meg *made* a trivet by gluing cork bottle stoppers together.

F. From your dictionary or a dictionary of synonyms, choose two synonymies that you find particularly interesting. Explain your reasons for thinking that it is important to know the distinctions among the synonyms given in each group. Make these distinctions clear by using each word in a sentence.

Part 2 Developing a Vocabulary of Criticism

By this time you should be aware of two important facts about English words.

1. Most words in common use have more than one meaning.
2. You never get all of the meaning of a word in any one encounter with it.

For example, take the word *criticism*. You have long been familiar with its meaning of "finding fault." However, the word is also used to name "the act of analyzing and of making judgments." This is the sense with which we are concerned at this point.

Making judgments is as common an act in your life as breathing. In fact, you cannot stay alive without making judgments. You have to analyze every situation in which you find yourself if for no other reason than to decide whether it is dangerous to you. In the classroom, the teacher asks a question. As a student, you must size up the question and determine whether you can make a reasonable answer. You must also reflect upon the importance to you of trying to make an answer. You may decide that you have not been carrying your weight in the classroom discussion and decide that it is time you did so. You may judge that you ought to make a try at an answer even though you are not sure of it.

This is one kind of analysis—the analysis of a situation. Every day you make countless other analyses and judgments. You judge the speech, actions, and character of friends and others you meet. You judge clothes, food, books, news accounts, and traffic conditions. For each of these judgments, there are exact and specific words that help you state your findings. More than that, these judgment words help you *think* about the things, people, and events in the world around you. They help to sharpen your perceptions and pinpoint your reactions.

You can make two kinds of judgments about things. You can react *subjectively*, which is to respond to your feelings about the thing you are criticizing. To say that something is "great," "okay," or "poor" is to give only the thinnest of subjective judgments. These words say nothing about the thing you are criticizing. They reflect only your feelings about the thing, and not very precisely at that!

As an alternative, you can judge something by trying to identify its qualities, or by being *objective*. To criticize something objectively is to use words that carry specific information to others about the thing you are judging. What can be said, for example, about another person? How can the person's personality, manner, intelligence, or character be described? Here is a sample of possibilities.

Words Useful for Describing People

Personality	Manner	Intelligence	Character
cold	forthright	quick	strong
aloof	outspoken	keen	reliable
reserved	frank	sharp	selfless
retiring	candid	agile	dependable
restrained	straightforward	fine	trustworthy
cool	debonaire	incisive	spotless
warm	ingratiating	acute	determined
vibrant	patronizing	brilliant	certain
buoyant	charming	bright	sure
bubbly	devil-may-care	nimble	selfish
vivacious	carefree	alert	demanding
outgoing	footloose	astute	thoughtless
attractive	brusque	clever	driven
compelling	curt	ingenious	calculating
charming	rude	creative	egoistic
magnetic	bluff	slow	self-serving
appealing	blunt	dull	vain
fascinating	abrupt	dim	weak
beguiling	short	limited	sheepish
adorable	sullen	ignorant	helpless
bewitching	surly	foolish	limp
repulsive	glum	silly	spineless
repelling	sulky	senseless	insipid
revolting	grouchy	shallow	listless
hideous	sharp	irrational	irresolute
vile	cross	unreasonable	uncertain
unsavory	irritable	mad	wishy-washy
disagreeable	cantankerous		fickle
unpleasant	testy		
obnoxious	calculating		
odious			

Similarly, an objective judgment of a motion picture or TV program can go far beyond the vague, subjective judgments that underlie *great*, *dull*, or *poor*. The characters can be discussed in the terms listed above. But what about the acting, the pace, the story, or the sound effects? Another sample of possibilities is shown below.

Words Useful for Criticism of Motion Pictures and TV Programs

Acting	Pace	Story	Sound Effects
inspired	brisk	contrived	complementary
natural	quick	artificial	supportive
realistic	lively	unbelievable	appropriate
relaxed	breakneck	calculated	jarring
truthful	hasty	maudlin	annoying
melodramatic	abrupt	clever	distracting
overblown	slow	bewildering	inappropriate
exaggerated	lethargic	baffling	intrusive
affected	leisurely	surprising	
unbelievable	relaxed	realistic	
unnatural	indolent		
wooden	halting		
uninspired	measured		
clumsy	irregular		
thoughtless	jerky		
careless			

Attempting to be objective in your judgments will have more than one benefit.

1. An objective criticism will carry more information and be more precise.

2. Making an objective criticism will require you to look at what you are criticizing with an open mind.

3. Searching for words to relay an objective criticism with precision and clarity will help you *think* more precisely and more clearly.

4. An objective criticism will earn the respect of your audience not only for the judgment you express but also for the critical effort that underlies it.

Exercises **Developing a Vocabulary of Criticism**

A. What can be said about a dress? Make a list of judgment words that convey precise information. These will be nouns as well as adjectives. Avoid words like *lovely, divine, adorable*. Consult fashion pages of newspapers and magazines for suggestions.

B. What can be said about a sports car? Make a list of judgment words that carry concrete information. Consult a sports car magazine for suggestions.

C. What can be said about the weather? You can describe the weather, and you can also describe its effects: *depressing, enervating*, for example. Consult the first stanza of "The Eve of St. Agnes" by John Keats for suggestions.

D. Think about a motion picture you have seen recently. What judgments can be made about it? What can you say more specifically than *great, dull*, or *poor?* What about the acting, costumes, sound effects? You might think of the aspects of a motion picture for which Oscars are awarded.

E. Substitute a precise judgment word for each of the italicized words in the following sentences.

1. It was a *good* game.
2. Bobby is a *neat* dancer.
3. *Stories from the Twilight Zone* is a *great* book.
4. The music at the party was *poor*.
5. The movie was *funny*.
6. The Mercedes-Benz is a *terrific* car.

F. Below are ten subjective criticisms. Write a paragraph of objective criticism for two of the items. Example: a good audience

> The audience was familiar with the music and became involved with the soloist's interpretation of the sonata. When the program was over, the audience rose for a standing ovation and demanded an encore, which the violinist obligingly gave.

1. an ideal vacation
2. bad news
3. a good friend
4. an elegant dinner
5. a friendly dog
6. nice hair
7. a comfortable house
8. soothing music
9. an appetizing meal
10. the perfect gift

Part 3 The Language of Literary Criticism

As you react with greater and greater maturity and sensitivity to the world around you, you will become more and more aware of the importance of a vocabulary of criticism—a vocabulary that will help you describe and evaluate the people, places, and things around you.

In your study of books, plays, motion pictures, and so on, you may already have become aware of the need for such a vocabulary. You need words to analyze the characters you meet—their words, actions, and motives. You need words to evaluate the style or form of a piece of writing.

For these purposes, you need more than just an understanding of the connotations of common words and a knowledge of common synonyms. You need a vocabulary with depth and scope, a store of words from which you can take the *one* word that best conveys the *precise meaning* you have in mind.

If, for example, you are criticizing a scene from a novel in which a character describes a childhood of suffering and deprivation, a scene in which you feel the writer successfully moves the reader to a feeling of pity for the character, will you characterize the scene as *pathos* or as *bathos?*

If you are discussing a protagonist who is roguish and appealing and appears in a series of humorous or satiric adventures, will you classify the character as a *romantic idealist* or as a *picaresque hero?*

If a writer includes a passage that is intended to represent the thoughts of a character, a passage that mixes memories, anxieties, and everyday concerns, will you say that the writer has used a *stream of consciousness technique* or *stark realism?*

If you are reading a novel described as in the tradition of the *Gothic novel* of Ann Radcliffe, will you expect it to be about the ancient Goths, to be set in a Gothic cathedral, or to have a mood of horror?

A good dictionary will answer these questions for you, but terms like those italicized above must become your stock in trade if you are to achieve that depth and breadth of language necessary to the understanding and enjoyment of literature.

Exercises **The Language of Literary Criticism**

A. The following sentences contain words that will be useful to you in expressing judgments about books, motion pictures, plays, and so on. Examine carefully each underlined word and be able to tell the class exactly what each sentence means. If you are not sure, consult your dictionary.

1. The <u>atmosphere</u> of Poe's "The Fall of the House of Usher" is one of mystery.

2. The <u>mood</u> of Barry's *Joyous Season* is not really one of joy at all but rather of a happiness that shows the leading character in tears at the final curtain.

3. Susan Glaspell builds up <u>suspense</u> in *Trifles* by skillfully introducing obstacles that the women must overcome to gain their ends.

4. Some people hold that Holden Caulfield in *Catcher in the Rye* is not fully <u>believable</u>.

5. The <u>imagery</u> of Keats's poems is very <u>rich</u>.

6. The <u>dialogue</u> in Hemingway's short stories is <u>racy</u> and <u>pungent</u>.

7. Robert Frost relies less upon metaphor than upon tone to achieve his effects.

8. The most important aspect of poetry is sound, and therefore a poem must be read aloud to be fully appreciated.

9. "The Purloined Letter," by Edgar Allan Poe, was the first of a new genre, the detective story.

10. Bernard Shaw was regarded by his contemporaries as an iconoclast.

11. Tennessee Williams frequently uses the South and its people as his milieu.

12. Because of the sensational action of the new play, critics classified it as outright melodrama.

13. *Oedipus Rex* is an outstanding example of irony.

14. The climax of *The Bridge of San Luis Rey* comes at the beginning of the book with the collapse of the bridge, and justifies the telling of the tale.

15. In "Stopping by Woods on a Snowy Evening," the horse, without losing its identity as a horse, also becomes a symbol.

B. A comprehensive knowledge of the words that describe people, places, and events is indispensable to good writing. Examine the words underscored below, define each exactly, and use each correctly in an original sentence. If you are not sure of any word, use your dictionary. Also, master the pronunciation of the word.

1. lethargic disposition
2. dour expression
3. vicarious enjoyment
4. mendacious personality
5. stentorian tones
6. scurrilous remarks
7. didactic literature
8. auspicious beginning
9. impeccably attired
10. indefensible conduct
11. sanguinary in nature
12. vacillating character
13. genteel manner
14. malodorous atmosphere
15. pertinacious individual
16. sophisticated manner
17. morbid obsession
18. abject poverty
19. ironic situation
20. poignant ending

C. Here is a test of your skill in evaluating people. Supply the name of a person—fictional or historical—who you feel would fit each adjective given below.

Example: procrastinating: Hamlet

1. garrulous	6. quixotic	11. senile
2. ambitious	7. compassionate	12. naive
3. cunning	8. treacherous	13. suave
4. magnanimous	9. subservient	14. egotistical
5. obsequious	10. implacable	15. humble

D. *The Hairy Ape,* by Eugene O'Neill, carries the following paragraphs in its preface. Read them thoughtfully; then answer the questions that follow.

> Eugene O'Neill is not only America's outstanding playwright: he is also chief of her dramatic rebels. But his rebellion is not against institutions or individuals; it is the more radical one aimed at spiritual slavery and effete convention. He is the dramatic apostle of a new vitality for man and art. His plays are a prologue to the great emancipation—the freeing of the human spirit. His leading characters are recruited from the ranks of those who, perhaps like himself, are the victims of a hypocritical civilization that represses and tortures the soul, while it romantically proclaims its liberty. Enmeshed in a confusion of restraints . . . they contend with tragic futility for self-expression. Even their goals of happiness are illusory. For most of them there is only defeat. But in the struggle each achieves a symbolic grandeur that is O'Neill's chief contribution to our theatre.
>
> Man's good, he seems to say, is in courageous striving if only he is true to his instinctive faith in his own spiritual value against the assaults of man-made conventions. In such strife he finds joy.
>
> O'Neill came to this rebellion from a sousing in the romantic sentimentality of the theatre. As son of a great romantic actor he early acquired a loathing for the stuff of his father's dramas, in several of which, like *The Count of Monte Cristo,* he had to act for his bread. He was soon at work on a series of short plays, the stark realism of which shocked his father and seemed unsuited to the polite theatre of that day.

This passage calls for careful reading. Examine each word or phrase below with reference to the context in which it appears, and tell the class what you think it means. There may be differences of opinion. Listen to them. Then let the class, with the aid of your teacher, decide which interpretation is correct.

1. dramatic rebel
2. rebellion not against institutions or individuals
3. radical
4. spiritual slavery
5. effete convention
6. dramatic apostle
7. prologue
8. great emancipation—the freeing of the human spirit
9. hypocritical civilization
10. represses and tortures the soul
11. romantically proclaims its liberty
12. tragic futility
13. goals of happiness are illusory
14. symbolic grandeur
15. instinctive faith in his own spiritual value
16. man-made conventions
17. in such strife he finds joy
18. romantic sentimentality of the theatre
19. stark realism
20. polite theatre of that day

E. Select a short story or play that you have read recently. Describe the following as clearly and specifically as possible.

1. the character of the protagonist
2. the character of the antagonist
3. the nature of the conflict
4. the style of writing
5. the effect of the piece upon you

Part 4 Getting Meaning from Context

Whether you go on to college or to a job, you are going to meet an increasing number of new and unfamiliar words. They may be the vocabulary of psychology, law, chemistry, or whatever other college course you are taking. They may be political or economic terms in the news. They may be technical terms related to the industry in which you are working.

Wherever an unfamiliar word appears, you have the problem of figuring out its meaning—not necessarily all of its meanings, but enough meaning to make the passage intelligible. If you are to understand what you read—and you must read in order to participate in the life around you—you must have a method of understanding unfamiliar words.

How do you get the meaning of an unfamiliar word that you come across in your reading? If you are reading a book or magazine in the backyard or on the bus, it is unlikely that you will have a dictionary close at hand. You will, therefore, need to use another method of getting the meaning of the word.

Sometimes you can get a clue to the meaning of a word from its root, prefix, or suffix. Sometimes you can get a clue from the **context,** the words with which the unfamiliar term is used. In using context clues, keep in mind that you are not trying to get the full meaning of the unfamiliar word. You are trying only to get enough meaning to go on with your reading, to make sense of the passage as a whole. Remember: you never get all the meaning of a word in any one encounter with it.

You may feel confident that you know the word *sensitive,* and yet you may not be aware of just how many ways it can be used. Each of the following sentences uses a different meaning of the word. In some sentences the word has a positive connotation, and in others a negative one. Compare the meanings of *sensitive* in each sentence.

> Millie was very *sensitive* about being called the baby of the family. (irritable, touchy)

A *sensitive* seismograph picks up earth tremors not felt by inhabitants of the area. (able to measure small changes)

Joe's sunburn was painfully *sensitive,* and he howled as Amy brushed by him. (tender)

Carol was a warm and *sensitive* person who really listened to other people's problems. (sympathetic)

The eye is *sensitive* to foreign objects. This sensitivity triggers blinking and a flow of tears to expel the intruder. (quick to react)

In each sentence you need only to grasp one meaning of the word *sensitive,* but to get full use of the word, you need to know its multiple meanings.

Exercises **Getting Meaning from Context**

A. From the context, work out the meaning of each of the following italicized words. Then consult a dictionary to find the other meanings for each word. In class, work out sentences illustrating these other meanings.

1. Ninety feet down I found the pig iron standing on a ledge. It did not appear in the torch beam as an object from the world above, but as something *germane* to the place.

2. On many occasions the smell of my pipe was my preservation and saved me from carrying in my clothes the *noxious* odors.

3. It became clear as the party progressed through the snow that Marcel was only an *indifferent* climber.

4. When we *cleared* the harbor entrance, I ordered full speed ahead.

5. The birds that Holbrook snared were a welcome *supplement* to our scanty rations.

6. At the station house an unemotional matron divested the famous *impersonator* of the last and best of her disguises.

7. Now the tree under which he had done this carried a weight of snow on its boughs. No wind had blown for weeks, and each bough was fully *freighted.*

8. And he did for me the unnecessary thing, the gracious thing, that we find done only by the great of heart. Things no training can teach, for they are done on the instant, with no *predicated* experience.

9. Spring made a man feel good and sad, too, and wild sometimes, wanting to howl with the wolves or *strike* north with the ducks.

10. The car careened on, charged the cliff face, rebounded, attacked the lower wall furiously with all its unwieldy weight like a great bumble bee, and tumbling over, crashed with a brief and distant *report* into the depths below.

B. The adjective *gross* has several meanings. Taking clues from the context, tell what it means in each sentence below.

1. The committee charged the Congressman with *gross* negligence in the execution of his duties.

2. If the *gross* weight of the package is given, remember that you must subtract the weight of the packaging to determine how much the contents weigh.

3. Trevor lost sight of the fleeing raccoon in the *gross* underbrush.

4. The *gross* form of the sculpture was now apparent, although the artist still had much of the detail to complete.

5. He was not invited to the party because no one could tolerate his *gross* language.

Part 5 Context Clues

Sometimes the context of an unfamiliar word will give you a definite clue to the meaning of the word. Professional writers, particularly textbook writers and newspaper reporters, take pains to explain unfamiliar words. An awareness of the devices writers use to provide an explanation will help you read smoothly through a passage without being interrupted by an unknown word. Six common types of context clues are explained and illustrated in this section.

How Context Reveals Meaning

1. **Definition.** The most obvious and straightforward method of revealing meaning is by outright definition. A form of the verb "to be" signals a definition.

Cinéma vérité is a technique used to make a documentary film appear natural and spontaneous.

The *sycophant* can be found wherever there is power; he is the person who works his way into favor with flattery.

2. **Restatement.** Sometimes a writer will explain a term by restating it in other words. A restatement can take many forms. Certain words act as signals that a restatement will follow. Be alert to such signal words as these: *in other words, that is, to put it another way, or, this means.*

One astronomer claims there is a total absence of *plasma,* or gaseous matter, in certain parts of the corona.

Scientists are curious about the *optical properties* of the clouds covering Venus. In other words, they wonder whether sunlight filters through the clouds and reaches the surface of the planet.

The words *this, that, these,* and *those* also signal a restatement.

Irv was getting a degree in *topology.* This branch of mathematics deals with the properties of geometric figures that remain unchanged even when under distortion.

Commas, parentheses, or dashes may signal an appositive, which is another kind of restatement.

A doctor will usually check the functioning of the *thyroid,* the gland that regulates body growth and metabolism, if the patient has a weight problem.

Many of the more familiar metals are *malleable* (capable of being hammered into sheets) and *ductile* (capable of being drawn into wire).

With attentive reading of the context, you may find a restatement that helps you understand a word, even if no signals are present.

Sara was *ambivalent* about Jack. She couldn't decide whether she admired him for leaving medical school to paint, or whether she considered him reckless and immature.

In my home town there is a law against smoking in public, but the law has fallen into *desuetude*. Until recently, people have not felt it was their concern whether another person was smoking or not, and the law has not been used in forty years. Now people are beginning to ask that the law be enforced.

Part of the effectiveness of her narrative is in her *understatement*. You know that being the only child living with these two crazy old people with their sleepwalking and fits of rage is very strange growing up, but she treats it as just a little bit odd, no more.

3. **Example.** Sometimes a writer will give one or more examples to show the meaning of a word. Words that signal an example are these: *such, such as, like, other, especially, particularly, for example, for instance.*

Like Manhattan, each of the other *boroughs* is an administrative unit of New York City.

There must be international agreement on punishment for hijacking and kidnapping. Such *terrorist tactics* cannot be tolerated by one nation without all nations being threatened.

4. **Modifiers.** A writer may clarify the meaning of a term in a modifying phrase or clause.

It is hoped that both presidential nominees will be on their guard against the *chauvinistic* patriot who carries devotion to obnoxious and pathological lengths and permits no criticism of any of our national institutions or methods.

5. **Contrast.** Occasionally a writer will make a contrast that enables you to grasp the meaning of an unfamiliar word.

Both women were good writers, but each approached her work from a different standpoint. One was a *dilettante*; the other had to write for her daily bread.

Unlike the other members of the band, who resurfaced in other groups in later years, James was lost to the public after his *meteoric* fame as the lead singer.

6. **Connecting words.** A connecting word links two thoughts in a way that can shed some light on the meaning of an unfamiliar word. Study the examples to see how an unfamiliar word is illuminated both by the words to which it is connected and by the connecting word itself. Do the connecting words indicate the similarity or dissimilarity of the thoughts they connect?

> An ungraduated income tax takes money from the rich person at the same rate as from the poor person. A person who is paid enough to buy many luxuries may not miss twenty percent of his or her salary; however, a person on a *subsistence* wage cannot be as offhand about giving up twenty percent to the government.

> There are disadvantages to color film for the professional photographer. No color film *renders* colors exactly as we see them. Moreover, the color results from any one film will vary, depending on the age and storage conditions of the film.

> One major objection to the proposed disarmament treaty was that there was no provision for inspection of *arsenals*, and therefore no assurance that weapons were not again being stockpiled.

Exercises **Using Context Clues**

A. The following passages are taken from newspaper columns or from college textbooks. They are typical of passages you will meet in adult life. For each passage, do these two things: (1) figure out from the context the meaning of the italicized words, and (2) identify the method by which the context reveals the meaning.

1. *Plant pathology* treats abnormalities in the life of the plant.
2. The movement of soil by water, wind, and ice is called *erosion*.
3. Louis Pasteur investigated *rabies*, the disease that makes dogs go "mad."
4. The points at which bones make contact or unite with one another are called *articulations*.

5. The fact that the lower vertebrates do not depend very much on the *cerebrum* can be demonstrated by removing this part of the brain and observing the general behavior of the animal.

6. To understand the principles involved in the treatment of cataract, it is first necessary to understand the *etiology*, or causes, of cataract.

7. The horizontal branches of the *banyan tree* and other species of fig often form numerous *prop roots*, which grow downward until they enter the soil, where they branch and develop as ordinary roots.

8. The *marine* fishes respond only to notes of low frequency; fresh-water species are sensitive to frequencies of several thousand cycles per second.

9. Colbert was a defender of the economic theory known as *mercantilism*. According to this theory, a nation should make itself wealthy by taking in more *specie* (gold and silver) from selling and exporting its goods abroad than it spends abroad by buying and importing.

10. Theatre people in New York are always sighing for a *repertory theatre*—an institution with a permanent company of actors, a permanent staff of technicians, an intelligent and, no less important, intelligible policy.

11. All the organisms that cause red tides are *photosynthetic*; they use visible light to convert water and carbon dioxide into oxygen and food.

12. Milk contains a type of amino acid—*tryptophan*—that when given to volunteers produces a pronounced sedative effect.

13. The Indians carried provisions on their persons that could keep them for days, but the English were hampered by the necessity for frequent *replenishment* of supplies.

14. Although this Einstein model of the universe was an intriguing one and was based on a rather firm mathematical foundation, an important development occurred in 1929 that completely *invalidated* it.

15. If taxes sometimes seem *onerous*, what we get for them is probably the best bargain of our lives.

B. Choose a newspaper or magazine article in which the writer's purpose is to inform readers about some subject. Be aware of how the writer provides clues to the meanings of terms that readers may not be familiar with. Copy sentences from the article in which the writer uses context clues to clarify words and phrases. After each sentence, define the word or phrase as you understand it from the context.

Inferring Word Meanings

The six kinds of context clues you have just studied are visible and clear clues to word meaning. Many other contexts convey meaning in a more subtle way. In such contexts you must **infer** the meaning of an unfamiliar word.

Inference involves reasoning from known facts. When you encounter an unfamiliar word, search the context to see what can be known. Then try to determine what the connection is between the known facts and the unknown word. Rather than being steered by a specific device, you will have to derive the meaning of a word from the whole context.

Study the following examples. Do you see the reasoning that leads to a definition of each italicized word?

> He kept the *talisman* on a chain around his neck at all times. Once he had gone out to shovel the driveway without it, and he had fallen and broken his arm. It didn't pay to take chances with a thing like that.

A talisman, which can be worn around the neck, is apparently an object that is supposed to bring good luck, since going out without it brought bad luck.

> In a series of settling tanks the solid waste *precipitates* out of the water, but the *effluent* is still too acidic to return to the river.

Since solid waste precipitates out of water in settling tanks, *precipitates* must mean something like *settles*. The *effluent* is water that is to be returned to the river, or water from the river that has been dirtied by some process.

> His drawing talent must be *intrinsic*, for he has never taken an art lesson in his life.

Since this artist did not acquire his skill from an outside source, *intrinsic* must mean that the talent came from within him.

Exercises Inferring Word Meanings

A. In the following sentences you are to infer the meaning of the words in italics. Be ready to explain to the class what clues in the context led you to your definition. Compare a dictionary definition for each word with the definition you have constructed.

1. Eleanor, who has always suffered from *acrophobia,* could not be induced to go to the top of the Washington Monument.

2. Each of these pianists is an erstwhile *prodigy*. Gould is supposed to have been able to read notes before he could read the printed word. He started playing the piano at the age of three, and gave his first recital at fourteen.

3. Americans have extended their high standard of living to more citizens since the days of the Poverty Program of President Johnson, and yet it is still possible to find people living in *destitution* in the land of plenty.

4. An *indefatigable* worker, Thomas Edison often spent days and nights on his experiments, not even taking time to eat and sleep.

5. Moths and butterflies are the insects to which budding *entomologists* are first attracted.

6. Roots may extend both much farther downward into the soil and much wider *laterally* than most people realize.

7. In 1921 the Soviet government turned against modern art, and Kandinsky thought it wise to leave his native land for good, settling again in Germany which, in turn, he left after the Nazis came to power. According to him, since the artist's first loyalty is to the satisfaction of an inner need, these displacements, despite their sadness, were *peripheral* to the creation of a lifework.

8. Of the American artists of the thirties and forties, some were traditionalists following *canons* of taste well formulated in the past; others were audacious innovators.

9. People's response to the decline in fish harvest has been to try harder—an action more suicidal than *sapient*.

10. There has been speculation about why the first national parks were established. In this period of relentless *disposition* of the *public domain,* it was reasonable to fear that even the most magnificent scenic sites might be plowed or grazed out of existence.

B. Examine the following passages, paying special attention to the italicized words. What is the special meaning of each word *in this context?*

1 Although it is difficult to generalize, too many of our universities have become huge circuses in which the sideshows overshadow the main attraction. "When a university president makes a speech calling for intellectual leadership," writes Dr. Hutchins, "he cannot be heard over the din his publicity man is making about the newest campus queen." Our colleges have involved themselves in activities that have only the most *tenuous relation* to the *academic function.*—MARTIN B. MARGOLIES

2 Certainly, some amount of criticism of the *bathos* and *sentimentality* that constitutes so great a part of our theatre fare today is justifiable. Serious students of literature should indeed maintain a *skeptical* attitude toward the commercially successful *floss;* they should be wary of gulping down uncritically the *mawkish sentiments* of the few who, by gently patting their audience on the head, comfort them with cheap and empty solutions.—LEONARD FLEISCHER

3 Burns brings an *element of complication* into what is otherwise the relatively simple *evolution* of English poetry. The influence of a half-foreign nationality, and the racy vigor of a son of the soil, quicken in him the germs of an unexpected originality. He is an *innovator,* but not after the manner of his English *contemporaries.* —LEGOUIS AND CAZAMIAN

4 Languages die but words tend to be *immortal.* Catchwords, slang, and technical terms often disappear after a *brief run,* but many become established parts of the language, and once so established they persist. *Hosts* of Greek and Latin words are in use in dozens of the world's present-day languages.—JOHN CIARDI

5 The English language is an unpredictable medley, but no other can communicate such subtle shades of thought and feelings, such fine discriminations of meaning. The riches of its *mingled derivations* supply a multitude of synonyms, each with its own *distinction of implications.*—ELIZABETH DREW

6 Sincerity in the fullest sense must be more than a *temperamental disposition* to be frank. It is a simplicity of spirit that is preserved by the will to be true. It implies an obligation to *manifest* the truth and to defend it.—THOMAS MERTON

7 The *faculty* of creating is never given to us all by itself. It always goes hand in hand with the gift of observation. The true creator may be recognized by his ability always to find about him, in the commonest and *humblest* thing, items worthy of note.—IGOR STRAVINSKY

8 One of the great *visionaries* of the architectural world is Paolo Soleri, who came to the United States from Italy thirty-one years ago. Soleri's fame does not rest on the structures he has actually built, for these are few in number: a striking glass-domed house, a ceramics factory on the Amalfi coast, and the so-called earth colony where he and his followers lived in Arizona. His impact on the world of design has been made almost entirely through his *intricate*, detailed drawings for the city of the future—in which he fully intends to live. These drawings have astonished and *mesmerized* visitors to museum shows around the country.—JOSEPH J. THORNDIKE, JR.

Chapter 2

Sentence Combining

Writing is a process of making choices. You choose what ideas you want to express, which words will best express them, and how those words can best be arranged. Because writing occurs in sentences, the sentence is the basic tool of writing. Learning to write sentences that are clear and direct is the first step toward making yourself understood in writing. The next step is to combine related ideas in your sentences.

A sentence is a group of words that expresses a single main idea. However, some main ideas are made up of smaller ideas. If each smaller idea is expressed in a sentence of its own, the result is choppy and monotonous. In addition, your reader may get only a vague idea of how the smaller ideas are related. The following group of sentences shows this kind of choppiness and vagueness.

> We bundled up in warm clothing. That would protect us from the north wind. It was icy. We set out for Park Hill.

The ideas can be combined in one sentence.

> We bundled up in warm clothing to protect us against the icy north wind, and we set out for Park Hill.

Notice that the new sentence has only one main idea, but that the main idea has several parts. Notice also that the new sentence flows smoothly and shows how the ideas are related. The new sentence is much more effective than the group of sentences.

There are many ways to express any idea; one way may be more effective than another. Good writers choose the way that communicates an idea most clearly. This chapter will show you how to combine related ideas to create more effective sentences. It will also give you practice in making the choices that a good writer must make.

Part 1 Joining Sentences

When two sentences express similar ideas that are of equal importance, they can usually be joined by a comma and the word *and.*

Mark was home by six o'clock. Ted arrived an hour later.
Mark was home by six o'clock, and Ted arrived an hour later.

When two sentences express contrasting ideas of equal importance, they can usually be joined by a comma and the word *but.*

The phone was ringing. I could not hear it.
The phone was ringing, but I could not hear it.

When two sentences express a choice between ideas of equal importance, they can usually be joined by a comma and the word *or.*

Is Sue going to the meeting? Is she staying home with you?
Is Sue going to the meeting, or is she staying home with you?

Exercises Joining Sentences

A. Join each pair of sentences by following the directions in parentheses.

1. Can you help me repair this fence? Do you have too much other work to do? (Join with **, or.**)

2. We arrived at the airport exactly on time. The plane was an hour late. (Join with **, but.**)

3. I mowed the lawn. Lucy clipped the shrubs. (Join with **, and.**)

4. Leroy is not as tall as Will. He is more agile. (Join with **, but.**)

5. The subway is faster than the bus. It is not as comfortable. (Join with **, but.**)

B. Join each pair of sentences by using **, and** or **, but** or **, or**. Be prepared to explain your choices.

1. Greg had thought that he would enjoy fishing. He found that he was not patient enough.

2. Allison hesitated for a moment at the door. Finally she decided to go on in.

3. Clamp the pieces tightly. Then allow the glue to dry.

4. Do you want to decide now? Do you want a day to think it over?

5. The noise from the road work outside was deafening. Diana tried to shout over it.

Part 2 Joining Sentence Parts

Sometimes the ideas expressed by two sentences are so closely related that some words are repeated in the two sentences. The repetition is unnecessary and awkward. The ideas would be much better expressed if they were joined in one sentence and the repeated words were eliminated. When the sentence parts express similar ideas of equal importance, they can usually be joined by *and.*

Ben Franklin was a diplomat. *He was also* an inventor.
Ben Franklin was a diplomat *and* an inventor.

When the sentence parts express contrasting ideas, they can usually be joined by *but.*

We searched everywhere. *We* could not find the keys.
We searched everywhere but could not find the keys.

When the sentence parts express a choice between ideas, they can usually be joined by *or*.

> The typical Colonial town grew around a coastal harbor. *It might also have grown around* a river junction.
>
> The typical coastal town grew around a coastal harbor or a river junction.

Exercises **Joining Sentence Parts**

A. Join the related parts in each pair of sentences by following the directions in parentheses. Eliminate the italicized words.

1. We will study pollution this term. *We will also study* solar energy *this term.* (Join related parts with **and**.)
2. Karen found a defect in the wiring. *Karen* couldn't repair it without special tools. (Join related parts with **but**.)
3. You can stake the tomato plants. *You can* string them to an overhead wire. (Join related parts with **or**.)
4. Frank prepared baked ham for our victory dinner. *He also prepared* sweet potatoes. (Join related parts with **and**.)
5. Charlie lay down on the sofa. *He* fell asleep. (Join related parts with **and**.)

B. Join the related parts in each pair of sentences by using *and, but,* or *or*. Eliminate repeated words.

1. I plan to grow carrots in the garden. I also plan to grow squash.
2. You can walk six blocks to the subway entrance. You can wait for the next bus that stops here.
3. Judge Kendall was appointed to the bench seventeen years ago. She retired last month.
4. Ben walked slowly onto the stage. He turned to face the audience.
5. I would like to write movie reviews. I would also like to write theater reviews.

Part 3 Adding Single Words

Sometimes only one word in the second sentence in a pair is really important to the meaning. All the other words in the sentence are unnecessarily repeated. The one important word can be added to the first sentence, resulting in one sentence that is a much tighter and more effective way of expressing the overall idea.

> Maria bought a sweater. *It is* green.
> Maria bought a green sweater.
>
> First we removed the paint. *It was* peeling.
> First we removed the peeling paint.

Sometimes the form of the important word must be changed slightly before it is added to the other sentence.

> First we removed the paint. *It had begun to* peel.
> First we removed the peeling paint.

You may be able to add several single words to a sentence. Adding several words will allow you to combine more than two sentences if one states the main idea and each of the others adds only one important detail to the main idea.

> Ms. Clark demonstrated her discovery to an audience of scientists. *The discovery was* amazing. *It was* new. *The scientists were* skeptical.
> Ms. Clark demonstrated her amazing new discovery to an audience of skeptical scientists.

Sometimes you will have to use a comma when you add more than one word to a sentence.

> Tim Reed ran an inn on the edge of town. *It was* small *and* quiet.
> Tim Reed ran a small, quiet inn on the edge of town.

Sometimes you can join the words with *and.*

> I was impressed by Donna's serve. *It was* smooth. *It was also* powerful.
> I was impressed by Donna's smooth and powerful serve.

Exercises Adding Single Words

A. Combine each of the following pairs of sentences by adding the important words. Eliminate the italicized words and follow any special directions given in parentheses.

1. Anne glanced at the line of clouds. *The clouds looked* threatening.

2. Michiko admired the blue water. *It* sparkled. (End the important word with **-ing**.)

3. In the armchair, a cat purred softly. *It was* content. (End the important word with **-ed**.)

4. The music calmed Russell's nerves. *The music was* soothing. *Russell's nerves were* shattered.

5. Chris gave a summary of the book. *The summary was* detailed. *It was* accurate. (Use a comma.)

6. A man sprang to his feet. *He was* nervous *and* young. (Do not use a comma.)

7. The finance committee reached a conclusion after a debate. *The debate was* long. *It was also* heated. (Join the important words with *and*.)

8. We began the climb up the observation tower. *The tower was* made of wood. *The climb was* strenuous.

B. Combine each of the following pairs of sentences by adding the important word from the second sentence. Decide on your own whether to change the form of the important word.

1. We were depressed by the room. It was dingy.

2. Use this paper for your report. It has lines.

3. Kate found her glasses under a pile of papers. She had misplaced them.

4. Brad is a young lawyer. He has determination.

5. I noticed a girl on the bus. She was nervous, and something was distracting her.

Part 4 Adding Words with *-ly*

When you take a single important word from one sentence and insert it into another sentence, you may have to change the word so that it ends with *-ly*.

> Lydia performed the ballet routine. *Her performance was* perfect.
> Lydia performed the ballet routine perfectly.

Often, the word ending in *-ly* can be placed in any of several positions in the sentence.

> Josh knocked over a can of paint. *It was an* accident.
> Accidentally, Josh knocked over a can of paint.
> Josh accidentally knocked over a can of paint.
> Josh knocked over a can of paint accidentally.

Exercise **Adding Words with *-ly***

Combine each pair of sentences by adding the important word, ending it with *-ly*. Eliminate the italicized words.

1. Warren listened to Ms. Jackson. *He was* attentive.
2. Maureen visited the Museum of Modern Art. *Her visits were* frequent.
3. The ship's guidance computer began to buzz. *This was* ominous.
4. Marcy trained her dog in three days. *The training was* effective.
5. Dan moved from table to table. *His movements were* brisk.

Part 5 Adding Groups of Words

You may find that one sentence contains an important group of words that can be added to another sentence. When the group of words gives more information about someone or something, it should be added near the words that name the person or thing.

A case stood in the middle of the shop. *It was* filled with cheeses.
A case filled with cheeses stood in the middle of the shop.

I was surprised by a shaggy gray dog. *It was* rounding the corner.
I was surprised by a shaggy gray dog rounding the corner.

I was surprised by a shaggy gray dog. *I was* rounding the corner.
Rounding the corner, I was surprised by a shaggy gray dog.

In some cases you will have to separate the group of words from the rest of the sentence with a comma or a pair of commas.

The recipe calls for saffron. *Saffron is* a very expensive spice.
The recipe calls for saffron, a very expensive spice.

The Grand Canyon is in Arizona. *It is* the earth's largest gorge.
The Grand Canyon, the earth's largest gorge, is in Arizona.

When the group of words describes an action, it should be added near the words that name the action.

The crowd had been waiting for hours. *They had been waiting* outside the theater.
The crowd had been waiting outside the theater for hours.

When the group of words adds more information to the entire main idea of the other sentence, it may be added at the beginning or at the end.

The snow had disappeared. *It had disappeared* by the time the sun set.
By the time the sun set, the snow had disappeared.
The snow had disappeared by the time the sun set.

Exercises **Adding Groups of Words**

A. Combine each group of sentences by adding a group of words or groups of words to one of them. Eliminate the italicized words.

1. Gretchen was resting. *She was resting* on the sofa.
2. A reporter stood beside Juan Carlos. *She was* holding a portable tape recorder.

3. *I was* looking through current magazines. I discovered four articles. *They were* about nutrition.

4. The rabbits scattered and ran. *They had been* startled by a sudden noise.

5. Phil encountered a group of eighty backpackers. *This happened* during a stroll downtown.

B. Combine each group of sentences.

1. We spotted a flock of ducks. We were walking near the river.

2. Margaret Sterns introduced the cast. This occurred during the intermission. She is the play's director.

3. Every Sunday Dad makes chili. Chili is my favorite meal.

4. I read a fascinating book. It was about the greatest years of American clipper ships. I read it during the summer.

5. The Mariana Trench is the deepest known spot in the world. It is in the Pacific Ocean.

Part 6 Combining with *-ing*

Read the following pair of sentences.

He packed only the essentials. *This* enabled him to travel lightly.

Notice that the word *This* in the second sentence refers to the entire idea expressed by the first sentence. This pair of sentences, and others like it, can be combined into one smoothly flowing statement.

Packing only the essentials enabled him to travel lightly.

The word *packed* was changed to *packing,* and the italicized words were eliminated. Here is another example of two sentences combined by using *-ing.*

She had had her meals brought to her every day. When she left the hospital, Sara missed *that.*

When she left the hospital, Sara missed having her meals brought to her every day.

Notice that the word *had* was changed to *having,* and that the italicized words were eliminated.

In some cases, the necessary changes are a bit more complicated. Notice the changes that must be made in the following example.

> Mr. Judson volunteered to coach the soccer team. *That* meant that we would be able to start the season on schedule.
>
> Mr. Judson's volunteering to coach the soccer team meant that we would be able to start the season on schedule.

The word *volunteered* has been changed to *volunteering,* and *Mr. Judson* has been changed to *Mr. Judson's.* If the words *Mr. Judson's* had not been included in the combined sentence, an important part of the original meaning would have been lost. Notice the similar changes in the following example.

> She hummed the same tune over and over again under her breath. *That* drove me crazy.
>
> Her humming the same tune over and over again under her breath drove me crazy.

The word *hummed* has been changed to *humming,* and *She* has been changed to *Her.* Notice that if the word *Her* were not included in the combined sentence, the meaning would be different from what was originally intended.

Exercises **Combining with *-ing***

A. Combine each group of sentences by using **-ing**. Eliminate the italicized words, and follow any special instructions in parentheses.

1. *Mr. Denby* used a high-speed drill. *That* made Mr. Denby's work more efficient.
2. *Sylvia* worked on her report until three in the morning. *This* made Sylvia sluggish the next day.
3. *People* litter. *This* wastes time, money, and resources.
4. Clark sang. *That* made the people in the front rows wince. (Combine with **'s** and **-ing**.)
5. *You can* read about a sunset. *You can* see a sunset. *The first* can never take the place of *the second.*

B. Combine each pair of sentences by using **-ing**. Decide on your own what words should be eliminated.

1. He designed the Imperial Hotel in Tokyo, Japan. That brought Frank Lloyd Wright international acclaim.
2. People should get some exercise every day. That is an important part of being physically fit.
3. Carol met the requirements for a car loan. That was a personal triumph for Carol.
4. We eat our catch every evening. That is the best part of our fishing trips.
5. We postponed the trip. That was the right thing to do.

Part 7 Combining with *who* and *that*

In some cases, when a group of words is added to a sentence, the group of words must begin with the word *who* or the word *that*.

The tall man must have taken the plans. *He* slipped out the side door.
The tall man who slipped out the side door must have taken the plans.

In effect, the word *who* takes the place of the word *he*.

The plans reveal every detail of my invention. He took *them*.
The plans that he took reveal every detail of my invention.

In effect, the word *that* takes the place of the word *them*.

In the two preceding examples, the group of words added to the first sentence in each pair is necessary to make it clear which man and which set of plans are meant. In some sentences, the added group of words is not absolutely necessary, but merely adds additional information. When the group of words merely adds additional information, combine with **, who** or **, which**.

The coach let me play in every game. *He* happens to be my father.
The coach, who happens to be my father, let me play in every game.

His first record has become a collector's item. *It* sold only a few thousand copies.

His first record, which sold only a few thousand copies, has become a collector's item.

Exercise **Combining with *who* and *that***

Combine each of the following pairs of sentences by following the directions in parentheses. Eliminate the italicized words.

1. Kevin gave up only one run. *He* walked four batters in the first inning. (Combine with **, who**.)
2. Marilyn wore the skirt. I made *it* for her. (Combine with **that**.)
3. I always enjoy visiting my uncle. *He* runs an ice cream store. (Combine with **, who**.)
4. This paint must be thinned with turpentine. *Turpentine* is a highly flammable solvent. (Combine with **, which**.)
5. Dan broke the vase. *It* had been on the piano. (Combine with **that**.)

Part 8 Combining with *since, because, therefore,* and *as a result*

Often in your writing you will want to explain to your readers that something happened because of something else or that one thing caused another. If you do not make the cause-and-effect relationship clear, your reader may not realize that one exists. Notice that in the following examples the combined sentence makes the relationship clear.

The price of oranges has gone up. I have stopped buying them.

Because the price of oranges has gone up, I have stopped buying them.

It is raining today. The tennis match has been postponed.

Since it is raining today, the tennis match has been postponed.

The words *because* and *since* are added before the sentence that states the cause. There is another way to combine sentences to show a cause-and-effect relationship. The words *as a result* or *therefore* can be added before the effect. If you use this method, you will also have to use a semicolon (;).

> The price of oranges has gone up; as a result, I have stopped buying them.
>
> It is raining today; therefore, the tennis match has been postponed.

Exercise **Combining with *since, because, therefore,* and *as a result***

Combine each of the following pairs of sentences in two ways. First use either *because* or *since*. Then use either *therefore* or *as a result*.

1. Denise spilled coffee on her first three customers. She decided to try another line of work.
2. Jack hadn't repaid the money he borrowed from me a month ago. I wouldn't lend him money for lunch today.
3. We hadn't had any rain for three weeks. We cheered the line of clouds on the horizon.
4. Jim had worked tirelessly on his project for three weeks. He felt that he deserved a few days of rest.
5. The Jacksons didn't want to lose touch with their old friends and neighbors. They continued to subscribe to our local paper after they moved away.

Part 9 Applying Sentence Combining Skills

You have learned several ways to combine related ideas in your sentences. Your next step is to use these combining skills to eliminate choppiness, monotony, and vagueness from your writing.

Notice how the following paragraph has been revised.

Mahalo is an island. It exists only in my dreams. It is a place of beauty. It is a place of wonder. Streams run down from the mountains. The streams are crystal-clear. They cascade through the forests. They empty into the ocean. The ocean is blue. The forests are filled with wonderful plants. They are also filled with exotic animals. Everyone on the island lives in peace. Everyone on the island lives in happiness. No one ever goes hungry.

Mahalo is an island that exists only in my dreams. It is a place of beauty and wonder. Crystal-clear streams run down from the mountains, cascading through the forests and emptying into the blue ocean. The forests are filled with wonderful plants and exotic animals. Everyone on the island lives in peace and happiness, and no one ever goes hungry.

When you read something that you have written, think about how it can be improved. Remember that there are many ways to express any idea; one way may be more effective than another. Good writers choose the way that communicates an idea most clearly.

Exercise **Applying Sentence Combining Skills**

Use the combining skills you have learned to revise the following paragraph. Be prepared to explain your choices.

I went to bed early. I could not get to sleep. I tossed. I turned. I could not find a comfortable position. I heard people. They mumbled. I slipped out of bed. I was quiet. I noticed a light. It was dim. It was coming from the living room. I pressed my ear to the door. That allowed me to hear what the people were saying. They shouted "Surprise!" That told me what was going on. Jack Parker flung the door open. He had organized the party. It had been easy to arrange. I had told him in school that I'd be going to bed early.

Review Exercises **Sentence Combining**

A. Join each pair of sentences by using **, and** or **, or** or **, but**.

1. Would you like to take the subway? Would you rather walk?
2. Kim included snacks in her weekly budget. Elena didn't.
3. Do you want to camp here for the night? Do you want to keep going?
4. Elena completed the five-mile walk. Carlos didn't.
5. Keiko types faster than anyone else in the office. She makes many errors.

B. Join the related parts of each pair of sentences by using **and**, **or**, or **but**. Eliminate the italicized words.

1. Melody figured out her expenses. *Melody* forgot to include transportation costs.
2. We can use the wok to cook dinner. *We can use* the skillet *to cook dinner.*
3. Ms. Finley is a professional musician. *Ms. Finley is* a chemist.
4. The course on computer programming sounds informative. *It does* not *sound* very exciting.
5. You can vote for the proposed bill. *You can vote* against *the proposed bill.*

C. Combine each of the following pairs of sentences by adding the important word or words. Eliminate the italicized words and follow any special directions in parentheses.

1. Coach Wong gave me a signal. *It was* frantic.
2. The car was towed to the South Street Service Station. *It had* damage. (End the important word with **-ed**.)
3. I enjoy listening to Miki's voice. *It is* clear *and* mellow. (Use a comma.)
4. A bee made me nervous. *The bee* circled. (End the important word with **-ing**.)
5. The coat suits you well. *It is* gray. *It is* tweed. (Do not use a comma.)

D. Combine each pair of sentences by using **-ly**. Eliminate the italicized words.

1. Herb marched to the center of the stage. *He was* confident.

2. Don reported on the progress of his experiment. *His reports were* frequent.

3. Donna dropped an earring in the cake batter. *It was* unintentional.

4. Dr. Taylor found her way back to the campsite. *It was* miraculous.

5. The cubs wrestled with each other. *Their wrestling was* playful.

E. Combine each group of sentences by adding a group of words or groups of words to one of them. Eliminate the italicized words.

1. The cat was sleeping. *It was* on top of the television.

2. Marge sauntered down the spiral staircase. *She was* singing at the top of her lungs.

3. The contestants stood quietly on the stage. *They were* anxious to hear the results.

4. I was interrupted. *This was* while I was reading a good mystery.

5. *I was* turning toward the door. I noticed a pair of yellow eyes. *They were* peering at me in the dark.

F. Combine each group of sentences by using **-ing**. Eliminate the italicized words, and follow any special instructions in parentheses.

1. *We* contributed to the renovation of the historic district. *That* gave all of us a sense of pride.

2. *Anna* had her book published. *That* was Anna's crowning achievement.

3. *Jesse* monograms sweaters. *This* has earned Jesse spending money for school next year.

4. *Adam* outlined his proposal for the new business district. *That* brought Adam both criticism and support.

5. *People* save money regularly. *This* is a good habit.

G. Combine each of the following pairs of sentences by following the directions in parentheses. Eliminate the italicized words.

1. I lived down the street from Sam Jones. *He* was a famous basketball player. (Combine with **, who**.)

2. The bear ate all our food. *It* wandered into camp last night. (Combine with **that**.)

3. Harry brags. *That* has cost him many friends. (Combine with **'s** and **-ing**.)

4. I suggest that you make the table out of ash. *It* is a light-colored wood with a nice grain. (Combine with **, which**.)

5. The fire was started by a careless camper. *It* destroyed the forest. (Combine with **that**.)

H. Combine each of the following pairs of sentences in two ways. First use either *because* or *since*. Then use either *therefore* or *as a result*.

1. Everyone took some responsibility for organizing the trip. It went off smoothly.

2. Interest in the life-saving course has grown considerably. We have decided to offer it three times a year.

3. We planted lettuce, cucumbers, radishes, and onions. We were able to make salads that were entirely home-grown.

4. Elaine hopes to become an architect. She has been trying to get a summer job in construction work.

5. This glue can cause skin irritation. Any spilled glue should be washed from the skin immediately.

Chapter 3

Effective Sentences

Many of the problems of writing are sentence problems. These problems are of two kinds:

1. Problems of grammar
2. Problems of meaning and sense

Sentence improvement is therefore treated at length in this book, both from the standpoint of grammar and from the standpoint of sense.

This chapter is devoted to those sentences that, though grammatically correct, are nonetheless unsatisfactory. These are the empty sentences, the circular sentences that say nothing. They are the overloaded sentences, the sentences that try to say too much. They are the illogical sentences, created by unrealized gaps in thought. These unsatisfactory sentences arise from clearly identifiable causes that can be isolated and presented to you without dependence on grammatical principles.

Part 1 Avoiding Empty Sentences

The function of a sentence is to convey facts, ideas, or feelings.

Writing cannot be done well in haste. It cannot be done well without thought. **Empty sentences,** like the following, result from haste and from failure to think before beginning to write.

> In cities and everywhere else there is too much traffic because there are too many cars and trucks and many of the cars and trucks take up too much room because they are so big.

This sentence starts out well: "*In cities and everywhere else there is too much traffic because* . . ." The writer promises to explain why there is too much traffic. This is worth hearing about. What reason is given? ". . . there are too many cars and trucks . . ." The writer clearly does not know any reason. She is simply saying, "There is too much traffic because there is too much traffic." As an afterthought, the writer added something about the size of cars.

This point about the size of many automobiles is a good one. It is related to traffic conditions in city streets. The writer's problem was to *think through* the relationship and to express it clearly. If she had *thought*, she would not have written "there is too much traffic because. . . ." She might have written this:

> The existence of so many full-size luxury cars is increasing the tangle of traffic in our city streets.

Here is another example of an empty sentence.

> I think it is unfair to charge higher automobile insurance rates for men under twenty-five because it is not fair to charge men higher rates than women.

This sentence says only that higher automobile insurance rates are unfair because they are unfair. Why are they unfair? If the writer had reasons, he should have given them. If he did not have reasons, he should merely have expressed his opinion. By using "because," he led the reader to expect reasons and details. He might better have written this:

> I think it is unfair to charge men higher rates for automobile insurance than women.

Exercise **Avoiding Empty Sentences**

Rewrite the following empty sentences. Add any facts or ideas that you think will improve them.

1. I want to go to college because going to college will satisfy my long-felt desires.
2. Going to college is a necessity for entering the profession that I want to enter, for my profession requires a college education.
3. I thoroughly enjoyed the concert at the Auditorium because I liked the music.
4. The world is beautiful in the early morning, for everything takes on added beauty when the sun is just coming up.
5. My teachers are not what I expected because I didn't know what to expect.
6. Having planned for a long time to buy a car, I was finally able to buy one as a result of my planning over a long time.
7. Athletics of all kinds should be provided in high school because all high schools need athletic teams to develop school spirit among the high school students.
8. If you're just starting, a Gibson guitar would be just right for a beginner.
9. Everyone who drives should drive carefully because reckless driving is dangerous.
10. Everyone needs a large vocabulary if he or she wishes to be successful in the future, for a large vocabulary is necessary for the person who wishes to go to the top in his or her career.
11. I believe in always trying my best in vollyball because I think that in that sport one must always give one's all and really try.

12. The excitement of the final quarter became so unbearable that I could hardly stand it any more.

13. That was the best novel I ever read because it wasn't boring at any time.

14. Being a paramedic would be a worthwhile and vital job because what they do is really important.

15. Once you have learned to swim and ride a bike, you can always swim or ride a bike because they are skills that stay with you and you can't forget them.

Part 2 Avoiding Overloaded Sentences

The guides to writing effective sentences are few and simple:

1. Say one thing at a time.
2. Say it clearly and directly.

Everyone has the experience of writing sentences that try to say too much. They become so crowded that the writer cannot remember what he or she started to say, and the reader becomes fatigued from trying to follow the thought. Such sentences are **overloaded sentences.**

When you find an overloaded sentence in your own writing, examine it carefully. Look for the main idea. Start over again with this subject-verb combination. Drop irrelevant details entirely. If the leftover details are important, start with a new subject-verb combination and pull the details together around it.

OVERLOADED Everyone should learn a second modern language today because in a shrinking world we need to know what is going on in other countries where there are many opportunities for young people to find interesting work.

IMPROVED Everyone should learn a second modern language today because in a shrinking world we need to know what is going on in other countries. A second language will open opportunities for young people to find interesting work abroad.

OVERLOADED I prefer a large university because there you can meet many kinds of people with different interests from many parts of the country where there are different ideas, and a wide experience with many kinds of people is an important part of education.

IMPROVED Experience with many kinds of people is an important part of education. In a large university you can meet people from many parts of the country and people with different interests. I prefer a large university because it provides this experience.

Exercise **Avoiding Overloaded Sentences**

Rewrite the following overloaded sentences. There is no one right way to improve them. You may find it necessary to add words and details.

1. All colleges should be coeducational because men and women can work together with mutual respect for each other and interact socially as well as academically by being together on the campus.

2. Everyone wants to be a success, and this means making enough money to fulfill material needs and to pursue the goals that will make a person happy, which is the greatest thing in the world.

3. I like winter better than any other season of the year, for in winter I can skate and ski without getting too hot and too tired as I do in the summer, and I like to go to parties in the winter, and even school is exciting and interesting in the winter.

4. Hobbies can be a source of pleasure and relaxation from business, and they can even lead to success in a vocation, and a student who enjoys designing, drawing, or even building aircraft models may become a pilot of an executive in an aircraft company.

5. Dogs are the best pets of all because they are friendly and intelligent, and they are easy to care for, and when you own a dog, the dog is always glad to see you when you get home.

6. Participation in one or two extra-curricular activities in high school can be enjoyable and beneficial to the student if he or she doesn't join too many and neglect classwork, but maintaining good scholastic standing is necessary for a future vocational or college career.

7. A satisfying work is one of the ingredients of a happy life, so when you choose a career, be sure that it is something you will enjoy doing and that it will give you a feeling of fulfillment, self-worth and achievement.

8. Everyone should learn to cook because knowing how to cook makes one more appreciative of good food, and cooking a good dish brings a feeling of great satisfaction, and it is also useful to be able to prepare a meal in an emergency.

9. Trying to be an amateur painter, musician, or writer is better than simply studying art appreciation, music appreciation, or literature, though these have their rewards too, but trying to paint or write will make a person even more appreciative of the arts.

10. Juanita was chairperson of the committee, and under her leadership more was accomplished than ever before, including an all-day educational forum and a fund-raising dance, both of which attracted many new members and brought the group much favorable publicity.

11. On the first day of our trip we drove as far as Chicago, and just as we were about to stop for the night the car gurgled and stopped, and we learned from the mechanic that it would take a day or two to repair the motor and that we'd have to stay over in Chicago.

12. A tunnel under the English Channel would be a good thing because it would make travel between England and the continent easier and more convenient and cheaper and many people cannot afford the passage now but would be able to drive from England to the continent and back.

Part 3 Avoiding Wordiness

A sentence that uses more words than necessary is boring. The extra words smother the meaning. The writer with a sharp eye can spot excess words and delete them during revision of the work.

One kind of wordiness arises from needless repetition of a word or from needless use of words with a similar meaning.

> We thought we had an *adequate* supply of *food* with *enough* for everyone *to eat.*
> Hard work *alone* is not the *only* thing you need.
> Jack is an *honest* person who *never tells a lie.*
> Carlene is the *kind* of person of the *sort* you can trust.

Another kind of wordiness arises from the repetition of *that.*

> I thought *that* if I came *that* I might be able to help.
> We knew *that* Matt felt *that* he had been cheated.

In the last two sentences, the second *that* may be dropped.

In general, wordiness results simply from the use of too many words. The writer may use a clause or a phrase when a single word would suffice. Methods of avoiding or repairing wordiness are considered in Chapter 4 under the heading *Reduction.*

WORDY In the case of physics, you would probably agree that physics is too hard for most young people in the tenth grade.

IMPROVED You would probably agree that physics is too hard for most tenth-grade students.

WORDY A year after we graduated we could look back and see that what we thought was an attitude on Ms. Stein's part of being very severe and demanding was really good training for later life.

REVISED When we looked back a year after graduation, we could see that Ms. Stein's severe and demanding attitude was good training for later life.

Awkward Repetition

Sentences lose their effectiveness if a word or phrase is repeated carelessly. Sometimes there is no substitute for a word, and it must be repeated. Awkward repetition is the use of a word or phrase a second or third time when it need not be repeated.

Awkward repetition can be corrected by using a synonym, by using pronouns in place of nouns, or by rewriting the sentence.

AWKWARD I have chosen a *topic* that is a frequent topic of conversation today. My *topic* is developing our natural resources.

IMPROVED I have chosen a topic frequently heard in conversation today—developing our natural resources.

AWKWARD My point is that too much *emphasis* is placed *on college education,* and this *emphasis on college education* makes many people go to college who don't need or want a *college education*.

IMPROVED My point is that too much emphasis on college education makes many people go to college for education they don't need or want.

AWKWARD *Hamilton and Jefferson* had entirely different ideas about government, but *Hamilton and Jefferson* both contributed much to our government.

IMPROVED Hamilton and Jefferson had entirely different ideas about government, but they both contributed much to our country.

Exercise Avoiding Wordiness

The following sentences are wordy or needlessly repetitive. Revise them to eliminate these faults.

1. The mirror was round in shape.
2. Maya Angelou wrote an autobiography of her life.

3. The League of Women Voters is a non-partisan organization and is not in favor of any one political party or candidate.

4. A play that is very interesting and that is very unusual is the play *The Effect of Gamma Rays on Man-in-the-Moon Marigolds* by Paul Zindel.

5. Such factors as the right to own and sell property and the right to make a profit are characteristic of the free enterprise system in a capitalistic society.

6. It is my belief that the greatest invention since the wheel is, I think, the television.

7. Mary Ann was a great help to her team because of the fact that she had a willing spirit and wanted to help the team.

8. The committee held a lengthy discussion in respect to the matter of raising money for the prom.

9. Many nations in the world are anxious to improve their economic conditions, to rise from their present levels of poverty.

10. The graduating class heard much good advice and counsel from the commencement speakers on the occasion of their commencement exercises.

11. Since my parents spoke two languages, my mother speaking German and my father speaking French, I grew up learning both French and German from them and English in school.

12. The class discussed not only the problems of water conservation but also the problems of water pollution and the wastes that are poured into water from industrial plants.

Part 4 Avoiding Awkward Beginnings

The normal, easily readable pattern of English sentences is subject—verb—complement. A great many awkward sentences occur when this pattern is abandoned. Certain expressions create awkwardness when used at the beginnings of sentences. They delay the thought, and they add nothing to it. Usually, they are not needed at all. The most common of these offending expressions are *The fact that, What I believe is, What I want is, Being that, The reason is.*

AWKWARD *The fact that* Mary was sick should be taken into account.

BETTER Mary's sickness should be taken into account.

AWKWARD *What I believe* is that no one should be compelled to go to school.

BETTER I believe that no one should be compelled to go to school.

AWKWARD *What Terry needs* is a little encouragement.

BETTER Terry needs a little encouragement.

AWKWARD *Being that* there was no school yesterday, we have no homework assignments.

BETTER Since there was no school yesterday, we have no homework assignments.

AWKWARD *The reason* I chose this book *is* because of its title.

BETTER I chose this book because of its title.

Exercise Revising Sentences with Awkward Beginnings

Revise these sentences to remove their awkward beginnings.

1. Being that he was a new student in the high school, Bob felt lonely and apprehensive.
2. What I think is that everyone should work a ten-hour day and a four-day week in order to conserve our resources.
3. The fact that too many extra-curricular activities are often too time-consuming should be considered by the student before he or she joins too many clubs.
4. The reason I liked my summer work was because the work itself was pleasant.

5. What the stock market crash in 1929 did to many people was to make them bankrupt.

6. Being unhappy about losing my job, I lost my appetite too.

7. The reason there are so many accidents on the highways today is because people drive too fast.

8. What all Americans should do is learn to conserve energy.

9. The fact that many colleges have language requirements makes it necessary that one study one or two languages in high school.

10. The reason that Lori has been studying Russian and Spanish is because she wants to go into the diplomatic service.

11. What every diplomat needs is to be able to speak several languages.

12. The fact that the weather looked threatening made us postpone our picnic.

13. Being that the picnic was postponed, we decided to have a party indoors.

14. The reason that Jon is now working hard is that he nearly failed two of his midterm tests.

15. The old man being unable to keep up with the others, the group left him sitting by the roadside.

Chapter 4

Sentence Revision

Everyone is called upon at times to speak without preparation. In conversation and discussion, in class meetings, faculty meetings, or business conferences, a question will arise on which you must say something. In these situations there is little time to arrange your thoughts. You do your best, and the quality of your "best" depends upon previous experience and training.

In writing, the situation is different. There always comes a point at which you can go back over what you have written and put it in order. You can reorganize, you can rearrange your paragraphs, you can revise your sentences. This chapter discusses the kinds of revisions you will find it profitable to make in your sentences.

Part 1 Omitting Unrelated Details

The function of a sentence is to state an idea, to present facts, or to describe feelings. When unrelated details appear in a sentence, they interrupt the flow of thought.

In sentence revision, keep your mind on the main idea. Delete any detail that is not closely related to this idea.

> I would like to be an engineer like my brother, *who has a Mercedes* and works on big construction jobs all over the world.

Clearly, the Mercedes has nothing to do with being an engineer. It has a great deal to do with "my brother's" success as an engineer, but his success is another matter. It belongs in another sentence.

> It was so foggy over New York, *where we expected to spend two weeks,* that our plane could not land.

The expectation of spending two weeks in New York has nothing to do with the fog over the airport. If it is important at all, it belongs in another sentence.

Exercise Omitting Unrelated Details

Rewrite these sentences, omitting details that are not related to the main idea.

1. We spent our vacation in Virginia, where George Washington lived, and we liked the state very much.
2. We usually go shopping on Saturday, which is the last day of the week, and buy our groceries for the next week.
3. The truck, which had burned on the highway and which was a Ford truck, was being dragged away by a crew of men who wore red shirts and caps.
4. Reading good books, which can fill our leisure time, is helpful in acquiring knowledge and an extensive vocabulary.

5. The new magazines, which came yesterday, are filled with articles on foreign policy and international affairs.

6. Important problems in American history are discussed by a panel of experts, one of whom is a friend of ours, on a weekly television program.

7. I had been absorbed in a television program, which was about the forthcoming election, and I had failed to notice that someone had entered the room.

8. The students at Roosevelt High School, located in the center of the city, can choose many courses from a varied curriculum.

9. The most beautiful scenes in Europe, which we visited last summer, are the lakes and mountains in the Alps.

10. TV weather forecasts, which are usually part of a news program, are based on scientific observation and knowledge.

11. Tourists love Florence, Italy, the home of the Medici, where Sue lost her purse when we were there last summer.

12. Ryan, who last year won the soccer award, went skiing in Aspen.

13. Much of the poetry of seventeenth century England, which suffered from great plagues, fires, and political revolutions, is called metaphysical.

14. They were afraid that the cold front, which was moving southward, would damage the orchards, located in Orlando where I was born.

15. San Francisco, where my sister lives, is one of the most colorful cities I have ever visited.

Part 2 Keeping Related Sentence Parts Together

In effective English sentences, the verb is closely tied to the subject; it is also closely tied to the complement. Similarly, the parts of a verb phrase are tied closely together. When these related sentence parts are widely separated by intervening words, the sentence is difficult to read. In general, keep closely related sentence parts together.

AWKWARD The *fog*, after closely hugging the ground all day long, *lifted* at last.
(subject and verb separated)

REVISED After closely hugging the ground all day long, the fog lifted at last.

AWKWARD Jack *had* never in the four years of his high school career *received* such poor marks.
(parts of a verb phrase separated)

REVISED Jack had never received such poor marks in the four years of his high school career.

AWKWARD You *have had*, whether you know it or not, your last chance. (verb and object separated)

REVISED Whether you know it or not, you have had your last chance.

Exercise Keeping Related Sentence Parts Together

Revise these sentences to bring related parts closer together.

1. The newest discoveries in science are to the average person awe-inspiring.
2. The refugees, after having been shunted around from one camp to another, were finally settled into homes of their own.
3. The TV announcer began, after a few opening remarks, his usual morning broadcast of the news.
4. The team had never, in all the games it had played, been so lucky as in this last game.
5. The family had, after a long vacation at the beach, returned to their home in the city.
6. The Student Council had, after much weighing of pros and cons, gone to the convention.
7. The foreign ministers' conference will be, everyone hopes, of great significance.

8. The program committee has, even though several members believe it is not feasible, voted to give the choral concert.

9. The house across the street has, for the last four years, been unoccupied.

10. Computer programing is, according to an article I read, extremely complicated.

11. Because United States Presidents had fewer duties, they often vacationed for whole summers early in the nineteenth century.

12. Gary volunteered to give the oral presentation in history because he frequently enjoyed attention.

13. He regretted only having two hands.

14. The Breitzmans were, having planned to go to Sweden after the Christmas season, disappointed that they were not granted their visas.

15. Because there was a fuel shortage, many big businesses were forced to close down this winter.

Part 3 Coordinating Related Ideas

There are times when ideas are so closely related that they should be joined in a single sentence. If the ideas seem of equal importance, they can be joined by a conjunction or by a semicolon in a compound sentence.

The coordinating conjunctions used to form compound sentences are *and, but, or, for, nor*. Each of these conjunctions has a specific meaning and therefore relates the parts of a compound sentence in a specific way: *and* and *nor* mean "in addition"; *or* means "an alternative"; *but* means "an exception"; *for* means "because."

The seniors will take their tests on Monday, *and* the juniors will take theirs on Wednesday.

Beth cannot solve the problem, *nor* can anyone else.

Our team started last, *but* we gathered the most paper.

Kate should apply now, *or* she may be too late.

Bob decided to try, *for* he was sure there had been a misunderstanding.

Conjunctive abverbs and connecting phrases are also used to tie ideas in compound sentences.

ADDITION	ALTERNATIVE	EXCEPTION OR CONTRAST
indeed	on the other hand	yet
in fact	at the same time	still
furthermore		however
moreover		nonetheless
also		
besides		

RESULT

consequently
as a consequence
therefore
hence
then

The choice of a conjunctive adverb depends upon the meaning the writer wants to convey. Each conjunctive adverb specifies a particular meaning, just as each coordinating conjunction does. The correlative conjunctions (*either–or; neither–nor; both–and; whether–or; not only–but also*) may be used to tie together the parts of a compound sentence.

Note: A comma is used before the coordinating conjunction in a compound sentence. A semicolon is placed before a conjuctive adverb, and a comma is usually placed after it. Here is an example of each.

The ballet opens this weekend, and the tickets will go on sale tomorrow.

The traffic was heavy; nevertheless, we arrived on time.

There are times when ideas do not need a conjunction between them. This is particularly true when the idea of "in addition to" is quite clear. The semicolon alone is better than *and* in these sentences.

It is raining here again; it was raining yesterday; it will rain tomorrow.

The outcome of the election was decisive; it was never in doubt.

Exercises Coordinating Related Ideas

A. From the conjunctions given in parentheses, choose the one that best fits the meaning.

1. Usually the lake is still and placid, (and, but, or) today it is in constant motion.
2. Please buy me a straw pocketbook in Italy, (or, for, but) bring me some perfume from Paris.
3. Spices were once one of the world's most desired possessions, (but, or, and) they are now available to everyone at reasonable prices.
4. She cannot read her own handwriting, (nor, and, but) can anyone else read it.
5. Kathy looked after the children, (and, but, for) her mother was sick.
6. The wind roared in the treetops, (but, and, or) the windows of the old house rattled.
7. The Supreme Court gives a majority opinion, (or, and, but) it often gives a minority opinion as well.
8. We can go to Europe by ship, (and, or, for, but) we can go by jet.
9. Our weekend hike in the mountains was a great adventure, (and, or, but) the sudden thunderstorms forced us to return home early.
10. Steve cannot go to the soccer match, (but, nor, and) can he go to dinner with us.

B. Supply a suitable conjunctive adverb from the list on page 62. Copy the sentences, punctuating properly.

1. We had read all the news stories _____ we had even read all the advertisements.
2. The Senator's constituents wrote him about the legislation _____ he ignored the letters.
3. Lori had never learned to swim _____ she nearly drowned when the boat overturned.
4. Keith did not meet us at the appointed time _____ we waited.

5. We want to be in Salzburg for the Music Festival _____ we want to see the ruins of ancient Greece.

6. The seniors usually take their examinations early _____ they are free for a week before Commencement.

7. We waited expectantly _____ the speaker did not appear.

8. The books were piled on the table and on the floor _____ the bookshelves were filled to overflowing.

9. The sun shines most of the time _____ the state is called the Sunshine State.

10. Violets grow wild in this region _____ they even come up through cracks in the pavement.

Part 4 Avoiding Faulty Coordination

When ideas are closely related, they can be read together with ease. One idea seems to complete the other; in fact, the second idea may help to explain the first. The main use of a compound sentence is to help the reader see a close relationship.

If unrelated ideas are joined in a compound sentence, the reader is confused, and the writer's point is lost. Sometimes the fault of joining unrelated ideas occurs because the writer has omitted something essential to the sense. His mind has raced ahead of his pen; consequently, a step has been left out.

CONFUSING The airport was closed in by fog, and we missed the game.

IMPROVED The airport was closed in by fog. *We were four hours late in arriving* and missed the game.

CONFUSING I took the aptitude tests last spring, and I am not going into engineering.

IMPROVED The aptitude tests I took last spring *showed that I am weak in mathematics.* I am not going into engineering because it requires mathematical skill.

Exercise **Avoiding Faulty Coordination**

Revise the following sentences in order to avoid faulty coordination.

1. Six inches of snow fell during the night, and we were late to school.

2. The cost of living has risen sharply during the past few years, and personal incomes have risen too.

3. The admission requirements of the colleges have become more stringent, and the number of students entering college has increased.

4. The new Music Center cost six million dollars, and the city has increased the tax rate.

5. The sky is overcast, and we cannot go on our picnic.

6. The experts had predicted that Bartow would never get into office, and she ridiculed them in her acceptance speech.

7. Mother had completely forgotten to take the turkey out of the freezer, but fortunately the shrimp made a hit with the guests.

8. The last-minute camping trip was fun, and Jane and I needed an extra blanket.

9. Jack auditioned for the band yesterday, and he will choose a different activity.

10. Our team won the state tournament, and school was canceled the next day.

11. Jason won first place in the photography competition, and he is now our newspaper photographer.

12. Megan's car broke down, and we still arrived at the airport on time.

13. Illinois is called "The Land of Lincoln," and President Lincoln spent much of his life there.

14. The sky was dark and threatening, and the cross country meet was postponed.

15. Alex Haley spoke about his ancestry to a large crowd in Texas, and he is the author of the highly publicized *Roots*.

Part 5 Avoiding Stringy Sentences

Some sentences become overloaded because the writer strings a number of ideas together, placing an *and* between each idea. The result is that no one idea stands out; there seems to be no organization. You can revise stringy sentences in two ways.

1. Choose the conjunction that will show the real relationship between the ideas you are presenting.
2. Divide the sentence into two or more sentences.

STRINGY There is a water shortage in many parts of the country, and this shortage is causing concern, and the U.S. Department of the Interior is trying out methods of changing sea water to fresh water.

REVISED The water shortage in many parts of the country is causing concern; *consequently*, the U.S. Department of the Interior is trying out methods of changing sea water to fresh water.

STRINGY Scientists today are working in an invisible world, and they are dealing with genes, atoms, ions, and electrons, and no one has ever seen them, and some of them may not exist, but to understand modern science, we must understand the scientists' ideas of these invisible things.

REVISED Scientists today are working in an invisible world of genes, atoms, ions, and electrons. No one has ever seen them; *indeed*, some of them may not exist. To understand modern science, however, we must understand the scientists' ideas of these invisible things.

Exercise Revising Stringy Sentences

Revise the sentences on the next page. They have too many *and*'s. In each case, you will need to make two or more sentences.

1. Many scientists have dreamed of transmitting power through the air without the use of wires, and they have experimented for many years, trying to develop their ideas, and at last they seem to have come near the realization of their dream.

2. Recently the small colleges have been sorely pressed financially, and they need more money for salaries for their teachers, and they do not want to raise the costs of tuition to supply the needed funds.

3. Students nowadays may want to learn such languages as Arabic, Russian, and Hindustani, and these are not taught in many schools, and students may have to wait until they are graduate students to learn them.

4. They were to entertain their family and friends that night, and they decided to go on with it and try it and make the best of it.

5. She was a scholarly and accomplished book critic for a large newspaper and when she decided to write her own novel and had to quit the job, her co-workers wondered who could replace her.

Part 6 Subordination

The main clause is the basic structure in any sentence. It states the main idea of the sentence. Modifying clauses and phrases are used to add details or to explain the conditions that define or limit the meaning of the main clause.

The writer alone knows what the main idea is in each sentence he or she writes. If he or she writes only compound sentences, or only main clauses, the writer gives the reader no guidance; hence, the effectiveness of the writing is lost.

MAIN IDEA	LIMITING, EXPLAINING, OR DEFINING DETAILS
We can go to the concert (at any time?)	if the tickets aren't sold out. (under this condition)
Gary may need an assistant (why?)	to help with the correspondence. (explaining)
Raleigh went to his death (how?)	proclaiming his innocence. (defining details)

Ideas of less importance can be subordinated (put in their proper place) by use of clauses. Adverb clauses are introduced by subordinating conjunctions, which express a great variety of relationships. (See Section 1.7 in your Handbook.) Nothing improves a sentence quite so much as substituting the right subordinating conjunction for a meaningless *and* that has been dropped thoughtlessly between two clauses.

WEAK Jim took the heaviest pack, *and* he staggered slowly up the hill.

BETTER *Taking* the heaviest pack Jim staggered slowly up the hill. (participle)

WEAK Mari was dressed in tennis dress, *and* she looked like a pro at the court club.

BETTER *Dressed* in a tennis dress, Mari looked like a pro at the court club. (past participle)

WEAK Pam worked hard for Sue's election, *and* she knew all along that Sue had no chance to win.

BETTER Pam worked hard for Sue's election, *although* she knew all along that Sue had no chance to win. (adverb clause)

Subordination may also be used to join two related sentences smoothly and economically.

FAIR Peg worked all night. She wanted the job completed on time.

BETTER Peg worked all night to complete the job on time. (infinitive)

FAIR Jack LeClerc is our guidance counselor. He did personnel work in the Navy.

BETTER Jack LeClerc, *our guidance counselor*, did personnel work in the Navy. (appositive)

BETTER Jack Le Clerc, *who did personnel work in the Navy*, is our guidance counselor. (adjective clause)

Upside-Down Subordination

This is the fault of placing an important idea in a subordinate clause or phrase.

FAULTY The sailboat capsized, *nearly drowning the crew.* (The near drowning of the crew is more important.)

REVISED The crew nearly drowned when the sailboat capsized.

FAULTY Mrs. Brown was crossing at the corner *when a cyclist knocked her down.*

REVISED Mrs. Brown was knocked down by a cyclist as she was crossing at the corner.

FAULTY Jon lost control, *falling off the cycle.*

REVISED Losing control, Jon fell off the cycle.

Exercises Subordinating Ideas

A. Combine these sentences, converting one into either a phrase or a clause. Be careful to avoid upside-down subordination.

1. The match suddenly came to an end. The weary challenger fell against the ropes.
2. The scaffolding had been built beside the church. A workman had fallen off the scaffolding.
3. Last Sunday we were at home. Some guests came in for dinner.
4. We will vote next Tuesday for our favorite candidates. The candidates have made no promises of patronage to their supporters.
5. These plates are replicas of the marble squares in the floor of the cathedral. The cathedral is in Siena, Italy.
6. The chairperson of the committee left the meeting. The members of the committee stayed to finish the discussion.
7. The guests had been entertained well. They thanked their host and hostess profusely.
8. The team has played well throughout the season. It will probably win the championship game.

9. Egypt became a province of Rome. Cleopatra committed suicide in 30 B.C.

10. The haiku is a Japanese poem usually on some subject in nature, and consists of three lines totalling seventeen syllables.

B. Change each of the following compound sentences by subordinating one of the clauses. You may change it to either a subordinate clause or a phrase.

1. The new books are reviewed each Sunday in *The New York Times Book Review*, and the reviewers are important writers and critics.
2. The foreign ministers' conference was held in Geneva, and the ministers from many nations attended the conference.
3. Science education is encouraged by the federal government, and many grants are given to improve science instruction in the high schools.
4. Golfing requires skill and experience, and many people take up golfing as a means of getting exercise.
5. The actor forgot his lines, and he went into an impromptu performance.
6. The color of the water changed from a dull gray to a bright blue, and the sun came from behind a dark cloud and shone brightly on the lake.
7. The air feels cold, but the outside thermometer registers sixty-six degrees.
8. We picked the flowers yesterday and arranged them, but they are wilted today.
9. Cross-country skiing requires strength and stamina, and many people have found cross-country skiing a way to stay physically fit.
10. Newly-released movies are reviewed each week in *Time*, and the reviewers are often well known critics.

C. Correct the upside-down subordination in these sentences.

1. He was walking in the woods when he was struck by lightning.
2. The woman who fell from the second-story window and fractured her leg was a window cleaner.
3. The book, which has caused a nation-wide sensation, is a novel about a small town.

4. The orchestra had begun the last number when someone shouted, "Fire!"

5. The politician, who was never elected to office, had tried five times.

6. Words, which can often be dangerous, are in reality only sounds in air or black marks on white paper.

7. The dancers, who seemed to be poetry in motion, presented a ballet.

8. The driver, who was killed when his car crashed into a tree, had fallen asleep at the wheel.

9. The outbreak of measles, which reached epidemic proportions, affected many children.

10. The special art exhibit was at The Art Institute of Chicago which included only Van Gogh originals.

Part 7 Reduction

Reduction is the means by which bulky sentences are made compact and effective. Reduction can be achieved by changing a clause to a phrase or a phrase to a single modifier.

CLAUSE We live in a house *which has high ceilings.*

PHRASE We live in a house *with high ceilings.*

PHRASE One of the players *on the Detroit team* was hurt.

WORD One of the *Detroit* players was hurt.

CLAUSE The people *who drive the buses* are on strike.

WORD The *bus* drivers are on strike.

CLAUSE The class elected José, *who is my closest friend.*

APPOSITIVE The class elected José, *my closest friend.*

If the clauses of a compound sentence have the same subject, the compound sentence can be reduced by using a compound predicate. Similarly, two clauses with the same verb can be reduced by using a compound subject.

SAME SUBJECT The men arrived at the camp late, *and they went right to bed.*

REDUCED The men *arrived* at the camp late and *went* right to bed.

SAME SUBJECT The tires are wearing thin, *and they will soon be useless.*

REDUCED The tires *are wearing* thin and *will* soon be useless.

SAME VERB The cups *were broken,* and the saucers *were broken.*

REDUCED The cups and saucers *were broken.*

Exercise **Reducing Sentences To Make Them Effective**

Rewrite each of these sentences, reducing the italicized words to a shorter construction.

1. Mr. Smith, *who is a banker and philanthropist,* gave a million dollars to Aurora College.
2. The boys and girls hiked up the mountain, *and when they were up there, they ate their supper there.*
3. The 1984 Olympics, *which will be held in Los Angeles,* are to be televised live throughout the world by satellite.
4. Karen, *who is the valedictorian of her class,* has been accepted by several universities *that are well known.*
5. The house had been burned, and *the garage had been burned too.*
6. Then men and women in the choir sang a selection *that was very beautiful.*

7. The Student Government Association sent delegates to the annual convention, *which was meeting in Denver, Colorado.*

8. The pencils, *which are a special kind with soft lead,* are lying on the table, *which is in the living room.*

9. Canoeing on the Kankakee River, *which is in northern Illinois,* is an enjoyable summer activity.

10. Organizing a paper *that is long and difficult* requires an outline, *which may be a tentative one.*

11. Source material must be acknowledged, *and it can be acknowledged in a footnote or in the body of your paper.*

12. Questionnaires *that were long and involved* were sent to the high school seniors.

13. An analogy, *which is an extended simile or metaphor,* may be helpful in clarifying an issue.

14. The Sears Tower, *which is one of the world's tallest buildings,* is 1,454 feet high.

15. James Hoban, *who was an Irish-born architect,* designed the White House.

Part 8 Parallelism

The word *and* should be used to join sentence parts of the same kind. It may join two nouns, two adjectives, two prepositional phrases, and so on. Similar sentence parts so joined are **parallel.** If the sentence parts joined by *and* are not of the same kind, **faulty parallelism** has occurred.

FAULTY The child needs *sleep* and *to be fed at regular hours.* (noun joined to phrase)

REVISED The child needs sleep and food at regular hours.

FAULTY Nancy worried about the *test* and *if she would do well.* (noun joined to clause)

REVISED Nancy worried about how she would do on the test. (When a parallel is impossible, change the sentence.)

FAULTY The police officer told the driver to park his truck and *that he must go to the police station.* (phrase joined to clause)

REVISED The police officer told the driver to park his truck and go to the police station.

FAULTY We go into town *to dance, to buy food,* or *for a movie.*

REVISED We go into town to dance, to buy food, or to see a movie.

And Which; And Who

A special kind of faulty parallelism occurs with *which* and *who.* The *and* should never appear before these words unless *which* or *who* appears earlier in the sentence.

STANDARD Dr. Granjon was a person *who* loved people and *who* devoted her life to their care.

NONSTANDARD There is a new sign over the entrance *and which* will direct you to our studio.

STANDARD There is a new sign over the entrance *which* will direct you to our studio.

NONSTANDARD We took our problem to the old repairman *and who* had never failed us before.

STANDARD We took our problem to the old repairman, *who* had never failed us before.

Exercise **Parallelism**

Correct the faulty parallelism in these sentences.

1. She is ambitious, intelligent, and has persistence.

2. The ambitious executive wants success in business, an active social life, an active family life, and he or she works for the community.

3. The teacher told the students to write the answers to the questions and that they must finish within the hour.

4. In the park I saw old people playing checkers, families picnicking, and students who were absorbed in reading textbooks.

5. Every town and city needs more parking space, more recreational facilities, and to have more money for these needs.

6. The class in reading learned to read faster and also reading with greater comprehension.

7. The explorers expected to find gold, to get rich, and an easy life.

8. The Puritans, a brave group and who suffered many hardships, influenced greatly the character of the American people.

9. All drivers using the turnpike and who cross the drawbridge must pay a toll.

10. The class read "Chicago," a poem by Carl Sandburg and who was an American poet.

11. The university attempts to teach students to think by requiring that they study logic, and they solve problems, and organizing in outline form their written work.

12. Preparing a manuscript for publication is an arduous task and that requires care and accuracy.

13. She asked for help with her geometry and that I explain the theorem again.

14. Mrs. Watkins asked for votes and to be elected.

15. This is an exciting novel and which you can get at the library.

Part 9 The Weak Passive

The subject of an active verb is the doer of the action. The subject of a passive verb is the receiver of the action. (See Section 1.3 in your Handbook.) There are many occasions when a passive verb form is useful and desirable. Sometimes the doer of an action is unknown or cannot be named.

The old house had been torn down.
The President was warned of the conspiracy.

Sometimes the passive verb is used to describe a common or ongoing experience.

The Yankee games are played in the Stadium.
The mail is delivered at one o'clock.

Sometimes the passive verb is used to avoid giving a direct order. Generally, in your Handbook, for example, rules and usages are stated with passive verbs.

A participial phrase at the beginning of a sentence *is followed* by a comma.
In standard usage, *bad is always used* after linking verbs.

The *weak passive* is the use of the passive when the active verb is more natural and direct.

WEAK A good time was had by everyone.
BETTER Everyone had a good time.

WEAK Much time is lost by students through poor planning.
BETTER Students lose much time through poor planning.

WEAK The ball was hit by Pete Rose right out of the park.
BETTER Pete Rose hit the ball right out of the park.

WEAK My homework is not given enough attention by me.
BETTER I do not give my homework enough attention.

Exercise **The Weak Passive**

Revise these sentences to eliminate the weak passive verbs. Four of the passive verbs are acceptable as they stand.

1. The book was discussed by the senior class.
2. Many gifts were brought by Mother when she went to town.
3. Dinner is served promptly at six o'clock.
4. The car was washed by us in the morning.

5. At the end of the program, a song was played by the ensemble.
6. A letter was written by the class to the town's mayor.
7. Litter boxes have been placed at every corner.
8. The old house was bought and remodeled by us.
9. The store window was crashed into by a runaway car.
10. Arrangements had been made by me for the club to meet at our house.
11. My tennis game is not given enough attention by me.
12. The dinner was enjoyed by all of the guests.
13. The article was printed in five languages.
14. The trailer court was destroyed during the storm.
15. A petition was written by the townspeople to the governor.

Chapter 5

Sentence Clarity

A writer's purpose is to state his or her thoughts and feelings as exactly as possible. The more carefully they are stated, the greater effect they will have. If necessary words are left out, the meaning is incomplete. If modifiers are misplaced or left dangling, the writer's meaning is distorted. If there is a sudden shift in point of view, the reader is thrown off the track of the argument.

All of these errors can be caught in the process of revision. This chapter will help you to become alert to such errors and, by correcting or avoiding them, to write with ever-increasing clarity.

Part 1 Avoiding Omissions of Necessary Words

Omission of *That*

In some sentences the *that* introducing a noun clause must be stated to avoid confusion. When it is omitted, the sentence can be read in two different ways.

CONFUSING We heard all transportation, even Amtrak, was halted by the snowstorm.

IMPROVED We heard *that* all transportation, even Amtrak, was halted by the snowstorm.

CONFUSING We heard the team members, coming off the field, were complaining about the referee.

IMPROVED We heard *that* the team members, coming off the field, were complaining about the referee.

CONFUSING Lee found all the employees were unhappy about working on Saturday.

IMPROVED Lee found *that* all the employees were unhappy about working on Saturday.

Omission of Part of a Verb Phrase

The subjects in the two clauses of a compound sentence often differ in number. The verb in each clause must agree with its subject. When both verbs have auxiliaries, the second auxiliary is sometimes omitted, resulting in confusion. The complete verb phrase must be used for clarity.

CONFUSING The gas tank was filled, and the tires checked. (tank *was;* tires *were*)

REVISED The gas tank *was* filled, and the tires *were* checked.

CONFUSING The drawing *was* made, and the winners announced. (drawing *was;* winners *were*)

REVISED The drawing *was* made, and the winners *were* announced.

Omissions in Comparisons

A comparison becomes awkward and confusing if necessary words are omitted.

CONFUSING Pat is one of the fastest, if not the fastest, student on the team. (Pat is not one of the fastest student.)

REVISED Pat is one of the fastest *students* on the team, if not the fastest.

CONFUSING The storm will be as bad or worse than last week's blizzard.

REVISED The storm will be as bad *as* last week's blizzard or worse.

Omission of Words in Idioms

An idiom is a group of words with a meaning different from the literal meanings of the words taken one by one.

The fisherman *held up* his catch.
The pilot *held up* her departure.

Many idioms like *hold up* are composed of a verb followed by an adverb. Here are some examples of idioms.

Idioms with *up*	**Idioms with *down***	**Idioms with *for***
hold up	turn down	love for
tie up	put down	need for
break up	hold down	respect for

Idioms with *in*	**Idioms with *on***	**Idioms with *off***
trust in	turn on	put off
pride in	put on	hold off
interest in	take on	turn off

When two idioms are used together in a compound construction, there is a temptation to drop the adverb from one of them. This omission is awkward and confusing.

FAULTY We were putting and taking off our coats all day.

CORRECTED We were putting *on* and taking off our coats all day.

FAULTY Mr. Andrews had no desire or need of more money.

CORRECTED Mr. Andrews had no desire *for* or need of more money.

FAULTY Carrie had a pride and respect for her work.

CORRECTED Carrie had a pride *in* and respect for her work.

Exercise Avoiding Omissions of Necessary Words

Revise these sentences to correct the omissions.

1. We understood the guests were coming in a few days.
2. The house was empty and the windows cracked and broken.
3. Have you heard the concert has been postponed?
4. The clothes were packed, and the house turned over to its new occupants.
5. The basketball team is one of the best, if not the best, team in the entire state.
6. The food on the boat will be as good or better than the food in the hotel.
7. She has a liking and pride in her music.
8. The paralegal is enthusiastic and thrilled with her new position.
9. Mary Pickford was one of the most popular, if not the most popular, motion picture star of the silent films.
10. She heard her name had been mentioned for the Cabinet post.
11. My dog is one of the most intelligent, if not the most intelligent, dog on our block.
12. The pilots were briefed on the flight, and the order given to proceed.
13. This novel by Faulkner is one of the best, if not the best, novel I have ever read.
14. The principal of the school decided the players could go to the game in the school bus.
15. The cakes looked and were similar to baking powder biscuits.

Part 2 The Placement of Modifiers

Single adjectives are usually placed just before the words they modify. Adjective phrases and clauses follow immediately after the words they modify. The only exceptions occur in sentences in which a phrase and a clause modify the same word. In this situation, the phrase precedes the clause.

We talked to the man at the store whom we met yesterday.

Many adverb modifiers can be moved from one place in a sentence to another without a change of meaning. Occasionally, however, moving an adverb produces unexpected effects. In general, be careful to place adverb modifiers so that they will express your meaning exactly.

CONFUSING Linda was learning to dive *slowly*.

REVISED Linda was *slowly* learning to dive.

CONFUSING *Happily*, the play ended. (just in time!)

REVISED The play ended *happily*. (happy ending)

CONFUSING All the students can*not* get into the room.

REVISED *Not* all the students can get into the room.

CONFUSING Amy was praised for heroism *by the mayor*.

REVISED Amy was praised *by the mayor* for heroism.

BETTER The mayor praised Amy for her heroism.

Exercise The Placement of Modifiers

Revise these sentences to correct the misplaced modifiers.

1. The children sat looking at the parade in the window.
2. The class only has five dollars to spend for decorations.
3. The party never hopes to lose another election.
4. The dentist looked at the person who sat in the chair stealthily.

5. Did you see the article about the new school in the paper?

6. All of the spectators cannot get into the stadium.

7. Pulitzer prizes are given annually for outstanding work in journalism, established by Joseph Pulitzer.

8. Her gift for her sister was a book of drawings on her birthday.

9. There is a package from Grandpa in your mailbox.

10. The thieves were arrested soon after the bank had been robbed by the police.

11. The ushers brought in chairs for the guests with cushioned seats.

12. Terry was praised for pitching a no-hitter by the coach.

13. Everyone should see a doctor to stay healthy at least once a year.

14. Wally Chambers talked about his football experiences during dinner.

15. I saw some geese eating my lunch at the lagoon.

Part 3 Avoiding Dangling Modifiers

When a phrase or clause is placed next to a word that it cannot modify sensibly, it is called a **dangling modifier.** Dangling modifiers often appear at the beginning of sentences.

PARTICIPLE Opening the door, chaos met our eyes. (This says that *chaos* opened the door.)

INFINITIVE To be perfectly safe, good tires are necessary. (This says that *tires* are *perfectly safe.*)

ELLIPTICAL CLAUSE While swinging a bat, his wrist broke. (This says the *wrist* swung a bat.)

To correct a dangling participle, supply a word for it to modify sensibly, or change the participle to a main verb and give it a subject. The phrase is thus turned into a clause.

FAULTY Walking in the dark, my foot struck something soft.

CORRECTED As I was walking in the dark, my foot struck something soft.

FAULTY Standing on tiptoe, the inside of the room could be seen.

CORRECTED Standing on tiptoe, *we* could see the inside of the room.

FAULTY Hoping for prompt aid, this letter is addressed to you.

CORRECTED I address this letter to you, hoping for prompt aid.

To correct a dangling infinitive, supply a word for the phrase to modify sensibly.

FAULTY To see the show this season, tickets must be ordered now.

CORRECTED To see the show this season, *you* must order tickets now.

To correct dangling elliptical clauses, supply the omitted words.

FAULTY When frozen, place the cream in a tray.

CORRECTED When the cream is frozen, place it in a tray.

Exercise **Avoiding Dangling Modifiers**

Revise these sentences to correct the dangling modifiers.

1. Eleanor said, "I smelled oysters going downstairs for supper."
2. Entering the English classroom, four windows can be seen.
3. Looking at television, the electricity went off suddenly.
4. Looking up, the brilliant stars can be seen in the dark sky.
5. While walking in the park, the lake can be seen in the distance.
6. At the age of five, my parents sent me to camp.
7. Being rushed to the hospital, the siren of the ambulance made a weird noise.
8. After seeing Rome, other cities seem lacking in grandeur.
9. To hear well, the auditorium must be built properly.
10. When thoroughly cooked, serve the food in a casserole dish.
11. Paul found a wallet walking home from school.

12. Hoping to see the President, the streets were packed with people.

13. I knocked over the plants walking in the dark.

14. Driving toward the west, the sun was in our eyes.

15. We saw the Goodyear blimp driving down the expressway.

Part 4 Avoiding Needless Shifts

If you were looking at a movie and suddenly found that the pictures were showing upside-down, you would have at least a momentary feeling of confusion. Something like this occurs when a writer begins a sentence in one tense and suddenly shifts without warning to another tense. Shifts in number or person, and shifts from active to passive verb forms produce the same confusion.

There are times when it is necessary to shift from one tense to another or from active to passive. The need on these occasions will be readily apparent to the reader. It is the needless shift that causes confusion.

Shifts from Active to Passive

A sentence that starts out in one voice should usually continue in that voice. Remember that the subject of an active verb is the doer of the action; the subject of the passive verb is the receiver of the action. To change from active to passive is therefore a considerable change in point of view.

SHIFT IN VOICE The district attorney *questioned* the bank president, and his files *were examined*.

IMPROVED The district attorney questioned the bank president, and examined his files.

SHIFT IN VOICE We *telephoned* all our friends, and even strangers *were called*.

IMPROVED We telephoned all our friends and even called strangers.

Shifts in Tense

If a sentence begins in the present tense, it should usually continue in that tense. If it begins in the past tense, it should not shift to the present.

FAULTY We *are standing* in the street when the door *began* to open.

REVISED We *were standing* in the street when the door *began* to open.

ALSO ACCEPTABLE We *are standing* in the street when the door *begins* to open.

FAULTY The class *was studying* quietly, and suddenly Jeff *lets* out a yell.

REVISED The class *was studying* quietly, and suddenly Jeff *let* out a yell.

FAULTY There *were* two seconds left when Laura *makes* the basket.

REVISED There *were* two seconds left when Laura *made* the basket.

Shifts in Person and Number

The indefinite pronoun *one* is in the third person. It is referred to by the personal pronouns *he, his* and *him;* or *she, her,* and *her;* or by *he or she.* If you start a sentence with *one,* do not refer to it with the pronouns *you* or *your.*

SHIFT If *one* hears a baseless rumor, *you* can either ignore it or try to find out how it started.

CORRECTED If *one* hears a baseless rumor, *he or she* can either ignore it or try to find out how it started.

Many collective nouns like *group, class, club, crowd, team,* and so on, may be regarded as either singular or plural. As the writer, you may decide whether the word is to be singular or plural, but once having decided, you must abide by your decision.

SHIFT The club *has* (singular) decided that *they* (plural) will not elect new members this fall.

CORRECTED The club *has* (singular) decided that *it* (singular) will not elect new members this year.

SHIFT The crowd roared *its* (singular) approval, and then *they* (plural) broke up the meeting.

CORRECTED The crowd roared *their* (plural) approval, and then *they* (plural) broke up the meeting.

Exercise **Avoiding Needless Shifts**

Revise these sentences to correct the needless shifts in number, person, tense, or voice.

1. Paula prepares the food for the party, and the house was filled with flowers.
2. The boys were on their way to Riverfront Stadium and are happy to be going to a World Series game.
3. I think that if one goes to college, you should do your best to succeed.
4. The team was playing brilliantly when suddenly they begin to collapse.
5. The members of the class sold tickets for the homecoming dance, and the money was collected.
6. I was sitting alone in the house when suddenly someone begins to pound on the door.
7. Ed wrote his weekly theme by hand, but it was typed before it was given to the teacher.
8. The family plans a trip each year, and usually they go to some interesting place.
9. I heard a step on the porch, and then the dogs, hearing it also, begin to bark.

10. The mayor campaigned hard, but the election was won by the party in favor of the Charter-Council form of government.

11. When one reads a newspaper, you should read the important news and editorials as well as the sports page.

12. Sally and Jean were lying on the beach, and suddenly the tide begins to come in around them.

13. The army offers many courses of study for the enlisted personnel and they are offered also vocational training.

14. The class is studying frogs now, but they will study insects next week.

15. It has been my experience that if one wants to learn to write, you must write a composition of some kind each week.

Chapter 6

Sentence Variety

This section is for students who have mastered the basic elements of good sentences. It is for students who understand the subject-verb-complement order of English sentences and use this order to write clear sentences. It is for students who know where modifiers usually appear in a sentence and for those who regularly avoid ambiguities created by faulty omissions, faulty pronoun reference, and the like. In short, this section is for students who have achieved clarity in their writing and now wish to compose effective and interesting sentences.

In natural English speech, we use three devices to secure interesting expression: the rise and fall of the voice, stress or accent, and rhythm. The voice falls between clauses, at the close of an introductory phrase or clause, and at the end of a sentence. We accent certain syllables in order to pronounce words correctly, and we also stress words to which we want to give special emphasis. Rhythm is achieved by a combination of voice falls and accents.

Speech is a natural expression; writing is not. Some of the cleverest conversationalists we encounter will have little formal schooling. They speak easily with varying rhythms, but they may be totally incapable of recording these rhythms in written sentences. It follows that the smoothest writing, when read aloud, sounds like normal speech, for the successful writer gives the reader the feeling of speaking directly in conversation.

In writing, as in speech, variety in rhythm is pleasing. Varied rhythm is achieved by using a combination of sentence patterns—by changing the kinds and positions of modifiers, by varying the lengths and kinds of sentences.

Sentence variety is usually desired. However, *deliberate* repetition of the same pattern is a good device for securing emphasis and clarity. Note the repeated pattern in the first paragraph of this section.

The methods of securing variety suggested here are best used in revision. They are a means of curing monotonous passages. The writer who sets out in a first draft to begin each sentence in a different way is likely to find that the sentence structure interferes with natural speech rhythms, producing self-conscious and awkward passages.

Part 1 Variety of Sentence Beginnings

Usually when every sentence in a passage begins in the same way, the effect is monotonous. A succession of sentences beginning with the same word or with the same kind of phrase or clause lulls the reader to inattention. As you read the two following passages, note the points at which your voice drops.

Sentences beginning with the same kind of phrase

Leaving the road, we plunged into the brush. *Coming to a creek,* we waded across. *Fighting our way through a tangle of vines,* we at last reached a path. *Turning left,* we climbed steadily uphill for an hour.

Sentences beginning with the same word

He was puzzled by the reaction of the crowd. *He* had tried to say something that would win their approval. *He* could not understand why they seemed hostile. *He* decided finally that it would not have mattered what he said.

Sentence variety can be achieved by beginning a succession of sentences in different ways—with adverb modifiers; infinitive, prepositional, or participial phrases; or with adverb clauses.

Jill worked conscientiously at the job until evening.
(subject-verb)

Conscientiously, Jill worked at the job until evening.
(adverb modifier)

To finish the job, Jill worked until evening.
(infinitive phrase)

Until evening, Jill worked conscientiously at the job.
(prepositional phrase)

Working conscientiously, Jill stayed at the job until evening.
(participial phrase)

Until evening came, Jill worked conscientiously at the job.
(adverb clause)

Exercises Varying Sentence Beginnings

A. Rewrite the following sentences, beginning each in accordance with the suggestion in parentheses.

1. Walter walked over to the bank in the morning to cash the check. (prepositional phrase)
2. Someone had evidently notified the Coast Guard about us. (single-word modifier)

3. Harry held the precious package in his arms and climbed into the back seat. (participial phrase beginning with *holding*)

4. Drivers' licenses are issued in Alabama and Georgia to sixteen-year-olds. (prepositional phrase)

5. Dad drives twenty miles to work every day. (adverb modifier)

6. Linda earned a thousand dollars during the summer by working at two jobs. (prepositional phrase)

7. Beth scored high on the test and won a valuable scholarship to the state university. (participial phrase beginning with *having scored*)

8. We will hire you if there is a job open. (adverb clause)

9. The Yankee pitching staff was in a state of collapse by midsummer. (prepositional phrase)

10. The rain came down suddenly in torrents. (adverb modifier)

B. Follow the directions for Exercise A.

1. We had been afraid of fire from the beginning. (prepositional phrase)

2. Mike left the pool early and hurried home. (participial phrase beginning with *leaving*)

3. The old motor was clearly not equal to the task. (adverb modifier)

4. The little movie house closed because of poor attendance. (prepositional phrase)

5. Only one of all our neighbors has a new car this year. (prepositional phrase)

6. Virginia Woolf was among the first authors to make use of the stream-of-consciousness technique in writing. (prepositional phrase beginning with *among*)

7. William Wordsworth celebrated nature in his poetry; he felt that nature was a source of "joy and purest passion" for man. (participial phrase beginning with *celebrating*)

8. Hitler's forces were conquering Russia until winter set in. (adverb clause)

9. The President issued the warning sternly. (single-word modifier)

10. They do not give courses in home economics in the first semester. (prepositional phrase)

Part 2 Variety of Sentence Structure

In student writing, a monotonous style arises chiefly from overuse of compound sentences. A succession of compound sentences is boring because the rise and fall of intonation is so regular. As you read the following passage, note the points at which your voice drops.

> The storm arose without warning, and waves started to bounce our boat around. Herb pulled in the anchor, and I reeled in our lines. It was impossible to get back to our dock, so Herb steered for the point. The wind was behind us, or we would never have made it. We got fairly close, and then we jumped into water up to our hips and pulled the boat ashore.

A succession of compound sentences can be avoided by changing one of the clauses. The clause may be made into a subordinate clause or a participial phrase. Some compound sentences can be changed into simple sentences with a compound predicate.

COMPOUND SENTENCE	We were delayed by a flat tire, and we missed the first touchdown.
PARTICIPIAL PHRASE	Delayed by a flat tire, we missed the first touchdown.
SUBORDINATE CLAUSE	Because we were delayed by a flat tire, we missed the first touchdown.
COMPOUND PREDICATE	We were delayed by a flat tire and missed the first touchdown.

Exercises Varying Sentence Structure

A. Rewrite the following compound sentences, changing one of the clauses in each in accordance with the suggestion in parentheses.

1. The lecturer spoke about cancer, and he said that cancer could turn out to be several diseases. (compound predicate)

2. Many people do not want to go to college more than two years, and junior colleges are growing rapidly. (subordinate clause)

3. Sue has been an exchange student in France and she speaks French fluently. (participial phrase)

4. I knew that the plane was late, and I took my time in getting to the airport. (subordinate clause)

5. We flew at an altitude of 20,000 feet, and we passed over a bad electrical storm. (participial phrase)

6. The Indian visitor was delighted by the students' knowledge of life in his land, and he stayed for three days. (participial phrase)

7. Paul Norwood read the morning newspaper, and he discovered that he had not been elected after all. (subordinate clause)

8. There is plenty of rainfall in this country, but it is not evenly distributed. (subordinate clause beginning with *although*)

9. Everyone was late to work this morning, and there was a fire on the subway. (subordinate clause beginning with *because*)

10. The disassembled Statue of Liberty was brought here in 210 wooden cases, and it arrived at Bedloe's Island in June, 1885. (participial clause beginning with *brought*)

B. Rewrite the following compound sentences. Change one of the clauses in each in accordance with the suggestions in parentheses.

1. Pam heard about the job early, and she was first to apply. (participial phrase)

2. The American clipper ships appeared, and they swept other ships from the seas. (subordinate clause beginning with *when*)

3. The book is long, and it requires careful reading. (compound predicate)

4. News of the gold strike reached San Francisco, and there was a mad dash out of the city. (subordinate clause)

5. The band uniforms have been delivered. They are packed for the trip. (compound predicate)

6. The severe winter weather caused food and fuel shortages, and many people suffered greatly. (subordinate clause beginning with *because*)

7. The mayor spoke to the district attorney and he urged him to proceed with the investigation. (compound predicate)

8. The crowd left, and the hall was searched thoroughly. (subordinate clause beginning with *after*)

9. Influenza vaccine is available to everyone, but we are still having epidemics. (subordinate clause beginning with *although*)

10. Pittsburgh was still a small city, and Willa Cather came there in 1910. (subordinate clause beginning with *when*)

Part 3 Variety of Sentence Length

A passage in which all the sentences are of about the same length, whether long or short, is monotonous. The insertion of a sentence of different length varies the rhythm and revives the interest of the reader. In the following passage from Hemingway's "Big Two-Hearted River," note how the short sentences are relieved by long sentences.

> He walked along the road feeling the ache from the pull of the heavy pack. The road climbed steadily. It was hard work walking uphill. His muscles ached and the day was hot, but Nick felt happy. He felt he had left everything behind, the need for thinking, the need to write, other needs. It was all back of him.

Avoiding a Series of Short Sentences

Monotony is created especially by a succession of short sentences. There are times when a conscious use of a series of short sentences is very effective, as in narrative, when it has the effect of building up suspense. The unconscious use of a succession of short sentences, however, creates an awkward effect. The effect can be overcome by combining the sentences. As you read the two passages on the next page, note the points where your voice drops.

ORIGINAL Quietly we walked into the hall. It was very dark. Bob found a lamp. He turned it on. We sat down to wait for Mr. Manning. We waited for an hour. He didn't come.

REWRITTEN Quietly we walked into the dark hall. After Bob had found a lamp and turned it on, we sat down to wait for Mr. Manning. We waited for an hour, but he didn't come.

Short sentences may be combined in a number of ways:

1. By using a compound sentence.

TWO SENTENCES The plane stopped in Okinawa for repairs. We landed in Tokyo three hours late.

COMBINED The plane stopped in Okinawa for repairs, so we landed in Tokyo three hours late.

2. By using a simple sentence with a compound predicate.

TWO SENTENCES I stained the cabinet. Then I coated it with shellac.

COMBINED I stained the cabinet and then coated it with shellac.

3. By using a subordinate clause.

TWO SENTENCES Jeff sprained his ankle. He was practicing the javelin throw.

COMBINED Jeff sprained his ankle when he was practicing the javelin throw.

4. By using a participial phrase.

TWO SENTENCES We were worried by some strange noises. They were coming from the engine.

COMBINED We were worried by some strange noises coming from the engine.

5. By using a prepositional phrase.

TWO SENTENCES The concert will take place at County Center. The date is February 10.

COMBINED The concert will take place at County Center on February 10.

6. By using an appositive.

TWO SENTENCES Susan Stein won first prize in the state instrumental competition. She is a soloist in our orchestra.

COMBINED Susan Stein, a soloist in our orchestra, won first prize in the state tournament competition.

7. By using a single-word modifier.

TWO SENTENCES Quietly we walked into the hall. It was very dark.

COMBINED Quietly we walked into the dark hall.

Exercises **Varying Sentence Length**

A. Combine each of the following sets of short sentences in accordance with the suggestions in parentheses.

1. Ellen turned through the book. It was old. (single-word modifier)

2. The judge came in. (subordinate clause beginning with *when*) The spectators stood up.

3. We left Jean at home. She was watching television. (participial phrase)

4. I read about your illness in the paper. (subordinate clause beginning wiith *when*) I was reminded that I had not written you.

5. The engineers landed in helicopters on Ellesmere Island. It was the dead of winter. (prepositional phrase beginning with *in*)

6. The doctor decided on an operation. She realized that it might not succeed. (participial phrase)

7. I am going to Triton College in River Grove, Illinois. It is a junior college. (appositive) It specializes in technical subjects. (participial phrase)

8. We were delayed by an accident on the expressway. (subordinate clause beginning with *because*) We missed the first act of the play.

9. The magnificent Bayeux Tapestry is a strip of embroidered linen that depicts the incidents preceding the Battle of Hastings. The Tapestry was commissioned in 1077. (participial phrase)

10. We attended a lecture on consumer fraud. It was informative. (one word)

11. We have been building millions of houses a year. (subordinate clause beginning with *although*) There are still not enough. Every year a greater number of new families is started. (subordinate clause beginning with *because*)

12. Grover Cleveland was elected to a second term. (subordinate clause) The country was on the verge of financial panic. People were jittery. (main clause)

13. Sir Georg Solti is one of the finest conductors in the world. He directs the Chicago Symphony. (appositive)

14. The play will open at the Shubert Theatre. The date is July 1. (prepositional phrase)

15. Doctors discovered that Cleveland had cancer of the jaw. They decided on an operation. (compound predicate) They put him on a battleship. They performed the operation secretly in New York Harbor. (compound predicate)

B. Rewrite the following paragraph. Using the methods shown in this chapter for achieving sentence variety, make changes in sentence structure to create fluent, readable prose.

> Many of today's novelists write as if by rote. Their works all appear to be taken from the same pattern. Readers must be more critical in their choice of books. The shelves of bookstores are

teeming with mediocre if not inferior tales. The books are praised by their publishers as being "the greatest romance of the time" or "the year's most suspenseful novel." Even the writing is poor. Many writers are interested only in making money and not in producing good, solid literature. Few writers today are interested in contributing to the growth of the novel as a literary genre. At no other time have there been so many literary works available to the public.

Chapter 7

The Process of Writing

As you mature, you bring new ideas and experiences to bear on your writing. The process of writing becomes more complex because you have larger ideas to sort out and a more subtle kind of refining to do. You need to do more thinking before you write to find a sharp focus for your writing.

You are beginning to find your own voice and are more aware of style. Sensory appeal and figurative language achieve a new level of sophistication. You become more critical in your choice of precise vocabulary. You strive to achieve a greater variety of sentence structure. You are better able to test the unity and coherence of a piece of writing.

Writing as often as possible to free yourself for writing is a continuing challenge. One procedure, however, remains constant: the process of writing. The stages in the process are pre-writing; writing a first draft; and rewriting, or revising. These steps are critical to the process. They help you decide what to write about, how to organize what you write, and how to rewrite, or revise, what you have written.

Pre-Writing

1. Possible Topics
the botanical gardens
coaching the Special Olympics
an evening at the lake

2. Selected Topic
coaching the Special Olympics

Writing the First Draft

The happiest time I have ever spent was last Sunday, ~~was really great.~~ ~~That was~~ the day I coached the Special Olympics. ~~It was a day of happiness.~~ The happiness came

Rewriting, or Revising

The happiest time I have ever spent was last Sunday, the day I coached the Special Olympics. The happiness came from the fact

Part 1 Pre-Writing

The pre-writing step is important. It is the physical aid to thinking about and planning what you are going to write. It helps you collect your ideas, sort them out, and organize them in a meaningful way.

First, concentrate your thinking on possible topics to write about or on the assignment given. Write the topics as they occur to you. Study your list. After you have chosen a topic that interests you or one that fulfills the requirements of the assignment, narrow the topic so that you can handle it in a given length.

Next, make a list of interesting and meaningful details to use in developing your topic. List as many as you can. You can select the most workable ones later.

Finally, jot down any ideas or questions related to your topic. Use whatever is meaningful. If you need to learn more about your topic, do so.

Here is an example of pre-writing notes.

PRE-WRITING NOTES

1. Possible Topics

visiting a college
my tryout for cheerleader
my photography assignment
missing the plane
my driving test
my visit to Hawaii

2. Selected Topic

my photography assignment

3. Specific Details

sunny, warm day
woods and small hills
expensive new camera
proud of it
birthday present
leather equipment bag
stout hiking boots
walked for hours
grove of trees
headache
bruises
pheasant in field

4. Notes

narrative paragraph?
vivid details, sensory
chronological order
show feelings
first person
topic sentence at end?

Part 2 Writing the First Draft

Now that you have thought about your topic sufficiently and focused on your main idea, you are ready to write your first draft. Using your pre-writing notes to guide you, let your ideas and feelings flow on paper. Do not stop to correct mistakes or reorganize ideas. Just free yourself to write. This is only your first draft. You will rewrite, or revise, later.

Here is an example of a first draft of a paragraph.

FIRST DRAFT

I had a mouthful of dirt. I had a headache. My face was numb. I tried to open my eyes, but everything was black. I lay there, trying to come to. Where was I? What happened? Soon I realized that I was lying face down on the ground. I forced myself up and lifted my head. In the distance I saw my equipment bag. Its contents were spilled all over. The bag looked like a lump of dough. My camera was nowhere in sight. I looked up. My camera was dangling above me. Its leather strap was caught on a rock. Then I remembered what happened. I was photographing some trees for my photography class and I stumbled over a root and fell down the hill.

Part 3 Rewriting, or Revising

Now read what you have written. At this stage of the process, you will need to think critically about what you have written.

Did you stick to your topic? Did you include everything you wanted to? Did you leave out unnecessary details? Do you like what you have written? Does it come alive, or is it static? Now read aloud what you have written. Do your ideas flow smoothly? Do you have variety in your sentence structure?

Concentrate on every word. Are your ideas clearly expressed? Is each word the right word? Did you *show* your reader what you want to say? Have you involved the reader in your experience?

Is your writing organized logically? Is there a beginning, a middle, and an end to the development of your idea?

Here is the rewritten, or revised, paragraph. Think about how the added details help the reader to share the immediacy of the experience. Notice how the short sentences at the beginning help to convey the disjointed feelings and actions of the speaker. Notice the words that convey the physical condition of the speaker. Finally, notice how suspense is created by placing the topic sentence at the end.

REWRITTEN, OR REVISED PARAGRAPH

~~I had a mouthful~~ My mouth was full of dirt. ~~I had a headache.~~ My head ached, but my face ~~was~~ seemed numb. When I tried to open my eyes, ~~but~~ everything ~~was~~ looked black. I lay ~~there~~ quietly, trying to ~~come to~~ gather myself together. Where was I? What had happened? ~~Soon~~ As my senses returned, I realized that I was lying face down on ~~the~~ ground, covered with coarse dirt and small stones. I forced myself ~~up~~ onto my hands and lifted my throbbing head. ~~In the~~ A short distance away I saw my equipment bag, ~~I~~its contents ~~were~~ spilled ~~all~~ over the ground. The bag itself looked like a lump of brown dough. My camera was nowhere in sight. Painfully, I looked up. My camera ~~was dangling~~ dangled above me, ~~I~~its long leather strap ~~was~~ caught on a projecting rock. ~~Then~~ With effort, I remembered what had happened. As I was photographing ~~some~~ trees as an assignment for my photography class, ~~and~~ I had stumbled over a gnarled root and ~~fell~~ had fallen down the side of the hill.

Proofreading

After you have critically analyzed and carefully revised your first draft, you need to proofread it to make sure that everything is correct. Check the spelling. Check capitalization and punctuation. Use whatever references you have available to check accuracy.

Finally, when you are satisfied that your writing is clear and correct, write it in its final form. Write carefully. Make your work as neat as possible. Be sure to follow the manuscript form that your teacher requires, including headings and margins.

When you have finished your final copy, proofread it again to make sure you have written it correctly. Read it aloud, to yourself, one more time.

Here is the final copy of the paragraph.

FINAL COPY

My mouth was full of dirt. My head ached, but my face seemed numb. When I tried to open my eyes, everything looked black. I lay quietly, trying to gather myself together. Where was I? What had happened? As my senses returned, I realized that I was lying face down on ground covered with coarse dirt and small stones. I forced myself onto my hands and lifted my throbbing head. A short distance away I saw my equipment bag, its contents spilled over the ground. The bag itself looked like a lump of brown dough. My camera was nowhere in sight. Painfully, I looked up. My camera dangled above me, its long leather strap caught on a projecting rock. With effort, I remembered what had happened. As I was photographing trees as an assignment for my photography class, I had stumbled over a gnarled root and had fallen down the side of the hill.

Guidelines for the Process of Writing

Pre-Writing

1. Make a list of possible topics.
2. Select a topic that interests you and narrow it.
3. Make a list of interesting and meaningful details that you could use to develop your topic.
4. Jot down ideas or questions related to your topic.
5. Learn more about your topic if you need to.

Writing the First Draft

1. Begin to write.
2. Continue to write, without stopping to fuss over or correct anything at this stage. Let your thoughts flow freely.

Rewriting, or Revising

1. Read what you have written.
2. Did you stick to your topic?
3. Did you include everything you wanted to? Did you leave out unnecessary details?
4. Do you like what you have written? Is it interesting? Does it come alive, or is it static?
5. Read aloud what you have written. Do your ideas flow smoothly? Do you have variety in your sentence structure?
6. Are your ideas clearly expressed? Is each word the right word?
7. Did you *show* the reader what you want to say? Have you involved the reader in your experiences?
8. Is your writing organized logically, with a beginning, a middle, and an end?
9. Analyze your writing. Rewrite, or revise, wherever necessary.

Proofreading

1. Read your rewritten, or revised, first draft.
2. Check for correct capitalization.
3. Check spelling. Use a dictionary, if necessary.
4. Check to see that all punctuation is correct.
5. Make a neat, final copy, following required manuscript form.

Chapter 8

The Paragraph: Its Structure

A paragraph is a unit of writing complete in itself. A single paragraph is like a brick. Just as a brick is solid and substantial, so is a paragraph. Just as a brick is usually combined with other bricks to form a wall, a walk, a foundation, or a patio, so is a paragraph combined with other paragraphs to form a composition, an article, a story, or a book. In this chapter, the basic structural elements of the paragraph—the topic sentence and the body—are analyzed. In the next chapter, other characteristics inherent in the well written paragraph are explored.

Part 1 Defining the Paragraph

A paragraph is a group of related sentences that develop a single idea. A paragraph usually has a topic sentence that states the main idea and a body made up of sentences that explain or support the idea in the topic sentence.

Like most definitions, this definition of an ideal paragraph has some exceptions. They are introduced later in the chapter, but for the present, the discussion is based on the criteria set forth in the preceding definition.

Analysis 1

> Herbert Hoover established the image of himself as an Iowa farm boy steeped in the traditions of rural America. He spoke of the swimming hole under the willows, of trapping rabbits in cracker boxes in the woods down by the Burlington track, and of belly-whopping down Cook's Hill on winter nights. He recalled being taught by a neighboring Indian boy how to bring down pigeons and prairie chickens with a bow and arrow. Fishing, wrote Hoover, was "good for the soul," for everyone was equal before fishes. He sung the praises of "the willow pole with a butcher'd-string line, fixed with hooks ten for a dime, whose compelling lure is one segment of an angleworm and whose incantation is spitting on bait." When he wrote his letter accepting the Republican nomination in 1928, Hoover referred to himself as "a boy from a country village, without inheritance or influential friends."
> —William E. Leuchtenburg

This is a good example of a well constructed paragraph. The first sentence tells the reader that Hoover represented himself as a simple farm boy. Having said that, the writer then explains, or enlarges upon, this idea. He does so in sentences two, three, four, and five. In the final sentence he restates Hoover's view of himself as a country boy, the subject he introduced in his first sentence.

Analysis 2

> One of the things I recall most clearly about my first nervous days of research in a Cambodian peasant village—as I struggled to adjust myself to an alien tropical setting, a blur of unfamiliar faces, and a language I could barely comprehend—is the old women. When I wandered timidly through the village, most

people seemed to stand back and stare. However, the old ladies smiled and greeted me, patted my arms, and drew me into their houses with graceful invitations. There they would offer me sweets, pat me some more, and speak to me slowly and simply as to a child, saying how nice it was that I had come to stay in their village. Filled with anxiety about my acceptance into the community, I clung to these expressions of hospitality like a drowning woman. The old "grandmothers" buoyed me through those difficult first weeks, giving a foretaste of the warmth and generosity that I would eventually receive from all the villagers; and I shall always be grateful for their kind welcome.—May Ebihara

This paragraph also fits the definition of an ideal paragraph. The topic sentence introduces the setting, describes the writer's feelings of alienation and nervousness, and indicates the importance of the old women to her first days in Cambodia. The body sentences explain the main idea by describing the gestures of friendship made by the women and the writer's reaction to these gestures. Each sentence adds something to the development of the paragraph.

Analysis 3

Quite recently the peasants of Transylvania, a mountainous Rumanian province, discovered that they harbor a considerable tourist attraction. For the past few years visitors from the West have been coming round to inquire the whereabouts of Castle Dracula, home of the celebrated literary and cinematic vampire. The resulting confrontation between peasant and tourist is a sort of mismeeting between a surviving folk culture and a thriving mass culture.

This paragraph has a serious flaw. While it opens with a strong topic sentence, the body stops short of completely developing the main idea. The reader is left wondering about the nature of the confrontation between the peasants and the tourists and about its impact on both groups.

Analysis 4

Winter memories are the best memories of all. To sit before a roaring fireplace when the snow is on the ground and to remember the laughter of summer is to remember joyously. The wind howls but doesn't penetrate your warmth or security. Yes, winter memories are the best of all.

This paragraph is not only inadequately developed, but it also contains a sentence that strays from the idea of winter memories, the main idea stated in the topic sentence. In addition, the paragraph concludes with a sentence that can be best described as a "space filler" or an afterthought.

Exercise Analyzing Paragraphs

Examine the following paragraphs. Identify those that are well developed, unified paragraphs and those that are not. Be prepared to give reasons for your decisions.

1 For those of you who are not familiar with her, Lassie was only the greatest dog on earth, a collie like no other collie, a canine like no other canine. She lived with the Millers on a farm and she slept with their son, Jeff. If necessary, in the dead of a winter night she would force the window open with her nose and leap out into the cold to run for miles to save a dog friend of hers who had accidently fallen into an abandoned well and was lying there dying of fright. Many was the time she would disappear from the farm, only to return barking frantically and turning in a particular direction. The whole family would drop whatever they were doing, jump into the pickup truck, and follow her down the road where she would lead them to their best friend who had fallen out of a tree while he was trying to save his neighbor's cat and had broken his leg and couldn't move. At the end of each show, Lassie would be hugged by the family and everyone was happy.

2 Skiing demands strong legs. As all professional athletes know, it is the legs that go first as the body ages. Skiers can't count on many years in the sport and must start very young if they are to put in much time at the sport. Women have entered skiing in ever-increasing numbers. Children also are appearing on the slopes with greater frequency. Boxers need strong legs, too. When you see a fighter's legs turn "rubbery," you know that he no longer has full control over his body.

3 At the risk of stating the obvious, it is worth remarking that success of communication depends upon the charm (I use the word in its most serious sense) of the narrative. "Writings are useless," declared Theodore Roosevelt, speaking as president of the American Historical Association in 1912, "unless they are read, and they cannot be read unless they are readable."

4 If you relish paradoxes, consider the career of Horatio Alger, Jr. He made his fame writing books in which boys rose "from rags to riches"—yet he himself did not begin life in rags and did not die rich. The boys in his books got ahead by outwitting thieves and sharpers—yet he himself, a mild and generous little man who gave freely of his earnings to newsboys and bootblacks on the New York streets (the sort of boys who were his favorite heroes) —was an easy mark for impostors. His books were, and are, generally regarded by the critical as trash, yet their sales mounted into the millions. He was one of the most popular of all American authors, if not of all authors of all time; and there can be little doubt that he had a far-reaching influence upon the economic and social thought of America—an influence all the greater, perhaps, because it was innocently and naïvely and undogmatically exerted.

5 While "instant" cameras of various types offer you "no muss, no fuss" convenience, they all have limitations. Cartridge-loading cameras are simple to handle, but they raise your film costs. Cameras that process a picture seconds after you've shot it have a very high film cost, don't give you the best possible prints, and cause problems when you want duplicates or enlargements. Cameras with automatic exposure prevent mistakes, but they can also prevent you from experimenting and improving your skill. In short, if you want the most for your money, don't buy convenience alone. In photography the "inconvenience" can be half the fun—and educational as well.

Part 2 The Topic Sentence

A topic sentence presents the reader with the main idea of a paragraph. Following is an example of a topic sentence.

The children were excited.

After reading this sentence, you expect that the rest of the paragraph will describe or explain the excitement of the children, not hunting big game in Africa or shooting the rapids of the White River. This topic sentence has a subject, children. It also presents a point of view toward that subject; the point of view is expressed in the word *excited*. All topic sentences must contain both a subject and a point of view if they are to be expanded into satisfying, well developed paragraphs.

This next sentence has no point of view.

Christmas arrives on December 25.

While the sentence has a subject, Christmas, it does not contain a word or phrase that reveals the writer's attitude toward the subject. Therefore, once the statement is made, there is nothing more to say. Suppose, though, that the sentence were revised as follows:

Christmas is the most exciting season of the year.

The sentence now has a point of view, expressed by the word *exciting*. The idea of excitement can be developed with details about the colorful window displays, the happy smiles of little children, the jam-packed streets, or the thrill of giving and receiving gifts.

The following topic sentence has the same subject, but a different point of view.

Christmas can be an unhappy season.

Because point of view determines the details that can be included in a paragraph, a paragraph developed from this topic sentence would be entirely different from one developed from the preceding example. The body of this paragraph might describe the loneliness of elderly people with no families, or children whose families are too poor to buy presents for them.

Earlier, the sentence "Christmas arrives on December 25" was used as an example of a statement that would not work as a topic sentence. A writer, though, might choose to open a paragraph with that sentence and to follow it with a second sentence such as, "It is a truly festive day." She would then give details that develop the idea of Christmas as a festive day. In this paragraph, the topic sentence would not be the first sentence but rather, the second sentence.

This example points out the fact that although the topic sentence usually is the first sentence in a paragraph, it can also be placed somewhere in the middle or at the end. Many writers occasionally alter the usual pattern of opening with a topic sentence in order to introduce variety and interest into their writing styles. They might also choose an unusual placement for a topic sentence to elicit an emotional response in the reader or to emphasize an idea. For example, a writer might create suspense by building to a final general statement; or a writer might emphasize the central, or main, idea of the paragraph by actually placing the topic sentence in a central position.

Exercises **Working with Topic Sentences**

A. Find the topic sentence in each of these paragraphs, and note whether it is at the beginning of the paragraph, in the middle, or at the end. Explain why you think the writer chose that particular position for the topic sentence.

1 My mother used to tell me how once a prairie wolf had stalked her as she walked home alone from school, over miles of abandoned stubble. I always felt cheated when I looked at the faded photograph of my father sitting on a horse, his hat higher than some telephone wires. He had ridden that horse right to the top of a gigantic snowbank, packed so hard that the horse's hoofs hardly dented its crust. It was true that there was usually a bank in our yard that reached to the top of the clothesline pole, but this was hardly satisfying when I knew what grander things had been. Why couldn't something happen *after* I was born, I wondered.

2 It happened in Singapore. It was a wonderful, sleepy afternoon, tinted with crimson and gold. The air was laden with the sweet scent of multicolored flowers. Leaving the Hotel Raffles, the scene of so much literary international intrigue, I walked to the Singapore General Hospital where I was to meet its director. The flowering gardens spread out like peacocks' tails. The azure sky resembled a Fabergé Easter egg. Ships' sirens in the harbor sounded distant but fascinating, like the songs of Nausicaä in the *Odyssey*. Rickshas, automobiles, bicycles competed with the eager procession of pedestrians. When I arrived at the General Hospital, I was told I would have to wait a few minutes for my colleague. And while I waited on the sun-drenched patio, watching some birds singing near a bed of flowers—whether they sang in Malay or in the universal language of birds, I do not know—I saw the little girl.—FELIX MARTI-IBAÑEZ, M.D.

3 Charles Bedou, at the age of forty, stands four and a half feet tall. When the towheaded Bedou was born, he weighed nearly nine pounds and was the size of any normal baby. Five years later, however, he was less than two feet tall; at ten, he was three feet; when he celebrated his eighteenth birthday, he was four-foot-six; and in the ensuing twenty-two years, he did not grow another inch. His body is all out of whack. His head and torso are the size of a much taller person; his arms and legs are much too small. He is what is known as a dwarf.—SONNY KLEINFIELD

4 Pink was moving around in the bedroom. William cocked his head on one side, listening to her. He could tell exactly what she was doing, as though he were in there with her. The soft, heavy sound of her stockinged feet as she walked to the dresser. The dresser drawer being pulled out. That meant she was getting a clean slip. Then the thud of her two hundred pounds landing in the rocker by the window. She was sitting down to comb her hair. Untwisting the small braids she'd made the night before. She would unwind them one by one, putting the hairpins in her mouth as she went along. Now she was brushing it, for he could hear the creak of the rocker; she was rocking back and forth, humming under her breath as she brushed.—ANN PETRY

5 It was a bucket of bolts and barnacles. The staterooms were little more than cramped closets with iron bunks. The debris and litter of countless voyages were scattered about its deck. The *Vulcania* was a tired old ship. Her engines broke down in mid-voyage. Her third-class travelers had only one rusty shower room, its plumbing obsolete and its floors covered with fungus.

B. Here are ten sentences that would make good topic sentences for paragraphs. Each has both a subject and a point of view toward that subject. Rewrite each sentence, retaining the subject but changing the point of view. Keep your sentences for use in Exercise C and in Part 3, Exercise B.

1. Dancing is superb conditioning for your body.
2. I enjoy listening to the patter of rain on the roof.
3. Do you believe everything you read in the newspapers?
4. My mother concocts tantalizing soups.
5. Despite your cynicism, you will like this play.
6. You will find bargains if you shop carefully.
7. The referee was unfair.
8. In my opinion, bowling is a boring sport.
9. Dave seems to be an unusually responsible member of the group.
10. Many adults are interested in comic books.

C. Select three topic sentences from the twenty available from Exercise B (the original sentences plus the rewritten versions) or write new topic sentences. Develop three paragraphs from these sentences. In each paragraph, place the topic sentence in a different position.

Part 3 The Body

The body of a paragraph is a group of related sentences that develop the idea in the topic sentence. The body proves, illustrates, supports, or explains the topic sentences.

Analyze the body of the following paragraph to determine how it develops the topic sentence.

> My work on the Plains brought me many friends, among them some of the truest and staunchest that anyone ever had. You who live your lives in cities or among peaceful ways cannot always tell whether your friends are the kind who would go through fire for you, but on the Plains one's friends have an opportunity to prove their mettle. I found out that most of mine would as cheerfully risk their lives for me as they would give me a light for my pipe when I asked for it.—BUFFALO BILL

The topic sentence is the first sentence in the paragraph. Its subject is friends; its point of view is expressed by the words *truest* and *staunchest*. The body, which is made up of sentences two and three, explains the point of view by comparing friendships on the Plains with friendships in other settings and by citing the willingness of friends on the Plains to perform the ultimate act of friendship.

Exercises Determining How the Body of a Paragraph Works

A. In each of the following paragraphs identify the topic sentence. Then explain how the body develops the idea stated in that sentence.

1 Whenever we children came to stay at my grandmother's house, we were put to sleep in the sewing room, a bleak, shabby, utilitarian rectangle, more office than bedroom, more attic than office, that played to the hierarchy of chambers the role of a poor relation. It was a room seldom entered by the other members of the family, seldom swept by the maid, a room without pride; the old sewing machine, some castoff chairs, a shadeless lamp, rolls of wrapping paper, piles of cardboard boxes that might someday come in handy, papers of pins, and remains of material united with the iron folding cots put out for our use and the bare floor boards to give an impression of intense and ruthless temporality. Thin white spreads, of the kind used in hospitals and charity institutions, and naked blinds at the windows reminded us of our orphaned condition and of the ephemeral character of our visit; there was nothing here to encourage us to consider this our home. —MARY MCCARTHY

2 In the whole galaxy of youth presented in the novels of Charles Dickens, those juveniles who play important roles in the stories are but a few stars. Many more youngsters contribute to the story lines of the various books without playing principal roles, and there are incidental children everywhere underfoot, sometimes put into the books to make crusading or philosophical points, more often merely for fun. Dickens *liked* to write about children. Whereas other authors of the era studiously ignored children even as incidentals in their books, perhaps seeing nothing of interest in them, Dickens sprinkled them everywhere.—FRANK DONOVAN

3 The forest was the source of life and every Iroquois was comfortable in it. The forest provided the Iroquois with deer, moose, beaver, bear, and every sort of fowl to hunt. Wild turkeys sometimes ran to forty pounds and pigeons numbered in the millions. Cod, sturgeon, mackerel, and salmon were available in inland waters or in the nearby ocean. Children and women could gather lobsters, crabs, clams, and other shellfish along the beaches; or they could enter the forest to get maple sugar, birds' eggs, and berries. As a guarantee that they would never be hungry, the Iroquois used clearings among the trees to plant corn, beans, and squash, which they called the Three Sisters.—DAN GEORGAKAS

4 Everywhere we turn, we see the symbolic process at work. Feathers worn on the head or stripes on the sleeve can be made to stand for military rank; cowrie shells or rings of brass or pieces of paper can stand for wealth; crossed sticks can stand for a set of religious beliefs; buttons, elks' teeth, ribbons, special styles of ornamental haircutting or tattooing, can stand for social affiliations. The symbolic process permeates human life at the most primitive and the most civilized levels alike. Warriors, medicine men, police officers, door attendants, nurses, cardinals, and kings and queens wear costumes that symbolize their occupations. American Indians collected feathers, college students collect

membership keys in honorary societies to symbolize victories in their respective fields. There are few things that people do or want to do, possess or want to possess, that have not, in addition to their mechanical or biological value, a symbolic value.—S. I. HAYAKAWA

5 Jim was a Jellybean. I write that because it has such a pleasant sound—rather like the beginning of a fairy story—as if Jim was nice. It somehow gives me a picture of him with a round, appetizing face and all sorts of leaves and vegetables growing out of his cap. But Jim was long and thin and bent at the waist from stooping over pool tables, and he was what might have been known in the indiscriminating North as a corner loafer. "Jellybean" is the name throughout the undissolved Confederacy for one who spends his life conjugating the verb *to idle* in the first person singular—I am idling, I have idled, I will idle.—F. SCOTT FITZGERALD

6 American he certainly was. Sam Clemens had the advantage, or disadvantage, of being brought up solely in his own country, remote from its coasts, with no contact with the outside world, in the days when America was still America. He lived, and died, before the motion picture had flickered the whole world with similarity, and before rapid transport had enabled every country to live on the tourists of all the others. His childhood was spent in an isolation from the outside world now beyond all conception. Nor was the isolation much relieved by mental contact. Like Shakespeare and Dickens, young Sam Clemens had little school and no college. He thus acquired that peculiar sharpness of mind that comes from not going to school, and that power of independent thought obtained by not entering college. It was this youthful setting which enabled him to become what he was.—STEPHEN LEACOCK

B. Go back to Exercise B on page 119. You have already used three of the topic sentences. Choose two of the remaining sentences, or write new ones, and develop each into a paragraph.

Part 4 Some Exceptions to Paragraph Form

Implied Topic Sentence

Often a paragraph has no actual topic sentence. Instead, it has an **implied topic sentence.** Here is an example of such a paragraph.

> As Pavlova's little bird body revealed itself on the scene, her instep stretched ahead in an incredible arch, the tiny bones of her hands in ceaseless vibration, her face radiant, diamonds glittering under her dark hair, her little waist encased in silk, the great tutu balancing, quickening, and flashing over her beating, flashing, quivering legs, every man and woman sat forward, every pulse quickened. She never appeared to rest motionless: some part of her trembled, vibrated, beat like a heart. Before our dazzled eyes she flashed with the sudden sweetness of a hummingbird in action too quick for understanding.—AGNES DE MILLE

This paragraph is a detailed observation of the dancing of Anna Pavlova, the famous Russian ballerina. A topic sentence written for the paragraph might be similar to this: "I once saw the great Pavlova dance in her superlative way." Notice the references to the excellence of Pavlova's dancing, expressed by the words *great* and *superlative*. This is the point of view developed by the details in the paragraph.

Exercise Determining an Implied Topic Sentence

Study the following paragraph to determine the subject and point of view developed by the details presented. Then write a topic sentence that could function as the controlling statement for the paragraph.

> Old Jeff Patton, the black share farmer, fumbled with his bow tie. His fingers trembled and the high stiff collar pinched his throat. A fellow loses his hand for such vanities after thirty or

forty years of simple life. Once a year, or maybe twice if there's a wedding among his kinfolks, he may spruce up; but generally fancy clothes do nothing but adorn the wall of the big room and feed the moths. That had been Jeff Patton's experience. He had not worn his stiff-bosomed shirt more than a dozen times in all his married life. His swallow-tailed coat lay on the bed beside him, freshly brushed and pressed, but it was as full of holes as the overalls in which he worked on weekdays. The moths had used it badly. Jeff twisted his mouth into a hideous, toothless grimace as he contended with the obstinate bow. He stamped his good foot and decided to give up the struggle.—Arna Bontemps

Dialogue

When the characters in a book talk to each other, they are engaging in dialogue. Each time a different character speaks, no matter how short or how long the speech is, a new paragraph must be started. The "he said" and "she said" are included in the same paragraph as the words spoken by the character. These signals as to who is speaking, called *tags*, can be omitted when the change of speakers is clear without them. The following passage is an example of how dialogue and tags should be paragraphed.

"Howard, I got something on my chest and I might as well get it off."

"What is it?" I asked from my bed.

"You been acting strange lately. Haven't been talking to me. If you got something on your chest, get it off now."

"I have nothing on my chest," I said.

"Then why don't you talk?"

I did not answer.

"You hardly speak to me in the kitchen. If you have something against me, tell me now."

"I have nothing against you."

"Why don't you talk, then?" He looked directly at me. "If a man doesn't talk, you think *something's* wrong!"

"I've been nervous lately, that's all. I got problems and I don't want to talk."

"Everybody's got problems. That's no reason for going around making a man feel guilty."—James Alan McPherson

Passages of dialogue usually include words, phrases, and sentences that qualify the dialogue in some way or that describe the speakers, their actions, or the setting. Sometimes a word or phrase is appended to a tag; for example, the word "hoarsely" might be added to the tag "she whispered" to give additional information about the way the dialogue was spoken. In the sample passage, the phrase "from my bed" added to the tag "I asked" indicates the place from which the words were spoken.

A descriptive sentence or sentences might interrupt dialogue spoken by a character. For example:

> "Laura, please pass the salt." I watched as Laura searched the table. "It's right in front of you," I said impatiently.

Descriptive material might either precede or follow the words spoken by a character, as in the following examples:

> "Come sit next to me, Joey." The old woman raised a skeletal hand and slowly beckoned the boy to come nearer. Her eyes remained fixed on a faded photograph propped on the bedside table.

> The old woman raised a hand and slowly beckoned the boy to come nearer. Her eyes remained fixed on a faded photograph propped on the bedside table. "Come sit next to me, Joey," she said weakly.

In general, descriptive material that relates directly to the character who is speaking is included in the same paragraph as the dialogue and the tag.

Often the words spoken by a character are either preceded or followed by descriptive material related to another character or to the scene in general. This material is paragraphed either with dialogue spoken by the other character or in a separate paragraph, depending on the context in which it occurs. The sentence "I did not answer" in the sample passage is an example of a descriptive sentence that is paragraphed separately because it does not relate to the character who is speaking. The following dialogue is paragraphed differently. Note that the new paragraph begins when the focus shifts from the speaker to the other character.

> "Come sit next to me, Joey," the old woman said weakly.
>
> Joey stood in the doorway. He lowered his eyes and shifted from one foot to the other, reluctant to approach the bed. Finally he said in a low voice, "Hi, Grams."

Exercise **Paragraph of Dialogue**

Each of the following is a passage of dialogue that has not been paragraphed. Determine where each new paragraph should begin.

1 "I'll be seeing you in court then tomorrow, Mr. Fergusson." "Yes, Patrick. Be there at quarter past ten." "If I get off, Mr. Fergusson, I may have some news for you." "Let's have your information now, then, Patrick." "I'd rather wait and see if I get off." "Your news wouldn't be about Socket, would it?" "I'd rather not say, Mr. Fergusson." "We need information about Socket. I don't mind admitting it," said Fergusson. "That statement I signed in August—you'll be using it in court?" Patrick said. "Yes, Patrick. We can't let you get away with that, I'm afraid. You've been useful to us, but a statement's a statement. It's filed."—MURIEL SPARK

2 "Now then, Podgers, I want to ask you about this clerk. What time does he arrive in the evening?" "At prompt six, sir." "Does he ring, or let himself in with a latchkey?" "With a latchkey, sir." "How does he carry the money?" "In a little locked leather satchel, sir, flung over his shoulder." "Does he go direct to the dining room?" "Yes, sir." "Have you seen him unlock the safe and put in the money?" "Yes, sir." "Does the safe unlock with a word or a key?" "With the key, sir. It's one of the old-fashioned kind." "Then the clerk unlocks his leather money bag?" "Yes, sir."

3 She could feel her father struggling within himself to speak, to appeal to her. Stubbornly, she did not want to help him. "Sylvia," he brought out at last, almost plaintively and without looking at her, "your mother is mad at me." She turned to stare at the back of his head, forcing her eyes to be noncommittal. It always shocked her to hear him utter in his Chinese accent such colloquial phrases as "mad at me" or "sore at them." He had a long face for a Chinese and a high, receding forehead; these expressions were wholly out of keeping with this fine and tailored face, and his rather remote air. "But that's not so serious, is it?" Sylvia asked, and regretted her tone immediately. He had often confessed to her that before his children he felt half relic, half contemporary. Of course, he often pointed out, children were one's equals in modern China, but today she felt he was prepared to reverse that —he was almost equal to his daughter. "Couldn't you—couldn't you just go in and say a word to her?" he asked. He turned around, smiling; his smile always grew in proportion to his distress. "It's so much easier for you, you see."—DIANA CHANG

4 Diessy raised his right shoulder toward his ear and held out one hand palm upward. "What have you on a ship? Swab deck, carry tray, wash dishes, push crates. Sometimes drink brandy with mate when he want a friend talking to him." He smiled at Father. "Luck is up and down. Once in Martinique I own Hispano." "Diessy is Senegalese, Father Witherby," said Madolyn. Since when had she started this "Father Witherby"? That was the last straw. Father stirred his demi-tasse. With a bored sigh he said to Diessy, "You received your education in France?" "In school all over world. Mostly school of life. But I been in a school sometimes. In Germany, France, Russia. I learn all three languages." He looked at Father for a minute and then winked. "But enough of any—you think?" He shrugged. "My father say I must be learned man. That is why I not go home—to Senegal. I rather my father think I am learned man, not dishwasher. Father like to be proud of son, *n'est-ce pas?* You have son you are proud of?" "Yes," said Margaret suddenly. "He has John Junior. John Junior is not exactly a learned man but—"

5 The door latch clicked, the bell tinkled, and a small boy walked in. He gaped at Ichiro with the doorknob still in his hand and said: "Who are you?" "I work here," he said. "Oh." The boy closed the door and proceeded to the bread rack, where he methodically squeezed each loaf of bread. "Day-old stuff," he grimaced and reluctantly selected a small loaf. He placed it on the counter and examined the coins in his hand. "Gimme two black-whips too," he said. "Black-whips? What are they?" "If you work here, how come you don't know? I know more'n you." "Yeah, you're smart. What are black-whips?" "Lik-rish. Them over there." He pointed behind Ichiro at the assortment of candy, indicating the long strips of red and black licorice. "I want the black ones." Without further comment, Ichiro took two strips from the box and handed them to the boy, who put his coins on the counter and departed after again eyeing him skeptically.—JOHN OKADA

Dramatic Effect

Occasionally you may encounter a piece of writing in which many of the paragraphs are one- or two-sentence statements of ideas rather than fully developed explanations of those ideas. The purpose of such a presentation is to emphasize each idea by surrounding it with extra white space. In the following passage, notice how the paragraphing enhances the drama of the old chief's words.

It was during the first hundred years of Canada's nationhood that we met defeat. Broken by wars and disease, we huddled on our reserves and nursed our wounds.

But our greatest wound was not of the flesh but in our spirit and in our souls. We were demoralized, confused, and frightened. We were left without weapons to defend ourselves, medicine to heal us, and leaders to guide us.

How easily despair comes when hope dies. How easily ambitions alter when goals slip from one's reach like the end of the rainbow.

But after the winter cold and icy winds, life again flows up from the bosom of mother earth; and mother earth throws off her dead stalks and the withered ends for they are useless, and in their place new and strong saplings arise.

Already signs of new life are rising among my people after our sad winter has passed. We have discarded our broken arrows and our empty quivers, for we know what served us in the past can never serve us again.—Chief Dan George

Exercise Locating Unusual Paragraphs

Search in books and magazines for examples of writing in which the paragraphs are shortened for dramatic effect. Try to find at least two examples. Copy the passage or bring the book or magazine to class.

Chapter 9

The Paragraph: Its Other Elements

You have worked with the basic structural elements of the paragraph—the topic sentence and the body. You are now ready to consider the other elements inherent in the well written paragraph. They consist of the following:

unity	adequate detail
coherence	tone
emphasis	mood

These five characteristics will be discussed in detail in this chapter.

Part 1 Unity

A well written paragraph is a unified paragraph. Each sentence relates to the one point of view that controls the paragraph. Each sentence contributes in some way to achieving the single end that is the purpose of the paragraph.

In attempting to explain an idea clearly or to examine all sides of a question or to express many thoughts and feelings on a subject, a writer may violate the unity of a paragraph. He or she may include ideas that relate only indirectly to the main idea of the paragraph or may shift the discussion away from the idea presented in the topic sentence.

Examine the following paragraph to see if every sentence is needed and works with the other sentences to develop the main idea of the paragraph.

> Up from the deep dusk of a cleared spot on the edge of the forest a mellow glow arose and spread fan-wise into the low-hanging heavens, and all around the air was heavy with the scent of boiling cane. A large pile of cane stalks lay like ribboned shadows upon the ground. A mule, harnessed to a pole, trudged lazily round and round the pivot of the grinder. Beneath a swaying oil lamp, a black man alternately whipped out at the mule, and fed cane stalks to the grinder. A fat boy waddled pails of fresh-ground juice between the grinder and the boiling stove. Steam came from the copper boiling pan. The scent of cane came from the copper pan and drenched the forest and the hill that sloped to factory town beneath its fragrance. It drenched the men in the circle seated around the stove. Some of them chewed at the white pulp of stalks, but there was no need for them to, if all they wanted was to taste the cane. One tasted it in factory town. And from factory town one could see the soft haze thrown by the glowing stove upon the low-hanging heavens.—JEAN TOOMER

The first sentence is the topic sentence. Its subject is *boiling cane*, and its point of view is expressed by the words *deep dusk, mellow glow, low-hanging*, and *heavy;* together these words evoke a mood of oppressiveness. The rest of the paragraph describes the pervasiveness of the heavy, cane-sweet air. Each sentence adds details that develop the point of view presented in the topic sentence. The paragraph contains no distracting "extra" ideas, nor does it shift away from the main idea. It is, therefore, an example of a unified paragraph.

Here is a paragraph that has unneeded sentences. Look for them as you read.

> In 1850, Pinkerton founded the country's first private detective agency, whose insomnolent logo (an open eye) and motto ("We Never Sleep") gave birth to the phrase "private eye." Of course, other people used Pinkerton's idea to start agencies of their own. Many made lots of money in those days because police officers were very limited in number. A few agencies, though, failed and went bankrupt. The Pinkertons pursued Jesse James, spied for Lincoln (himself a detective-fiction fan), and smashed the heads of striking steel workers for Andrew Carnegie before settling down to become a reputable multimillion-dollar corporation which now has some 37,000 employees. Only about five percent of Pinkerton's work today is investigative, but that still requires close to 1,000 detectives nationwide, including part-time help.

The writer of this paragraph made a common mistake. Although he started out to deal with one subject, the Pinkerton Agency, in sentence two he introduced the idea that other people set up agencies of their own. He then went on in sentences three and four to speak of the money made by many of these companies and of the bankruptcy of some of them. These three sentences do not develop the main idea of the paragraph and, therefore, do not belong there. To restore the unity of the paragraph, the writer would have to delete the three intruding sentences.

Exercises **Understanding Paragraph Unity**

A. Study the following three paragraphs and identify the one that has unity. For each paragraph that does not have unity, identify the sentences that do not work with the others to develop the main idea of the paragraph.

1 Of course, she, the woman I visit, is old and of her youthful beauty there is little left. Her face of today is coarse with hard water and there is no question that she has lived her life: given birth to six children, worked side by side with her man for forty years, working in the fields, working in the house, caring for the grandchildren, facing the summers and winters and also the springs and autumns, running the household that is completely her little world. When I came on the scene, when I discovered her in her little house on Seventh Street, all of her life was behind, all of her task in this world was tabbed, looked into, thoroughly attended, and all that is before her in life and the world, all that could be before her now was to sit and be served; duty done, work done, time clock punched; old-age pension or old-age security; easy chair; soft, serene hours till death take her. But this was not of her, not the least bit of her.—Toshio Mori

2 Traveling is an exciting, painless way to learn a history lesson. Touring the settings of historic events can make those events more real and more understandable than mere reading about them can. Whether strolling along the seafront in Boston or exploring Gettysburg or walking through the Alamo or retracing the steps of the Spanish missionaries through California, just being on the actual sites can recall voices and emotions from the past that caused history to be made. I made a wonderful visit to historic Williamsburg once. The weather was perfect, the crowds were not too large, and the food was excellent. Afterwards, I was glad I had chosen to go there instead of to the seashore for the weekend.

3 Poverty can often be a strong incentive for people. We all know, or have read stories about, people who were born in a slum area and who, because of the grinding poverty they experienced, made up their mind to work and study so they could live a more gracious life. My uncle had a friend who grew up in a ghetto and who now is chief engineer at a radio studio. My uncle seems to know all kinds of people. He is very open and outgoing and makes friends easily. He lives a successful life as head mechanic at a large garage, and he makes more money than you might guess. Poverty sometimes is an asset rather than a liability.

B. All three of the following paragraphs lack unity because they contain sentences that do not support or explain the idea in the topic sentence. Revise each paragraph, deleting the sentences that violate unity and, if necessary, adding sentences to fill out the paragraph.

1 I used to think I was a person, but I'm really just a bunch of numbers. In English class I sit in row 4, seat 2. If I'm not in that chair I am marked absent—even though I may be somewhere else in the room. The teacher doesn't know me; he merely knows if the chair is occupied. I'm a number on a driver's license. I'm an ID number, and I'm a locker number. I had a combination lock that was numbered. However, I changed to a lock that opens with a key. That kind of lock is much safer than a combination lock. Mine cost only a dollar, but it is a good, strong lock.

2 I enjoy being a joiner. My days and evenings are filled, and I avoid boredom. I belong to a stamp club, I play in the school orchestra, I am a member of the chef's club, and I belong to the city's drum and bugle corps. I get a lot of companionship and pleasure from being in these organizations, and I have made many friends. Friendship is a valuable thing. Everyone needs friends. You need someone in whom to confide, and you need friends when you are depressed. You can well believe that I love being a member of active groups.

3 We made an exciting trip to the West last summer. It was thrilling to observe what I had always been told—that America is as scenic as any country in the world. We saw the Rocky Mountains, which are huge masses on the landscape. They were surprisingly green. I had expected them to be solid rock. We saw lakes that we had never seen before except in travelogues. A highlight of our trip was seeing the Pacific Ocean for the first time. I will never forget the fun we had on that trip.

Part 2 Coherence

A well written paragraph is coherent; that is, the ideas in the paragraph are arranged in a logical order and are clearly related to each other. Coherence enables the reader to follow the writer's train of thought with ease.

Some subjects do not require a specific order of ideas. For example, if you wish to describe a party, you can write about the food first and the band second, or the opposite way around. If you were describing a raging storm, it would not matter if you first described the downpour of rain or the devastating power of the wind.

Other subjects, by their very nature, are developed with details that must be ordered in specific ways. There are three most frequently used ways of ordering ideas.

chronological order   spatial order   order of importance

Chronological Order

The Greek word *chronos* means "time." From this word comes the word *chronological,* which means "in the order of occurrence." Paragraphs that explain processes and those that relate incidents are almost always arranged in chronological order. For example, in a paragraph that presents the steps in assembling an engine, these steps would be listed in sequence. In a paragraph that describes an automobile accident, the events would be related in the order in which they occurred.

The ideas in the following paragraph are arranged chronologically. In this paragraph, the writer traces the melting of the polar ice caps in seasonal time, from early spring until midsummer.

> Easily the most conspicuous feature of the planet is the white caps that cover its polar regions. They display a fascinating rhythm of advance and retreat. At the end of winter in each hemisphere, the polar cap covers some four million square miles. As spring comes, it begins to diminish—rather slowly at first, then at an increasing rate. Near the middle of spring, dark rifts appear. They grow steadily and soon split the cap into several sections. Disintegration of the fragments then proceeds rapidly. The cap never disappears completely, however; even in midsummer a tiny, dazzling spot remains near the pole.—GERARD DE VAUCOULEURS

Spatial Order

Spatial order, the order of things as they are arranged in space, is used most often in descriptive writing. When planning a description in which the details will be arranged in spatial order, a writer must choose either a central focus or a position from which to view the object or scene. He or she can then decide on a way to present the details relative to that focus or position. For example, a writer wishing to describe a country church must decide whether to describe it from the outside or from the inside. If the position chosen is inside, he or she must decide whether to describe the interior from the altar to the front door, from the high ceiling to the parquet floor, from one side of the church to the other, or in some unique order that fits the particular content of the paragraph.

The writer of the following paragraph has chosen to view the lobby of her apartment building from a moving position; she goes methodically through the lobby, describing in detail each prominent feature.

> At that time we were living in a second-floor apartment on West 10th Street. The lobby was an asset to the tenants; large, faintly grand, a polished place that smelled strongly of Liquid Veneer and dimly of cats. It was illuminated by paired bracket-lamps, each with one eye blinded by economy, and the melting hues of their Tiffany glass shades reminded me of half-sucked candy. Two staircases—one for the tenants on the east side of the building and one for the tenants on the west—opened out and upward with expansive, old-fashioned gestures; and in each French window stood a twirled iron tripod holding a pot of those plants that somehow cling to life through all: spitting radiators, north light, neglect of janitors. For me, the lobby had a soothing elegance; it brought to mind the baronial halls in illustrations by Reginald Birch.—ELIZABETH ENRIGHT

Order of Importance

The order of importance is usually used in paragraphs of explanation, argument, and persuasion. Most often a writer moves from the least important to the most important idea, thus ending on a strong note. A writer may, however, use the reverse order, starting with the most important idea in order to catch the reader's immediate attention.

The following tongue-in-cheek passage from *Candide* builds to its conclusion, and though the conclusion is as faulty as the examples leading to it, the form is that of a logical argument.

> Pangloss taught metaphysico-theologo-cosmolonigology. He proved admirably that there is no effect without a cause and that in this best of all possible worlds, My Lord the Baron's castle was the best of castles and his wife the best of all possible Baronesses. " 'Tis demonstrated," said he, "that things cannot be otherwise; for, since everything is made for an end, everything is necessarily for the best end. Observe that noses were made to wear spectacles; and so we have spectacles. Legs were visibly instituted to be breeched, and we have breeches. Stones were formed to be quarried and to build castles; and My Lord has a very noble castle; the greatest Baron in the province should have the best house; and as pigs were made to be eaten, we eat pork all the year round; consequently, those who have asserted that all is well talk nonsense; they ought to have said that all is for the best."—VOLTAIRE

Combination of Orders

Many writers use not one, but a combination of orders to achieve effective paragraphs. The following writer, for example, combines spatial order with chronological order.

> These days our back porch was piled with baskets of peaches and grapes and pears, bought in town, and onions and tomatoes and cucumbers grown at home, all waiting to be made into jelly and jam and preserves, pickles and chili sauce. In the kitchen there was a fire in the stove all day, jars clinked in boiling water; sometimes a cheesecloth bag was strung on a pole between two chairs, straining blueblack grape pulp for jelly. I was given jobs to do and I would sit at the table peeling peaches that had been soaked in the hot water, or cutting up onions, my eyes smarting and streaming. As soon as I was done I ran out of the house, trying to get out of earshot before my mother thought of what she wanted me to do next.—ALICE MUNRO

Exercises Analyzing the Order of Ideas in Paragraphs

A. Each of the following paragraphs is developed in chronological order, spatial order, or order of importance, or in a combination of two of these orders. Determine the order of ideas in each paragraph and be ready to explain your choice.

1 He heard footsteps and crawled quickly into the coalbin. Lumps rattled noisily. The footsteps came into the basement and stopped. Who was it? Had someone heard him and come down to investigate? He waited, crouching, sweating. For a long time there was silence; then he heard the clang of metal and a brighter glow lit the room. Somebody's tending the furnace, he thought. Footsteps came closer and he stiffened. Looming before him was a white face lined with coal dust, the face of an old man with watery blue eyes. Highlights spotted his gaunt cheekbones, and he held a huge shovel. There was a screechy scrape of metal against stone, and the old man lifted a shovelful of coal and went from sight.—RICHARD WRIGHT

2 There are at least three good reasons for the study of Indian authors and themes in the English classroom: (1) The Indian is an essential part of our American history and literature. At the time that the Pilgrims arrived, Indian tribes had an oral tradition of storytelling and ceremony that integrated all of life. Only recently have the rest of us begun to realize the richness of this literature. (2) The Indian has always furnished inspiration and characters for the standard writers and works from American literature—from Freneau to Faulkner. Unfortunately, some of these writers have helped to create about the Native American certain stereotypes and generalizations that need to be dispelled. (3) American Indians, with their spiritual oneness, their concept of the sacred hoop, have much to teach modern youth, many of whom find their own world dreary and materialistic. The Indian's problem of trying to live in two worlds also strikes a responsive chord in teenagers who are trying to find out who they are.—ANNA LEE STENSLAND

3 There is a photo of the two of us on the second page. There's Maggie in Minnie Mouse shoes and a long, polka-dot affair with her stocking rolled up at the shins, looking like muffins. There's me with nothing much at all on, in her arms, and looking almost like a normal, mortal, everyday-type baby—raw, wrinkled, ugly. Except that it must be clearly understood straightaway that I sprang into the world full wise and invulnerable and gorgeous like a goddess. Behind us is the player piano with the spooky keys. And behind that, the window outlining Maggie's crosshatched face and looking out over the yard, overgrown even then, where later I lay lost in the high grass, never hoping to be found till Maggie picked me up into her hair and told me all about the earth's moons.—Toni Cade Bambara

4 You have heard it repeated, I dare say, that scientists work by means of induction and deduction and that, by the help of these operations, they wring from nature certain other things (which are called natural laws and causes), and that out of these, by some cunning skill of their own, they build up hypotheses and theories. And it is imagined by many that the operations of the common mind can be by no means compared with these processes. To hear all these large words, you would think that the mind of a scientist must be constituted differently from that of other human beings. However, if you will not be frightened by terms, you will discover that you are quite wrong, and that all these terrible apparatus are being used by yourself every day of your life.—Thomas Henry Huxley

5 She dressed her tiny self carefully, donning a clean white camisole and her black Sunday frock. After she had drunk her tea and eaten a slice of thinly margarined toast, she washed her cup and saucer in some water she had drawn from the bathroom the evening before and put them away on her "kitchen" shelf in the clothes closet. Then she tiptoed down the steep stairs to the bathroom and washed her face and hands—"a lick and a spit" as she called it.—Hugh Garner

B. The sentences in the following paragraphs are not in logical order. Study each paragraph; then write the numbers of the sentences in the correct order of ideas. Note whether the order is chronological, spatial, order of importance, or a combination of orders.

1 1. During 1902 we made upward of fourteen hundred flights, sometimes going up a hundred times or more in a single day. 2. I recall sitting in it, ready to cast off, one still day when the breeze seemed approaching. 3. Our runway was short, and it required a wind with a velocity of at least twelve miles an hour to lift the machine. 4. We had to go ahead and discover everything for ourselves. 5. That's just a sample of what we had to learn about air currents; nobody had ever heard of "holes" in the air at that time. 6. It came presently, rippling the daisies in the field, and just as it reached me I started the glider on the runway. 7. But the innocent-appearing breeze was a whirlwind. 8. I tilted my rudder to descend. 9. It jerked the front of the machine sharply upward. 10. Then the breeze spun downward, driving the glider to the ground with a huge shock and spinning me out headfirst.

2 1. Many evenings as I prepared the material for this chapter, I found myself drifting from my subject, the brain, to wander deep into the fascinating lives of electronic computers. 2. Exploring the living brain, however, proves to be a different kind of venture and makes enormous demands of our own brain. 3. No matter how remarkable and intricate the computer may be, humans made the computer, and so humans know what was put into it and how it functions. 4. The intricate details of computer structure and function by no means provide easy reading, but I soon realized that compared to the infinite mysteries of the living brain, computers are a logical and relaxing subject. 5. Fortunately the brain is the most adaptable organ in the body, and an examination of itself is inevitably the challenge the human brain must accept.

3 1. When I first started going to motor races, they were conducted mostly on small dirt tracks up to a mile in length, their curves modestly banked. 2. The straightaways were short, forcing cars to bunch up fiercely on the corners. 3. At the starting gun, the colossal rear tires kicked up magnificent rooster tails of dust. 4. At the peak of their maneuver, their front wheels were sideways to the direction in which the cars were traveling. 5. The herd hurtled into the turns in a fantastic blur of dust, heat, noise, speed. 6. Finally pulling back onto straight track, they drifted into long, graceful slides. 7. It was one of the most spectacular sights in sport.

4 1. Buying a loaf of bread usually involves thought processes no more complicated than those required for choosing among white, whole-wheat, and rye. 2. In pre-bread history, humans depended on hunting, fishing, and food-gathering, and they continually moved around to find new sources of food. 3. And with this settling down came the birth of towns, villages, and eventually cities. 4. A simple loaf of bread, though, can serve as the inspiration to consider the development of the human race from its primitive stages to today's technological societies. 5. This involved settling down in a spot long enough to watch the crop grow and to harvest it. 6. Then various groups began to cultivate wild plants and to grow crops, especially bread grains. 7. To progress from these first simple tools to the machinery involved in putting today's loaf of bread on the store shelf is again to retrace the history of the human race. 8. Farming also led to the slow development of tools, from digging sticks to hoes to plows.

Linking Words and Expressions

A writer achieves coherence by arranging the ideas in a paragraph in logical order. He or she often reinforces that coherence with **linking words and expressions** that help the reader follow the line of thought from one idea to another.

Some linking words and expressions are identified with particular logical orders; for example, such words as *next*, *then*, *soon*, and *later* are associated with chronological order. Words and phrases such as *above*, *below*, *next to*, and *across from* are associated with spatial order.

Other linking devices have more general applicability. Pronouns, for example, appear in many different kinds of writing. By referring to persons, places, things, and ideas in preceding sentences and clauses, pronouns help to join together the ideas in a paragraph.

In the following paragraph, note how each word in color refers to a previously mentioned person, place, or thing.

> Of course I had to live somewhere, and the somewhere turned out to be Montrouge, a worker's quarter, just beyond the Porte d'Orléans; for a friend sublet me his apartment there, in the Place Jules Ferry, where there were a few blocks of modern apartment buildings. My place, in one of these, was like that whole winter, curiously empty and curiously crowded. It was chiefly a studio, empty except for a large, glass bottle made into a lamp, a mattress on the floor beside it, a phonograph, and some records—my friend was a dancer. The living quarters were on a small balcony above this chill vacuum, and they were extremely crowded, containing as they did a bed, a desk, bookshelves, chairs, a fireplace, all in a small place. A tiny kitchen and bath opened off on one side of this balcony, and on the other side it gaped draftily onto the unheated studio. This strange apartment was on the ground floor, and I lived there, acutely aware of every footstep on the pavement outside. I was lonely at first, and frightened.—May Sarton

Linking expressions, or connectives, also help to clarify the relationships among the ideas in a paragraph. These expressions, like pronouns, move the reader smoothly from sentence to sentence. Here are some commonly used linking expressions.

Commonly Used Linking Expressions

TO ADD IDEAS

also	in addition	and then
too	likewise	further
besides	again	furthermore
in the second place	nor	as a result
equally important	moreover	in the same fashion

TO LIMIT OR CONTRADICT

but	however	at the same time
yet	although	on the other hand
and yet	nevertheless	on the contrary
still	otherwise	nonetheless

TO ARRANGE IN TIME OR PLACE

first	at this point	afterward	here
second	meanwhile	at length	nearby
presently	eventually	beyond	opposite to
finally	sooner or later	there	adjacent to

TO EXEMPLIFY

for example	for instance	in fact	in other words

TO SUM UP

in short	on the whole	for the most part	in any case
in brief	to sum up	in any event	as I have said

In the following paragraph, note how the linking expressions, shown in color, show the relationships between ideas.

> I don't live in the past very much. In fact, I hardly live there at all. My memory is just awful for things that happened last week, let alone what happened fifteen, twenty, or twenty-five years ago. I've never kept a diary or journal or even a scrapbook. I don't know exactly; there just never seemed to be time. Every now and then, though, I'll run across an old newspaper clipping my parents saved, or maybe a school yearbook, and that'll trigger the memory of some experience or feeling I had many years ago. I rarely remember details—what I was wearing or what somebody said to me or whether the sun was shining—and I'm sure that the few things I do remember vividly are colored by the way I feel about them now, today. Still, certain incidents stand out, and they're important to me, at least right at this moment. How important they were to me when they actually happened, I don't really know.
> —BILLY JEAN KING

Exercise Identifying Linking Words and Expressions

Read the following paragraph carefully. Identify the pronouns and linking expressions that help to make the paragraph coherent. Copy them in order, numbering each with the number of the sentence in which it appears. Some sentences have more than one linking word or expression; others do not contain any pronouns or connectives.

> 1. Animals talk to each other, of course; there can be no question about that; but I suppose there are very few people who can understand them. 2. I never knew but one man who would. 3. I knew he could, however, because he told me so himself. 4. He was a middle-aged, simple-hearted miner who had lived in a lonely corner of California among the woods and mountains a good many years, and had studied the ways of his only neighbors, the beasts and the birds, until he believed he could accurately translate any remark that they made. 5. This was Jim Baker. 6. According to Jim Baker, some animals have only a limited education and use only very simple words and scarcely ever a comparison or a flowery figure; whereas certain other animals have a large vocabulary, a fine command of language, and a ready and fluent delivery. Consequently, these latter talk a great deal, they like it, they are conscious of their talent, and they enjoy "showing off."—MARK TWAIN

Part 3 Emphasis

Many devices are available to the writer who wishes to emphasize an idea or ideas within a paragraph. The following paragraphs exemplify the most common of these devices.

Example 1

> The orchard to the east of the house was full of gnarled old apple trees, worm-eaten as to trunks and branches, and fully orna-

mented with green and white lichens, so that it had a sad, greenish-white, silvery effect in moonlight. The low outhouses, which had once housed chickens, a horse or two, a cow, and several pigs, were covered with patches of moss as to their roof; and the sides had been free of paint for so long that they were blackish gray as to color, and a little spongy. The picket fence in front, with its gate squeaky and askew, and the side fences of the stake-and-rider type were in an equally run-down condition. As a matter of fact, they had aged synchronously with the person who lived here, old Henry Reifsneider and his wife Phoebe Ann.—THEODORE DREISER

In this paragraph each detail is presented in relation to the house, the implied central focus of the scene. The orchard, the outhouses, and the fence are positioned around the house, thus emphasizing its importance.

Example 2

About half way between West Egg and New York the motor road hastily joins the railroad and runs beside it for a quarter of a mile, so as to shrink away from a certain desolate area of land. This is a valley of ashes—a fantastic farm where ashes grow like wheat into ridges and hills and grotesque gardens; where ashes take the forms of houses and chimneys and rising smoke and, finally, with a transcendent effort, of ash-gray men who move dimly and already crumbling through the powdery air. Occasionally a line of gray cars crawls along an invisible track, gives out a ghostly creak, and comes to rest, and immediately the ash-gray men swarm up with leaden spades and stir up an impenetrable cloud, which screens their obscure operations from your sight. —F. SCOTT FITZGERALD

In this paragraph, the word *ashes* is the key to the writer's point of view. By repeating the word several times, along with the related word *gray*, the writer makes his point of view the preeminent emphasis of the paragraph.

Example 3

> It is a compressed Vietnamese morning, hot, bright, and steamy. I feel the weight of air and sunlight. Flies buzz solidly. Odors have earthy textures. Everything in the shade rots and smells. Everything in the sunlight bakes and shimmers. The surrounding jungle resembles impervious, shiny, hot green vinyl. —David Grinstead

This writer also emphasizes his point of view, but he employs a more subtle repetitive technique. Rather than repeat the exact words *hot, bright, and steamy,* the words in the topic sentence that express the point of view, he uses words and phrases that extend the same idea to all five senses.

Example 4

> Who is there who isn't peddling himself to the devil in some way? There are those who do it according to the tradition: for knowledge and power. There are those who do it for fame and money. There are those who do it to maintain the *status quo* and those who do it for the sake of revolution. There are those who do it to keep their children fed, to quiet their own consciences, to make the sun rise tomorrow morning, or to torment their heirs. There are those who do it for what most of us might agree are sufficiently good reasons, and others whose reasons, well, leave something to be desired. Why do I do it? I do it for a .368 batting average.—Alvin Greenberg

In this paragraph, repetition is the stylistic device used to emphasize the final, most important sentence in the paragraph. By opening the five supporting sentences with "There are those who do it," the writer creates a comfortable rhythm that brings the reader up to the concluding questions and answers. At this point, the cadence of the paragraph changes and the approach shifts from objective to subjective, bringing the conclusion into sharp contrast with the rest of the paragraph.

Example 5

> His legs pump. His eyes are wild. His brows work fiercely. His hands are helpless fists. He leans against a wall, seeking the cool plaster. He darts to a chair, perches on its edge with hands clasped, as if imploringly, between his knees. He jumps up, fills his pipe, sets it down, lights a cigaret, puffs twice, it goes out, it remains between his lips. He nibbles his fingernails. He rubs his head. He explores a dental cavity. He pinches his nose. He plunges his hands into his jacket pockets. He kicks a chair. He glances at the headline of the morning newspaper on his desk but glances away heroically. He goes to the window and soon becomes interested in the scientific aspects of a fly crawling up the screen. He fingers the tobacco grains in his right pocket, rolls a grain in a wad of lint, places the wad in a piece of paper that happens to be in the same pocket. He folds the paper around it, takes the paper out, glances at it.—ELLERY QUEEN

The emphasis here is the staccato style in which the details of the paragraph are presented. This style parallels the nervous, disjointed movements of the character being described. It also reinforces the implied point of view developed by the details in the paragraph.

Exercise Planning a Paragraph

Choose a subject and a point of view and work these into a topic sentence. Then explain, in a sentence or two, how you would achieve emphasis in a paragraph developed from this topic sentence.

Part 4 Adequate Detail

Adequate details are necessary if a reader is to respond fully and intelligently to the content of a paragraph. Details allow the reader to share in a writer's experience. They help the reader to visualize the people, places, and things described by a writer. They help the reader to understand clearly the concepts that a writer is attempting to convey.

Writers weave details into the textures of their paragraphs by selecting strong, specific verbs and nouns. They use richly connotative adjectives and adverbs, alone or within descriptive phrases. They also use figurative language to express feelings and ideas. All writers have these same basic techniques available to them, yet each writer uses them in a highly individual way.

Some writers create paragraphs with a profusion of details. Following is an example of such a paragraph.

> Edinburgh is a city of pure drama. It sits on a natural terrain of ridges, hills, ravines, and stupendous rocks as sharp-edged as a piece of crumpled steel. An amalgam of light and shadow, brightness and gray mist, it joins two separate parts: an Old Town, whose craggy skyline is one of the most dramatic in the world, and a New Town, an eighteenth-century concept of fine residences that is Europe's largest stretch of Georgian houses. A subtle, somber, yet exciting city, it can thrill or chill a visitor, for its striking townscapes—its Castle, its sky-piercing churches, its superb crescents—are marvelously thrilling to the eye; but its inner life is pulled back out of sight. At night the city becomes a tomb, the yellow streetlamps flickering in the mist.—FRANCES KOLTUN

Other writers subordinate their details to the flow of ideas in their paragraphs. The following paragraph exemplifies this approach. Although the paragraph contains plentiful details, they are woven unobtrusively into the fabric of the narrative.

> The soldiers were forbidden to leave the train, but at every station they pushed the windows down so that they could call to girls on the platform or buy chocolate bars from a barrowman or jeer in transparent asides at the striding guard. When the train was still for a few minutes in this way, the bugler would begin to play—always the same air, an antiquated, sentimental tune that belonged, perhaps, to a regimental song. This wistful music filled the train and floated out on the cold dark station of every town they stopped at. The song never reached its conclusion, for the train would always start up again with the last refrain and the instrument would be violently shaken in the musician's mouth and grasp. But after each such departure, for a little while, the

bugler tried to keep playing, to reach the end of the song; and these last notes, wobbling and swaying, persisted out of the station and into the countryside until the train, gathering speed, made it impossible to play any longer.—SHIRLEY HAZZARD

Some authors write deceptively simple prose in which the details are spare but highly effective. Notice, in the following example, the striking use of such simple words as *dry, white, clear, blue, dust,* and *bare.*

In the late summer of that year we lived in a house in a village that looked across the river and the plain to the mountains. In the bed of the river there were pebbles and boulders, dry and white in the sun, and the water was clear and swiftly moving and blue in the channels. Troops went by the house and down the road, and the dust they raised powdered the leaves of the trees. The trunks of the trees too were dusty and the leaves fell early that year, and we saw the troops marching along the road and the dust rising and leaves, stirred by the breeze, falling, and the soldiers marching, and afterward the road bare and white except for the leaves. —ERNEST HEMINGWAY

Exercise **Supplying Adequate Details**

Here are some ideas for paragraphs. Choose three of them, or use your own ideas. Develop each into a paragraph that is rich with details.

1. The snow and cold of winter complicate my life.
2. Somehow, there doesn't seem to be enough time to read.
3. Saturday is the busiest day of my week.
4. I have many weaknesses.
5. I was completely exhausted after our Fourth of July picnic.
6. The program was wonderful.
7. The garbage at the camp site was scattered all over the area.
8. I received an unusual birthday present.
9. The car was fully loaded and we were ready to start our vacation.
10. The man who entered the kitchen looked cold and hungry.
11. The sky to the west was an ominous black.
12. The year 19— was an exciting year for cars.

Part 5 Tone

The tone of a piece of writing reveals the writer's attitude toward the subject. This attitude might be angry, joyous, disgusted, formal, amused, satirical, flippant, naive, bored, or sarcastic. Usually, the subject matter of the paragraph, combined with the writer's background and personal experiences, determines the tone chosen for a paragraph.

In oral communication, a speaker reveals attitude by the pitch and volume of his or her voice, by gestures and facial expressions, and by the vocal emphasis given to certain words. The writer chooses from a different array of techniques. They include the careful choice and placement of words, the use of figurative language, the selection of appropriate details and their arrangement within the paragraph, the creation of rhythm, and the conscious manipulation of sentence constructions. By employing these techniques, a writer can control the tone, or coloration, of a paragraph. Notice how tone is achieved in the following paragraph.

> The lazy, sinister summer evening thickened with dust and and petrol fumes, and the weariness of homeward-turning human beings drifted over Notting Hill like poison gas. The perpetual din of the traffic diffused itself in the dense light, distorting the facades of houses and the faces of men. The whole district vibrated, jerked, and shifted slightly, as if something else and very nasty were trying, through faults and knots and little crazy corners where lines just failed to meet, to make its way into the ordinary world.—Iris Murdoch

The words *sinister, fumes, weariness,* and *poison* in the opening sentence set the tone for the entire paragraph. Through the careful selection of words and details with negative connotations, the writer creates a paragraph that reveals her aversion to the place called Notting Hill. It is not the aversion of a resident of Notting Hill, immersed in its poisonous atmosphere, but that of an observer who is in a position to generalize about the entire district.

Consistency of tone within a paragraph is as important as consistency, or unity, of idea. Good writers maintain the same tone from the beginning to the end of their paragraphs. They avoid the inclusion of sentences written in a tone incompatible with the rest of the paragraph; for example, the placement of a humorous statement within an otherwise serious paragraph. Following is another good example of a paragraph whose tone is completely consistent.

> Our Southern springs are filled with quiet noises and scenes of growth. Apple buds laugh into blossom. Honeysuckles creep up the sides of houses. Sunflowers nod in the hot fields. From mossy tree to mossy tree—oak, elm, willow, aspen, sycamore, dogwood, cedar, walnut, ash, and hickory—bright green leaves jut from a million branches to form an awning that tries to shield and shade the earth. Blue and pink kites of small boys sail in the windy air. —RICHARD WRIGHT

The writer of this paragraph lovingly describes the beauty, joy, and richness of the Southern spring. There is no mistaking his attitude of wonder and appreciation for the many signs of rebirth, an attitude uncompromised by any element in the paragraph.

Exercises **Analyzing Tone**

A. Determine the tone of each of the following paragraphs and be able to explain how the tone is created.

1 On December 20 there flitted past us, absolutely without public notice, one of the most important, profane anniversaries in American history—to wit: the seventy-fifth anniversary of the introduction of the bathtub into these states. Not a plumber fired a salute or hung out a flag. Not a governor proclaimed a day of prayer. Not a newspaper called attention to the day.—H. L. MENCKEN

2 It is sometime before dawn, in the late spring, as I write this. The seagulls have more than an hour before it will be their moment to fly in from the river, screeing and crying, and then fly back. After them, the pigeons will murmur, and it will be day, perhaps a hot and sticky day. Right now the air is deliciously cool, but I find myself shivering. I find myself imagining the cold, the bitter cold, of that morning when Death came in full panoply, like one dressed for dinner. That morning so very long ago. —AVRAM DAVIDSON

3 Old and crumbling, the squat-built adobe mission of El Tordo sits in a hollow high up near the snow-capped Truchas. A few clay houses huddle close to it like tawny chicks about a ruffled old hen. On one of the steep slopes, which has the peaks for a background, sleeps the ancient graveyard with all its inhabitants. The town itself is quite as lifeless during the winter months, when the few folks that live there move down to warmer levels by the Rio Grande; but when the snows have gone, except for the white crusts on the peaks, they return to herd their sheep and goats, and with them come a stream of pious pilgrims and curious sightseers that lasts throughout the spring and summer weather.—FRAY ANGÉLÍCO CHAVÉZ

4 Mrs. Brennan took snuff. She got it out of her grandson's store, going in and helping herself from the big tin on the second shelf. It was a habit her family deplored. Mrs. Brennan did not like snuff much. It was one of the things she had got over. It made her cough. But the fact that her family deplored her taking it prevented her from giving it up completely. She drank a little, too, Not much; just enough to get "tiddly." That was what she called it, "I'm a little tiddly today," she'd say, and the family didn't like that either. Nor did she, save for the fun of shocking them and the interest outwitting them gave her.—STUART CLOETE

5 Into each life, it is said, some rain must fall. Some people have bad horoscopes, others take tips on the stock market. McNamara created the TFX and the Edsel. Churches possess the real world. But Indians have been cursed above all other people in history. Indians have anthropologists.—VINE DELORIA, JR.

6 It's a story they tell in the border country, where Massachusetts joins Vermont and New Hampshire. Yes, Dan'l Webster's dead—or, at least they buried him. But every time there's a thunderstorm around Marshfield, they say you can hear his rolling voice in the hollows of the sky. And they say that if you go to his grave and

speak loud and clear, "Dan'l Webster—Dan'l Webster!" the ground'll begin to shiver and the trees begin to shake. And after a while you'll hear a deep voice saying, "Neighbor, how stands the Union?" Then you better answer the Union stands as she stood, rock-bottomed and copper-sheathed, one and indivisible, or he's liable to roar right out of the ground. At least, that's what I was told when I was a youngster.—Stephen Vincent Benét

7 These are the times that try men's souls. The summer soldier and the sunshine patriot will, in this crisis, shrink from the service of his country; but he that stands it NOW, deserves the love and thanks of man and woman. Tyranny, like hell, is not easily conquered; yet we have this consolation with us, that the harder the conflict, the more glorious the triumph. What we obtain too cheap, we esteem too lightly: 'tis dearness only that gives every thing its value. Heaven knows how to put a proper price upon its goods; and it would be strange indeed, if so celestial an article as FREEDOM should not be highly rated. Britain, with an army to enforce her tyranny, has declared that she has a right (*not only to* TAX) but "to BIND *us in* ALL CASES WHATSOEVER," and if being *bound in that manner*, is not slavery, then is there not such a thing as slavery upon earth. Even the expression is impious, for so unlimited a power can belong only to God.—Thomas Paine (1776)

8 A clear, racy day with the wind smelling of leaves. Even grubby sparrows in the gutter showed not uniformly sooty but brown-capped and blackthroated. Content to be alone, Anna walked toward the lake, a blanket over her arm and a book Leon had pressed on her—an interpretation of Blake he claimed was his theory of film—tucked in her cow of a purse. As she passed under the echoey railroad viaduct, she wondered in which lakeside tower Leon was lunching with his mother, in these blocks almost entirely white and largely vertical. The managers, the lawyers, and middle echelon administrators lived over here in grandiose, well kept apartment hotels or new glass walled skyscrapers. Cliffs of money on the lake.—Marge Piercy

9 Sometimes at evening I sit, looking out on the big Missouri. The sun sets, and dusk steals over the water. In the shadows I seem again to see our Indian village, with smoke curling upward from the earth lodges; and in the river's roar I hear the yells of the warriors, the laughter of little children as of old. It is but an old woman's dream. Again I see but shadows and hear only the roar of the river; and tears come into my eyes. Our Indian life, I know, is gone forever.—Buffalo Bird Woman

10 It was a beautiful college. The vines and the roads gracefully winding, lined with hedges and wild roses that dazzled the eyes in the summer sun. Honeysuckle and purple wisteria hung heavy from the trees and white magnolias mixed with their scents in the bee-humming air. I've recalled it often, here in my hole: How the grass turned green in the springtime and how the mocking birds fluttered their tails and sang, how the moon shone down on the buildings, how the bell in the chapel tower rang out the precious, short-lived hours; how the girls in bright summer dresses promenaded the grassy lawn. Many times, here at night, I've closed my eyes and walked along the forbidden road that winds past the girls' dormitories, past the hall with the clock in the tower, its windows warmly aglow, on down past the small white Home Economics practice cottage, whiter still in the moonlight, and on down the road with its sloping and turning, paralleling the black powerhouse with its engines droning earth-shaking rhythms in the dark, its windows red from the glow of the furnace, on to where the road became a bridge over a dry riverbed, tangled with brush and clinging vines; the bridge of rustic logs, made for trysting, but virginal and untested by lovers; on up the road, past the buildings, with the southern verandas half-a-city-block long, to the sudden forking, barren of buildings, birds, or grass, where the road turned off to the insane asylum.—Ralph Ellison

B. Choose a subject, then write two paragraphs about it. Have each paragraph reveal a different attitude toward the subject. Describe the tone of each paragraph and explain, in a few sentences, how you achieved that tone.

Part 6 Mood

Tone is the writer's attitude toward a subject; mood, on the other hand, is the attitude that is evoked in the reader. This paragraph illustrates the difference between the two.

> Michael Lowes hummed as he shaved, amused by the face he saw—the pallid, asymetrical face, with the right eye so much higher than the left, and its eyebrow so peculiarly arched, like a "v" turned upside down. Perhaps this day wouldn't be as bad as the last. In fact, he knew it wouldn't be, and that was why he hummed. This was the bi-weekly day of escape, when he would stay out for the evening, and play bridge with Hurwitz, Bryant, and Smith. Should he tell Dora at the breakfast table? No, better not. Particularly in view of last night's row about unpaid bills. And there would be more of them, probably, beside his plate. The rent. The coal. The doctor who had attended to the children. Jeez, what a life. Maybe it was time to do a new jump.—CONRAD AIKEN

The paragraph describes a self-satisfied man. He is "amused" by his face and is not ashamed of its asymetrical features, as is revealed by his humming as he looks in the mirror. He is somewhat upset about unpaid bills, but they are little more than passing annoyances. Uppermost in his mind is that evening's card game, which he decides to keep secret from his wife. The thought passes through his mind that he should duck out on his wife and his bills. The writer does not judge Michael Lowes' attitudes or behavior; his tone is one of acceptance.

The reader, on the other hand, senses something sinister in the "pallid" face with its rakishly formed eyebrow. He or she responds to the writer's revelations with feelings of dislike toward Lowes. Dislike, then, is the mood of the paragraph.

What mood is created in the following paragraph?

> Aristide Valentin, Chief of the Paris Police, was late for his dinner, and some of his guests began to arrive before him. These were, however, reassured by his confidential servant, Ivan, the old man with a scar, and a face almost as gray as his moustaches,

who always sat at a table in the entrance hall—a hall hung with weapons—Valentin's house was perhaps as peculiar and celebrated as its master. It was an old house, with high walls and tall poplars almost overhanging the Seine; but the oddity—and perhaps the police value—of its architecture was this; that there was no ultimate exit at all except through this front door, which was guarded by Ivan and the armory. The garden was large and elaborate, and there were many exits from the house into the garden. But there was no exit from the garden into the world outside; all round it ran a tall, smooth, unscalable wall with special spikes at the top; no bad garden, perhaps, for a man to reflect in whom some hundred criminals had sworn to kill.—GILBERT K. CHESTERTON

The writer of this paragraph presents many bizarre details about Valentin's house—"the old man with a scar," "a hall hung with weapons," "no ultimate exit," and "a tall, smooth, unscalable wall with special spikes"—in a completely matter-of-fact tone. The reader, though, suspects that the guests should be far from reassured by Ivan's presence and that their evening, spent in such a setting, will be anything but ordinary. The mood is one of expectation and of curiosity.

Exercises **Recognizing and Creating Mood**

A. Turn back to Exercise A at the end of Part 5. Identify the mood of each paragraph and explain how that mood is created.

B. Write two paragraphs, each designed to evoke a different mood. Ask a classmate to read your completed paragraphs and to describe his or her response to each. Revise your paragraphs until they elicit the desired mood from your reader.

Chapter 10

Types of Paragraphs

When a professional writer sits down to write a paragraph, he or she has an idea and a purpose in mind. These two variables determine the type of paragraph that the writer will use. Common types of paragraphs include the following:

- the paragraph of description
- the paragraph of comparison
- the paragraph of contrast
- the paragraph of analogy
- the paragraph of narration
- the paragraph of explanation
- the paragraph of argument
- the paragraph of persuasion
- the paragraph of definition

Usually, the selection of paragraph form is unconscious. For instance, a writer would not think, "I'll write a paragraph of persuasion today." Rather, he or she would first decide to convince people of the need to conserve natural resources, and then would write a paragraph of persuasion.

You, too, might automatically select the proper form for the ideas you wish to convey. However, because you are a relatively inexperienced writer, you can control your paragraphs more successfully if you are conscious of the form in which you are writing.

Part 1 The Paragraph of Description

Persons, places, and things are the subjects for paragraphs of description. Usually, a writer describes more than just the external characteristics of the subject. He or she also attempts to capture its essence, or internal qualities. For example, in describing a woman, a writer might indicate that she is five feet six inches tall, that she is Caucasian, and that she has blue eyes and black hair. These facts reveal nothing about the kind of person she is. The writer might go on, though, to note that she has a shy smile, that her hands and eyes are in constant motion, and that she always looks away from the person who talks to her. These details provide the reader with a glimpse of the woman's inner qualities.

Descriptions of places and things also go beyond inventories of external facts. For example, a writer describing the Statue of Liberty might convey the idea that the immigrants who sailed into New York harbor were heartened by the symbolic strength of her welcoming smile and thrilled by her quiet dignity and uplifted torch of freedom.

Describing a Person

Read the following description of a person. Note how the writer uses physical details as the vehicle through which he reveals inner qualities.

> Before the prisoner left for Texas, the police took the traditional mug shots of him. In these photographs, Abel looks something like an unfrocked monk who had been caught blaspheming. A scowl clouds his ascetic face, and the sparse fringe of brownish-gray hair around his ears and the back of his head is disarranged. He is looking down an aquiline nose with tired eyes, and his receding chin is darkened by a one-day growth of beard. The collar of his white shirt is unbuttoned, and his striped tie is askew. Looking at this face, one might think immediately of a clerk who has worked too long in the same department. The photograph brings

to mind an observer's remark: "He has a genius for the inconspicuous." The foreman of the Abel jury, John T. Dublynn, exclaimed when he first saw the defendant: "He could be walking down the street and he could be anybody."—SANCHE DE GRAMONT

The writer concentrates almost exclusively on Abel's unpleasant characteristics, noting his scowling expression; sparse, disarranged hair; tired eyes; receding, unshaven chin; and rumpled clothing. If Abel has attractive features, such as a pleasant smile, or an easy self-assurance, you would not know it from this description. By maintaining such a consistent point of view, the writer communicates his own dislike for the man and arouses the same feelings in the reader.

The writer of the following description takes a different approach to details.

> Her face was drowned in the shadow of an ugly, rolled-brim brown felt hat, but the details of her slight body and of the struggle taking place within it were clear enough. It was an intense, unrelenting struggle between her back, which was beginning to bend ever so slightly under the weight of her eighty odd years, and the rest of her, which sought to deny those years and hold that back straight, to keep it in line. Moving swiftly toward us (so swiftly it seemed she did not intend stopping when she reached us but would sweep past us out the doorway that opened onto the sea and, like Christ, walk upon the water!) she was caught between the sunlight at her end of the building and the darkness inside. For a moment she appeared to contain them both: the light in the long, severe, old-fashioned white dress she wore, which brought the sense of a past that was still alive into our bustling present, and in the snatch of white at her eye; and the darkness in her black, high-top shoes and in her face, which was visible now that she was closer.—PAULE MARSHALL

The writer of this description is highly selective in the details that she has chosen to include in the paragraph. She views the old woman as the embodiment of contrasts—between an aging body and a youthful spirit, between sunlight and darkness, between the past and the present, between black and white—and presents only those details that reinforce this central idea.

Exercise **Describing a Person**

Write a paragraph describing someone you know. Include details that reveal his or her inner qualities and your own attitude toward that person.

Describing a Place

You have five senses—touch, taste, smell, hearing, and sight—and ideally a description will appeal to at least one of the five. In other words, a description paragraph will enable you to "feel," "taste," "smell," "hear," or "see" whatever the writer is describing. Most descriptions appeal primarily to the sense of sight. Some descriptions also include details that appeal to other senses as well. These details work together to develop the point of view of the paragraph. In a description of a place, the details convey the feeling or atmosphere that imbues the place, as in the following description.

> It was a lovely morning. The last stars withdrew while we were waiting, the sky was clear and serene, but the world in which we walked was somber still, and profoundly silent. The grass was wet; down by the trees where the ground sloped, it gleamed with the dew like dim silver. The air of the morning was cold; it had that twinge in it which in Northern countries means that the frost is not far away. However often you make the experience—I thought—it is still impossible to believe, in this coolness and shade, that the heat of the sun and the glare of the sky, in a few hours' time, will be hard to bear. The gray mist lay upon the hills, strangely taking shape from them; it would be bitterly cold on the Buffalo if they were about there now, grazing on the hillside as in a cloud.—ISAK DINESEN

The words *serene*, *somber*, and *silent* capture the feeling of the place in the hours before the heat and glare of the day. This point of view is expanded with details that appeal to the senses of touch, hearing, and sight—"profoundly silent," "wet grass," "dim silver," "coolness and shade," "gray mist."

Exercises Describing a Place

A. Write a paragraph describing what you see around you at this moment. Then write a second paragraph in which you add details that appeal to one of the other five senses. For example, you might describe smells or sounds.

B. Write two paragraphs, each describing the same place from a different point of view. In one description include details that reveal a liking for the place; in the other description present details that reveal a dislike. Appeal to as many senses as you can without overwriting your descriptions.

Describing a Thing

Describing a thing is much the same as describing a place. In this kind of description, a writer utilizes details with sense appeal to communicate a point of view toward an object. A writer might also make use of similes and metaphors, comparing the thing being described with some other thing. For example, he or she might describe a stone as looking like a plump little pillow embroidered in tiny black stitches.

Read the following description of a thing, noting the sense appeal of the details and any comparisons used by the writer.

> The object that most drew my attention, in the mysterious package, was a certain affair of fine red cloth, much worn and faded. There were traces about it of gold embroidery, which, however, was greatly frayed and defaced; so that none, or very little, of the glitter was left. It had been wrought, as was easy to perceive, with wonderful skill of needlework; and the stitch (as I am assured by ladies conversant with such mysteries) gives evidence of a now forgotten art, not to be recovered even by the process of picking out the threads. This rag of scarlet cloth—for time and wear and a sacrilegious moth had reduced it to little other than a rag—on careful examination, assumed the shape of a letter. It was the capital letter A. By an accurate measurement, each limb proved to be precisely three inches and a quarter in length. It had been

intended, there could be no doubt, as an ornamental article of dress; but how it was to be worn, or what rank, honor, and dignity, in by-past times were signified by it, was a riddle which (so evanescent are the fashions of the world in these particulars) I saw little hope of solving. And yet it strangely interested me. My eyes fastened themselves upon the old scarlet letter, and would not be turned aside. Certainly, there was some deep meaning in it, most worthy of interpretation, and which, as it were, streamed forth from the mystic symbol, subtly communicating itself to my sensibilities, but evading the analysis of my mind.—NATHANIEL HAWTHORNE

The 'thing" described in the paragraph is the famous "A" worn by the heroine of *The Scarlet Letter*. Notice how the writer invests it with mystery. There is something strange and compelling about the letter that makes him unable to take his eyes off it. It is, for him, a "mystic symbol."

Exercise **Describing a Thing**

Write a paragraph describing a thing that has some unusual qualities. Try to include in your description at least one comparison and details that appeal to two or more senses.

Mixing Descriptions

A writer often mixes two or more descriptions. In writing about a dance, for example, a writer might describe a thing (the music) and the people (the dancers). In describing a picnic, a writer might talk about a place (the park) and a thing (the food). In the following paragraph, a writer describes a place (the hall) and a person (the subject of a portrait).

On the east side of the hall a free staircase, tile-paved, rose to a gallery with a wrought-iron railing and another piece of stained-glass romance. Large, hard chairs with rounded, red plush seats were backed into the vacant spaces of the wall round about. They didn't look as if anybody had ever sat in them. In the middle of the west wall there was a big, empty fireplace with a brass screen in four hinged panels, and over the fireplace a marble mantel with cupids at the corners. Above the mantel there was a large oil portrait, and above the portrait two bullet-torn or moth-eaten cavalry pennants crossed in a glass frame. The portrait was a stiffly posed job of an officer in full regimentals of about the time of the Mexican war. The officer had a neat black imperial; black mustachios; hot, hard, coal-black eyes; and the general look of a man it would pay to get along with. I thought this might be General Sternwood's grandfather. It could hardly be the General himself, even though I had heard he was pretty far gone in years to have a couple of daughters still in the dangerous twenties.—RAYMOND CHANDLER

Exercise **Writing Descriptions**

Here are some subjects for paragraphs of description. Choose two of these subjects, or use your own ideas. Write two paragraphs, one describing either a person, place, or thing exclusively, the other combining two of these kinds of subjects. Use as many details with sense appeal as you can.

1. A well baked pizza is a work of art.
2. At 4:00 the traffic on the expressway started bunching up, and we were slowed to fifteen miles per hour.
3. The garden showed all shades of the rainbow in its lavish display of flowers.
4. There is one comedian I like better than all others.
5. Fall is a lovely season.
6. The smell and sound of the ocean can lull me into sleep.
7. The beginners' ski slope is a wild confusion of people, noise, and color.
8. There is nothing else like the shine and smell of a new car.
9. At the touchdown, the stands exploded with frenzied cheers.
10. Puppies are cuddly creatures.

Part 2 The Paragraph of Comparison and Contrast

Using Comparison

In a paragraph of comparison, a writer shows the similarities between two or more people, places, or things. The primary purpose of such a paragraph can be the comparison itself. To achieve this purpose, a writer would present several points of similarity, along with supporting details. For example, a writer setting out to compare Earth and Mars might note similarities in temperature, pressure, atmospheric gasses, and topography.

Comparison can also play a secondary role in a paragraph, being used to clarify the main idea. In the following paragraph, for example, the writer's purpose is to describe the surface of Mars, a purpose achieved largely through comparison.

> In appearance, at least, Mars is not so different from the Earth. Many regions of the Earth must resemble Mars so closely that you could not tell which was which from a photograph. An artist friend of mine who has made a name for himself depicting planetary scenes tells me that Mars is his hardest subject. Editors balk at paying for a picture supposedly representing Mars when their readers are likely to mistake it for the country around Reno or Las Vegas, for Mars is practically all dry land and most of that land is desert.—ROBERT S. RICHARDSON

The writer of this paragraph used a brief anecdote to develop the comparison between Earth and Mars. This is one of many available techniques used to support or explain both comparisons and and contrasts. Other techniques include the use of one or more examples and the presentation of facts and statistics.

Using Contrast

In using contrast, the writer shows how two things differ. The writer of the following paragraph, for example, makes a sweeping contrast between the inspiring and the challenging aspects of Indian history.

> The history of India provides both an inspiration and a challenge to the historian. It inspires by its vast range and scope, its color, its variety, its rich cluster of personalities; it challenges with its complexities, its long periods of obscurity, its unfamiliar movements, and its stark contrasts between luxury and poverty, between gentleness and cruelty, creation and destruction. For the few with gorgeous processions and rainbow pageantry there were the many with mud huts and a handful of rice or millet a day, with the burning heaven for a canopy and the stifling dust for perfume.—PERCIVAL SPEAR

This paragraph captures the duality of Indian life through three different types of contrasts: the contrast of broad generalizations (its variety versus its complexities), the contrast of narrower ideas (luxury versus poverty), and the contrast of specific information (the few with gorgeous possessions versus the many with mud huts). The paragraph exemplifies the type of writing in which broad concepts are distilled into a few descriptive sentences supported with one or more specific examples.

The writer of the following paragraph focuses on a much more limited topic.

> How does one determine whether a law is just or unjust? A just law is a man-made code that squares with the moral law or the law of God. An unjust law is a code that is out of harmony with the moral law. To put it in the terms of St. Thomas Aquinas: An unjust law is a human law that is not rooted in eternal law and natural law. Any law that uplifts human personality is just. Any law that degrades human personality is unjust.—MARTIN LUTHER KING, JR.

The writer presents criteria for judging the justice of a law with definition-like clarity. Each statement about just laws is contrasted with a corresponding statement about unjust laws.

Combining Comparison and Contrast

Often, writers combine comparison and contrast in the same paragraph. In the following example, the writer first presents the similarities between the experiences of the Indian and the white person, then draws a sharp contrast between their value systems.

> At the time of the Creation, the Cherokee say, the white person was given a stone, and the Indian a piece of silver. Despising the stone, the white person threw it away. Finding the silver equally worthless, the Indian discarded it. Later the white person pocketed the silver as a source of material power; the Indian revered the stone as a source of sacred power. This prophetic story underscores the profound differences in Indian and white value systems. In time, the Indian would be forced to use the white person's currency as a medium of exchange, but the white person would never appreciate the Indian's sense of the cosmic power invested in an ordinary pebble.—PETER NABOKOV

The writer of the following example takes a different approach to organizing a paragraph of comparison and contrast.

> It is to be assumed that if people were to live this life like a poem, they would be able to look upon the sunset of their lives as their happiest period, and instead of trying to postpone the much feared old age, be able actually to look forward to it, and gradually build up to it as the best and happiest period of existence. In my efforts to compare and contrast Eastern and Western life, I have found no differences that are absolute except in this matter of the attitude toward age, which is sharp and clearcut and permits of no intermediate positions. The differences in our attitude toward sex, toward women, and toward work, play, and achievement are all relative. The relationship between husband and wife in China is not essentially different from that in the West, nor even the relationship between parent and child. Not even the ideas of individual liberty and democracy and the relationship between the people and their ruler are, after all, so different. But in the matter of our attitude toward age, the difference is absolute, and the East and the West take exactly opposite points of view.—LIN YUTANG

Instead of separating the sentences of comparison and the sentences of contrast, this writer has inserted the sentences describing smilarities between the statements about the key difference between Eastern and Western life.

The next paragraph illustrates a third approach to comparison and contrast.

> Many experts believe that the chimpanzee is next to the human being in intelligence. The Yerkes, however, reasonably expect that the gorilla would be, in view of the more pronounced resemblance in structure of the nervous systems in the gorilla and the human being. It may be that the former judgment is colored by human performances. The gorilla is sullen, untamable, and ferocious, shy, wary, and slow-moving. The chimpanzee, on the other hand, is more lively, tractable, gregarious, and "humanizable"—besides being of smaller size, and less dangerous to people than the gorilla. The fact is that psychologists know a great deal about the intelligence of the chimpanzee, whereas the gorilla's is relatively unknown. Meanwhile, it should be stated that gregariousness and amiability are not quite identical with intelligence. And if gorillas do not go out of their way to show affection for their human hunters and captors, this can scarcely be adduced as evidence against a respectable I.Q.—WESTON LA BARRE

The writer begins by setting up a comparison between the human being and two members of the ape family in regard to intelligence. He then notes the similarity between the gorilla and the human nervous systems. In the rest of the paragraph, he contrasts the gorilla with the chimpanzee to explain why the similarity between the gorilla and the human being is often discounted in favor of the chimpanzee. The writer uses contrasts to support a comparison, a technique that is difficult to employ successfully.

Exercises Writing Paragraphs of Comparison and Contrast

A. Write a paragraph in which you compare or contrast two places you know well. Be sure that your topic sentence makes clear whether you are focusing on similarities or differences.

B. Select one of the following subjects, or one of your own, and develop it into a paragraph that combines comparison and contrast.

1. novels and short stories
2. riding a skateboard and roller skating
3. riding in a small car and riding in a large car
4. animals in zoos and animals in their natural habitats
5. stage plays and movies
6. life in a small town and life in a large city
7. motor cycles and motor bikes
8. two popular performers or musical groups
9. a hit-and-run driver and a murderer
10. traveling on a train and traveling on a bus

Part 3 The Paragraph of Analogy

An analogy is a comparison in which something unfamiliar is compared with something similar but more familar to the reader. Often, an analogy is used to classify an abstract concept that would otherwise be difficult to explain. In the following paragraph of analogy, the participants in the agricultural system in California's San Joaquin Valley are compared with parts of the human body. As you read, notice how this analogy helps to explain the relationship between the growers and the farm workers.

> The backbone of the valley's prosperity is the farmer who grows the many fruits and vegetables. But if the farmer, or grower, is the backbone, the blood and sinew are supplied by the farm worker, usually a migrant, who labors long and hard to make the dream of a "Golden State" a reality. Without farm workers, there would be no four-billion-dollar-a-year agribusiness. Without them, the soil, perhaps, would revert to its condition of 150 years ago—an arid, wind-sucked land covered with sagebrush and inhabited mainly by the coyote, bobcat, and ring-tailed pheasant.—JAMES SANTIBAÑEZ

The analogy in this paragraph is a detail, used along with other details to support the main idea: the farm worker is essential to California's agriculture. In the next example, the analogy between the art of war as practiced by human beings and by ants *is* the main idea, which is explained by the details that are included in the paragraph.

> It is a curious phenomenon of nature that only two species practice the art of war—human beings and ants, both of which, ironically, maintain complex social organizations. This does not mean that only humans and ants engage in the murder of their own kind. Many animals of the same species kill each other, but only humans and ants have practiced the science of organized destruction, employing their massed numbers in violent combat and relying on strategy and tactics to meet developing situations or to capitalize on the weaknesses in the strategy and tactics of the other side. The longest continuous war ever fought between countries lasted thirty years. The longest ant war ever recorded lasted six-and-a-half weeks, or whatever the corresponding units would be in ant reckoning.—NORMAN COUSINS

Exercise **Writing a Paragraph of Analogy**

Select one of the following subjects for comparison, or one of your own, and develop it into a paragraph of analogy. As you write, keep in mind that your purpose is to clarify an unfamiliar or abstract idea by comparing it with one that is more familiar or concrete.

1. Civilization and a beehive
2. Tools and parts of the human body
3. Reading and sailing in a hot air balloon
4. Vacation and having a battery charged
5. Friendship and a boxing match
6. Life and a card game
7. A factory and a household
8. The human circulatory system and city streets
9. Hope and a distant star
10. The passage of time and waves on the ocean

Part 4 The Paragraph of Narration

A narrative paragraph is a short account of something that happened. In this type of paragraph, a writer relates an event or a brief series of events, concentrating solely on the unfolding of the simple plot. Usually, the characters are merely named and the setting is either implied or mentioned in passing.

Following is an example of a paragraph of narration. Note how simply and directly it is written.

> During the night we had already prepared our rescue net, and when with a rising sea Skipper Mees brought the *Insulinde* alongside the wreck, four persons were able to jump into the net. At the second attempt, three succeeded in jumping across. In the meantime the day had fully dawned. Again we tried. Everything cracked and creaked as we touched the wreck, but we got nobody across. We tried anew for the fourth time. The *Insulinde* thumped against the doomed ship, seeming to tear everything on board from its moorings, but no one jumped. The fifth attempt—again in vain. The sixth: no one saved. Six attempts in the furious surf in a raging storm—and five sailors still aboard the lost ship! Six times hurled against the wreck, again seeking space, again up and through the breakers to the waiting sailors, again alongside the ship. Six times under almost impossible circumstances, through ground swells and a treacherous surf, each time the *Insulinde* scraping the hard sand of the reef. I can assure you that it wasn't much fun.—Klaas Toxopeus

This paragraph, a kind of story in miniature, represents one common type of narrative paragraph. The next example represents a second type, in which an anecdote is used to illustrate a general principle or idea.

> Statistics, it is sometimes said, can be made to prove anything. If you play around with the right figures in the right way you will always get the right answer. A good example of this once arose in

a firm that made vitamin pills. Its sales department found that there was a definite relationship between the number of pills sold and the death rate. As the former increased the latter decreased in strict proportion. On this basis, the firm had only to step up production and sales enough to bring the death rate down to zero and then below zero, by which time it would have brought about the resurrection of the dead. On their own the statistics were sound enough, but the conclusions they led to were obviously absurd.—HENRY C. KING

Although this type of paragraph can be classified as a narrative paragraph, it can also be identified as an explanatory paragraph because the narration is used to explain or clarify an idea.

Exercise **Writing Paragraphs of Narration**

From the following list of ideas, choose one that lends itself to development as a brief story and one that lends itself to explanation by anecdote. Then write two paragraphs of narration.

1. Everyone who drives a car needs a course in auto mechanics.
2. A careless remark can hurt a sensitive person.
3. Two people can communicate even though they speak different languages.
4. My father's love of moving furniture around upsets the entire family.
5. I have one, only one, true friend.
6. She worked hard for her promotion.
7. Once I awoke at five o'clock in the morning.
8. My trip to New York was highly eventful.
9. Attending a live concert opened a new world to me.
10. I'll never forget the day I started ninth grade.
11. I find it hard to believe what an expert can do with a skateboard.
12. I was late for band practice today.
13. Not everyone has a family like mine.
14. Practice makes perfect.
15. The day was blustery and altogether miserable.

Part 5 The Paragraph of Explanation

The paragraph of explanation is a broad classification that includes a variety of paragraph forms. Three of these forms are described in Part 5; three additional forms are examined in Parts 6 and 7. The distinctions among them are based on the differences in their purposes and in their methods of development.

Explaining Why

A simple kind of explanatory paragraph is one in which you give reasons for something that happened once or that happens regularly, or for a conclusion that you have reached. For example, you can explain why your football team lost, why you were late for an appointment, why you forgot to return a phone call, why you failed a test, why you chose physics over chemistry, why hurricanes occur at certain times of year, why presidential primaries are held, or why corn grows well in the Midwest. Explanations of this kind can be reconstructed from your own experience, from general knowledge, or from research.

The following paragraph is an explanation of why the writer considers herself lucky.

> I'm one of the lucky people. My Otoe-Pawnee-Wyandot parents and ancestors endowed me with a sureness of identity I will never lose. The Wyandots have been terminated as a tribe, and there are indeed no fullblood Wyandots now. Even so, enrolled Wyandots if called upon to do so, would have no problem identifying as a definite tribe. Their history even today is distinct. The beauty of their heritage is still to be felt and seen in the early morning mists that refresh the luxuriant greenery of the Wyandot countryside in Oklahoma and Kansas. And I, blessed one, can still know firsthand the strengths and beauties of my seventy-nine-year old Wyandot mother.—MIFAUNWY SHUNATONA HINES

Explaining a Process

To explain how to do something or how something works requires a logical presentation of ideas and enough information to enable the reader to understand each step in the process. The following paragraph is an explanation of how a dictionary editor goes about writing a definition.

> To define a word, the dictionary editor places before himself the stack of cards illustrating that word. Each of the cards represents an actual use of the word by a writer of some literary or historical importance. He reads the cards carefully, discards some, rereads the rest, and divides up the stack according to what he thinks are the several senses of the word. Finally, he writes his definitions, following the hard-and-fast rule that each definition *must* be based on what the quotations in front of him reveal about the meaning of the word. The editor cannot be influenced by what *he* thinks a given word *ought* to mean. He must work according to the cards or not at all.—S. I. HAYAKAWA

Explaining an Idea

A common kind of explanation is one in which details—in the form of facts, statistics, examples, and anecdotes—are used to develop the idea or concept presented in the topic sentence of the paragraph. Following is an example of this type of explanation.

> A unique idea that pervades all Hindu thinking and forms, as it were, the mental atmosphere that the traditional Hindu breathed, is the concept of *karma*. *Karma* is literally "action" and the concept may be described as the law of consequences. Every action, good or bad, has its consequence or fruit. The consequence comes back to the individual, the fruit must be plucked or the crop reaped, by a law from which there is no escape. This idea is closely linked with that of transmigration of the soul, or reincarnation, since the fruits of one's actions clearly cannot all be experienced in a single physical existence. These two ideas are intimately

interwoven into the texture of the Hindu mind, from the prince to the peasant, from the philosopher to the worldly wise merchant. They serve as a justification of the whole system of caste, justifying both the claims of the privileged and the disabilities of the lowly.—PERCIVAL SPEAR

After reading this paragraph, you can understand why explaining ideas can sometimes be a difficult undertaking. Considering that the topic is philosophical in nature and foreign to our culture, the writer has achieved a truly fine explanation, clear, intelligent, and interesting.

Exercises **Writing Paragraphs of Explanation**

A. The following subjects are starting points for paragraphs of explanation that involve reasons. Choose one of these, or one of your own, and write an explanatory paragraph.

1. He was unable to keep up with the rest of the class.
2. The Paris world of fashion no longer dictates clothing styles.
3. The rights of victims are now being recognized.
4. When it is winter in the United States, it is summer in Australia.
5. Diet pills can have harmful side effects.
6. Pilots often try to get into the jet stream.
7. Automobile insurance is costly.
8. Color photography is more popular than black and white.
9. I enjoy bird watching.
10. A circus appeals to young and old alike.
11. Athletes are much admired.
12. Many people take their dogs to obedience school.

B. Write a paragraph that explains a process; for example, how a helicopter can stay in the air, how a tornado develops, how to grow tomatoes, or how to bowl. When you are choosing a subject, be certain that it can be developed as an explanatory paragraph.

C. Choose a broad subject such as brotherhood or sisterhood, charity, respect, prejudice, selfishness, or self-denial, and limit the subject so that it can be handled in a single paragraph. Then write a paragraph explaining that idea or concept.

Part 6 The Paragraph of Argument or Persuasion

Paragraphs of argument and persuasion are essentially the same form of writing. In each, reasons are presented to support a point of view that is open to question or debate. Where these two kinds of paragraphs differ is in intent. In a paragraph of argument, the writer explains a point of view without expecting the reader to act upon or to embrace his or her way of thinking. For example, Ellen attacks Maria for being a conservationist. Maria then writes a paragraph in which she argues in favor of practicing conservation. She does not attempt to persuade Ellen to buy soft drinks in reusable bottles, to organize a car pool, or to initiate some other appropriate action. She does try to get Ellen to acknowledge the validity of her point of view.

In a paragraph of persuasion, the writer's purpose is to convert the reader to his or her point of view. Paragraphs of persuasion are much more common than paragraphs of argument because writers seldom argue without also trying to persuade. For example, a writer is not likely to write an editorial for the student newspaper arguing the case for shorter school days or less homework without also trying to persuade someone to take action on these issues. Following is an example of a paragraph of persuasion.

> In our day the Constitution has been used to shield racketeers, gangsters, and those suspected of radicalism from the necessity of testifying about their activities before courts and legislative investigating committees. It has prevented the censorship of books, magazines, and movies offensive to many groups; upset the con-

victions of criminals found guilty by juries; and blocked religious instruction in the public schools. Constitutional restraints (Fourth Amendment) on police make warrants necessary for searches of homes and offices for evidence of crime and forbid the police to use intensive interrogation or drugs to get confessions from persons accused of crimes. As a result, some citizens believe that the courts are soft on criminals and that constitutional rights that protect enemies of society and members of despised political minorities should be abolished or, at least, limited. The ordinary law-abiding citizen has no need of such protection, they argue. With crime rising in our major cities, with juvenile delinquency spreading among youth, with the spread of illegal gambling, drug addiction, and sex offenses, with the competition between the United States and the Soviet Union for world leadership, should we not strengthen the powers of government and law-enforcement officers?

The writer introduces his point of view toward constitutional rights by citing several controversial applications of the Constitution. These facts gain the attention of the reader and arouse curiosity as to the purpose of the paragraph. The writer then describes the desire of some citizens to abolish or limit constitutional rights and the current social and political situation. He ends with a question that invites the reader to agree with his idea that the powers of government and law enforcement officers should be strengthened.

Although the writer relies heavily on facts, he also uses many words and phrases that appeal to a reader's emotions; for example: "racketeers," "gangsters," "soft on criminals," "despised political minorities," "ordinary law-abiding citizen," "juvenile delinquency," "illegal gambling," "drug addiction," "sex offenses," "competition between the United States and the Soviet Union." Such words and phrases play on the readers' fear of crime and criminals, their desire to be considered law-abiding citizens, and their patriotic feelings.

This next paragraph, written by the same author, has an even stronger emotional appeal.

> We reject the implication that a responsible citizen must participate in the political process. Those who vote simply because they have been told that they should—and feel guilty if they do not—may be among those who vote for mules, favor the first names on the ballot, and elect the dead to offices that have been abolished. We believe that people who are mature and responsible will vote because they sense the relationship between the quality of the society in which they live and their own well-being. They will want, therefore, to cooperate with others in order to ensure that the conditions of progress for themselves and the society are maintained. By eliminating the burden of guilt about political participation, we may be able to arrive at an understanding whereby free, willing individuals spontaneously take part in the political process in order to extend the area of creativity for themselves, in order to express more adequately the obligation they feel toward the society, and to discharge more handsomely the debt they believe they owe society.

In this paragraph, the writer begins with a direct, uncompromising statement of what he believes and then gives the reasons to support that statement. He makes little attempt to construct an objective argument. Instead, he appeals to the reader's desire to be counted among the "mature and responsible" citizens. Can you identify the words and phrases that create the strong emotional appeal of this paragraph?

Exercise Writing the Paragraph of Persuasion

Write a paragraph of persuasion in which you develop your point of view on some controversial issue; for example: the women's movement, nuclear power, ecology, or an issue in your local community. Support your point of view with facts, statistics, examples, anecdotes, comparisons, contrasts, analogies, or any other kind of information that will increase the effectiveness of your presentation. Wherever possible, make the paragraph even more powerful by using words and phrases that will appeal to your readers' emotions.

Part 7 The Paragraph of Definition

Some words can be defined within the context of a paragraph. Their definitions are brief, often consisting of a synonym or a short descriptive phrase, and are tangential to the ideas being presented in the paragraph. Other terms, though, must be defined more completely because of the complexity of their meanings, their openness to misinterpretation, their unusual use by a writer, or because a writer chooses to explain them in some detail. When the need for an extended definition occurs, a writer can develop a paragraph of definition. Following is an example of this type of paragraph.

> A metaphor is a game in which the wit of the writer and the wit of the reader are matched. The mind of the poet fastens on an object and then rushes halfway across the world to establish a relation between that object and some hitherto unrelated object. Although the objects are not in the least alike, the reader is quick to see the likeness at the point of comparison. My love, says the poet, is like—and, in the spirit of play, he looks about him for something resembling his lady as little as possible—like, he announces triumphantly, a red, red rose. To the solemn scientific eye there is no reasonable resemblance between the figure of a woman and the shape of a rose, but the reader is as little interested in laboratory realism as is the poet. It is an intellectual game, this saying one thing and meaning another, a verbal sportiveness; the poet points the way, and the reader's mind romps along.—LOUIS UNTERMEYER

This definition of a metaphor is broader and more informal than the dictionary definition of the same term. The writer uses the example of a poet describing his lady to clarify his personal conception of a metaphor as an intellectual game.

The use of examples is one technique available to a writer wishing to define a term. Other techniques are the inclusion of a dictionary definition, the discussion of connotations, the exploration of a word origin, the discussion of synonyms and their differing connotations, and the identification of inappropriate interpretations of a word.

The following paragraph exemplifies a highly subjective approach to defining a term. The writer makes no attempt to construct an objective definition of the word *reservation*, but rather, explains the meaning of the concept in her own life.

> To me, *reservation* means a wide network of related people through time. I have relatives through blood and marriage on all the South Dakota reservations, mainly the Standing Rock Sioux where I am enrolled, and the Cheyenne River Sioux. At the moment, my here and now is New York City, but I can return to the reservation at any time, and I do. I return to the reservation for strength and direction, to find what I am seeking, which enables me to "keep going on." I know that I am in the midst of a wide circle of a journey. I knew when I was able to come into the world again and I will know when I am to leave it. I am young enough to have many challenges yet to meet, and things to accept which are not all of my own making. But I feel a wholeness in the relationship between reservation and urban people; I respect the link; it sustains me.—Dawn Kathleen Good Elk

Exercises **Writing Paragraphs of Definition**

A. Choose a simple subject such as a yard, a chicken, a head cold, a pair of eye glasses, or a ballpoint pen, and write a paragraph of definition. Use at least two of the techniques described in this lesson.

B. Here is the beginning for a paragraph of definition. Examine it closely and then complete the paragraph by explaining your personal view of both the positive and negative sides of liberty.

> In the dictionary, *liberty* is defined as freedom from external restraints or compulsion. The definition is not incorrect but is too narrow, because liberty means freedom *from* having to do something, as well as freedom *to* do something. In this sense, liberty may be said to possess two sides—a positive and a negative.

Review Exercise Analyzing Paragraphs

Study the following paragraphs and determine the specific type (or types) of paragraph that each represents. Be ready to support your answers.

1 That the insects have adapted is obvious. Their failures to adapt, however, are dazzling. It is hard to believe that nature is partial to such dim-wittedness. Howard Ensign Evans tells of dragonflies trying to lay eggs on the shining hoods of cars. Other dragonflies seem to test a surface, to learn if it's really water, by dipping the tips of their abdomens in it. At the Los Angeles la Brea tar pits, they dip their abdomens into the reeking tar and get stuck. If by tremendous effort a dragonfly frees itself, Evans reports, it is apt to repeat the maneuver. Sometimes the tar pits glitter with the dry bodies of dead dragonflies.—ANNIE DILLARD

2 Earthquakes are caused by stresses that develop within the upper layers of the earth, usually within the crust. As the stresses build up, the rocks are increasingly distorted until they can no longer withstand the pressure. Suddenly they fracture, or break, and spring back toward their original positions. The sudden fracture of the rocks causes the development of the shock waves that we call an earthquake. The shocks of a severe quake may last for several minutes, its waves spreading out in every direction from the original break. Often the first violent break is followed by aftershocks as other stresses fracture other rocks in the area. Sometimes these aftershocks are very severe and very frequent and they may take weeks or months to die away.—KEITH CLAYTON

3 By the summer of A.D. 79, life in Pompeii and Herculaneum must have been very pleasant. Set in a fertile countryside with a warm climate, both towns could offer visitors delicious fruits in abundance and a variety of delicate wines from the vineyards that flourished on the slopes of Vesuvius. Pompeii, with its shops, offices, and busy market, its amphitheatre, public baths, and taverns, had all the bustle of a typical Roman country town. Herculaneum was smaller, quieter, and more secluded. There were no chariots rattling through its cobbled streets as they did through the streets of Pompeii, and its inhabitants—mainly wealthy people—were content to live away from the hurly-burly of trade and commerce. Life was carried on in quiet dignity.—HENRY GARNETT

4 About my interests: I don't know if I have any, unless the morbid desire to own a sixteen-millimeter camera and make experimental movies can be so classified. Otherwise, I love to eat and drink—it's my melancholy conviction that I've scarcely ever had enough to eat (this is because it's *impossible* to eat enough if you're worried about the next meal)—and I love to argue with people who do not disagree with me too profoundly, and I love to laugh. I do *not* like people whose principal aim is pleasure, and I do not like people who are *earnest* about anything. I don't like people who like me because I'm black; neither do I like people who find in the same accident grounds for contempt. I love America more than any other country in the world, and, exactly for this reason, I insist on the right to criticize her perpetually. I think all theories are suspect, and that the finest principles may have to be modified, or may even be pulverized by the demands of life, and that one must find, therefore, one's own moral center and move through the world hoping that this center will guide one right. I consider that I have many responsibilities, but none greater than this: to last, as Hemingway says, and get my work done.—J. SAUNDERS REDDING

5 On reaching Hispaniola, Captain Lowther sighted and approached a French vessel which had a cargo of wine and brandy. Pretending that he was a merchant who desired to purchase certain wines and brandies of the Frenchman's ample stock, he went on board to view the liquors. The pirate then carried his deception further by offering a price for the greater part of the cargo, which the Frenchman refused. This annoyed the buccaneer, so he stepped closer to the French captain and whispered in his ear that they were going to take all the cargo anyway without paying anything. Terror-stricken, the Frenchman collapsed, and Lowther ordered the immediate removal of thirty casks of brandy, five hogsheads of wine, and other valuable goods in the cargo. As the Frenchman had given in so easily, Lowther presented him with five pounds for his trouble.—EDWARD ROWE SNOW

6 The river was dark and swift, and there were jagged panes of ice along the banks, encrusted with snow. The valley was gray and cold; the mountains were dark and dim on the sky, and a great, gray motionless cloud of snow and mist lay out in the depth of the canyon. The fields were bare and colorless, and the gray tangle of branches rose up out of the orchards like antlers and bones. The town lay huddled in the late winter noon, the upper walls and vigas were stained with water, and thin black columns of smoke rose above the roofs, swelled, and hung out against the low ceiling of the sky. The streets were empty, and here and there were drifts of hard and brittle snow about the fence posts and the stones, pocked with soil and cinders. There was no telling of the sun, save for the one cold, dim, and even light that lay on every corner of the land and made no shadow, and the silence was close by and all around and the bell made no impression upon it. There was no motion to be seen but the single brief burst and billow of the smoke. And out of the town on the old road southward, the snow lay unbroken, sloping up on either side of the rocks and the junipers and the dunes. A huge old jack rabbit bounded across the hillside in a blur of great sudden angles and settled away in the snow, still and invisible.—N. SCOTT MOMADAY

7 What I mean by education is learning the rules of this mighty game. In other words, education is the instruction of the intellect in the laws of Nature, under which name I include not merely things and their forces, but people and their ways; and the fashioning of the affections and of the will into an earnest and loving desire to move in harmony with those laws. For me, education means neither more nor less than this. Anything that professes to call itself education must be tried by this standard, and if it fails to stand the test, I will not call it education, whatever may be the force of authority or of numbers upon the other side.—THOMAS HENRY HUXLEY

8 Wit is a lean creature with sharp inquiring nose, whereas humor has a kindly eye and comfortable girth. Wit, if it be necessary, uses malice to score a point—like a cat it is quick to jump—but humor keeps the peace in an easy chair. Wit has a better voice in a solo, but humor comes into the chorus best. Wit is as sharp as

a stroke of lightning, whereas humor is diffuse like sunlight. Wit keeps the season's fashions and is precise in the phrases and judgments of the day, but humor is concerned with homely eternal things. Wit wears silk, but humor in homespun endures the wind. Wit sets a snare, whereas humor goes off whistling without a victim in its mind. Wit is sharper company at table, but humor serves better in mischance and in the rain. When it tumbles, wit is sour; but humor goes uncomplaining without its dinner. Humor laughs at another's jest and holds its sides, while wit sits wrapped in study for a lively answer. But it is a workaday world in which we live, where we get mud upon our boots and come weary to the twilight. It is a world that grieves and suffers from many wounds in these years of war; and therefore as I think of my acquaintances, it is those who are humorous in its best and truest meaning rather than those who are witty who give the more profitable companionship.—CHARLES S. BROOKS

9 I usually find myself talking about my father, telling my friends and any strangers what he does and where he has been, trying to describe with exactness his activities, trying to grasp his life through what little information I have of him. Doing this, I feel like a small child pressing a string of hard beads to my chest, a rosary of sorts, chanting the same phrases and images a thousand times in order to derive an order, a strength out of them. But the polished beads do not yield a thing; it is a repetition of uselessness. Nothing comes out of them.—WALLACE LIN

10 She tried to be sexy and stylish, and was, in her fashion, with a predominant taste for pastel taffetas and orange shoes. In the summertime she paid twenty dollars for big umbrella hats with bows and flowers on them and when she wore black and white together she would liven it up with elbow-length gloves of red satin. She was genuinely undecided when she woke up in the morning whether she really outstripped the other girls in town for beauty, but could convince herself that she was equally good-looking by the time she had breakfast on the table. She was always talking with a lot of extra movement to her thick, coarse mouth, with its hair tufts at the corners; and when she drank coffee she held the cup over the saucer with her little finger sticking out, while she crossed her short, hairy legs at the knees.—ALICE WALKER

Checklist for Writing Paragraphs

This Checklist will help to remind you of the qualities necessary for good paragraphs. However, your writing procedure should also follow the steps listed in Guidelines for the Process of Writing on page 109.

1. Is the paragraph a group of sentences dealing with only one main idea?
2. Does the paragraph have a topic sentence that states the main idea?
3. Does the topic sentence have a subject? Does it have a point of view that is expandable?
4. Does the body of the paragraph support or explain the main idea in the topic sentence? Does the paragraph have unity?
5. Is the paragraph coherent? Are the ideas presented in a logical order and clearly linked to one another? Is the order of ideas appropriate for the subject of the paragraph?
6. Are there linking words and expressions that reinforce coherence by showing relationships among the ideas in the paragraph?
7. Are there enough details to engage the reader's interest?
8. Does the paragraph have a carefully constructed emphasis?
9. Does the tone of the paragraph convey the desired attitude toward the subject?
10. Does the paragraph work to evoke the desired mood in the reader?
11. If it is a paragraph of description, does it capture the essence of a person being described? the atmosphere of a place? the quality of a thing?
12. If it is a paragraph of comparison, does it compare similarities? If contrast, does it show differences?
13. If it is a paragraph of analogy, does it compare something unfamiliar with something familiar?
14. If it is a paragraph of narration, does the story or anecdote achieve the purpose of the paragraph?

15. If it is a paragraph of explanation using details, do the details adequately explain the main idea? If explaining a process, does the paragraph follow a step-by-step order? If explaining an idea, do the details clarify the idea? If supporting an opinion, are the reasons logical and valid?

16. If it is a paragraph of persuasion, is it developed by the kinds of information that would effect your purpose?

17. If it is a paragraph of definition, does it clarify a concept or a term for the reader?

Chapter 11

The Composition

A composition is a piece of writing that develops an idea or expands a topic in a coherent and unified manner. The paragraphs in a composition must adequately develop the topic or idea, must be logically connected, and must form a complete whole.

In this chapter you will study the following basic steps involved in writing a composition.

1. Choosing and limiting your subject
2. Writing down your ideas
3. Organizing your ideas
4. Outlining
5. Writing your first draft
6. Revising
7. Writing your final draft

Following this step-by-step procedure will enable you to write an effective composition, one that proceeds in an orderly manner toward the goal you wish to achieve.

Part 1 Choosing Your Subject

The first step in writing any composition is to decide on a subject. What is worth writing about? It is anything worth thinking about. What is a worthwhile subject for your composition? It is anything that interests you. Remember, however, that you must develop your subject in a coherent and unified manner. Therefore you must ask yourself whether you know enough about your subject to discuss it in some depth. If you do not, are you willing to research the subject enough to allow you to develop it more fully? Will you be able to do the required research? Is the information available? Do you know where to find it? The range of subjects available to you is limited only by your own interests and the available information.

If you are interested in social problems, you may wish to write about efforts to revitalize the residential areas of large cities or the difficulties retired people encounter when living on a fixed income or the prospects for programs of preventive medical care.

If you watch television, you may wish to write about the portrayal of American family life on situation comedy series or the quality of network news programs.

Your composition will benefit from your genuine interest in the subject you choose to write about. On the other hand, your composition will suffer if your interest in it is slight.

Limiting Your Subject

The composition you will write will consist of five paragraphs and will total approximately 500 words. Because you will not be able to develop any broad or general subject within those limits, you will have to limit or narrow the scope of your subject. Consider the subject of communication. It is a boundless subject, and an adequate treatment of it would fill many volumes. If you were to limit it, you might follow a process similar to the following, continually dividing each large subject into two smaller ones. In each pair, the subject in boldface type is the one chosen for further subdivision.

UNLIMITED:	Communication
SLIGHT LIMITATION:	History of Communication **Modern Communication**
2000-WORD LIMITATION:	Postal Service Today **Television Today**
1000-WORD LIMITATION:	Television Entertainment Today **Informative Television Today**
500-WORD LIMITATION:	Consumer Information *via* Television **The Limitations of Network News**

Exercise Limiting the Subject

The following list of subjects is too large for adequate treatment in a 500-word composition. Within each subject, find three narrow subjects suitable for a composition of that length. Keep your list of subjects for a later exercise.

1. Energy
2. Government
3. Superstition
4. Cities
5. Transportation
6. Sports
7. Art
8. Rivers
9. Stars
10. Literature

Determining the Controlling Purpose of Your Composition

It is important to write down a clear statement of your controlling purpose and to keep it in front of you through all stages of your composition. If the nature of your subject forces you to revise your original controlling purpose, make the necessary change, but be sure that all parts of your composition reflect that change. Your composition and your controlling purpose must work hand in hand: your composition should achieve what your controlling purpose sets out to do. Keep referring to your controlling purpose and employ it as a guide as your work progresses.

In a statement of controlling purpose, the most common verbs are *to explain, to show, to demonstrate*. For example, if you chose to write on the subject of network news, your controlling purpose might be stated like this:

> The controlling purpose of this composition is to show that network news programs do not adequately inform the public.

This statement will not appear in your composition, at least not in the form of a statement of purpose, nor will it be your title. It is intended for your own use as a way of controlling your thinking and writing, helping you to stick to the point. Such a statement is sometimes called a **thesis statement.**

Exercises Determining the Controlling Purpose of a Composition

A. In the exercise on page 191 you limited each of ten broad subjects to three possible subjects for compositions of 500 words. Choose three of these limited subjects and write for each a statement of the controlling purpose that you would follow in developing the composition. Save your statements for use in a later exercise.

B. Choose a subject for your own composition and limit it sufficiently for a 500-word paper. Then write a one-sentence controlling purpose for your composition.

Part 2 Writing Down Your Ideas

You have chosen a subject and limited it. You have also established a controlling purpose for your composition. Your next step is to write down your ideas on the subject you have chosen. This is the first step in The Process of Writing.

The purpose of this step is to get as many ideas as possible down on paper. You will organize and polish those ideas later, so do not concern yourself with order, relative importance, or phrasing. At the top of your paper, write your title if you already have one. If not, leave the space blank, to be filled in later. Write your controlling purpose below your title space so that you can use it to guide your thinking. Then begin to jot down whatever ideas come to mind.

As you begin to write down ideas, you may find that you do not have as many ideas on your subject as you thought you had. You may have to do more extensive reading or research in the subject you have chosen. You may find that you are not certain of the accuracy of some points. If so, you will have to check these points in reference books or other source material. (See Chapter 15 on The Library and Its Reference Materials.) When you have completed any additional research, you can add to your list of ideas.

Your first list of ideas might look something like this (ignore the asterisks):

TENTATIVE TITLE

CONTROLLING PURPOSE The controlling purpose of this composition is to show that network news programs do not adequately inform the public.

a half hour of news is too short
television too dependent on visual stories
*everybody watches television
*television polls have an undue influence
oversimplification in TV news
shallowness
depth possible in newspapers
television dependent on brief stories
paternal newscasters
newspapers more idea-oriented
television more personality-oriented
Jefferson's notion of an informed populace

uninformed or misinformed public will act foolishly
intrusive commercials
*rise in newspaper cost
decline in newspaper readership
public dependence on TV news
*economics of television
*emergency programing
*famous newscasters
*famous reporters
*portable cameras
*history of TV news
*ratings of news shows

A review of the list of ideas will show you that some are not closely related to the controlling purpose of the composition. The unrelated ideas, marked with asterisks, should be eliminated so that the focus of the composition remains clear and well-defined.

everybody watches television
television polls have an undue influence
rise in newspaper cost
emergency programing
famous newscasters
famous reporters
portable cameras
ratings of news shows

Two ideas are too broad to be treated within the limit of 500 words. The unmanageable ideas should also be eliminated.

economics of television
history of TV news

When reviewing your list of ideas, ask yourself the following questions.

1. Is this idea directly related to the controlling purpose?

2. Can this idea be developed adequately, along with the others, in 500 words?

If the answer to either question is no, the idea should be eliminated.

After you have reviewed your list of ideas and eliminated all those that are unrelated or unmanageable, study those that remain in search of ideas for your tentative title. Try to write two or three possible titles at this time. They will also help to focus your work as you write, and you can eliminate two later. Possible titles for this subject include the following.

What's the Use of Network News?
Sorry, Mr. Jefferson
Network News Is Not Enough

As you develop your composition further, you may find that some of the remaining ideas are not so appropriate to your purpose as they had seemed earlier, or that some ideas cannot be adequately developed within the limits of your composition. If so, do not hesitate to eliminate those ideas. Your composition will be further improved by the elimination of every inappropriate or unmanageable idea.

Exercises **Writing Down the Ideas**

A. In Exercise A on page 192, you wrote a controlling purpose for each of three limited subjects. Select two of these controlling purposes and list under them all the ideas that come to your mind for developing that subject. After studying your lists, (1) eliminate every idea that is irrelevant to the controlling purpose, and (2) eliminate every idea that cannot adequately be developed in a 500-word composition. Save these lists for use in a later exercise.

B. Do the same as above for the subject you have chosen for your composition.

Part 3 Organizing Your Ideas

You have eliminated those ideas that are unmanageable within the 500-word limit of your composition and those that are not directly relevant to your controlling purpose. The ideas that are left are those that are manageable and relevant. It remains now to order them into a coherent pattern for development.

First, examine your remaining list of ideas in search of major points. Look for three major points, corresponding to the three paragraphs that will make up the body of your composition.

In the ideas on the subject of network news programs, notice that "oversimplification in TV news" is a major point in support of the controlling purpose. The ideas below are related to this point.

a half hour of news is too short
television too dependent on visual stories
shallowness
television dependent on brief stories
paternal newscasters
intrusive commercials

A second major point is "depth possible in newspapers," and the following ideas are directly related.

newspapers more idea-oriented
television more personality-oriented
decline in newspaper readership
public dependence on TV news

The third major point seems to be "Jefferson's notion of an informed populace," with the related idea that "uninformed or misinformed public will act foolishly."

There are now three major ideas to be developed.

oversimplification in TV news
depth possible in newspapers
Jefferson's notion of an informed populace

The first job of organization has been accomplished: grouping into three major categories. The second job is to determine in what order each of the major points should be developed in order to present the reader with an orderly and logical piece of reasoning. To determine a logical order of development, ask yourself which of the major points, if any, cannot be understood without the others. Clearly these must follow the others.

The controlling purpose of the composition on the subject of television news is as follows:

> The controlling purpose of this composition is to show that network news programs do not adequately inform the public.

Since the composition will be building to the conclusion that network news programs do not adequately inform the public, it seems logical that the major idea of oversimplification in television news should come last. Jefferson's notion of an informed populace would logically come first, since it establishes a reason for concern over the inadequacy of television news. The comparison of the depth possible in newspapers can fall between the two, partly as a link between the past—the informed populace that Jefferson had in mind—and the present—the ill-informed public of the television age. Thus the final order of ideas in developing the composition will be as follows:

> Jefferson's notion of an informed populace
> depth possible in newspapers
> oversimplication in TV news

The groups of subordinate ideas can now be organized into a logical order of development under their respective major points. New ideas are almost certain to come to you at this time, and the act of organizing the ideas is likely to make some of them seem less potent than they had seemed at first. Do not hesitate to add or eliminate at this stage.

At this point in the organization it was necessary to do some additional reading on Jefferson's notion of an informed populace because that idea lacked sufficient supporting ideas. The grouped ideas for the composition on the subject of television news programs might now resemble the list on the following page.

Jefferson's notion of an informed populace
- vital to democracy
- political decisions based on reason
- uninformed public would focus on personality
- fear of demagogues

depth possible in newspapers
- long, careful analyses of issues
- declining newspaper readership
- increasing dependence on television

oversimplification of TV news
- television too dependent on visual stories
- intrusive commercials
- dependence on brief stories
- shallowness
- paternal newscasters

Exercises **Organizing the Ideas**

A. Refer to the lists of ideas you developed for two subjects in Exercise A on page 195. Organize each set of ideas into three major points and related subordinate ideas. Then order the ideas in the sequence in which you would expect to develop them in a 500-word composition. Save this work for use in a later exercise.

B. Do the same as above with the ideas for your own composition.

Part 4 Outlining

Your preliminary organization of your ideas will now serve as the basis for an outline. The outline will show all the ideas in a sequential and logical relationship to one another. An outline is, in effect, a schematic diagram of the relationships among ideas.

Two outline forms are in wide use. One is the **sentence outline,** in which all ideas are expressed in complete sentences; the other, briefer form is the **topic outline,** in which the ideas are expressed in words or phrases. Use a topic outline for your composition.

Outlining Procedure

1. Leave space at the top of the page for a final title.
2. Write the statement of your controlling purpose two spaces below the line allotted for the title.
3. Use standard outline form. The following example is a sample arrangement of numerals and letters that will constitute the form of your outline.

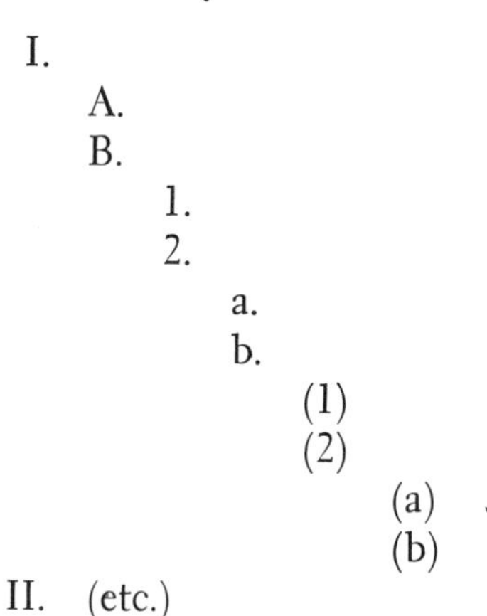

I.
    A.
    B.
        1.
        2.
            a.
            b.
                (1)
                (2)
                    (a)
                    (b)
II. (etc.)

4. Number your main headings with Roman numerals. Use capital letters for subtopics under each main heading. Divide your subtopics in descending order of importance: first Arabic numerals, then small letters, then Arabic numerals in parentheses, then small letters in parentheses.
5. Indent subtopics, placing the letters or numerals directly below the first letter of the first word in your preceding topic or subtopic.
6. Do not use the words *Introduction*, *Body*, and *Conclusion* in your outline. These are merely organizational terms used in planning a composition.
7. Use only one idea for each topic or subtopic.
8. Do not use a single subtopic. Use either two or more or none at all. A topic cannot be divided into fewer than two parts.

9. Begin the first word of each topic and subtopic with a capital letter. Do not use periods after topics or subtopics.
10. Make all main topics parallel in form. Make each group of subtopics parallel in form. For example, if the first main topic is a noun, all the other main topics must be nouns. If the first subtopic under the main topic is an adjective, the remainder of that group of subtopics must also be adjectives.

Example of an Outline

Following is a completed outline, sharpened and refined, for the body of the composition on the subject of television news programs. Notice that parts I and V have not yet been completed; these will be, respectively, the introduction and the conclusion. Notice also that the title has not yet been decided.

> The controlling purpose of this composition is to show that network news programs do not adequately inform the public.
>
> I.
>
> II. The function of news in a democracy
>
> A. Jefferson's notion of an informed populace
> 1. Capable of evaluating political issues
> 2. Capable of basing decisions on reason
>
> B. Jefferson's fears for an uninformed populace
> 1. Inability to make intelligent decisions
> 2. Inclination to focus on personalities
> 3. Tendency to follow demagogues
>
> III. Newspapers and television as sources of news
>
> A. Traditional dependence on newspapers
> B. Advantages of newspapers
> C. Decline in newspaper readership
> D. Increasing dependence on television

IV. Limitations of television news reporting

    A. Brevity
    B. Dependence on visual stories
    C. Interruption by commercial breaks
    D. Focus on personalities

V.

Exercises **Making an Outline**

A. In the following list you will find all the ideas necessary for a topic outline on the subject of oil.

Arrange the ideas in outline form, using every item and numbering and lettering each item properly as a main topic or a subtopic. Which item could serve as a title?

Supports modern technology
In everyday life
Effect of oil on our economy
Creates jobs
Chemical composition
In international trade
Possible substitutes for oil
History of oil
The uses of oil
Varieties
In transportation
Important facts about oil
Energy value
In industry
Viscosity
Creates pollution problems
Oil and Society

B. Briefly review the following outline and then correct it, keeping in mind the following points: (1) Every topic and subtopic must relate to the controlling purpose. (2) Main topics should be parallel in form; each group of subtopics should be parallel in form. (3) Subtopics should never be fewer than two. (4) Organizational terms should never be used. (5) In a topic outline, complete sentences should not be used.

LIFE IN AN INSTANT CITY

I. Introduction: The instant city a relatively new phenomenon

II. Profile of typical instant city

   A. Residential area
      1. Single-family dwellings
      2. Contrasting with suburban homes
   B. May also include industrial area
   C. Commercial areas included by design

III. Describe the population

   A. Economic mix
   B. Backgrounds—blue-collar workers and professionals

IV. These cities are luring people away from suburbs and more established urban areas.

   A. Convenience
      1. Self-contained transportation network
   B. Leisure activities
      1. Boating
      2. Social organizations
      3. Many provide entertainment complexes
   C. They provide some of the advantages of a city with the feeling of a small town.
   D. Education
      1. Centralized schools, for economy
      2. Recruiting teachers

C. In Exercise A on page 198, you organized the ideas for two subjects into the major points and their related ideas in the order you would develop each of them in a five-paragraph composition. Now put the ordered ideas for these two subjects into proper topic outline form.

D. Do the same as above with the ideas for your own composition.

Part 5 Writing Your First Draft

You now have a statement of controlling purpose and an outline of the body of your composition to work from. You are ready to begin the actual writing of a first draft, which will include all the information in your outline and also an introduction and a conclusion. This is the second step in the Process of Writing.

While the work you have already done will serve as a base for the writing itself, you may find that you have a difficult time beginning. If you find it so, begin with the second paragraph, which is the first paragraph that appears on your outline. The information for this paragraph is already at hand, and therefore ready to be put in your first draft. The introduction can be written later, even as the last writing you do for the composition.

Keep in mind that you are writing a first draft. Concentrate on getting your ideas expressed in a logical manner, and do not worry too much about sentence structure, word choice, or punctuation. These matters can be adjusted when you rewrite, or revise the first draft.

Remember that the composition will have three basic parts—a beginning, a middle, and an end. These basic parts are usually called the introduction, the body, and the conclusion. The composition as a whole will be only as strong as the weakest of these parts. The following sections will consider the writing of each part in turn.

The Introduction

The introduction to a composition serves two purposes: it *introduces* the reader to the subject, and it *interests* the reader in the subject. In a five-paragraph composition, the introduction should be limited to a single paragraph. Many techniques can be used to construct an effective introduction. For example, a writer may choose to use a quotation, startling statistics, or an interesting anecdote.

The composition on the subject of television news programs might begin with any of the following introductions.

QUOTATION Mails from the North—the East—the West—the South—whence, according to some curious etymologists, comes the magical word NEWS. THOMAS DE QUINCEY

STATISTIC According to a recent survey conducted by The Center for the Study of Public Information, a full sixty percent of American voters get all their information about political issues from nightly television news programs.

ANECDOTE In conversation over lunch one day last week, I asked a friend of mine whether she thought the water control bill should pass. "I don't know anything about it," she said. "Was it on TV?"

Each of these introductions goes beyond merely getting the reader's attention; each tells the reader what the subject of the composition will be: specifically, the news. But two of the three, the final two, are stronger than the first because they raise the key issue of the composition: the question of the adequacy of television news programs as the public's primary source of political information. The first might be strengthened by the addition of a statement like the following.

> It is certainly true that news comes from all directions, but if we get our news solely from television, it might be said that we are getting more magic than fact.

Regardless of the device used to open a composition, the introduction should never be merely a lifeless restatement of the controlling purpose such as the following.

> This composition will discuss the shortcomings of television news programs.

Remember that the controlling purpose is a device that the writer of a composition uses to keep the composition focused on a single purpose; it will never serve the two functions of an adequate introduction—to introduce the subject and to interest the reader.

Exercises Writing an Effective Introduction

A. Choose three of the following introductions to rewrite and expand in order to make them both informative and interesting. Use a quotation, a statistic, or an anecdote.

1. It seems to me that the invention of the camera changed our understanding of cultures around the world.
2. Everyone should know something about the history of his or her local community.
3. We really know very little about this small and fragile planet we live on.
4. Many people underestimate the skill required to train animals to perform in films.
5. The Nobel Prizes have an interesting history.

B. Keeping in mind the purposes and possibilities for effective introductions, write a first paragraph for your composition. Remember that it should both introduce the subject and interest your reader. Review your introduction to decide whether it completely covers the controlling purpose of your composition. The first sample introduction by Thomas de Quincey, for example, would have been misleading without the additional statement. The reader would have expected the composition to treat news in general rather than television news specifically.

The Body

The body of the composition is the longest section. Here the points are made, the issues raised and discussed. In a five-paragraph composition the body consists of the three paragraphs in the middle, and the writer must accomplish his or her purpose within that body. The following concerns should serve as a guide in the writing of the body.

1. **Use your outline as a guide.** The outline was written as an aid to establishing a clear and appropriate pattern of development for the ideas that the composition is meant to express. If you do not follow the outline, you will lose the logical structure that the outline was designed to provide.

2. **Keep your purpose in mind.** Make the body of your composition accomplish what your controlling purpose promises you will accomplish. If you set out to demonstrate the truth of an assertion, be certain that you demonstrate it forcefully, clearly, and fully.

3. **Divide your writing into paragraphs.** Develop each main topic in your outline into a single paragraph in your composition. Begin each paragraph with a topic sentence, and support each topic sentence with the information you have included in your subtopics. Develop each topic and subtopic fully.

4. **Provide clear transitions.** Transitional devices at the beginning of paragraphs indicate how each idea is logically related the ideas in preceding paragraphs. It is crucial that your reader be able to follow the development of your thoughts if he or she is to be able to understand them.

Using Transitional Devices

Transitional Words and Phrases. Just as the linking expressions or connectives in Chapter 9 are used to achieve coherence within a paragraph and to help the reader move smoothly from one idea to another, certain words and phrases are used to help the reader move smoothly from one paragraph to another. The following transitional words and phrases are the ones most often used in the first sentence of a new paragraph.

TO INDICATE TIME RELATIONSHIPS

before	earlier	once	sooner or later
during	later	then	at this point
after	soon	in time	at the same time
afterward	first	eventually	until
at last	next	finally	recently

TO INDICATE LOGICAL RELATIONSHIPS

since	besides	furthermore
therefore	consequently	and then
because	inevitably	as a result

TO INDICATE SIMILARITY

as	also	similarly	in the same way
like	again	another	equally important
and	likewise	moreover	
too	equally	in addition	

TO INDICATE CONTRAST

but	however	otherwise
yet	although	in contrast
nor	nevertheless	on the contrary
still	nonetheless	on the other hand

Each of the following sentences is the first sentence of a paragraph. Notice how the transitional devices serve, in each case, to link the new topic to that of the preceding paragraph. You can even guess what the preceding paragraph was about without having read it.

> *Still,* solar power will never totally eliminate the need for other sources of energy.
>
> *Later,* the Romans established an outpost of the Empire near what is now the border of England and Scotland.
>
> His attitude toward freedom of speech was *equally* contemptuous.

Pronouns. The use of a pronoun to refer to an idea in the preceding paragraph can also create a link in the mind of the reader. The words *this, that, these,* and *those* are frequently used as transitional devices, sometimes as pronouns and sometimes as adjectives.

Great care must be taken in the use of these words as adjectives. They must be followed by a noun that makes the reference clear to the reader. Consider the sentence "This cannot continue indefinitely." The reader would be justified in wondering, "This *what* cannot be continued indefinitely?" Such a sentence must make it clear what is being referred to; for example, "This waste," or "This conduct."

Other pronouns can also function as transitional devices. The following sentences, which could serve as opening sentences of paragraphs, demonstrate how the technique works.

> *That* attitude soon changed, however.
>
> Never before have *these* issues seemed so critical or *their* resolution so important.
>
> *This* procedure has been effective in the past, but stronger measures are required today.

Repetition. The flow of meaning from one paragraph to the next can be smoothed by the repetition of a key word in the opening sentence. Notice how repetition of a word is used as a transitional device in the following examples.

1 Mass production has made it possible for a great number of people to own reproductions of significant works of art. It is now only a matter of taste that determines whether a person hangs an inexpensive reproduction of a lithograph by Picasso or a cat calendar on that blank spot on the living room wall.

But taste is not the only consideration for collectors of high-priced original prints.

2 The people who spend their time wondering about such things predict that the next boom in home entertainment will not be swimming pools or television tennis games but computers.

The typical home computer setup will be no larger than a component stereo system and will serve equally well as an accountant, a family nutritionist, a heating engineer, or a chess opponent.

Repetition need not be limited to a single word; sometimes a writer will use a single word or phrase in the second of two paragraphs to refer to the whole idea developed in the first. In such cases, the repetition serves much the same purpose as the use of a pronoun. Notice how this device works in the following examples.

3 To the manufacturers, the recall rate for American cars is startling testimony to the overall ability of the industry to turn out a product that does what it is supposed to do in a dependable and predictable manner. To the owner of a car recalled for a defective seat-belt harness, however, the recall rate is a shocking indictment.

Reliability, it would seem, is in the eye of the beholder.

4 On an increasingly large number of golf courses in the winter months, one can see lines of weekend skiers gliding along without fear of broken legs or the price of the next lift ticket.

However, safety and economy are not the only reasons for the rise in popularity of ski touring.

Exercises The Body of the Composition

A. Find a magazine article on a subject that interests you and examine it for transitional devices. Write down the opening sentences of ten paragraphs from the article that make use of the transitional devices discussed in this section. Explain how the devices work in each paragraph.

B. The body of your composition will consist of three paragraphs. Write the body now, keeping the following points in mind.

1. Test your ideas against your controlling purpose as you write.
2. Use your outline as your guide.
3. Develop the ideas in each paragraph completely.
4. Provide clear transitions between paragraphs.

The Conclusion

As its name implies, the conclusion of the composition should bring matters to a close. The reader should be left with a sense that what should have been said has been said. It is always a good technique to return in the conclusion to the ideas you used in your introduction. This reiteration serves to remind the reader of the key ideas and leaves him or her with a feeling of completeness.

If the paragraphs in your composition have adequately developed your topics and are logically connected, your concluding paragraph will form the complete whole, making the structure complete and stable.

The model composition might have a conclusion like the following.

> The situation is deplorable, but what are people to do? People cannot be forced to read newspapers. People cannot be forced to study political and economic issues in detail. The power of the television image will remain, no matter what people do, but television news programs might be improved to the point where they provided more of the substance of information. Network news programs could be expanded to an hour. The focus of the programs could be directed to larger issues, not just to the events of the day. Instead of one or two paternal newscasters, the public could be offered a variety of men and women, reporting from a variety of political perspectives. These changes are small, but they would go a long way toward making television news contribute to a truly informed populace.

Notice that the conclusion begins with the use of the word *situation* as a repetitive device, providing the transition from the preceding paragraph. The writer offers suggestions for improvement of the situation and returns to a key idea of the introduction and the composition as a whole: that an informed public is essential to a democratic society. The reader has, in the course of reading the composition, learned why an informed public is necessary, why dependence on television news has made for an inadequately informed public, and now learns in the conclusion what might be done about it.

With the draft of the entire composition complete, the writer is at last in a position to select a final title for the work. The title, like the introduction, should both inform and interest the reader. It should not be clever without substance, but neither should it be accurate without life.

Exercises **Writing an Effective Conclusion**

A. Write the concluding paragraph of your composition, including in it an echo of the ideas and techniques you used in your introduction. Refer again to your controlling purpose and try to include all its essential ideas in your conclusion.

B. Choose a title for your completed composition.

Part 6 Rewriting, or Revising

The best compositions are largely the products of work done in this final stage of The Process of Writing. It is in revision that your ideas will achieve their best and most succinct expression. Following the steps listed below will enable you to make visible improvements in your first draft.

1. **Read your composition aloud.** The importance of this step cannot be overemphasized. Nothing else will show you so clearly where your ideas were not fully developed or where your thinking was fuzzy or where your sentences were awkward. If possible, read your work to someone who will be critical of it. Use the criticism in your revision.

2. **Revise for content.** Is your purpose clear from the outset? Have you said enough? Is your information accurate? Are your ideas laid out clearly?

3. **Revise for form.** Have you organized your composition clearly and logically? Have you given each main idea its own paragraph and introduced it with a topic sentence? Are your paragraphs coherent? Are all your ideas clearly related to each other? Have you made connections between ideas by using transitional devices?

4. **Revise for wording.** Have you used the most precise words to express your ideas? Review the information on synonyms and antonyms in Chapter 1. Use a dictionary or thesaurus to check the

meanings of key words in your composition and to locate synonyms for them. If you find synonymous words with meanings closer to what you had intended, revise the wording.

5. **Check for capitalization, punctuation, and spelling.** Obviously, faults of these kinds will distract your reader from the content of your work. If necessary, consult Sections 10–16 in the Handbook.

A Model Composition

Following is a revised, completed composition based on the outline that appears on pages 200 and 201.

NETWORK NEWS
IS NOT ENOUGH

According to a recent survey conducted by the Center for the Study of Public Information, a full sixty per cent of American voters get all their information about political issues from nightly television programs. A democracy that gets most of its news from such shows is a democracy in great jeopardy, for half-hour news programs provide the public with the illusion of information, not the substance. This insubstantiality is the result not of a conspiracy to misinform or under-inform; it is an inherent shortcoming of television as an information medium, at least as currently organized.

The introduction offers a statistic and asserts the purpose of the composition: to show that television news programs, as currently organized, are not a sufficient means of informing the citizens of a democracy.

The importance of solid information to a democracy did not escape Thomas Jefferson, who felt most strongly that a democracy could survive only when the public was well informed about current affairs. In his view, an informed public would have the ability to evaluate po-

The first paragraph of the body of the composition corresponds to topic II and its subtopics in the outline. The first sentence is the topic sentence; the rest of the paragraph develops the statement it makes.

litical issues and make political decisions on the basis of reason, not on preconception or whim. He feared a public that received false or inadequate information. They would be unable to make intelligent decisions; instead they would focus on personalities, not issues, and would be likely to follow demagogues. Jefferson could not have foreseen television, but he clearly anticipated its impact.

Repetition of the key word *information* serves as a transition from the introduction.

Until recently, the dominant source of information in America has been the newspaper. By its very nature—the fact that it is in print and can be read at the reader's own pace—a newspaper can provide long and careful analyses of issues and events. However, recent polls show a precipitous decline in newspaper readership. Each year, more and more Americans get most of their information not from a newspaper, but from television.

Again, the key word *information* is repeated, linking this paragraph to the preceding one and to the introduction. The words *until recently* locate the paragraph in time. The paragraph corresponds to topic III in the outline.

Television, however, unlike a newspaper, is by its very nature an inadequate medium for communicating information. Because it is a visual medium, relying on stories that can be filmed, it cannot probe the complexity and interrelatedness of the issues that confront the citizens of a complex world. Television news programs are prisoners of time, dominated by periodic commercial breaks and dependent on brief stories that can never provide the depth that is possible in newspapers. The visual image encourages a focus on personalities rather than issues, a focus that is demonstrated by the attitude of the newscasters themselves, who adopt a wise

Two words, *however* and *unlike*, provide a transition from the preceding paragraph and indicate a contrast between its topic and the topic discussed here. The paragraph corresponds to topic IV in the outline.

and paternal manner. This focus on personalities is exactly what Jefferson feared from an ill-informed public.

The situation is deplorable, but what are people to do? People cannot be forced to read newspapers. They cannot be forced to study political and economic issues in detail. The power of the television image will remain, no matter what people do, but television news programs might be improved to the point where they provided more of the substance of information. Network news programs could be expanded to an hour. The focus of the programs could be directed to larger issues, not just to the events of the day. Instead of one or two paternal newscasters, the public could be offered a variety of men and women, reporting from a variety of political perspectives. These changes are small, but they would go along way toward making television news contribute to a truly informed populace.

The final paragraph constitutes the conclusion of the composition. The writer returns to the problems posed in the introduction, echoes a phrase from the introduction in the words *the substance of information,* and returns to Jefferson's concerns in the closing words. As a whole, the conclusion is prescriptive, offering the reader a possible solution.

Exercise Revising a Composition

Revise your composition, following the suggestions in this section. Prepare a clean, final version, carefully proofread.

Checklist for Writing Compositions

As you write a composition, follow the steps in Guidelines for the Process of Writing on page 109. Use this Checklist after you have written your composition.

1. Has the subject been narrowed to a topic that can be covered in a few paragraphs?
2. Does the composition deal with a single topic or idea?
3. Does the composition follow the outline? Have you used your major topics as the main idea of each paragraph? Have you used the subtopics to develop the main idea of each paragraph? Does the composition have an introduction, a body, and a conclusion?
4. Does the introduction present the main idea of the composition? Does it catch the reader's interest?
5. Does the body explain or support the main idea?
6. Does the conclusion restate the main idea, summarize the information, or comment upon it? Does it leave the reader with a sense of completeness?
7. Do the paragraphs work together to develop the single topic or idea that is the subject of the composition?
8. Is the composition appropriate for the audience for which it is intended? Is the purpose clear?
9. Are the ideas presented in a clear, logical order?
10. Does the composition have unity? Are the supporting ideas in each paragraph related to the topic sentence? Is each paragraph directly related to the main idea in the introductory paragraph? Does the composition relate directly to the idea set forth in your controlling purpose?
11. Are there transitional devices that tie the paragraphs together?
12. Is the title meaningful and interesting?

Chapter 12

The Paraphrase and the Summary

The paraphrase and the summary are altered or shortened versions of difficult or longer pieces of original writing. They are a way of recording the essentials of a reading assignment. Unlike notetaking, they provide a prose version of the original selection. You will find both paraphrasing and summarizing useful techniques.

This chapter will provide a guide to these skills.

Part 1 The Paraphrase

Paraphrasing is the technique of putting a difficult reading assignment into your own words. A paraphrase helps you to understand what you are reading. It also provides an excellent basis for reviewing ideas.

The paraphrase requires a careful reading and rephrasing of the original material. The paraphrase simplifies; it does not necessarily shorten the selection. The step-by-step procedure, outlined below, will show you how to approach this type of writing.

How To Write a Paraphrase

1. Read the material.

   a. Read the selection through once to get the central meaning.
   b. Look up any words you do not understand.
   c. Reread the selection at least twice more. Think of simple words to substitute for any long or difficult ones.

2. Write the paraphrase.

   a. Follow the same order that the writer uses in presenting the ideas.
   b. Put the material into your own words. Shorten long sentences. Use simple vocabulary.
   c. Check your paraphrase to be sure that it expresses the ideas of the original.

A Sample Paraphrase

Read the paragraph below. Then work through the steps that lead to a finished paraphrase.

> On the weekend of the Kennedy assassination, Walter Cronkite's sober mien—his natural strength—reflected the mood of the country. His earnest, almost reverent approach, often criticized as being stuffy, now struck many viewers as solid and reassuring. This was the start, for Cronkite, of a new persona or, to be more precise, what was perceived as a new persona. In the years ahead, as the country continued to reel through difficult times (a despised war, urban riots, more political assassinations), Cronkite always seemed to be there, on the TV screen, in moments of crisis

or travail. Thus the image of solid integrity was steadily reinforced until, eventually, his reputation grew so immense that it extended well beyond the limits of broadcast journalism.—GARY PAUL GATES

Applying the Techniques

Step 1. Reread the selection for the main idea. Usually the key sentence comes first in a paragraph. Here, it is the third sentence. This sentence summarizes the preceding two and prepares us for what follows. The writer is showing how Walter Cronkite's handling of a crisis changed the public's view of his personality.

Put into your own words, the idea of the paragraph might read like this:

> The country's view of Walter Cronkite as a journalist of integrity and strength began as a result of his sober, earnest handling of the Kennedy assassination.

This sentence may not appear in your finished paragraph, but it is helpful to keep it in front of you as you work. It will give focus and coherence to your writing.

Step 2. Several words in the paragraph need defining. The dictionary will give you more than one synonym for each. Select the one that is best for the context. Whenever possible, choose the word with which you are familiar and comfortable.

For example, *travail* is defined as (1) toil (2) drudgery (3) agony (4) effort. Clearly, what the writer has in mind is the mental agony of the nation.

Following is a list of the more difficult words in the selection and their appropriate synonyms.

sober	serious
mien	manner
reverent	deeply respectful
persona	image
perceived	viewed
reel	stagger
integrity	honesty

Step 3. As you reread, substitute the synonyms above. Look for other words and phrases that can be simplified or even omitted.

Writing the Paraphrase

Step 1. Structure your paragraph in the same way the writer does. Begin with Cronkite's TV handling of the Kennedy assassination. Contrast this view with what had been the view of Cronkite as a stuffy person. Conclude with the new view in the years that follow.

Step 2. Here is the completed paraphrase.

> On the weekend of the Kennedy assassination, Cronkite's serious manner mirrored the feeling of the country. Although viewers had once seen him as stuffy, they were now reassured by his serious, deeply respectful approach. This was the beginning of a changed view of him—a new image. As the country staggered through its times of crisis and agony (a hated war, unrest in the cities, more assassinations), Cronkite was reassuringly present. Thus the sense of his honesty was strengthened and expanded into areas beyond TV broadcasting.

Exercises Practice in Writing Paraphrases

A. Paraphrase this selection on bats. Follow the steps that are outlined after the selection.

> Bats are obliged to make sounds almost ceaselessly, to sense, by sonar, all the objects in their surroundings. They can spot with accuracy, on the wing, small insects, and they will home onto things they like with infallibility and speed. With such a system for the equivalent of glancing around, they must live in a world of ultrasonic bat-sound, most of it with an industrial, machinery sound. Still, they communicate with each other as well, by clicks and high-pitched greetings. Moreover, they have been heard to produce, while hanging at rest upside down in the depths of the woods, strange, solitary, and lovely bell-like notes.—LEWIS THOMAS

Step 1. Here the key sentence is the first one. Rephrase it in your own words.

Step 2. Do any words need defining? What synonyms can you substitute for *sonar, home onto, infallibility, equivalent, ultrasonic, solitary?*

Step 3. Reread the selection and in your mind substitute the synonyms you have selected. Does it sound right? Now rewrite the paragraph as simply and clearly as you can.

B. Using the same procedure, paraphrase each of the following selections.

1 Of the great American popular singers, Bing Crosby has been among the most profoundly and decisively influential. It might be more accurate to say that he has been among the most immediately influential. The impact of earlier innovators, notably Al Jolson, Bessie Smith, and Ethel Waters, was indirect, filtered to a considerable extent through Bing—and the microphone. The two elements contributing to a new, distinctive vocal idiom—an Afro-American approach to phrasing, and radio, bringing with it the microphone—met in him. They were synthesized in his singing, and passed on to all who came after him.—HENRY PLEASANTS

2 For a great tree, death comes as a gradual transformation. Its vitality ebbs slowly. Even when life has abandoned it entirely, it remains a majestic thing. On some hilltop a dead tree may dominate the landscape for miles around. Alone among living things, it retains its character and dignity after death. Plants wither; animals disintegrate. A dead tree, however, may be as arresting, as filled with personality, in death as it is in life. Even in its final moments, when the massive trunk lies prone and it has moldered into a ridge covered with mosses and fungi, it arrives at a fitting and a noble end. It enriches and refreshes the earth. And later, as part of other green and growing things, it rises again.—EDWIN WAY TEALE

3 The lion tamer's will must be stronger than that of his or her beasts. How often has one been to the circus and suddenly felt a certain tension in the cage when a beast is proving difficult? There is clearly a battle of wills going on. The most observant in the audience will watch fascinated; the rest will sense that a moment of crisis is upon them, and the trainer must impose both will and mastery on the recalcitrant animal. The trainer may turn quickly upon it as though making quite clear that it has earned his or her displeasure, and, if not careful, will earn some chastisement; the trainer may merely look in the direction of the animal or may point imperiously with a whip—not that that would prove any real protection should the animal attack—it is more an instrument for instruction. Then with a snarl, or with a whimper, or with defiance, the beast will do as it should have done, and everyone will sigh with relief. The battle of wills is over; the human has won, and the other animals in the act will be as aware of that all-important fact as the wayward beast itself.—PETER VERNEY

4 The storms and high seas that generations of sailors have cursed, fought, and sometimes succumbed to have provided us with historical and archeological treasures. People have been sailing the seven seas, or at least some of them, for nearly 10,000 years, and the number of ships that have sunk is untold. True, the ancient wooden vessels would seem to be highly susceptible to the forces of destruction in the sea—the rot of the timbers, the drilling or gnawing organisms, and the relentless pushing and pulling of the water itself. However, most of these ships were rapidly covered by sediment, which protected them against further decay. Enough sunken ships, or their cargoes, have been found to spur archeologists and anthropologists into increasing their efforts to recover historical evidence buried beneath the sea.—JACQUES COUSTEAU

Part 2 The Summary

The summary, unlike the paraphrase, cuts a selection down to about one-third of its original length. Its purpose is to condense without losing the basic meaning of the original. Being able to summarize material will be particularly helpful in your research paper. In most cases, you will have to condense material from your reading in order to prepare your note cards.

The summary is not new to you. Radio and TV broadcasts summarize important events of the day. The last paragraph of a textbook chapter often summarizes the main points of the chapter. In fact, you read and listen to summaries daily.

How To Write a Summary

1. Read the material.
   a. Read the selection carefully. There usually is a key sentence that expresses the main point. Sometimes a topic sentence will summarize a whole paragraph for you.
   b. Note the important ideas, the order in which they occur, and the way the writer has connected them. You may want to write these ideas briefly in your own words.

2. Write the summary.
   a. Omit unnecessary details, examples, anecdotes, and repetitions. You may want to retain some of the key words or technical language of the original, but the bulk of the summary should be in your own words.
   b. Check your first draft to see that it includes all the important ideas of the original. Any unnecessary or repetitious details should be omitted.
   c. You may need to revise and rewrite. Your final summary should be about one-third the length of the original. It should give all the essential information in such a way that the reader can use it without referring to the original.

A Sample Summary

Read the paragraph below. Then work through the steps that lead to a finished summary.

> About a hundred years ago, Thomas Henry Huxley, the English biologist, could say with confidence: "I believe that probably all the great sea fisheries are inexhaustible; that is to say that nothing

we do seriously affects the numbers of fish." Huxley, of course, did not foresee the technological advances that would be made and applied within a century to fishing, as well as to every other aspect of man's activities. Sadly, Huxley's prediction has proved wrong. Today's fishing fleets consist of entire flotillas equipped with electronic devices and include floating ships that process the catch at sea. Planes are used as spotters to locate schools of fish. Radio telephones direct the boats to the fish. Radar and echo sounders find schools that cannot be seen from the air or on the water's surface. Moreover, oceanic sciences have determined the conditions of salinity and temperatures required for various species to thrive. Today, thermometers and salinometers are used by fishing fleets. These ultramodern fishing fleets can stay in the open water almost indefinitely, sweeping the sea of much of its life. The herring population in the Atlantic, the most heavily fished area of the world, is decreasing. Haddock may have been wiped out. Similarly, modern whaling methods have all but eliminated several types of whales from the face of the earth. Helicopters and swift, engine-driven catcher boats with sounding equipment spot the whales. Explosive harpoons fired from guns mounted on the catchers find their mark. Humans have become by far the greatest predators of all time.—JACQUES COUSTEAU

Apply the Techniques

Step 1. The writer begins this paragraph with a quotation from the past, reflecting an optimism about the abundance of nature. The rest of the paragraph refutes this optimism with a hard-headed look at the present reality. Two things have worked to deplete the resources of the ocean: technology and scientific advancement. The writer develops each of these points with examples and then cites specific kinds of fish that are either threatened or extinct. His concluding sentence places the responsibility squarely on humans.

Step 2. By omitting unnecessary details, examples, and repetitions, you can reduce long phrases and even whole sentences to short phrases or single words.

Original	Summary
Sentence 1. Lengthy quotation from Huxley	brief paraphrase
Sentence 10. "These ultra-modern fishing fleets can stay in the open water almost indefinitely."	year-round fleets
Sentences 4, 5, 6, 7.	electronic detectors, radar, echo sounders and spotter planes
Sentences 8, 9.	Advances in oceanic sciences have further improved their efficiency.
Sentences 11, 12, 13.	As a result, the herring population has been seriously decreased; haddock and several kinds of whales have been almost wiped out.

The final sentence of this paragraph indicts humans.

Following is the finished summary. It is eighty-six words compared with the original two hundred and fifty-five. Does it include all of the important ideas of the original?

> A hundred years ago, the English biologist Thomas Henry Huxley predicted that despite anything we might do, our supply of fish would remain inexhaustible. Technological and scientific advances have proved him wrong. Today's year-round fleets are aided by electronic detectors, radar, and echo sounders and spotter planes. Advances in oceanic sciences have further improved their efficiency. As a result, the herring population has been seriously decreased; haddock and several kinds of whales have been almost wiped out. Humans are the greatest destroyers of all time.

Exercises Practice in Writing Summaries

A. Summarize the selection on computers that appears on the next page. Follow the steps that are outlined after the selection.

You can make computers that are almost human. In some respects they are superhuman; they can beat most of us at chess, memorize whole telephone books at a glance, compose music of a certain kind and write obscure poetry, diagnose heart ailments, send personal invitations to vast parties, even go transiently crazy. No one has yet programmed a computer to be of two minds about a hard problem, or to burst out laughing, but that may come. Sooner or later, there will be real human hardware, great whirring, clicking cabinets intelligent enough to read magazines and vote, able to think rings around the rest of us.

Well, maybe, but not for a while anyway. Before we begin organizing sanctuaries and reservations for our software selves, lest we vanish like the whales, here is a thought to relax with.

Even when technology succeeds in manufacturing a machine as big as Texas to do everything we recognize as human, it will still be, at best, a single individual. This amounts to nothing, practically speaking. To match what we can do, there would have to be three billion of them, with more coming down the assembly line; and I doubt that anyone will put up the money, much less make room. And even so, they would all have to be wired together, intricately and delicately, as we are, communicating with each other, talking incessantly, listening. If they weren't *at* each other this way, all their waking hours, they wouldn't be anything like human, after all. I think we're safe, for a long time ahead.—LEWIS THOMAS

Step 1. Reread the selection.

a. Look for the sentence that expresses the basic idea. You will find that in this selection it is the topic sentence of paragraph three.

b. Note the structure of the selection and list the important ideas in the order in which they occur. In paragraph one, Thomas somewhat humorously warns us that computers may be developing superhuman qualities. In paragraph two, he reassures us about the unlikelihood of such a development. In paragraph three, he explains why we may feel safe.

Step 2. Summarize the selection in your own words, keeping to the structure outlined above.

a. Omit unnecessary details.
b. Read your summary and check for accuracy.

B. Using this same procedure, summarize each of the following selections.

1 The sense that humans depend upon the least is the one most highly developed in dogs. Perhaps this is the reason that every known civilization, culture, and subculture throughout history has included dogs at the hearth and home and in the fields. Although dogs as companions and work-mates offer us much more than just a compensation to our weak sense of smell, the combination of human and dog in the pursuit of game has been a super-efficient hunting team since ancient times. Each partner contributes to the best of his or her ability to compensate for shortcomings in the other.

Of course, nearly all four-legged predators have extremely good senses of smell, but more than that is required from a domesticated dog. The modern dog has a genetic history of sociability. Wolves, dingos, and other wild dogs live in highly social pack structures in which each member knows who the boss is, what the territorial limits are, and where to stand in line at suppertime. These social concepts have been carried over, and in many cases even enhanced by selective breeding, so that your dog is usually very well adjusted to the basic concepts of teamwork and obedience. Most dogs will usually make a distinct effort to let you know when they smell something worth bringing to your attention.—DENNIS G. WALROD

2 When the first European settlers arrived in this country, the passenger pigeon was the most abundant bird on the continent and probably the most plentiful creature ever to inhabit this earth. It was not at all uncommon for migrating flocks to number over a billion birds. Yet, by the early twentieth century, they were gone from the face of America—every last one of them.

Early Americans, who thought there could be no end to the vast number of passenger pigeons, hunted the beautiful, slate-blue dove into oblivion. Martha, the last of the passenger pigeons, died in the Cincinnati Zoo in 1914. In the Smithsonian today, she is a stuffed reminder of what once was.—*American History Illustrated*

3 We have an abiding impression of the outlaw as a low-life renegade, a violent fool who lived off luck and the gun. We view him as one of society's misbegotten, who had to be hunted down like an animal by morally superior men in white hats. That was not so, however. In truth, the line between the "good guy" and the "bad guy" in the West was often blurred, and many of the outlaws, in spite of their errant and often violent natures, were men of extraordinary skill and cunning, who by comparison made lawmen look pathetic.—Robert Redford

4 Nobody knows the name of the first farmer who piled some surplus fruits and vegetables on a picnic table in front of the farmhouse and thereby started the first roadside market, an institution that has never left the scene and has grown and prospered in the past several years. Roadside markets began in the second decade of this century when city families with automobiles began taking Sunday drives into the countryside. They were soon knocking at farmhouse doors to buy vegetables or fruits or eggs fresher and better than they could find at the corner grocery store.

Today there are upward of eight thousand markets—about twice the number existing in 1965—clustered in the East, Midwest, Texas, and California, according to a survey of agricultural economists and horticulturists at land-grant universities in twenty-nine states. The survey's estimates are conservative, since several states did not respond. If they had, the figure might be closer to twelve thousand markets that sell substantial amounts of produce and generate a significant portion of the family income. If spare-time casual markets were counted too, the tally would be much higher.—Ken and Pat Kraft

5 Members of a dreamer's family constitute a fairly high percentage of dream characters. For younger dreamers, those in their late teens and early twenties, mother and father are dreamed about more often than any other family members, while among middle-aged dreamers, the dreamer's mate and his children play important roles. Why should we dream about our family? We believe that people who enter our dreams are ones with whom we are emotionally involved. The emotion may be one of love, fear, or anger, or a mixture of these feelings. For young people who are not married and do not have children, the most significant members of the family and the ones with whom they are emotionally involved are their parents. Young people are trying to break family ties and assert their independence, yet they are apprehensive about leaving the security of home for the hazards of the world. Moreover, they often feel guilty about deserting their parents. On the other hand, older dreamers, having resolved these particular conflicts, find themselves involved with their husbands or wives and with their children. It is rather ironical that while children are dreaming about parents, parents are dreaming about children, and while husbands are dreaming about wives, wives are dreaming about husbands. It might be said that if anyone wants to know who is dreaming about him or her, one will find the answer by consulting one's own dreams. The people in one's dreams are likely to be those who are dreaming about him or her.—Ralph L. Woods and Herbert B. Greenhouse

Chapter 13

Writing About Literature

Writing about literature is an important way of studying literature. It forces you to read more carefully and more critically. In order to find a focus for an analysis, you must understand the structure of a piece of literature. You must sort out the elements that the writer has used to achieve the meaning.

Once you have determined your focus and the general point you want to make about it, you will find that the Process of Writing about literature is similar to other composition work you have done. As in all expository writing, you develop your main idea with specific details. When your subject is a literary work, your supporting details come from the work itself.

Part 1 Writing About a Short Story

Certain steps are essential to successful writing about a short story. First, it is necessary to read and reread the story carefully, taking notes as you read. The next step is to decide upon a focus. Your focus will probably be one or more of the elements of the short story—plot, character, setting, point of view, theme, and style. The final step is the developing of a controlling purpose and the selecting of specific details from the story to develop it. After you have completed these three steps, you are ready to organize your paper.

Elements of a Short Story

Here is a brief review of the elements of a short story.

Plot. A short story shows characters living through a single experience or several closely related ones. This action is the plot of the story. It need not be exclusively physical. Sometimes the writer is primarily concerned with the thoughts of the characters and the insights they gain. The plot begins with the presentation of a situation that needs to be resolved. As the characters act and react, the plot moves to its resolution.

Character. The characters in a story are the persons who initiate or go through the experiences of the plot. Their qualities emerge and your understanding of them develops as the story progresses. Sometimes a character is more universal than individual, representing a basic human type.

Setting. Setting is the environment in which the characters live and move. It may include such things as time of day, natural surroundings, elements of weather, and even sounds and smells. Sometimes setting is incidental to the story; it serves as a mere location for events. In other stories, setting is essential to the action.

Point of View. This refers to the position from which the writer views his subject. Two different points of view are common in short stories.

1. **First-person narrator.** The story is told by an "I." All the action is seen through the eyes and mind of this character.

2. **Third-person limited.** The writer uses *he, she,* and *they,* not *I* in telling the story. The narration is limited, however, to the observations, feelings, and behavior of one character. Most short stories use this third-person limited point of view.

Theme. Short stories do more than show characters in action in a particular place and time. Most serious stories develop a theme, a deeper meaning underlying the human experience of the story. Discovering thematic significance is one of the most satisfying aspects of reading fiction.

Style. Style refers mainly to the way in which a writer uses language. It includes the qualities of word choice, sentence structure and variety, imagery, rhythm, repetition, coherence, emphasis, and arrangement of ideas. It also includes the use of irony and the surprise ending, which help to establish the central meaning.

Step 1. Read the following story and then work through the procedures that follow it. The first reading will give you the story line, the incidents that lead to the climax, and the resolution.

THE SNIPER

The long June twilight faded into night. Dublin lay enveloped in darkness, but for the dim light of the moon that shone through fleecy clouds, casting a pale light as of approaching dawn over the streets and the dark waters of the Liffey. Around the beleaguered Four Courts the heavy guns roared. Here and there through the city, machine guns and rifles broke the silence of the night, spasmodically, like dogs barking on lone farms. Republicans and Free Staters were waging civil war.

On a rooftop near O'Connell Bridge, a Republican sniper lay watching. Beside him lay his rifle, and over his shoulders were slung a pair of field glasses. His face was the face of a student—thin and ascetic, but his eyes had the cold gleam of the fanatic. They were deep and thoughtful, the eyes of man who is used to looking at death.

He was eating a sandwich hungrily. He had eaten nothing since morning. He had been too excited to eat. He finished the sandwich, and taking a flask of whiskey from his pocket, he took a short draft. Then he returned the flask to his pocket. He paused for a moment, considering whether he should risk a smoke. It was dangerous. The flash might be seen in the darkness and there were enemies watching. He decided to take the risk. Placing a cigarette between his lips, he struck a match, inhaled the smoke hurriedly and put out the light. Almost immediately, a bullet flattened itself against the parapet of the roof. The sniper took another whiff and put out the cigarette. Then he swore softly and crawled away to the left.

Cautiously he raised himself and peered over the parapet. There was a flash, and a bullet whizzed over his head. He dropped immediately. He had seen the flash. It came from the opposite side of the street.

He rolled over the roof to a chimney stack in the rear, and slowly drew himself up behind it, until his eyes were level with the top of the parapet. There was nothing to be seen—just the dim outline of the opposite housetop against the blue sky. His enemy was under cover.

Just then an armored car came across the bridge and advanced slowly up the street. It stopped on the opposite side of the street fifty yards ahead. The sniper could hear the dull panting of the motor. His heart beat faster. It was an enemy car. He wanted to fire, but he knew it was useless. His bullets would never pierce the steel that covered the grey monster.

Then round the corner of a side street came an old woman, her head covered by a tattered shawl. She began to talk to the man in the turret of the car. She was pointing to the roof where the sniper lay. An informer.

The turret opened. A man's head and shoulders appeared, looking toward the sniper. The sniper raised his rifle and fired. The head fell heavily on the turret wall. The woman darted toward the side street. The sniper fired again. The woman whirled round and fell with a shriek into the gutter.

Suddenly from the opposite roof a shot rang out, and the sniper dropped his rifle with a curse. The rifle clattered to the roof. The sniper thought the noise would wake the dead. He stooped to pick the rifle up. He couldn't lift it. His forearm was dead. "I'm hit," he muttered.

Dropping flat on to the roof, he crawled back to the parapet. With his left hand he felt the injured right forearm. The blood was oozing through the sleeve of his coat. There was no pain—just a deadened sensation, as if the arm had been cut off.

Quickly he drew his knife from his pocket, opened it on the breastwork of the parapet and ripped open the sleeve. There was a small hole where the bullet had entered. On the other side there was no hole. The bullet had lodged in the bone. It must have fractured it. He bent the arm below the wound. The arm bent back easily. He ground his teeth to overcome the pain.

Then, taking out his field dressing, he ripped open the packet with his knife. He broke the neck of the iodine bottle and let the bitter fluid drip into the wound. A paroxysm of pain swept through him. He placed the cotton wadding over the wound and wrapped the dressing over it. He tied the end with his teeth.

Then he lay still against the parapet, and closing his eyes, he made an effort of will to overcome the pain.

In the street beneath all was still. The armored car had retired speedily over the bridge, with the machine gunner's head hanging lifeless over the turret. The woman's corpse lay still in the gutter.

The sniper lay for a long time nursing his wounded arm and planning escape. Morning must not find him wounded on the roof. The enemy on the opposite roof covered his escape. He must kill that enemy, and he could not use his rifle. He had only a revolver to do it. Then he thought of a plan.

Taking off his cap, he placed it over the muzzle of his rifle. Then he pushed the rifle slowly upwards over the parapet, until the cap was visible from the opposite side of the street. Almost immediately there was a report, and a bullet pierced the center of the cap. The sniper slanted the rifle forward. The cap slipped down into the street. Then, catching the rifle in the middle, the sniper dropped his left hand over the roof and let it hang, lifelessly. After a few moments he let the rifle drop to the street. Then he sank to the roof, dragging his hand with him.

Crawling quickly to the left, he peered up at the corner of the roof. His ruse had succeeded. The other sniper, seeing the cap and rifle fall, thought that he had killed his man. He was now standing before a row of chimney pots, looking across, with his head clearly silhouetted against the western sky.

The Republican sniper smiled and lifted his revolver above the edge of the parapet. The distance was about fifty yards—a hard shot in the dim light, and his right arm was paining him like a thousand devils. He took a steady aim. His hand trembled with eagerness. Pressing his lips together, he took a deep breath through his nostrils and fired. He was almost deafened with the report and his arm shook with the recoil.

Then, when the smoke cleared, he peered across and uttered a cry of joy. His enemy had been hit. He was reeling over the parapet in his death agony. He struggled to keep his feet, but he was slowly falling forward, as if in a dream. The rifle fell from his grasp, hit the parapet, fell over, bounded off the pole of a barber's shop beneath, and then cluttered onto the pavement.

Then the dying man on the roof crumpled up and fell forward. The body turned over and over in space and hit the ground with a dull thud. Then it lay still.

The sniper looked at his enemy falling and he shuddered. The lust of battle died in him. He became bitten by remorse. The sweat stood out in beads on his forehead. Weakened by his wound and the long summer day of fasting and watching on the roof, he revolted from the sight of the shattered mass of his dead enemy. His teeth chattered. He began to gibber to himself, cursing the war, cursing himself, cursing everybody.

He looked at the smoking revolver in his hand and with an oath, he hurled it to the roof at his feet. The revolver went off with the concusion, and the bullet whizzed past the sniper's head. He was frightened back to his senses by the shock. His nerves steadied. The cloud of fear scattered from his mind and he laughed.

Taking the whiskey flask from his pocket, he emptied it at a draft. He felt reckless under the influence of the spirits. He decided to leave the roof and look for his company commander to report. Everywhere around was quiet. There was not much danger in going through the streets. He picked up his revolver and put it in his pocket. Then he crawled down through the skylight to the house underneath.

When the sniper reached the laneway on the street level, he felt a sudden curiosity as to the identity of the enemy sniper whom he had killed. He decided that he was a good shot, whoever he was. He wondered if he knew him. Perhaps he had been in his own company before the split in the army. He decided to risk going over to have a look at him. He peered around the corner into O'Connell Street. In the upper part of the street there was heavy firing, but around here all was quiet.

The sniper darted across the street. A machine gun tore up the ground around him with a hail of bullets, but he escaped. He threw himself face downwards beside the corpse. The machine gun stopped.

Then the sniper turned over the dead body and looked into his brother's face.—LIAM O'FLAHERTY

Step 2. Reread the story. As you read, take notes on anything that seems significant, whether related to plot, character, setting, theme, or style.

Notes on "The Sniper" might look like this:

a. Setting is one of contrasts: peaceful scene and roar of heavy guns.
b. The Republican sniper has the look of a student, but he has grown accustomed to death.
c. He provokes danger by lighting his cigarette. He seems excited by the war.
d. The story is told in the third person from the point of view of the sniper. Thus we see through his eyes and share his feelings.
e. The enemy sniper is similar to the Republican sniper. He, too, keeps undercover on a rooftop.
f. The enemy sniper is alert and quick. He sees the light of the match and fires immediately.
g. Neither man is given a name by the writer.

h. The Republican sniper kills both the soldier in the armored car and the old woman who betrayed his hiding place.
i. He seems to do this with little feeling.
j. The major character shows great courage, endurance, and ingenuity.
k. He dresses his own wound after he is shot.
l. He carries out a clever ruse, despite his pain.
m. The real death of the enemy parallels the fake death of the sniper. The dead man's rifle falls to the ground.
n. The sniper is revolted by his enemy's death. He curses the war and seems to feel an identity with his fallen enemy.
o. He almost kills himself.
p. The ending is ironic. The sniper turns over the dead body and finds it is his brother.
q. The theme seems to be that in civil war brother kills brother.

Step 3. Read over your list. Several patterns emerge. This is a story about courage under duress, about the brutalizing effect of war on a city's inhabitants, about the self-destructive quality of civil war. Important in the development of these themes is the technique of the writer.

A critical analysis cannot deal with every aspect of the story nor can it tell its entire plot. A good analysis must be sharply focused and include only such details as support and develop the main idea. In writing about a piece of literature, always stay inside the work itself.

Look through the list and find those items that interest you. Suppose, for example, that you choose letters a, b, e, g, m, n, p and q. For these items, an appropriate controlling purpose would take note of the structure of the story as it develops and reinforces the idea of the self-destructiveness of civil war. A workable controlling purpose might be stated like this:

> The controlling purpose of this critical analysis is to examine the techniques that the writer uses to reinforce the theme of the self-destructiveness of civil war in Liam O'Flaherty's "The Sniper."

Step 4. Plan the organization of your analysis, using the items you have chosen. You do not need to follow the sequence of your notes. Some items can be incorporated into others, giving you major topics and supporting details.

Sample Outline

Here is a sample outline. At this point, you may not have formulated your idea for your introductory paragraph.

I. (Introduction—to come)

II. Difference versus similarities
   A. Contradictory quality of setting
   B. Similarities of snipers

III. Critical point of story
   A. Republican's feigning of death
   B. Republican's killing of enemy
   C. Republican's revulsion toward killing

IV. Ironic ending
   A. Republican's descent to street
   B. Republican's recognition of brother

V. Conclusion of story
   A. Both men nameless
   B. Universal meaning in anonymity

Step 5. Write the first draft of your critical analysis. Keep your controlling purpose in front of you as you write. Note how each major division of the outline becomes a paragraph and the subdivisions act as supporting details. Note, too, that letter *g* in the notes, the anonymity of the snipers, has been used to create a concluding idea that extends the meaning of the story. As you write, remember that a work of literature is always discussed in the present tense.

Step 6. Rewrite, or revise, your paper and proofread it carefully. Title your paper appropriately.

Critical Analysis of the Short Story

Here is a final version of the critical analysis.

STYLE AND STRUCTURE IN "THE SNIPER"

In Liam O'Flaherty's "The Sniper," style and structure reinforce the theme of the unnatural and self-destructive quality of civil war. The initial description of the contradictory aspects of the setting sets the tone for the events that follow. The parallel actions in the structure of the story, along with the irony of the conclusion, serve to emphasize the dehumanization of war.

The language of the opening paragraph emphasizes the contradition between a peaceful, natural setting and the sounds of war. O'Flaherty talks of "June twilight" and of the moon shining through "fleecy clouds." Violating the serenity are the sounds of roaring guns and of rifles "like dogs barking on lone farms." A "Republican sniper," a young man with the "face of a student," watches over this scene. He is not at his studies, however; he is armed with a rifle, a revolver, and field glasses. On a neighboring roof, similarly armed, is another young man, also on the alert for enemy attack. Here, their seeming kinship ends. They are enemies, stalking each other in the environs of a great city.

The critical point of the story is reached when the Republican sniper, shot at by his enemy, feigns death and lets his rifle fall to the ground below. Off his guard, the Free State sniper stands up and is killed by the Republican with a single shot. What follows is a scene that parallels what was enacted moments before the deception. The Free Stater's rifle, too, falls to the ground, but not in pretense. He has been killed, and his body crumples and falls over the parapet of the roof. At this point, the Republican sniper has a moment of revelation. He recognizes how easily he himself could have been the victim, and he is revolted by his murderous act.

Total insight, however, comes only at the end. The Republican sniper descends to the street and turns over the dead body. He looks "into his brother's face." The ironic ending clarifies the insight that has been building throughout the story: In nations torn by internal strife, brother destroys brother.

The reader may carry this insight a step further. The author leaves the snipers unnamed, thus giving the story universal application. Not just civil wars but all wars deny humanity and turn man against his brother man.

Exercises Writing About a Short Story

A. Look over the list of notes again and find a different focus. Two mentioned earlier were the brutalizing effect of war and the courage and strength shown by the young sniper despite his pain and the danger of his situation. You might also consider, as a topic for analysis, the effect of the point of view on the reader. Because you experience the story only as the Republican sniper experiences it, your sympathies are with him. The third-person narration, however, provides a kind of detachment that affects your perception.

Follow the step-by-step pattern, ending with an analysis of about 250 to 350 words. Bear in mind that a critical analysis does *not* retell the story. Include only such details as are necessary to develop your main idea. Be careful not to move outside of the story in your analysis. Write an appropriate title.

B. Choose a story you like. Using the techniques you have learned, formulate a controlling purpose and then write an outline and a final analysis.

Part 2 Writing About a Poem

Writing about a poem is similar to writing about a short story. However, poetry is shorter and more concentrated than prose. Because the poems are short, you can read each one many times before writing about it. Because they are concentrated, you must read very carefully, paying close attention to each stanza, line, and word. Vital meaning and power can be packed into a single word.

The poet uses words for their sounds as well as their meanings. Rhythm, rhyme, and other sound effects bring poetry close to music. Poetry has visual appeal as well, creating word pictures through its imagery. Prose uses poetic devices too, but in prose they are often incidental. In poetry they are central.

When you write about a poem, be sure to consider its poetic devices and the feeling it evokes, as well as its theme. In fact, you might choose any one of these three as the focus for a critical analysis.

Analysis of Poem 1

Here is a step-by-step analysis of a poem. First, read the poem carefully several times. Then follow the procedure as it leads you to a final analysis.

OZYMANDIAS

I met a traveller from an antique land
Who said: Two vast and trunkless legs of stone
Stand in the desert . . . Near them, on the sand,
Half sunk, a shattered visage lies, whose frown,
5 And wrinkled lip, and sneer of cold command,
Tell that its sculptor well those passions read
Which yet survive, stamped on these lifeless things,
The hand that mocked them, and the heart that fed:[1]
And on the pedestal these words appear:
10 "My name is Ozymandias, king of kings:
Look on my works, ye Mighty, and despair!"
Nothing beside remains. Round the decay
Of that colossal wreck, boundless and bare
The lone and level sands stretch far away.

—Percy Bysshe Shelley

[1] Lines 6–8: The *passions* of Ozymandias *survive* (outlast) the hand of the sculptor and the *heart* of Ozymandias.

Can you see how this fourteen-line sonnet falls naturally into separate sections? The first eight lines introduce remnants of a mammoth statue, the legs and shattered face of a once-powerful king. The last six lines break into two parts. The first three lines present the proud king's boast. The last three lines show how time has dealt with it.

"Ozymandias" is a poem with a strong central idea. To find this idea, look at the elements that the poet presents.

1. *A king who boasted of his power and supremacy.* The character of Ozymandias lives on in "lifeless things." What do "wrinkled lip" and "sneer of cold command" reveal? What "passions" fed his heart? What do the words he chose for his pedestal show about him?

2. *The sculptor who created an awesome monument to the king.* The sculptor lives on through his art. His observations were keen and his skill considerable. What did he observe in the face of the king? What was it that his hand mocked?

3. *Time and its effects.* Time is a major element in this poem. Consider how time has destroyed the power of Ozymandias and altered the meaning of his boast. Originally, his words were backed by the magnitude of his works. Now, surrounded by empty sand, they proclaim a different message. You might express it like this: Worldly greatness—and the tyrant's power—will not outlast time. The monuments man builds to vanity all fall to dust.

However, the poem is more than this simple statement of truth. Reread the words of Ozymandias in lines 10 and 11. Notice the following:

1. The heavy, tramping sound of the one-syllable words
2. The harsh effect of repeated *k* sounds
3. The commanding second sentence
4. The powerful final word *despair*

Now contrast the quiet effect of the three-word sentence that follows: "Nothing beside remains."

Finally, notice how the *sound* of the last lines helps to describe endless desert sand. The word *boundless* stretches out in both sound and sense. The following vowel sounds emphasize length: long *o* in *lone*, broad *a* in *far* and long *a* in *away*.

Because the theme is so important to an understanding of this poem, our controlling purpose might be this:

> The controlling purpose of this analysis is to discuss the theme that world greatness will not outlast time in Shelley's poem "Ozymandias."

However, a good analysis must have a sharp focus. It must include more than a restatement of its theme. Your main idea, stated in the topic sentence might read as follows:

> Shelley's sonnet "Ozymandias" gives poetic force to the idea that worldly greatness will not outlast time.

Sample Outline

Here is a sample outline.

I. Poetic force of theme
   A. Language
   B. Irony

II. Details of wrecked statue
   A. "Trunkless legs"
   B. "Shattered visage"

III. Character of tyrant
   A. "Wrinkled lip"
   B. "Sneer of cold command"

IV. Irony of boast
   A. Contrast between wrecked statue and desolate sands
   B. Contrast of intended meaning to deeper truth

V. Poetic effects
   A. Quiet, matter-of-fact beginning
   B. Booming boast
   C. Slow, musical close

Critical Analysis of Poem 1

Here is a final version of the critical analysis.

THE ELEMENT OF TIME IN "OZYMANDIAS"

Shelley's sonnet "Ozymandias" gives poetic force to the idea that worldly greatness will not outlast time. The poem is basically a story told by an unnamed traveler about a strange scene he has come upon in the desert. The force of the irony, however, and the power of the language give universal significance to the story.

The poem presents a vivid picture—the remnants of a mammoth statue half-buried in desert sand. "Two vast and trunkless legs" still stand in the empty desert. Nearby, lies a "shattered visage." These two legs and a shattered face are all that remain of a monument to a once-proud king. The grotesque scene seems out of time and out of place.

The arrogance of the king lives on, however, in the "frown," the "wrinkled lip," and the "sneer of cold command" on the lifeless face. The sculptor seems to have understood this king well. His art has made a mockery of vanity. The art of the poet has recreated the mockery through the power of his language.

Paralleling the haughty face of the king are the boastful words on the pedestal.

> My name is Ozymandias, King of Kings.
> Look on my works, ye Mighty, and despair!

In the contrast between this boast and the endless, surrounding sand, the poet has created the basic irony of the poem. He uses time as the major element that destroys the power of Ozymandias and alters the meaning of his boast. The mighty ones will despair, not because they see Ozymandias's works, but because they see the devastation of them. So must we all despair if we hope to build lasting monuments to vanity and power.

The sonnet moves from a quiet, story-telling beginning to the booming boast of the king. The poetic language is powerful and compressed. The images build in force and power. The element of time is at work, however, on both the power of the king and the statue that was erected to honor him. Time has eroded all. "Nothing beside remains." The image is a "colossal wreck." The poem quickly falls away to a last line whose long vowels convey the feeling of endless waste.

Analysis of Poem 2

Here is another step-by-step analysis of a poem. Read the poem carefully and then follow the procedure as it leads you to a final analysis.

BY MORNING

Some for everyone
  plenty

  and more coming
Fresh   dainty   airily arriving
5 everywhere at once

Transparent at first
  each faint slice
  slow   soundlessly tumbling

  then quickly thickly a gracious fleece
10 will spread like youth   like wheat
  over the city

Each building will be   a hill
  all sharps made round

  dark worn noisy narrows made still
15 wide   flat   clean   spaces

Streets will be   fields
  cars be   fumbling sheep

A deep bright harvest will be seeded
  in a night

20 by morning we'll be   children
  feeding on manna

  a new loaf on every doorsill

—May Swenson

"By Morning" comes from a collection called *Poems To Solve*. It is a puzzle poem. In it, the poet describes but does not name a common natural occurrence—something almost everyone has either seen or heard about. It may take you several readings, however, to identify the subject of the poem.

The title makes it clear that something has happened during the night. By morning, says the poet, this is what you see. The word pictures provide clues. Consider these:

"airily arriving"	"soundlessly" falling
"transparent at first"	spreading like a "fleece"
"a faint slice"	altered look of buildings, streets, cars

May Swenson is describing the way that snowfall, overnight, magically transforms the city. The poet creates a feeling of childlike delight through a vivid and coherent imagery. The imagery is vivid in its imaginative comparisons. The snowfall makes ordinary things seem to be something else. It is coherent in its focus on two basic images—sheep and bread.

The sheep imagery is in lines 9, 16, and 17. The snow covers the city like "fleece" and cars become "fumbling sheep" on "fields" that were once streets. Look at lines 7, 10, 15, 16, and 18 to find images that center on bread. Another of the bread images, of course, is manna. How does the word *manna* deepen the meaning of the poem?

A controlling purpose for an analysis of this poem might focus on imagery.

> The controlling purpose of this critical analysis is to discuss May Swenson's use of vivid imagery to describe the magical transformation that a snowfall brings in her poem "By Morning."

Before limiting yourself to imagery, however, consider the verse form of the poem. Unlike "Ozymandias," with its metered and rhymed sonnet form, "By Morning" is free verse. The poet is not committed to any set pattern. Instead, she lines and spaces words in a way that best emphasizes the imagery, the emotion, and the meaning of the poem.

Notice how the spacing in lines 14 and 15 supports the sense of the lines. Consider how the pauses in lines 12, 16, and 20 suggest moments when the magic of the snowfall takes place.

A well focused topic sentence might be this:

> Through vivid imagery and skillful use of free verse, May Swenson creates the magic of a snowfall in her poem "By Morning."

Sample Outline

Here is a sample outline.

I. Puzzle poem

II. Vivid imagery
  A. Sheep
  B. Bread

III. Imaginative free verse

IV. Solution to the puzzle

Critical Analysis of Poem 2

A final version of the critical analysis appears on the following page.

IMAGERY AND SPACE IN "BY MORNING"

In "By Morning," May Swenson uses vivid imagery and imaginative free verse to create the magic of a snowfall. The poem is presented as a puzzle to solve. In it, the poet describes but does not name a common natural occurrence—something almost everyone has either seen or heard about.

The imagery is vivid in its imaginative comparisons. The poem shows a city transformed by snow. "Dark worn noisy narrows" are widened and cleansed by a thick "fleece." Streets become fields for "fumbling sheep." In addition to this sheep imagery is the imagery of bread. The snowflakes are "slices" that spread "like wheat," bringing a "deep bright harvest" that is "seeded in a night." The snow is manna, a gift from heaven for the children to "feed on." There's a "new loaf on every doorsill."

The free verse emphasizes this magic. In the following lines, appearance echoes sense.

> dark worn noisy narrows made still
> wide   flat   clean   spaces

Notice, too, the spacing in these lines taken from different sections of the poem.

> Each building will be   a hill
> Streets will be   fields
> By morning we'll be   children

Here the snow transforms and rejuvenates—in the silence of a pause.

All of the pieces of the puzzle make up the poem. The poem, however, moves far beyond the confines of a puzzle. The poet has created a feeling of childlike delight in the magical, overnight transformation of a city by the snow. The snowfall makes ordinary things seem to be something else. The poet has lined and spaced words in the way that best emphasizes the imagery, the emotion, and the meaning of the poem.

Exercise **Writing About a Poem**

Read the following poem carefully. Work through the questions on it and then write a critical analysis, as directed in question 5.

RICHARD CORY

Whenever Richard Cory went down town,
We people on the pavement looked at him:
He was a gentleman from sole to crown,
Clean favored, and imperially slim.

5 And he was always quietly arrayed,
And he was always human when he talked;
But still he fluttered pulses when he said,
"Good-morning," and he glittered when he walked.

And he was rich—yes, richer than a king—
10 And admirably schooled in every grace:
In fine, we thought that he was everything
To make us wish that we were in his place.

So on we worked, and waited for the light,
And went without the meat, and cursed the bread;
15 And Richard Cory, one calm summer night,
Went home and put a bullet through his head.

—Edwin Arlington Robinson

1. Like the surprise ending of "The Sniper," the ending of this poem makes a generalization about human nature. State the theme of the poem in a single, clear sentence.

2. Like the "people on the pavement," the reader sees Cory from the outside. This limited view is presented through images of royalty.

a. The use of *crown* instead of *head* in line 3
b. The word *imperially* in line 4 and *glittered* in line 8
c. Find the word in line 9 that is a key to all these images, giving them coherence.

3. The words *meat* and *bread* (line 14) are used symbolically to show the people's view of themselves in relation to Cory. What do the words stand for?

4. Consider the ironic contrast between the people's view of Cory and the surprise ending of the poem. Your statement of theme in question 1 should focus on this contrast.

5. Write a controlling purpose that relates the meaning of the poem to its surprise ending and effective imagery. Organize your material in outline form. Then refine your controlling purpose into a topic sentence with a sharp focus and develop it into a critical analysis of the poem. Be sure to support your main idea with specific details from the poem.

Chapter 14

The Research Paper

A research paper is a formal composition of some length based on information gathered from reliable sources, and organized and shaped by the writer's own thinking and judgment. The search for suitable source materials related to your subject, together with the planning and writing procedures you studied in connection with Chapter 11 (The Composition), requires an extended period of time. In order to use your time wisely, each step of the planning, research, and writing must be carefully controlled along the way.

Because a thorough research paper takes weeks to complete, choosing a subject for which reference books and articles are not readily available can be a costly error in terms of time. Careful attention to planning and organizing your paper is also important because mistakes become increasingly difficult to correct once you are involved in the actual writing. You must allow enough time to read your source materials and to judge the usefulness of that reading for your subject. You must allow enough time to write and revise your paper; and, finally, you must prepare accurate footnotes and a final bibliography.

While a research paper is a more ambitious undertaking than a composition, footnotes and a bibliography are the only aspects that are entirely new. When your teacher makes the research paper assignment, work out a time schedule, with your teacher's guidance, that will help you work through each stage in a thorough and unhurried way.

This chapter will discuss the procedures in writing a research paper. The basic steps are these:

EIGHT STEPS IN WRITING A RESEARCH PAPER

1. Choosing and limiting your subject
2. Preparing a working bibliography
3. Preparing a preliminary outline
4. Reading and taking notes
5. Organizing notes and writing the final outline
6. Writing the first draft
7. Writing the final draft with footnotes
8. Writing the final bibliography

Part 1 Choosing Your Subject

Choosing the right subject is extremely important to the success of your paper. To start your thinking, you may wish to make a list of ten subjects that come to your mind as possibilities for a research paper. Then check your list against the following guidelines.

1. **Choose a subject that interests you.** Choose a subject that you want to learn more about. If your subject does not really interest you, your paper will probably not be interesting to the reader either.

2. **Choose a subject for which a wide range of source materials is readily available.** Subjects that are too recent in development, or too technical in nature, will have few, if any, source materials. If you have doubts about source materials for any of the subjects on your list, consult your school librarian to find out how much information the library has.

3. **Choose a subject of some significance.** A subject of lasting interest will be challenging and gratifying to pursue. After all, you will be spending much time and effort on this assignment, and what you learn should be a significant addition to your store of knowledge as well as that of the reader.

4. **Choose a subject that can be presented objectively.** Your purpose is to sift through and reshape an accumulated body of information, not to indulge in arguments and persuasion. Argument and persuasion are right for debates, but not for a research paper. Your paper should be an objective presentation of your subject, not an emotional one.

5. **Avoid straight biography.** Biography requires long, intensive research, involving letters, interviews, and unpublished material not available to the average person. If the person is well known, biographies already exist and using them as resource material, even if they are in unusual quantity, results merely in a rehashing of already published information. Bringing your own thinking and direction to bear on a biography is virtually impossible.

Limiting Your Subject

As you learned in Chapter 11, limiting your subject is of vital importance in writing a good paper. A research paper will be approximately 2,000 words in length. Your subject must be limited so that your research can be handled within the time allotted, yet the coverage of your subject can be thorough.

Example 1

Suppose you were interested in art and wanted to do a paper on some aspect of it. Limiting your paper might proceed in the following steps:

1. Art
2. Painting
3. History of painting

At this point, stop to consider whether your subject can be handled in a 2,000-word paper. Obviously, the history of painting is far too large to be covered in that length, so you would have to narrow it further.

4. Turn-of-the-century realism in American painting
5. The Ash Can School
6. The paintings of John Sloan

If you examine the last two subjects, you will probably realize that your source material may be too limited to cover either of the subjects adequately. Whatever information you could find would tend to be repetitious and therefore frustrating. Subject number 4 might be exactly right. It has enough breadth for you to move around in, yet it is specific enough to concentrate on.

Example 2

Here is an example of a subject for a literary paper. Suppose you were interested in the works of Stephen Crane. Limiting your subject might proceed like this:

1. Stephen Crane
2. The works of Stephen Crane
3. The realism of Stephen Crane
4. *The Red Badge of Courage*

You have worked your way down to what seems to be a manageable subject: one book. However, the subject is still too general because there are countless ways in which to discuss a book. You need to focus on a particular aspect of the book that you feel will lend itself to a wide variety of source materials. You decide on the following subject for your paper.

The realism of Henry Fleming in Stephen Crane's *The Red Badge of Courage*

Exercise **Limiting Your Subject**

Bring to class three subjects that interest you as possible choices for a research paper. Limit each one properly and be sure that each one can be adequately researched. You will probably have to work in the library to complete this assignment. It is a vital first step in your research paper.

Part 2 Preparing a Working Bibliography

When you have decided on your subject, in consultation with your teacher, your next step is to search for and collect your source material. While the *Readers' Guide* and specialized reference books will be your best sources, you should first consult a good encyclopedia for a general overview of your subject.

If you have limited your subject properly, you will not find an article on your specific subject. Look for a general article on the larger subject of which yours is a part. This overview of the whole subject may suggest related ideas that you will want to consider as your subject takes shape. It may also suggest a modification in your original subject. While a shift in idea is not serious at this point, consult your teacher for approval.

Recommended Sources

At this point, you may wish to review Chapter 15 (The Library and Its Reference Materials) so that you can use your library time wisely. The following sources are the most important for a research paper.

1. **The card catalog.** Suppose you are doing a paper on William Faulkner. You would first look at all the subject cards with his name. In addition to all the books Faulkner has written, you will find major biographies and works of criticism mainly concerned with him. However, many books that may have informative chapters on Faulkner may not be entered. Look at "American Literature," "Twentieth Century Literature," "Literature of the South," "The Novel," "Literary Criticism," and any other general subjects that may seem related. The description of the book on the card will tell you whether the book is worth investigating.

2. **The *Readers' Guide*.** This source will list current magazine articles on your subject. For most subjects, past articles are as useful as present ones, and the library has cumulative bound volumes of past years.

3. **Specialized reference books.** Turn to Part 3 in Chapter 15 and review the list of reference books. If any of them relate to your subject, consult them in your library. They often suggest titles of additional books that may be useful.

In preparing a working bibliography, your object is to accumulate as many books and articles as you think might be helpful to you in some way. Beacuse you cannot always tell whether the information on a catalog card or in the *Readers' Guide* or in a bibliography will be helpful to you, it is wise to include sources you may be doubtful about at the moment. If some sources turn out to be of little help, you can later drop them from your bibliography.

Guidelines for Selecting Source Materials

These guidelines will help you in selecting source materials.

1. **Is the book or article included in any of the bibliographies you have consulted?** In addition to the bibliographies in reference books, many of the books from the card catalog will contain their own bibliographies. When you find such a bibliography, check your own working bibliography and add promising new sources. If the same books or authors appear in various bibliographies, they are probably worth investigating.

2. **Is the author an authority on the subject?** While you may not know this at the beginning, an author who has written several books or whose name is included in various bibliographies may be an authority on the subject. As you read, be on the alert for writers whose opinions are mentioned or quoted.

3. **What is the value of a promising book?** A book on the space age published in 1968 may not be as accurate as one published in 1980. A book on a famous scientist, written by a friend or relative, may not be as accurate as one written by an authority on scientific thinking. A third edition of a book would be more valuable than the first or second edition.

4. **If a magazine article looks promising, what kind of magazine does it appear in?** In general, popular interest magazines such as those on the newsstand are not suitable sources for a research paper.

5. **If a book looks promising, for what audience is it intended?** Many interesting books are intended for younger readers and are not suitable for research papers. Books of a highly technical nature are usually not suitable either.

Bibliography Cards

For each bibliography source, use a 3 x 5 card or slip of paper. Because you will be referring to each card time and again for specific information, be sure you fill out each card carefully and completely.

Bibliography cards have three purposes.

1. To record all the information needed to find the reference in the library when you are ready to take notes from it.
2. To record the information needed to prepare the footnotes for your paper.
3. To record the information needed to prepare the final bibliography for your paper.

Here are the correct forms of bibliography cards from three different kinds of sources: a book, a magazine article, and an encyclopedia article.

Book

Magazine Article

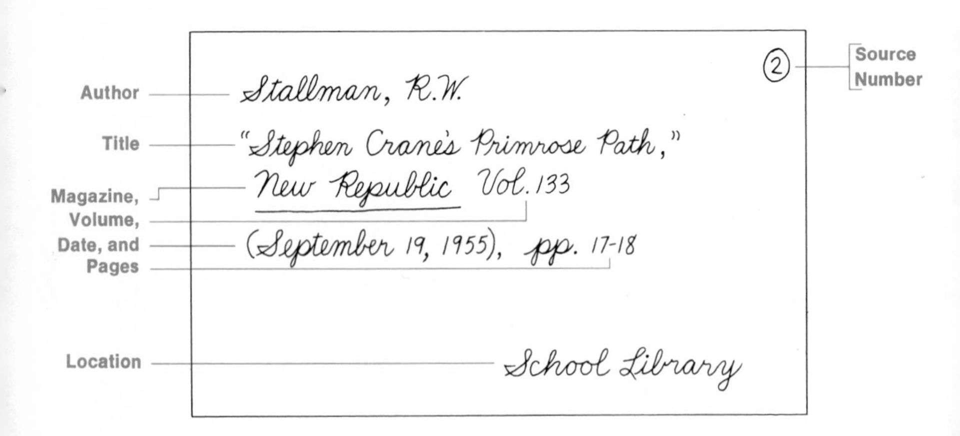

Encyclopedia Article

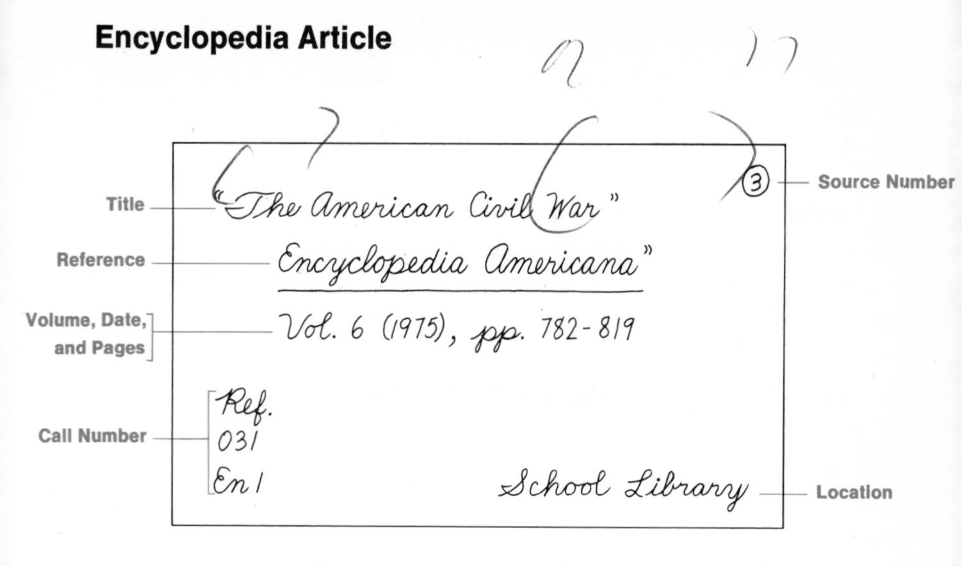

On these sample bibliography cards, note that the titles of books are underlined and the titles of articles are enclosed in quotation marks. Note also the correct abbreviations and punctuation.

Here is some additional information that will be helpful in preparing bibliography cards.

1. If a book has an editor rather than an author, use *ed.* (editor) or *eds.* (editors) after the name: *Todd, William, ed.*
2. If no publication date is given, use the copyright date: *c. 1970.*
3. If neither publication nor copyright date is given, use the abbreviation *n.d.* (no date).
4. Information such as the above is usually found on the title page of a book, encyclopedia, or pamphlet. Sometimes pamphlets have the information on front or back covers or on the last page. Magazines may have the information on the front covers or on one of the first few pages.
5. If you use a newspaper article, give the writer's name (if there is one); the title of the article in quotation marks; the name of the newspaper, underlined; and the date and the page number.

6. The source number in the upper right-hand corner of your card is important because it will save you a great deal of time as you are writing the first draft of your paper. Instead of having to write out all the information on the bibliography card every time you credit the use of an idea or a quotation, you can merely jot down the number of the card to identify the source.

As you continue the work on your paper, you will understand the importance of including the complete bibliographical data for each source.

Exercise Preparing a Working Bibliography

Using all available facilities, prepare a working bibliography for your chosen subject.

Determining the Controlling Purpose of Your Paper

Now that you have chosen your subject, prepared your working bibliography, and done some background reading, you are ready to bring your subject into sharper focus by deciding exactly what aspect of your subject you are going to write about. You need to formulate a controlling purpose for your paper—a formal, exact statement of what your paper is going to be about. Once you have refined your controlling purpose to the extent that it presents your purpose as clearly as you want it to, you can use it to direct your note-taking, and to help you write a good outline and a good paper.

It is possible that as you read you will want to revise your controlling purpose, but stating it as clearly as possible now will help you select the right material for your note-taking. Material that does not relate directly to your controlling purpose does not belong in your paper or your notes.

You will recall that on page 257, the student interested in Stephen Crane decided to write a paper on the realism of Henry Fleming in Stephen Crane's *The Red Badge of Courage*. While this statement may be suitable as a title, it is not sufficiently focused for a statement of controlling purpose. The statement must be recast into one that requires proof, such as the following.

Controlling Purpose: to demonstrate that Henry Fleming, the protagonist of Stephen Crane's *The Red Badge of Courage,* is an accurate portrayal of a Civil War soldier by comparing him with actual soldiers through their letters and diaries.

Exercise **Stating the Controlling Purpose**

Write out the controlling purpose for your paper, stating it as exactly as you can at this point in your procedure.

Part 3 Preparing a Preliminary Outline

The clear statement of your controlling purpose and the nature of the resources in your stack of working bibliography cards will help you prepare a preliminary outline for your paper. At this stage your outline will be only tentative and rough in form, but the major divisions and some subdivisions will suggest themselves. The first major topic will be devoted to your introduction and the last major topic to your conclusion, so at the present you need be concerned only with the topics in between.

This preliminary outline will function merely as a general guideline to your reading. As your reading progresses and you gain more information, you can revise and extend your outline accordingly. If you find that your source material does not contain enough information to develop a major topic sufficiently, you may have to delete that topic entirely and substitute one that is better covered. Your reading may also suggest an entirely new topic that you may want to develop. Make notes or revisions on your outline as you pursue your reading, so you have all the information in one place when you are ready to prepare your final outline.

Keep the statement of your controlling purpose before you at all times so that you can judge the relevance of your material when preparing your preliminary outline and also when taking notes on your reading. If you find that major topics need revising, you may need to revise your controlling purpose accordingly.

Here is an example of how a rough preliminary outline of the paper on Stephen Crane might look.

The Realism of Henry Fleming in Stephen Crane's *The Red Badge of Courage*

CONTROLLING PURPOSE: to demonstrate that Henry Fleming, the protagonist of Stephen Crane's *The Red Badge of Courage*, is an accurate portrayal of a Civil War soldier by comparing him with actual soldiers through their letters and diaries.

I. (Introduction—to come)

II. Soldiers in battle
  A. Risks
  B. Fears

III. Change in attitude
  A. Urgency
  B. Rage
  C. New Purpose

IV. Desertion
  A. Mental problems
  B. Physical problems
  C. Excuses

V. Expectations versus realities of battle

VI. Soldiers mature

VII. (Conclusion—to come)

Exercise Preparing a Preliminary Outline

Prepare a preliminary outline for your paper in the following form:

1. Put the title of your paper at the top.
2. Below the title, write your controlling purpose.
3. Follow standard outline form. (See pages 198–201.)
4. Keep the details of your outline to a minimum so you can revise and expand more easily as your reading progresses.

Part 4 Reading and Taking Notes

Keep your controlling purpose and your preliminary outline before you as you read and take notes, so you can keep a strong control over the direction of your paper. Take notes on 4 x 6 cards so they do not get mixed up with your 3 x 5 bibliography cards. Be sure to use a separate card for each note or for each set of related facts about one topic from the same source. Remember that the grouping of your cards under separate topics will be necessary when you write your final outline. For example, if you have two different ideas on one card, you may need one idea for the beginning of your paper and the other for the end of your paper. Sorting out your cards would be almost impossible with both ideas on one card.

A Sample Note Card

Here is a sample note card containing both a paraphrased idea and a direct quotation and showing the position and spacing for each part of a note card.

Sample Note Card

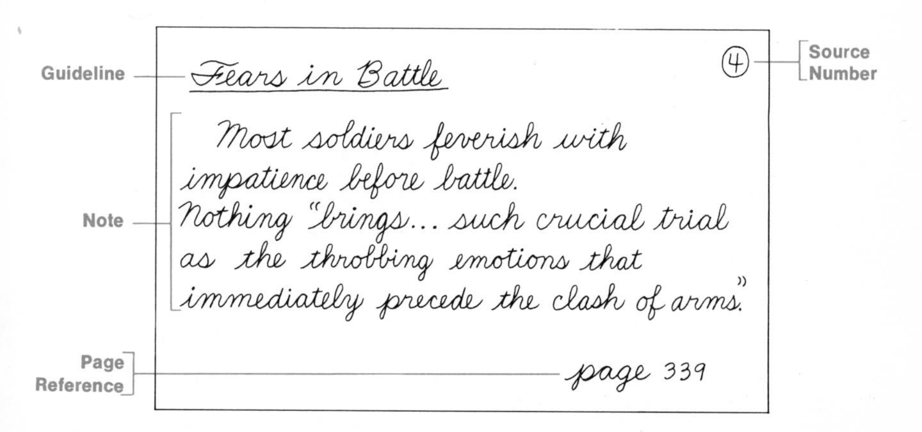

Here is an explanation of the parts of a sample note card.

1. **The guideline** is a heading that identifies the note on the card. It corresponds to a topic or subtopic on your preliminary outline. Include on the card only ideas pertaining to the guideline and use a different card for each source. If your reading does not yield enough information for your guideline, you may need to delete the topic from your outline and discard the corresponding note cards. If your reading yields new or different information, revise your outline and your guideline accordingly.

2. **The source number** corresponds with the number of your working bibliography card and is the source from which the note was taken. By checking the card in the working bibliography, you can obtain all the information on the source whenever you need it.

3. **The page reference** must be exact for two reasons: (1) You may want to refer again to the source to verify the facts, and (2) you may need the page reference for footnotes.

4. **The note,** of course, is the most important part of the card because it is this part that you are going to use in writing your paper. Except for direct quotations, all notes should be paraphrased in your own words to avoid plagiarism.

Plagiarism

Because plagiarism is intellectually dishonest and therefore a form of stealing, it is an extremely serious offense and can result in severe penalties, even no credit for the course. The following forms of plagiarism are the most frequent:

1. **Failure to document with quotation marks any material copied directly from other sources.**
2. **Failure to acknowledge paraphrased material (someone else's ideas).**
3. **Failure to provide a bibliography.**
4. **Use of others' work as one's own, particularly in the creative arts.**
5. **Use of others' ideas as one's own for themes, poems, musical compositions, or art work.**

Improving Your Skill at Taking Notes

Here are some ways to improve your skill in taking notes.

1. Be accurate. Double-check statistics and facts to make sure you have them right. When you summarize or paraphrase a writer's words, be sure you do not misinterpret or distort the meaning.

2. Distinguish between fact and opinion. Label opinions: "Dr. Graves thinks that . . ." or "According to Grace Jackson, . . ." Be careful to note differences in opinion and to point out such differences in your notes.

3. Take notes as quickly as possible. Omit all words or phrases not essential to meaning; use abbreviations. Be careful, however, not to take notes so brief that when you need to use them you cannot understand what you have written.

4. Copy a direct quotation exactly, including punctuation, spelling, and grammar. Be sure to use quotation marks both at the beginning and at the end of the quotation so that you can easily separate the quotation from paraphrased material.

5. Any words inserted by the writer in the text of a quotation must be enclosed in brackets. (See Section 12.13 in your Handbook.) Parentheses must not be used. Insert brackets in ink if your typewriter does not have them.

6. Indicate the omissions of nonessential parts of a quotation by ellipses. (See Section 12.14 in your Handbook.)

7. If you can't get all the information on one side of a card, write *over* in parentheses at the bottom of the card, flip the card over, and continue on the back. If you have more than two more lines, you probably have too much material for one card.

Exercise Reading and Taking Notes

Complete your reading and your note cards. Adjust or revise your preliminary outline, and make any final revisions of your controlling purpose.

Part 5 Organizing Notes and Writing the Final Outline

A research paper is longer and more complex than a short composition, and your outline will be correspondingly so. Remember, however, that much of your work has already been done. The guidelines on your note cards will provide the divisions and subdivisions of your outline, and your next step is to divide your note cards into separate piles in order to write your final outline.

Put each note card with the same guideline into a separate pile. Each of these piles of cards should relate to one of the major or minor divisions of your preliminary outline. Study these piles of cards to see what information each contains and the extent to which the information conforms to the information on your preliminary outline. Refer to your controlling purpose often as you study your cards.

Gradually, some topics will emerge as major divisions of your subject, some as subdivisions, and others as sub-subdivisions. If some cards reveal insufficient material on a subdivision and you feel that subdivision is important, you may have to do more reading. If the subdivision is not important, you can either combine it with another subdivision if it is closely related or delete the information and the card entirely.

This is the point at which you decide exactly what you are going to include in your paper and what you are going to leave out. Keep checking your controlling purpose to see that all your usable material is relevant to your subject. Do not be afraid to delete information that is not relevant. The decisions you make at this point will be reflected in your paper.

Finally, when you have chosen your main topics and subtopics and tested each note card for relevance to your controlling purpose, begin to organize the topics for your final outline. Try to decide in what order your topics would move most logically toward the conclusion you have determined in your controlling purpose. Feel free to move an entire main topic from one place to another or to shift your note cards to different positions.

Write down your main topics in various orders and study them, thinking about how logically you can make transitions between topics. If a transition from one topic to another seems forced, something is probably wrong. Either you need to rearrange your topics or you need to revise the emphasis or the direction of one of them.

When you are finally satisfied with the order of your material, test it once more against your controlling purpose in the following ways.

1. Does it begin at the beginning and move logically to the conclusion?
2. Are the main topics the most important ideas?
3. Do the subtopics relate specifically to the main topics?
4. Is there any unnecessary duplication of topics or subtopics?
5. Do all the main topics relate clearly to the controlling purpose?
6. Will the transition from one topic to the next be clear and logical?
7. Will the conclusion correspond to that of the controlling purpose?
8. Have you included too much information anywhere so that your paper will not be well balanced?
9. Have you included enough information to develop your ideas well?

When you are satisfied with the answers to these questions, you are ready to write your final outline. If you have any doubts about standard outline form, check pages 198–201. Remember that a good outline is not necessarily a long, elaborate one. Try to keep it within reasonable bounds.

Exercise Organizing Notes and Writing the Final Outline

Organize your note cards and write your final outline.

Part 6 Writing the First Draft

At this point you have the title of your paper, the statement of your controlling purpose, your final outline, and your note cards sorted to fit your outline. With all these in front of you, you are ready to write your first draft. This is the time to get all your information on paper as fully and freely as you can. Do not worry about style and form or the mechanics of punctuation. Your main purpose is to get all your ideas down in a form that you will be able to follow when you are ready to revise and polish your paper.

Follow your outline and keep your controlling purpose in mind. Begin a new paragraph for every topic and subtopic on your outline and make some attempt at paragraph transitions, although you can work these out more carefully later.

Write your entire paper in the third person. Never use *I*, *me*, or *my* because you will be in danger of injecting your own opinion, and personal opinion has no place in a research paper. Use the information on your note cards and be sure to include the source number in the upper right-hand corner of your note card when you use other people's ideas or direct quotations. You will need these sources for your footnotes. To save time, you can write the first few words of a direct quotation, and the source numbers will help you locate it quickly when you need to copy it carefully and completely on your final draft.

As you write, keep in mind that the first paragraph of your paper will constitute your introduction, in which you set forth your controlling purpose. Your final, or concluding, paragraph should round up all your ideas in a restatement of your controlling purpose.

Exercise **Writing the First Draft**

With your controlling purpose and your outline before you, and using your note cards, write the first draft of your paper.

Part 7 Writing the Final Draft with Footnotes

Before writing your final draft, you may wish to review the suggestions for revising a composition on page 211 and the recommendations for manuscript form in Section 18 of your Handbook. Because you have spent so much time and effort thus far, you will want to do your best job on revising your paper.

Long Quotations

If direct quotations are more than three typed lines long, indent them five spaces from both the left and the right margins. Single space each line and do not use quotation marks. If the quotation is the beginning of a paragraph in the source, indent the first word an additional two spaces.

Footnotes

Uses

1. To indicate source of material that is directly quoted
2. To give credit for other people's ideas even though you write them in your own words
3. To give the source of diagrams, figures, or statistics

Numbering

There are two common ways of numbering footnotes, both using Arabic numerals.

1. Consecutively throughout the paper, beginning with number 1 on the first page and ending with number 20 on the last page, if that is the total number of footnotes.

2. Numbering beginning over on each successive page: numbers 1 and 2 on the first page, numbers 1, 2, and 3 on the second

and successive pages. Check with your teacher to see which way he or she prefers.

Place the Arabic numerals slightly above the material to be footnoted, usually after the last word of a sentence or a direct quotation. For example:

```
     This same feeling was expressed by many Fed-
erals and Confederates. Bruce Catton, the Civil
War Historian, wrote that "the instinctive loy-
alty of all these men went...to the army."1
```

Position

Footnotes may appear in a paper in one of two ways: at the bottom of each page or on a separate page at the end. The actual form of each is the same.

If footnotes are to appear on each page, you must be careful to allow enough room at the bottom of each page for all the footnotes on that page. This will also include a one-inch margin of blank space at the bottom of each page.

When you have typed the last line of text on a page, skip a line. Then type a line that extends across the page, from the left margin to the right. Skip another space, and then type your first footnote. The bottom of your page will look like this:

```
     This same feeling was expressed by many Fed-
erals and Confederates. Bruce Catton, the Civil
War historian, wrote that "the instinctive loy-
alty of all of these men went...to the army."1
_________________________________________________

     1Bruce Catton, This Hallowed Ground, p. 360.
```

Form

1. Number each footnote with an Arabic numeral to correspond to the material in the text (See above).
2. Indent each footnote five spaces, just as you do for paragraphs. Observe the text margin at the right. If the footnote runs to a

second or third line, bring those lines back to the left margin.

[14]"Hypnotism Spots Epileptic Whose Fits Are Neurotic," Science News Letter, Vol. XX (May 13, 1970), p. 296.

3. Single space each footnote but double space between footnotes.
4. Place a period at the end of each footnote.
5. The first time a work is mentioned, the footnote should contain the author's first and last names, the title (magazines and book titles underlined to represent italics; articles and parts of works in quotation marks), the volume number (capitalize Vol. and put the number in capital Roman numerals), the date if the reference is a magazine, and the page or pages (in Arabic numerals).

[1]G. D. H. Cole, A Short History of the British Working Class Movement, Vol. III, p. 125.

[2]Robert A. Dahl, "Workers' Control of Industry and the British Labour Party," American Political Science Review, Vol. XLI (October, 1976), pp. 890–93.

6. To refer to sources already cited in previous footnotes in full form, use a shortened form for footnotes.

(a) To refer to a reference mentioned in the immediately preceding footnote, use *Ibid.*, the abbreviation for the Latin *ibidem*, meaning "in the same place." *Ibid* should be underlined because it is a foreign word. It can never be used as a first footnote on a page unless footnotes are numbered consecutively throughout a paper and an *Ibid.* just happens to refer to the preceding footnote which is on the preceding page. If the page number differs from that given above, place a comma after *Ibid.* and write the page number. The series of footnotes shown below demonstrate the proper form for this type of situation.

[15]Lawrence Battistini, _Japan and America_, p. 145.

[16]_Ibid_.

[17]_Ibid_., pp. 170-173.

(b) To refer to a work cited earlier in full form but not in the immediately preceding footnote, you should write the author's last name only and the page or pages.

[18]W. Pratt, "Japan and the Pacific Problem," _Newsweek_, Vol. XXXI (June 7, 1948), p. 22.

[19]Norton Ginsberg, _et al_., "What Future for the Japanese Economy?" _The Round Table_, Vol. DCCXVI (Dec. 16, 1971), p. 12.

[20]Pratt, p. 33.

Of course, if references by other authors with the same last name are used, you will also have to include the author's first name or initials.

If more than one work by the same author has been referred to, then you should write the author's last name and the title—in shortened form, if you desire.

[21]Thomas Hardy, _The Mayor of Casterbridge_, p. 56.

[22]Hardy, _Jude the Obscure_, p. 68.

[23]Hardy, _The Mayor_, p. 59.

If you refer to a reference with an extremely long title, you may use ellipses.

It is not necessary for identification purposes to give the complete title.

[24]Eva E. Dye, "Women's Part in the Drama of the Northwest," Transactions of the Twenty-second Annual Reunion of the Oregon Pioneer Association for 1894..., p. 42.

7. The last line of the last footnote in the paper should be one inch (6 spaces) from the bottom of the last page even though the text is not a full page.

Basic Forms for Footnotes

Books

1. One author:

[1]Robert Johnson, Battles and Leaders of the Civil War, Vol. II, p. 45.

2. Two authors:

[2]Otto Eisenschiml and Ralph Newman, The American Iliad, pp. 488–89.

3. Three authors:

[3]Otto U. Faulkner, Tyler Kepner, and Hall Bartlett, The American Way of Life--A History, p. 67.

4. Four or more authors. If you have more than three authors, you need list only the name of the first author and then use the abbreviation *et al.* (*et alii*), which means "and others":

[4]Rewey Belle Inglis et al., Adventures in English Literature, p. 57.

5. No author given. If you have a book with no author given, you start with the title:

[5]The Lottery, pp. 28–32.

6. If you wish to refer to a book written by an author using a pseudonym, you may supply the real name in parentheses:

[6]Mark Twain (S. L. Clemens), The Adventures of Huckleberry Finn, p. 20.

7. If you have an editor of a book, write the name followed by

(ed.). If you have two or more editors, write their names followed by (eds.):

[7]J. N. D. Anderson (ed.), The World's Religions, p. 143.

[7]J. E. Smith and E. W. Parks (eds.), The Great Critics, p. 143.

8. If you have a translator of an original work, put the name of the translator after the title of the book:

[8]Homer, The Odyssey, trans. E. V. Rieu, p. 129.

9. If you wish to note that you are using a particular edition of a book, put the information within parentheses:

[9]Sir Alan Gardiner, Egyptian Grammar (2d. ed. rev.), p. 27.

10. If you use a book or monograph that is part of a series, put the name of the series in quotes and, with other information, within parentheses:

[10]Virgil K. Whittaker, The Religious Basis of Spenser's Thought ("Stanford University Publications: Language and Literature," Vol. VII), p. 34.

11. If you wish to refer to only one volume with a special title that is part of a work of several volumes under one general title, list the author, title, and volume number, followed by the general title of the work:

[11]T. C. Chamberlin and R. D. Sailsbury, Geology, Vol. 1: Geologic Processes and Their Results (2d. ed. rev.), p. 153.

12. If you use a component part by one author of a larger work edited by other authors, list the particular author, the title of the part (in quotation marks), and then cite the title of the collection (underlined), followed by the names of the general editors:

[12]Roy P. Baler, "Psychological Pattern in 'The Love Song of J. Alfred Prufrock,'" Twentieth Century English, ed. William S. Knickerbocker, p. 384.

13. To refer to a volume of poems, write the name of the poet, the title of the poem in quotation marks, the title of the collection underlined, and the number of the page on which the poem appears:

[13]Edgar Lee Masters, "Ann Rutledge," Spoon River Anthology, p. 194.

14. Classical references. Books are indicated with small Roman numerals. If the classical work is not divided into books, all the divisions are indicated with Arabic numerals. There should be no punctuation between the author's name and the title of the work, and none after the title:

[14]Cicero Tusculanae disputationes ii. 2. 52–54.

[15]Aristotle Poetics 20. 35–37.

15. Scriptural references. The names of the books of the Bible, of the Apocrypha, and of the Apocalyptic, and the names of the versions of the Bible should be abbreviated when exact chapter and verse references are given. The names of the books should not be underlined:

[16]Acts 1: 1–3.

16. If you wish to refer to a book with several authors and more than one volume, write the names of the authors, the title of the book (underlined), the volume number, and page or pages:

    [17]Meriwether Lewis and William Clark, History of the Expedition of Captains Lewis and Clark, Vol. I, p. 291.

Magazines, Encyclopedias, Reports, Pamphlets, Newspapers

1. To refer to an article in a journal or periodical, give the author's name, the title of the article (in quotation marks), the name of the journal or magazine (underlined), the volume, if there is one, the date of issue, and the page or pages:

    [1]B. F. Trueblood, "Hague Conference and the Future of Arbitration," Atlantic Monthly, Vol. XCVII (June, 1906), p. 723.

    If an author's name is not given, put the title first:

    [2]"To End a Scandal," Time, Vol. LXXVII (May 26, 1971), p. 63.

2. To refer to an article in an encyclopedia, give the author's name, the title of the article, the name of the encyclopedia (underlined), volume and page:

    [3]Milton H. Erickson, "Hypnotism," Collier's Encyclopedia, Vol. X, p. 316.

    If an author's name is not given, put the title first:

[3]"Hypnotism," Collier's Encyclopedia, Vol. X, p. 316.

It is not necessary to give the names of the many editors of encyclopedias, such as the *Encyclopaedia Britannica*, but for a special encyclopedia with one editor, give the editor's name:

[4]E. E. Kellett, "Spinoza," Encyclopaedia of Religion and Ethics, ed. James Hastings, Vol. XI, p. 251.

3. If you wish to refer to a report or pamphlet, give the author's name, the title (underlined), the date and place of the report, and the pages:

[5]James W. Angell, Financial Foreign Policy of the U.S., A Report to the Second International Studies Conference on the State and Economic Life, London, May 29, 1933, pp. 8–10.

If the report is by an association rather than an author, start with the name of the association:

[6]American Medical Association, Medical Relations Under Workmen's Compensation, A Report Prepared by the Bureau of Medical Economics, p. 3.

4. To refer to an unsigned newspaper article, write the headline (in quotation marks), the name of the newspaper (underlined), the date, and the page. Sometimes the section and the column may also be given:

[7]"The Reading of Adults," Chicago Daily News, Aug. 6, 1975, p. 4.

[8]"The Influence of TV on Reading," The New York Times, Sept. 10, 1975, Sec. 4, p. 10.

Other Sources

1. To refer to an interview rather than a printed source, write the name of the person interviewed, the identification of the person, and the date:

    [9]Interview with Dr. Philip H. McDevitt, Superintendent of Evanston Township High School, Evanston, Illinois, May 15, 1977.

2. If you wish to refer to a letter that has not been published, write the name of the person who wrote the letter, the position he holds, and the date of the letter:

    [10]Letter from Hon. Jimmy Carter, President of the United States, Washington, D.C., May 22, 1977.

3. If you wish to refer to information in private files, put the name of the material and the place where it can be located:

    [11]Final Report on Plagiarism, by Clarence W. Hach and the Curriculum Committee of the English Department, Evanston Township High School,. May 23, 1961 (in the files of the English Department).

4. If you wish to refer to a thesis or dissertation, put the name of the author, title of work (in quotation marks), and the university where the work was completed, the date, and the page:

    [12]H. L. Reynolds, "The Number of Commas in Early Renaissance Poetry," (unpublished Ph.D. dissertation, Department of English, University of Chicago), p. 78.

5. When you wish to refer to a book review, include the name of the author of the work being reviewed, the title of the work, the name of the reviewer, the place where the review appeared, the date, the volume and the page:

    [13]Henry Aiken, "Review of The Moral Nature of Man," by A. Campbell Garnett, Ethics, Vol. LXIII (January, 1953), pp. 140–42.

6. When you wish to refer to a citation taken from a secondary source, write the name of the author and the title of the original source and the page and then the place where it was quoted:

    [14]Donald A. Stauffer, The Nature of Poetry, p. 58, quoted in Paul Engle and Warren Carrier, Reading Modern Poetry, p. 99.

Reference Words and Abbreviations Used in Footnotes

Here are some of the more common reference words and abbreviations used in footnotes.

bk., bks.	book or books
ca. (or *c.*)	*circa*, "about" or "near." Used with approximate dates: *ca.* 1776; "*ca.*" is preferable to "*c.*," which can also mean "chapter" or "copyright."
cf.	*confer*, "compare." Used, for example, when you wish to have your reader compare footnotes 22 and 23, which follow: *cf.* footnotes 22 and 23 or *cf. Ernest Hemingway, The Sun Also Rises*, p. 15.

c., ch., chs., (or chap., chaps.)	chapter(s)
col., cols.	column(s)
comp.	compiled or compiler
ed., eds.	editor(s), edition(s)
e.g.	*exempli gratia,* "for example"
esp.	especially (as in "pp. 208–232, esp. p. 220")
et al.	*et alii,* "and others"
et seq.	*et sequens* and *et sequentes,* "and the one following," "and those that follow." But cf. "f.," "ff."
ex., exs.	example and examples
f., ff.	and the following page(s) or line(s). These abbreviations are replacing *et. seq.*
fig., figs.	figure(s)
fn.	footnote (Cf. "n.")
ibid.	*ibidem,* "in the same place"; i.e., the single title cited in the note immediately preceding.
idem	(no period; sometimes *id.*) "the same." Used in place of *ibid.* when the footnote is to the same source on exactly the same page as that referred to in the note immediately preceding.
i.e.	*id est* "that is"
illus.	illustrated, illustrator, illustration(s)
l., ll.	line, lines
ms.	manuscript
mss.	manuscripts
n. or nn.	note or notes (as "p. 48, n. 2")

n.b., *N.B.*	nota bene, "note well"
n.d.	no date
no., nos.	number(s)
op. cit.	*opere citato*, "in the work cited." If several different items have come between the first mention of a book and a subsequent reference to it in a footnote, the last name of the author is repeated, followed by *op. cit.* and the correct page number.
p. or pp.	page(s)
par., pars.	paragraph(s)
passim	"throughout the work, here and there" (as pp. 79, 144, *et passim*)
pref.	preface
pseud.	pseudonym, a pen name: e.g., Mark Twain, pseud.
rev.	review, reviewed (by); revised (by), revision
sec. (or sect.), secs.	section(s)
ser.	series
sic	"thus, so" If the word "*sic*" in brackets [*sic*] is inserted in a quotation, it shows that you are recognizing and pointing out an error or a questionable statement. For example: "There were nine [*sic*] men on the bench at that time." Your own additions to quotations are shown by bracketing those words added: "He [Wouk] was a member of the New York Writers' Club."
st.	stanza
trans. (or tr.)	translator, translation, translated ("by" understood in context)
vol., vols.	volume(s)
vs.	*versus*, "against"; also verse

Exercise Writing the Final Draft with Footnotes

Write the final draft of your paper with the footnotes. Leave a three-inch margin at the top of your first page and number each page beginning with page 2. Reread your paper several times to check the following:

1. Does your introductory paragraph engage the reader? Is it well developed? Does it set forth the controlling purpose of your paper?
2. Does your paper follow your outline exactly? Is it well paragraphed? Do your ideas flow logically from sentence to sentence?
3. Are your paragraph transitions natural and logical?
4. Does your concluding paragraph sum up your ideas and restate your controlling purpose? Is it a logical result of what you set out to prove?
5. Have you numbered all the ideas and direct quotations in the text and footnoted them correctly?
6. Have you tested the force and accuracy of specific words? Do you have interesting sentence variety?
7. Have you checked spelling, punctuation, and usage?

Your final paper will be evidence of your intelligent understanding of your subject, your discrimination in research, your care in refining your paper, and your accuracy in footnote and bibliography form.

Part 8 Writing the Final Bibliography

Most research papers have at the end a bibliography, a list of references actually used in writing the paper. (Sources listed on your bibliography cards that were consulted but not referred to in the paper are not listed.) This bibliography serves two purposes: (1) it shows what research was done; (2) it provides a list of references for those who may be especially interested in your topic and wish to investigate it further.

In preparing your bibliography, arrange all of the items alphabetically by the last name of the author. If no author or editor is given, the first word of the title (ignoring *A*, *An*, or *The*) determines the order.

Use the following forms for the different types of entries.

1. For a book—one author:

Morris, Wright. Plains Song. New York: Harper and Row, 1980.

2. For a book—more than one author:

Strunk, William, and E. B. White. The Elements of Style. Toronto, Canada: Macmillan, 1959.

3. For a book—compiled by an editor:

Gold, Robert S. (ed.). Point of Departure. New York: Dell, 1972.

4. For a book—only one chapter used:

Wilson, J. Dover. "The Theatre," Life in Shakespeare's England. Middlesex, England: Penguin, 1970, pp. 197-237.

5. For a magazine article—author given:

Wills, Garry. "The Impeachment Man." Atlantic Monthly, Vol. 233 (May, 1974), pp. 79-84.

6. For a magazine article—no author given—alphabetized by title:

"Open Secret," Newsweek, Vol. XXI (Jan. 11, 1973), pp. 62-63.

Treat pamphlets or reports like magazine articles unless no author is given; then use the following form:

7. For a pamphlet or report—no author given:

American Medical Association. Medical Relations Under Workmen's Compensation, a Report Prepared by the Bureau of Medical Economics. Chicago: American Medical Association, 1976.

8. For an encyclopedia article—author given:

Baines, Anthony Cuthbert. "Bagpipes," Encyclopaedia Britannica, Vol. 2 (1968), pp. 1036-37.

9. For an encyclopedia article—no author given—alphabetized by title:

"Sarah Lawrence College," Collier's Encyclopedia, Vol. 20 (1968), p. 427.

10. For a newspaper article—no byline—alphabetized by title:

"Making the Most of Your Summer," Chicago Tribune, June 15, 1976, p. 56.

11. For a newspaper article—byline given:

Smith, John Justin, "Seeking the Trail of Jesus," Chicago Daily News, April 13-14, 1974, Sec. 2, pp. 19-20.

12. For a bibliographic entry for a casebook:

Marcus, Mordecai. "The Unity of The Red Badge of Courage," Stephen Crane's The Red Badge of Courage: Text and Criticism, eds. Richard Lettis, Robert F. McDonnell and William E. Morris. New York: Harcourt, Brace, 1970, pp. 189-95.

13. For non-print material:

"Shakespeare's Stratford," 76 frames, color with teaching guide, Literary Backgrounds, n.d.

14. For a book containing an article that first appeared in another source which is to be acknowledged:

Van Ghent, Dorothy. "On Pride and Prejudice," Pride and Prejudice: An Authoritative Text, Backgrounds, Reviews and Essays in Criticism, ed. Donald J. Gray. New York: Norton, 1971, pp. 362–73. Reprinted from Dorothy Van Ghent, The English Novel, Form and Function, New York: Holt, Rinehart, 1959, pp. 105–23.

Here are a few miscellaneous rules to follow.

1. If there are any facts of translation, editions, series, volumes, and the like, they should come immediately after the title, each item separated by a comma.
2. If the publication date is not given on the title page of a book, the copyright date should be used.
3. Page numbers are given only for articles from encyclopedias and periodicals and for single chapters from books.
4. Each entry should be single-spaced, and there should be a double space between entries.
5. The second and following lines of each entry should be indented five spaces so that the last name of the author stands out. This is exactly the opposite of footnote form.
6. Put a period at the end of each entry.
7. If you have two references by the same author, you need not repeat the author's name. A straight line will be sufficient:

Randolph, Vance. Ozark Mountain Folks. New York: The Vanguard Press, Inc., 1972.

______. Ozark Superstitions. New York: The Columbia University Press, 1977.

8. A bibliography may be divided into different classes in order to point out the types of sources used: books, pamphlets, periodicals, encyclopedias, and miscellaneous. In this plan, center each heading and arrange the sources alphabetically.
9. If no author is given, the entry should be alphabetized by the first important word of the title.

Here is a sample bibliography divided into different classes.

BIBLIOGRAPHY

Books

Anouilh, Jean. *The Lark*, tr. by Christopher Fry. London: Oxford University Press, 1956.

Fry, Christopher. *A Phoenix Too Frequent*. London: Oxford University Press, 1951.

Grierson, S. H. J. G. *Metaphysical Lyrics and Poems of the Seventeenth Century*. Oxford: Clarendon Press, 1961.

Rothe, Anna (ed.) *Current Biography*. New York: H. W. Wilson Co., 1977.

______. *Christopher Fry, An Appreciation*. London and New York: Peter Nevill Ltd., 1977.

Thor, with Angels. London: Oxford University Press, 1971.

Thrall, William Flint and Addison Hibbard. *A Handbook to Literature*. New York: Odyssey Press, 1966.

Whiting, B. J., *et al*. (eds.) *The College Survey of English Literature*. New York: Harcourt, Brace and Co., 1952.

Periodicals

Brown, John Mason. "Seeing Things," *Saturday Review of Literature*, Vol. XXXIII (Dec. 2, 1950), pp. 44-46.

______. "Theatre: Two Ladies," *New Republic*, Vol. LXXIII (Nov. 27, 1950), p. 22.

Downes, Mollie Panter. "Letters From London," *New Yorker*, Vol. XXIV (Feb. 11, 1970), p. 85.

"Enter Poet Laughing," _Time_, Vol. LVI (Nov. 20, 1970), p. 10.

Hobson, Harold. "Poetic Drama Ascendent," _Christian Science Monitor_, (March 25, 1970), Magazine Section, p. 10.

Willis, James R., Jr. "The Metaphysical Lyric," _Interpretations of The Lark_, ed. William O. Matterly. New York: Morgan Publishing Co., 1975, pp. 91–103. Reprinted from _The American Intellect_, Vol. X (Spring, 1971), pp. 16–30.

Unpublished Material

Lundgren, Ralph. "The Boy with a Cart," A production thesis, Washington University, August, 1974.

Shank, Jon Beck. "Saints in Question," A poetry play with preface. Unpublished Master's thesis, Department of English, Brigham Young University, June, 1973.

Other Sources

______. Personal interview with Christopher Fry, Playwright, London, England, May 22, 1970.

______. Letter from Christopher Fry, Playwright, London, England, June 10, 1971.

Exercise **Writing the Final Bibliography**

Following the correct form for your entires, prepare your final bibliography. Assemble your research paper in the following order.

1. Title page in whatever correct form your teacher requires
2. Page containing title at top, statement of controlling purpose beneath it, followed by your final outline
3. The text of your paper
4. The final bibliography

THE REALISM

OF

HENRY FLEMING

IN

STEPHEN CRANE'S

THE RED BADGE OF COURAGE

by

Craig Pirrong

[The following is a high school student's complete research paper. Use it as a model for preparing your own paper.]

3 English H
Mrs. Ichkoff
March 8

The Realism of Henry Fleming in Stephen Crane's *The Red Badge of Courage*

Controlling Purpose: to demonstrate that Henry Fleming, the protagonist of Stephen Crane's *The Red Badge of Courage*, is an accurate portrayal of a Civil War soldier by comparing him with actual soldiers through their letters and diaries.

I. A comparison of war experience
   A. Memoirs of actual Civil War soldiers
   B. Experiences of soldiers in *The Red Badge of Courage*
II. Soldiers' attitudes toward battle
   A. Risks of combat
   B. Fear of cowardice
   C. Nervousness before battle
III. Soldiers' change in attitude during battle
   A. Sense of urgency
   B. Feeling of rage
   C. Emergence of unity of purpose
      1. Abandonment of self
      2. Loyalty to army
IV. Problems of desertion
   A. Mental struggle
   B. Physical exhaustion
   C. Rationalizations
V. Differences between expectations and actualities of battle
   A. Physical
   B. Mental
VI. Growing maturity of soldiers
   A. Coping with stress
   B. Attitude toward death
VII. The reality of war experience
   A. In the Civil War
   B. In *The Red Badge of Courage*

Stephen Crane's The Red Badge of Courage was the first novel to explore the real feelings of a soldier going into action for the first time. Before The Red Badge, American fiction concerning the Civil War concentrated on the heroic deeds of soldiers and was marked by over-glorification and inaccuracy. However, the letters and diaries of actual Civil War soldiers reveal that these soldiers were more concerned with their feelings than their deeds. By examining the memoirs of Civil War soldiers and comparing them with experiences in The Red Badge, one can see that Stephen Crane's novel is an accurate portrayal of the reality of a soldier's emotions and resulting actions during the war.

Henry Fleming, the protagonist in The Red Badge, like many actual Civil War soldiers, feared the consequences of an impending battle. Henry thought that "as far as war was concerned he knew nothing of himself."[1] He also thought that "the only way to prove himself was to go into the blaze, and then figuratively to watch his legs to discover their merits and faults."[2] Many Civil War soldiers had the same feelings as Henry. Bell Wiley, a historian who has done extensive research on the Common Private of the Civil War, wrote that soldiers were more concerned with the question of how they would stand up in battle than they were over the chance of being wounded or killed.[3] One private wrote, "'I have a marked dread of the battle field, for I...have never seen a person die...& I am afraid

---

[1]Stephen Crane, The Red Badge of Courage, in The Complete Novels of Stephen Crane, ed. Thomas A. Gullason, p. 206.

[2]Ibid., p. 209.

[3]Bell Irvin Wiley, The Life of Billy Yank, p. 68.

that the groans of the wounded & dying will make me shake nevertheless I hope & trust that strength will be given me to stand & do my duty.'"[4]

The methods that soldiers devised to avoid battle or to alleviate their doubts about their courage were many. Some would self-inflict wounds; others would leave the front on the pretense of a broken musket, helping a wounded comrade, being ordered to do some special task by an officer, illness or a "call of nature." Many never returned.[5] Like Henry, some soldiers tried to relieve their fear of battle by calculating the odds of their being hit or their chances of running. Officers, as well as common soldiers, computed the risks of combat. Before the Battle of Perryville, three brigade commanders discussed the chances of their getting hit and of their troops' running. The generals predicted that their troops would stay and fight and that they themselves would not be hit, but all three were killed and their brigades were routed.[6] Like Henry's own calculations, the officers' calculations were wrong.

Some soldiers tried to hide their fear and go into the fight as bravely as possible. One of these real soldiers was Elbridge Capp. Like Henry, who felt that he had to "go into the blaze," Elbridge said to himself, "'I must face the danger.'"[7] Others resolved to let death solve their

---

[4]Bell Irvin Wiley, The Common Soldier of the Civil War, p. 56.

[5]Wiley, Billy Yank, p. 86.

[6]James M. Hillard, "'You Are Strangely Deluded': General William Terrill," Civil War Times Illustrated, Vol. XIII (February, 1975), p. 18.

[7]Elbridge Capp, Reminiscences of the War of the Rebellion, p. 135.

problems. One of these soldiers said, "'I'm willin ter die ...but I don't want ter be no coward.'"[8] Another private, Sam Watkins, said, "I had made up my mind to die."[9] Henry had these same feelings, thinking "that it would be better to get killed directly and end his troubles."[10] He thought it better to "fall facing the enemy, than to play the coward."[11]

The descriptions of Henry's feelings immediately before and during battle were consistent with the accounts of both Federal and Confederate soldiers. Before facing fire for the first time, Henry was "in a fever of impatience."[12] Most soldiers experienced this same feeling. One wrote that nothing "brings...such crucial trial as the throbbing emotions that immediately precede the clash of arms."[13] Another private said that "the knowledge of an impending battle always sent that thrill of fear and horror."[14]

Once the firing started, however, Henry's feelings, as well as those of most soldiers, changed. Henry had been advised that a man changed in battle, and he found it was true.[15] Before he went into action, Henry's main concern was for himself. After the battle opened in earnest, however, his outlook changed: "He suddenly lost concern

---

[8]William Hinman, Si Klegg and His Pard, p. 400.

[9]Sam R. Watkins, Co. Aytch, p. 234.

[10]Crane, p. 220.

[11]Wiley, Billy Yank, p. 68.

[12]Crane, p. 219.

[13]Hinman, p. 339.

[14]Capp, p. 140.

[15]Crane, p. 219.

for himself, and forgot to look at a menacing fate."[16] He became an automaton.

> He was at a task. He was like a carpenter who has made many boxes, making still another box, only there was furious haste in his movements. . .
> Following this came a red rage. He developed the acute exasperation of a pestered animal, a well-meaning cow worried by dogs. His impotency appeared to him, and made his rage into that of a driven beast.[17]

Civil war veterans' reminiscences echo Henry's change from fear to indifference, rage and urgency. One private wrote, "'Strange as it may seam to you, but the more men I saw killed the more reckless I became.'"[18] Henry Morton Stanley, the famous explorer, also described this feeling of urgency. He wrote, "We plied our arms, loaded, and fired, with such nervous haste as though it depended on each of us how soon this fiendish uproar would be hushed."[19] Oliver Norton, a Pennsylvania infantryman wrote, "I acted like a madman.... The feeling that was uppermost in my mind was a desire to kill as many rebels as I could."[20] A third soldier, like Henry, wished to grapple face to face with his enemies: "'I was mad...;how I itched for a hand-to-hand struggle.'"[21]

Gradually a feeling of unity—oneness—with the army, the corps, the regiment manifested itself in both the

---

[16] Ibid., p. 225.

[17] Ibid., pp. 225-226.

[18] Wiley, Billy Yank, p. 71.

[19] Henry Morton Stanley, "Henry Stanley Fights with the Dixie Grays at Shiloh," The Blue and the Gray, Vol. I, ed. H.S. Commager, p. 354.

[20] Oliver Norton, Army Letters, p. 91.

[21] Wiley, Billy Yank, p. 72.

average Civil War private and in Henry Fleming. Throughout The Red Badge Henry calls himself "part of a vast blue demonstration."[22] When he first came under fire, Henry thought that

> He became not a man but a member. He felt that something of which he was a part—a regiment, an army, a cause, or a country—was in a crisis. He was welded into a common personality which was dominated by a single desire. For some moments he could not flee, no more than a little finger can commit a revolution from a hand.
>
> There was a consciousness always of the presence of his comrades about him. He felt the subtle battle brotherhood more potent even than the cause for which they were fighting. It was a mysterious fraternity born of the smoke and danger of death.[23]

This same feeling was expressed by many Federals and Confederates. Bruce Catton, the Civil War historian, wrote that "the instinctive loyalty of all of these men went... to the army."[24] Henry Morton Stanley wrote that, "there were about four hundred companies like the Dixie Greys, who shared our feelings."[25] Sergeant Thomas H. Evans, a member of the regular army, said that an "abandonment of self"[26] emerged in battle. At the surrender of the Army of Northern Virginia, one private, "unwilling to outlive his army,"[27]

---

[22]Crane, p. 205.

[23]Ibid., p. 225

[24]Bruce Catton, This Hallowed Ground, p. 360.

[25]Stanley, p. 354.

[26]Thomas H. Evans, "'There is no use trying to dodge shot,'" Civil War Times Illustrated, Vol. VI (August, 1967), p. 43.

[27]William C. Davis, "The Campaign to Appomattox," Civil War Times Illustrated, Vol. XIV (August, 1975), p. 40.

shouted, "'Blow, Gabriel, blow!'"[28] These loyalties became "more potent even than the cause for which they were fighting."[29]

On the other hand, flight from the field of battle was not uncommon to Civil War soldiers. In fact, "there was a considerable amount of malingering, skulking, and running in every major battle."[30] Henry's own reasons for running were similar to those of many who fled from an actual battle. When the Confederates charged for the second time, Henry ran. He saw "a revelation."[31] When he fled, "There was no shame on his face."[32] A soldier in the Twelfth Connecticut was much like Henry. William DeForest described the soldier in these terms: "He did not look wild with fright; he simply looked alarmed and resolved to get out of danger;... he was confounded by the peril of the moment and thought of nothing but getting away from it."[33]

Soldiers who fled from the field of battle were generally beset with a conflict between their bodies and their souls. When the Rebels charged for the second time, Henry was exhausted and dismayed. "He seemed to shut his eyes and wait to be gobbled."[34] William Hinman echoed Henry's feelings, saying that a soldier had to

---

[28]Ibid.

[29]Crane, p. 225.

[30]Wiley, Common Soldier, p. 26.

[31]Crane, p. 230.

[32]Ibid.

[33]John William DeForest, A Volunteer's Adventures, p. 63.

[34]Crane, p. 230.

> ...go through the struggle...between his mental and physical natures. The instinct of the latter at such a time—and what soldier does not know it?—was to seek a place of safety, without a moment's delay. To fully subdue this feeling by the power of will was not... such an easy a matter as might be imagined....Some there were who could never do it.[35]

Soldiers who ran usually tried to rationalize their actions. Henry thought that he had been right in running because he

> ...was a little piece of the army. He considered the time, he said, to be one in which it was the duty of every little piece to rescue itself if possible. Later the officers could fit the little pieces together again, and make a battle front. If none of the little pieces were wise enough to save themselves from the flurry of death at such a time, why, then, where would be the army? It was all plain that he had proceeded according to very correct and commendable rules.[36]

Henry again tried to demonstrate to himself that he was right by "throwing a pine cone at a jovial squirrel."[37] When the youth saw that the squirrel fled rather than let the missile strike him, Henry felt that, "Nature had given him a sign."[38]

Actual combatants who ran from battle gave somewhat less symbolic and complicated, yet similar, excuses. George Townsend, a hospital steward, stumbled on a group of skulkers at the Battle of Cedar Mountain and recorded:

> Some of these miserable wretches...muttered that they were not to be hood-winked and slaughtered.
> "I was sick, anyway," said one fellow, "and felt like droppin' on the road."

---

[35]Hinman, p. 398.

[36]Crane, p. 233.

[37]Crane, p. 234.

[38]*Ibid.*, p. 235.

> "I didn't trust my colonel," said another; "he ain't no soldier."
>
> "I'm tired of the war, anyhow," said a third, "and my time's up soon; so I shan't have my head blown off."[39]

One soldier who deserted his comrades at the Battle of Corinth said on his return that he had not run, but had been detailed to guard a water tank. His comrades never let him live it down.[40] Another soldier, nicknamed "Spinney," said he had run because he thought that the bullets were calling his name.[41]

Henry found battle time to be very different from what he had conceived it would be. At first, he "had the belief that real war was a series of death struggles with small time in between for sleep and meals."[42] He learned later, however, that battle took up very little time in a soldier's life.[43] He also thought that "Secular and religious education had obliterated the throat-grappling instinct."[44] However, when the Confederates were attacking for the first time, and Henry "wished to rush forward and strangle with his fingers,"[45] he realized that this thought was wrong, too.

---

[39]George A. Townsend, "A Camp of Skulkers at Cedar Mountain." The Blue and the Gray, Vol. I, ed. H.S. Commager, p. 493.

[40]Wiley, Billy Yank, pp. 87-88.

[41]Warren Lee Goss, "Yorktown and Williamsburg," Battles and Leaders of the Civil War, Vol. II, eds. Robert U. Johnson and Clarence C. Buel, p. 197.

[42]Crane, p. 205.

[43]Ibid.

[44]Ibid.

[45]Ibid., p. 225.

Many actual soldiers also experienced a difference between their expectations and the realities of battle. Henry Morton Stanley wrote, "It was the first Field of Glory I had seen in my May of life, and the first time that Glory sickened me with its repulsive aspect, and made me suspect it was all a glittering lie."[46] Sam Watkins wrote, "I had heard and read of battlefields...but I must confess that I never realized the 'pomp and circumstance' of the thing called glorious war until I saw this."[47] Some were so naive about the realities of war that they were surprised that the enemy was firing bullets.[48] This difference between the untrained soldiers' image of war and the realities of combat was well portrayed in The Red Badge of Courage.

Under the stress of combat, both Henry Fleming and many actual Civil War soldiers rapidly matured. Henry's attainment of maturity was both quick and dramatic. Early in The Red Badge, Henry felt the need to make excuses to escape the reality of his cowardice, but by the end of the book, Henry was able to look upon his feats, both bad and good, objectively. He thought that "He could look back upon the brass and bombast of his earlier gospels and see them truly."[49] Earlier, when Henry had been walking with a wounded soldier called the tattered man, Henry felt guilty and embarrassed because he himself had no wound, while everyone around him had a "red badge of courage."[50] To escape his guilt and embarrassment, Henry ran from the

---

[46]Stanley, p. 357.

[47]Watkins, p. 42.

[48]Ibid. and Stanley, p. 353.

[49]Crane, p. 298.

[50]Ibid., p. 240.

tattered man, feeling that he "could have strangled"[51] his wounded companion. By the end of The Red Badge, however, Henry realized that the tattered man had actually been trying to help him, and he felt guilty for deserting this man who had cared for him and aided him.[52] When Henry had outgrown the selfishness of immaturity, he could finally say of himself that "He was a man."[53]

Henry's attainment of maturity was common to many adolescent soldiers. Bell Wiley wrote, "One of the most interesting things about the boy soldiers was the speed with which they matured under the stress and strain of army life."[54] Sam Watkins, a Confederate private, wrote that early in the war "we wanted to march off and whip twenty Yankees. But we soon found that the glory of war was at home with the ladies, not upon the field of blood and...death.... I might say the agony of mind were very different indeed from the patriotic times at home."[55] One soldier wrote:

> With the new troops, they have not been called on to train or restrain their nerves. They are not only nervous, but they blanch at the thought of danger.... What to them, on joining the service, was a terrible mental strain, is soon transformed into indifference.[56]

This view of the experience of war is also similar to Henry's. Before Henry had attained his maturity, he was nervous and afraid of how the strain of battle and the

---

[51]Ibid., p. 245.

[52]Ibid., p. 297.

[53]Ibid., p. 298.

[54]Wiley, Billy Yank, p. 301.

[55]Watkins, p. 21.

[56]Frank Holsinger, "How It Feels To Be Under Fire," The Blue and the Gray, Vol. I, ed. H.S. Commager, p. 308.

thought of death would affect him. After he had "become a man," however, Henry could say matter-of-factly that "He had been to touch the great death, and found that, after all, it was but the great death."[57]

Henry's final understanding of the meaning of life and death has emerged from his experiences during war. His diverse emotional experiences, his growth to maturity, and his eventual feeling of unity with his comrades all parallel the experiences that actual Civil war soldiers have recorded in their letters and diaries. These parallel experiences reveal that The Red Badge of Courage is an accurate representation of real life under the conditions of the Civil War.

---

[57]Crane, p. 298.

BIBLIOGRAPHY

Books

Capp, Elbridge. Reminiscences of the War of the Rebellion. Nashua, New Hampshire: The Telegraph Publishing Co., 1911.

Catton, Bruce. This Hallowed Ground. Garden City, New York: Doubleday and Co., Inc., 1956.

Crane, Stephen. The Red Badge of Courage, in The Complete Novels of Stephen Crane. Ed. Thomas A. Gullason. Garden City, New York: Doubleday and Co., Inc., 1967.

DeForest, John William. A Volunteer's Adventures. New Haven, Connecticut: Yale University Press, 1946.

Hinman, William. Si Klegg and His Pard. Cleveland: N. G. Hamilton and Co., 1892.

Holsinger, Frank. "How It Feels To Be Under Fire." The Blue and the Gray. Vol. I. Ed. H.S. Commager. Indianapolis: Bobbs-Merrill Co., Inc., 1950.

Johnson, Robert U. and Clarence C. Buel. (eds.) Battles and Leaders of the Civil War. Vol. II. New York: Thomas Yoseloff, Inc., 1956.

Norton, Oliver. Army Letters. Chicago: O.C. Deming Co., 1903.

Stanley, Henry Morton. "Henry Morton Stanley Fights with the Dixie Grays at Shiloh." The Blue and the Gray. Vol. I. Ed. H.S. Commager. Indianapolis: Bobbs-Merrill Co., Inc., 1950.

Townsend, George. "A Camp of Skulkers at Cedar Mountain." The Blue and The Gray. Vol. I. Ed. H.S. Commager. Indianapolis: Bobbs-Merrill Co., Inc., 1950.

Watkins, Sam R. Co. Aytch. New York: The Macmillan Co., 1962.

Wiley, Bell Irvin. The Common Soldier of the Civil War. Gettysburg: Historical Times Inc., 1973.

Wiley, Bell Irvin. The Life of Billy Yank. Indianapolis: The Bobbs-Merrill Co., Inc., 1951.

Periodicals

Davis, William C. "The Campaign to Appomattox," Civil War Times Illustrated, Vol. XIV (April 1975), p. 40.

Evans, Thomas H. "'There is no use trying to dodge shot,'" Civil War Times Illustrated, Vol. VI (August 1967), p. 43.

Hillard, James M. "'You Are Strangely Deluded': General William Terrill," Civil War Times Illustrated, Vol. XIII (February 1975), p. 18.

Chapter 15

The Library and Its Reference Materials

Knowing how to use library resources efficiently is an asset to every student. Whether you do research in literature, history, science, or other disciplines, the library is an indispensable tool.

To make effective use of the library, however, it is necessary for you to know (1) how books are classified and arranged, and (2) how to use the card catalog.

Reference books are also a valuable source of information. They include dictionaries, encyclopedias, almanacs, catalogs, atlases, biographical reference books, literary reference books, and magazines.

This chapter will give you the basic information you need to make the best use of the library.

Part 1 The Classification and Arrangement of Books

Finding any book you need requires a knowledge of how books are classified and how they are arranged on the shelves.

The Classification of Books

Fiction. Works of fiction (novels and anthologies of short stories) are usually arranged in alphabetical order by author. When there are two or more books written by the same author, you would find them shelved alphabetically by title. For example, Ray Bradbury's books would be found under *B*. His *Dandelion Wine* and *Fahrenheit 451* would be followed by *Martian Chronicles*.

Nonfiction. Most libraries—including high school libraries—use the Dewey Decimal System, named for its originator, the American librarian, Melvil Dewey. There are ten major classifications in the Dewey Decimal System; all books fit into one of these classifications.

THE TEN MAJOR CLASSIFICATIONS ARE THESE:

000–099 **General Works** (encyclopedias, handbooks, almanacs, etc.)
100–199 **Philosophy** (includes psychology, ethics, etc.)
200–299 **Religion** (the Bible, mythology)
300–399 **Social Science** (sociology, economics, government, education, law, folklore)
400–499 **Language** (languages, grammars, dictionaries)
500–599 **Science** (mathematics, chemistry, physics, biology, etc.)
600–699 **Useful Arts** (farming, cooking, sewing, nursing, engineering, radio, television, gardening, inventions)

700–799 **Fine Arts** (music, painting, drawing, acting, photography, games, sports, amusements)
800–899 **Literature** (poetry, plays, essays)
900–999 **History** (biography, travel, geography)

As you can see from the major categories of the Dewey Decimal System, each discipline has a classification number. For example, all books on the fine arts are classified between 700 and 799, and all history books will be found between 900 and 999. The system becomes more detailed as each of these major groups is subdivided. The table below subdivides works in literature as follows:

800–899 Literature	810 American literature
810 American literature	811 Poetry
820 English literature	812 Drama
830 German literature	813 Fiction
840 French literature	814 Essays
850 Italian literature	815 Speeches
860 Spanish literature	816 Letters
870 Latin literature (classic)	817 Satire and Humor
880 Greek literature (classic)	818 Miscellany
890 Other literature	819 Canadian-English literature

The numbers in a particular classification combined with the letter of the author's last name make up the **call number.** The call number helps you locate the book on the shelf once you have found it in the card catalog.

Arrangement of Books on the Shelves

You can see that books are arranged numerically on the library's shelves in order of classification. Most libraries prominently mark their shelves with the numbers indicating the books to be found in each particular section. Like fiction books, nonfiction books are arranged alphabetically by authors' last names under their subject classification.

Biographies are one of the most popular kinds of books in libraries. The Dewey Decimal System division for them is 920. However, large libraries will often place biographies in a separate section because of the large number of these books. In this case, they will have a "B" on the spine of the book and on the catalog card. If you are looking for a particular biography and are unable to locate it, ask the librarian for assistance.

Reference Books are located in the library's reference room or area. They are categorized in the Dewey Decimal System and often with the letter "R" or "Ref" above the classification number. Usually, a reference book may not be checked out from the library.

Exercise The Classification and Arrangement of Books

Using the Dewey Decimal Classification summary on pages 308 and 309, assign the correct classification number to each of the following books.

1. *The Book of Jazz*, by Leonard Feather
2. *Ancient Greece*, by Roger Green
3. *Economics and the Public Purpose*, by John Kenneth Galbraith
4. *The Concise Oxford Dictionary of Current English*, ed. J. B. Sykes
5. *The Treasury of House Plants*, by Rob Herwig
6. *Law and Everyday Life*, by Elinor Swiger
7. *Decisive Battles of the Civil War*, by Joseph Mitchell
8. *Fireside Book of Humorous Poetry*, ed. William Cole
9. *The Teenager and Psychology*, by Robert Gelinas
10. *Camping and Woodcraft*, by Horace Kephart
11. *Masters of the Drama*, by John Gassner
12. *Handbook of the World's Religions*, by A. M. Zehavi
13. *Explorations in Chemistry*, by Charles Gray
14. *Highlights of the Olympics*, by John Durant
15. *Tomorrow's Math*, by C. Stanley Ogilvy

Part 2 Using the Card Catalog

The **card catalog** will determine whether the library has the book you want and, if so, where you will find it. The card catalog is a cabinet of small drawers or file trays containing alphabetically arranged cards. Each card bears the title of the book and the classification or call number of the book. (Sample cards are found below and on page 312.)

There are usually three cards for the same book in the card catalog. These are the *author card*, the *title card*, and the *subject card*. The convenience of having three different ways of finding a book is described here.

The Author Card. Perhaps you are writing a paper on women. Narrowing your topic to one American woman, you choose to investigate a source on the subject by Charles W. Akers. You look up his name in the card catalog and find that the author card will appear like this:

BA
2111A

Akers, Charles W.

Abigail Adams: an American Woman/by Charles W. Akers. Boston: Little, Brown [1980]
207 p.: ill

Bibliography and index

Author cards for all books by an author will be filed together alphabetically according to title. Books *by* an author are followed by books **about** an author.

The Title Card. If you know the title of a book but not the author's name, the title card will help you locate the book. Look in the card catalog for a card bearing the title at the top of the card.

The place of the title card in the catalog is determined by the first letter of the first word in the title. (*A*, *An*, and *The* do not count as first words.)

BA
2111A

Abigail Adams: an American Woman

Abigail Adams: an American
Woman/by Charles W. Akers.
Boston: Little, Brown [1980]
207 p.: ill

Bibliography and index

The Subject Card. In your investigation of Abigail Adams you may not have a particular book in mind. However, you suspect there are many books on your particular subject. In the card catalog you will find a subject card similar to this:

BA
2111A

ADAMS, ABIGAIL (SMITH), 1744–1818

Abigail Adams: an American
Woman/by Charles W. Akers.
Boston: Little, Brown [1980]
207 p.: ill

Bibliography and index

Subject cards are most useful when you want information on a specific topic from a variety of sources. Cards for all books on a particular subject are cataloged together. The subject card may also indicate that a book has chapters on a single aspect of the topic you are interested in, and the publication date on the card will help you find the most up-to-date book on your subject.

The Information on Catalog Cards

The three types of catalog cards—author, title, subject—carry the same information.

1. The call number
2. The title, author, publisher, and date of publication
3. The number of pages, and a notation on whether the book has illustrations, maps, tables, or other features

Cross Reference Cards

Occasionally, while researching a particular subject, you will find a card that reads *See* or *See also*. The "See" card refers you to another subject heading in the catalog that will give you the information you want.

```
Conservation of energy resources

          see

Energy conservation
```

The "See also" card refers you to other subjects closely related to the one you are interested in. This card may be helpful to you in making sure that your research on a particular topic is complete.

Compare the cross reference cards and see how they both will be beneficial to you in doing thorough research on a topic.

```
Energy conservation

      see also

Energy policy
Solar energy
Waste heat
```

Guide Cards

Besides the catalog cards, you will find guide cards in the cabinet trays. The guide card bears a tab that projects above the other cards. It will aid you in finding other catalog cards quickly. For example, in researching the topic of television advertising, you will find catalog cards easily by means of alphabetically arranged guide cards like these:

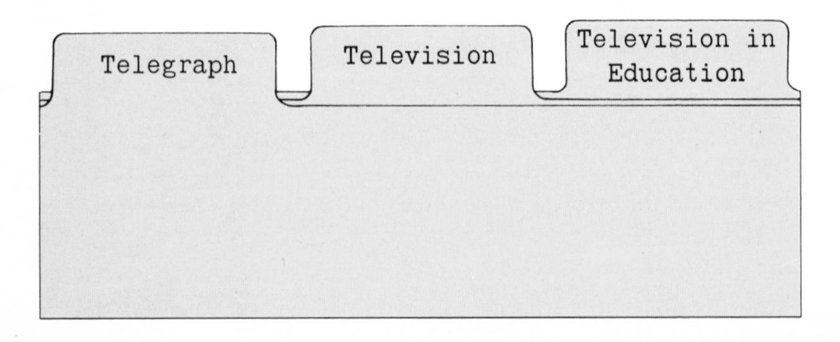

Exercise Using the Card Catalog

Use the card catalog to find the author, title, and call number of a book on the following subjects.

1. A history of Western music
2. A book about motorcycles
3. A novel on frontier and pioneer life
4. A collection of Greek myths
5. A book on Chinese cooking
6. A dictionary of usage and style
7. A book on playing chess
8. A book on the discovery of North America
9. A book showing how to draw maps
10. A biography of Henri Matisse
11. A source book of medieval history
12. A book of personal narratives of slaves
13. A history of firearms
14. A book on educational tests and measurements
15. A novel by William Faulkner

Part 3 Using Reference Materials

One of the best ways to obtain information on a particular topic is to consult a reference work. Libraries have either a reference section or a reference room. It is here that you will find just about everything you want, from a *Newsweek* article that reviews a recently published novel to a college catalog from a local junior college.

Reference works include the following: dictionaries; encyclopedias; pamphlets, handbooks, and catalogs; almanacs and yearbooks; atlases; biographical reference books; literary reference books; and magazines.

Reference works are tools, and like tools, should be used in definite ways. Most reference works have prefaces that describe how information is arranged, show sample entries, and explain the symbols and abbreviations used in the book. Before using any reference work for the first time, you would be wise to skim the preface.

The basic types of reference books are described in this section.

Dictionaries

The most widely used reference books in the library are the general dictionaries. General dictionaries fall into three major categories:

1. **Unabridged** dictionaries are dictionaries with over 250,000 entries.
2. **"College"** or **"desk" dictionaries** generally carry 130,000 to 150,000 entries.
3. **Concise** or **"pocket"** dictionaries are those with a smaller number of entries.

Unabridged Dictionaries. An unabridged dictionary may contain up to 500,000 words. It gives uncommon as well as common meanings of many words, and explains in detail how they are used. The best known unabridged dictionaries are the following:

Webster's Third New International Dictionary
The Random House Dictionary of the English Language, Unabridged Edition

You will find at least one—if not both—of these in your school or community library.

College or Desk Dictionaries. A college or desk dictionary is a quick and convenient reference. It provides information you would normally need about definitions, spellings, pronunciations, and matters of usage. It usually contains a special section that gives biographical information about well known people, and articles on such topics as pronunciation, spelling, and dialects.

Your school or local library probably carries several different college dictionaries. The best known are these:

The American Heritage Dictionary of the English Language
The Macmillan Dictionary

The Random House Dictionary of the English Language, College Edition
Thorndike-Barnhart Dictionary
Webster's New Collegiate Dictionary
Webster's New World Dictionary of the American Language

Dictionaries About Language. Another group of dictionaries is available to you. Each of these deals with a specific aspect of our English language: synonyms and antonyms, rhymes, slang, Americanisms, etymology, and so forth.

As a young writer, you need to be concerned with precision in your writing. A help in finding the precise word you are looking for is a **thesaurus,** or dictionary of synonyms.

A thesaurus should be used only as a "memory-jogger," to help you find words that are already in your vocabulary. You are treading on dangerous ground if you select from a thesaurus a word you do not know in place of a word you do know. From your study of Chapter 1, you know that most synonyms are not interchangeable.

A list of reliable thesauruses follows:

Roget's International Thesaurus
Roget's Thesaurus in Dictionary Form
Roget's Thesaurus of English Words and Phrases
Webster's Collegiate Thesaurus
Webster's Dictionary of Synonyms

Additional dictionaries dealing with our language are the following:

Abbreviations Dictionary: (Abreviations, Acronyms, Contractions, Signs and Symbols Defined)
Acronyms, Initialisms, and Abbreviations Dictionary
Brewer's Dictionary of Phrase and Fable
A Dictionary of American Idioms
Dictionary of American Slang
Dictionary of Literary Terms
A Dictionary of Slang and Unconventional English
A Dictionary of Word and Phrase Origins (3 volumes)
Harper Dictionary of Contemporary Usage

Mathews Dictionary of Americanisms
The Oxford Dictionary of English Etymology
Wood's Unabridged Rhyming Dictionary

Special-Purpose Dictionaries. Finally, there are special-purpose dictionaries that deal exclusively with music, medicine, foreign language, and many other subjects. These include the following:

FOREIGN LANGUAGE

Cassell's Dutch Dictionary
Cassell's French Dictionary
Cassell's German Dictionary
Cassell's Italian Dictionary
Cassell's New Latin Dictionary
Cassell's Spanish Dictionary

HISTORY

Concise Dictionary of American History
Dictionary of American History
A New Dictionary of British History

LITERATURE

Dictionary of Fictional Characters
Dictionary of Literary Terms
Dictionary of World Literary Terms
Webster's Dictionary of Proper Names

MATH AND SCIENCE

Compton's Illustrated Science Dictionary
Dictionary of Biology
Dictionary of Science and Technology
The International Dictionary of Applied Mathematics

MUSIC AND ART

Grove's Dictionary of Music and Musicians (10 volumes)
Harvard Dictionary of Music
Bryan's Dictionary of Painters and Engravers (5 volumes)
McGraw-Hill Dictionary of Art (5 volumes)

Encyclopedias

General Encyclopedias. An encyclopedia (from the Greek *enkyklios paideia,* which means "general education") is a collection of articles alphabetically arranged in volumes on nearly every conceivable subject. It is designed for quick reference and provides you with general information on various fields or branches of learning.

Guide letters on the spine of each volume and guide words at the top of the pages assist you in finding information. It is best, however, to check the general index when looking for information. It may list several good sources. For up-to-date information on a topic, check the yearbook that many encyclopedias include.

Never use an encyclopedia as your only source. Use it only to obtain a general survey of your subject. The library is a storehouse of information; an encyclopedia should be used only as a door to that storehouse.

Most libraries include the following encyclopedias in their reference section:

GENERAL ENCYCLOPEDIAS

Collier's Encyclopedia (24 volumes)
Publishes *Collier's Yearbook;* Volume 24 includes a bibliography and index

Encyclopaedia Britannica (30 volumes)
Publishes *Britannica Book of the Year;* includes separate Index and Atlas for the set (more details follow)

Encyclopedia Americana (30 volumes)
Publishes *Americana Annual*

World Book Encyclopedia (22 volumes)
Publishes annual supplement; Volume 22 includes Research Guide and Index

The *Encyclopaedia Britannica* is unique in its organization. In dealing with the great amounts of knowledge known to humankind, the *Britannica* is broken down into three parts: the *Propaedia* (*pro* meaning "prior to"), the *Micropaedia* (*micro* meaning "small") and the *Macropaedia* (*macro* meaning "big").

The *Propaedia*, or Outline of Knowledge and Guide to the *Britannica*, presents more than 15,000 different topics, arranged according to fields or areas of knowledge. For each topic in the Outline, there are references to the *Macropaedia* of three kinds: (1) whole articles, (2) sections of articles, (3) other references. These references make possible systematic study or reading on any subject in the encyclopedia.

The *Micropaedia*, consisting of 10 volumes, is a ready reference and index to the entire encyclopedia. As a ready reference, it is a short-entry encyclopedia. Its more than 100,000 entries, arranged in alphabetical order, give the most important and interesting facts about their subject. Often this is all you will want to know. When a subject is also treated in depth in the *Macropaedia*, the *Micropaedia* becomes an index.

The *Macropaedia*, which contains knowledge in depth, is the main body of the *Britannica*. The *Macropaedia's* 19 volumes contain 4,207 long articles by world-renowned contributors.

Encyclopedias on Specific Subjects. Encyclopedias on a wide variety of specific subjects fill library shelves. To give you some idea of the diversity of encyclopedias, here is a partial list:

ENCYCLOPEDIAS ON SPECIFIC SUBJECTS

ART

Encyclopedia of Modern Art
LaRousse Encyclopedia of Byzantine and Medieval Art
LaRousse Encyclopedia of Prehistoric and Ancient Art
LaRousse Encyclopedia of Renaissance and Baroque Art

HISTORY

An Encyclopedia of World History
Encyclopedia of World History

HOBBIES AND INTERESTS

Encyclopedia of Gardening
The Illustrated Encyclopedia of World Coins
The International Encyclopedia of Cooking

LITERATURE

The Concise Encyclopedia of English and American Poets and Poetry
The Concise Encyclopedia of Modern Drama
LaRousse Encyclopedia of Mythology
McGraw-Hill Encyclopedia of World Biography (12 volumes)
McGraw-Hill Encyclopedia of World Drama (4 volumes)

RELIGION AND OCCULTISM

Encyclopaedia of Occultism
Encyclopaedia of Religion

SCIENCE AND MATHEMATICS

The Concise Encyclopedia of Archeology
Encyclopaedia of Animal Care
The Encyclopedia of Chemistry
Grzimek's Animal Life Encyclopedia (13 volumes)
The Illustrated Encyclopedia of Aviation and Space
International Encyclopedia of Social Sciences (17 volumes)
The Mammals of America
The Pictorial Encyclopedia of Birds
Universal Encyclopedia of Mathematics

SPORTS

The Baseball Encyclopedia
Encyclopedia of Auto Racing Greats

Pamphlets, Handbooks, and Catalogs

The Vertical File. Pamphlets, handbooks, booklets, and clippings on a variety of subjects are available in most libraries. These subjects include information about vocations, travel, census data, and program schedules. It is here that you may find college catalogs, too. All of this information is kept in a set of file cabinets called the **vertical file.**

One of the most important ideas behind the vertical file is that the information in it is current. This file can be an invaluable source to you when writing a report on a contemporary topic, seeking current statistics, or looking up information on careers.

Information About Vocations, Colleges and Universities. The reference section of the library can be a starting point in seeking information about careers and about colleges. Again, depending on the size of your library, the availability of materials does vary. Here is a list of some resources you might use:

Encyclopedia of Careers and Vocations
Barron's Guide to the Two-Year Colleges
Barron's Profiles of American Colleges
Lovejoy's College Guide

The 300 section of your reference area will provide related material. Many libraries also have on reserve many college catalogs.

Almanacs and Yearbooks

Published annually, almanacs and yearbooks are useful sources of facts and statistics on current events, as well as on matters of historical record in government, economics, population, sports, and other fields.

Guinness Book of World Records
Information Please Almanac, Atlas and Yearbook
Statesman's Yearbook
Statistical Abstract of the United States
Women's Rights Almanac
World Almanac and Book of Facts

Atlases

We usually think of an atlas mainly as a book of maps, but it also contains interesting data on a number of subjects. The excellent *National Geographic Atlas of the World*, for example, lists some of the following topics in its table of contents: "Great

Moments in Geography," "Global Statistics," and sections on population, temperature, oceans, and place names. Below is a list of other widely used atlases.

Atlas of World History
Atlas of World Wildlife
The Britannica Atlas
Collier's World Atlas and Gazetteer
Goode's World Atlas
Grosset World Atlas
The International Atlas from Rand McNally
The Times Atlas of the World

Biographical References

There are brief biographical notations in dictionaries and longer biographical articles in encyclopedias. Often, however, a better source is one of the specialized works listed below.

Current Biography. Biographies of current newsworthy individuals are published here monthly. Each issue is indexed. All copies are bound in an annual volume with a cumulated index of people in that particular volume as well as previous annual volumes. Also found at the end of the annual volumes are the names of the people in *Current Biography* according to their profession. Biographies of internationally known persons are found here, but Americans are well represented throughout this reference.

Dictionary of American Biography. This is the most famous and most reliable of all American biographical dictionaries. Alphabetically arranged, this twenty-two-volume work carries articles on the lives and accomplishments of prominent deceased Americans. The work contains 14,870 biographies of Americans from the colonial days to 1940. It is kept up-to-date by supplements. The length of the articles varies from half-page sketches to chapter-length essays.

Dictionary of National Biography. This multi-volume dictionary is the most famous and the most reliable of British biographical dictionaries. Its accurate and concise information makes it a most valuable source. It includes only Englishmen who are no longer living.

The International Who's Who. Alphabetically listed, this source provides brief biographical sketches of prominent living people of all nations. This publication includes thousands of personalities and provides a valuable source for current biographies.

Webster's Biographical Dictionary. This is a source of biographical facts about past and present noteworthy people. More than 40,000 individuals are listed alphabetically and pronunciation keys are given for each name.

Who's Who. Principally concerned with British personalities, this source provides a very brief description of the life and accomplishments of each individual included. You would probably need to refer to another source if you needed information.

Who's Who in America. This volume provides biographical sketches, listed alphabetically, of prominent Americans who are known either for their positions or their accomplishments. Published every two years, this book can guide you to other sources in seeking detailed information about a particular person.

Who's Who in America also has regional editions: *Who's Who in the East (and Eastern Canada), Who's Who in the Midwest, Who's Who in the South and Southwest,* and *Who's Who in the West.*

Who's Who in American Women. Unusual in its title, this book not only lists outstanding American women, but women of international acclaim.

Books About Authors. For biographical information about authors, and critical evaluations of their works, the following sources are especially useful.

American Authors: 1600–1900
British Authors Before 1800
British Authors of the Nineteenth Century
Contemporary Authors

Cyclopedia of World Authors
Twentieth Century Authors
Twentieth Century Authors: First Supplement
World Authors: 1950–1970

Literary Reference Books

The following are valuable reference books on the history of literature, on quotations and proverbs, for locating poems and stories, and for finding information about writers.

Bartlett's Familiar Quotations
Book Review Digest
Contemporary Poets
Cyclopedia of Literary Characters
Encyclopedia of World Drama
Granger's Index to Poetry and Recitations
Illustrated Encyclopedia of the Classical World
A Literary History of England
A Literary History of the United States
Mencken's *A New Dictionary of Quotations*
The Oxford Companion to American Literature
The Oxford Companion to Classical Literature
The Oxford Companion to English Literature
The Oxford Companion to the Theatre

From the above list, three widely used reference works are the following:

Bartlett's Familiar Quotations. This is one of the best known of the dictionaries of quotations. Its completeness and accuracy have made it notable for over a century.

Quotations are arranged chronologically by author in the main section of the book. A shorter section of passages from the Bible, Koran, and the Book of Common Prayer follow. To find the complete source of a quote, you should use the main index in the back of the book. Whether you know the entire quotation or simply have a general idea of its topic, you would be able to find it in the index.

For example, study this quotation from a poem by the American poet, Walt Whitman:

> "I hear America singing, the varied carols I hear."

You may find a reference to this quotation in three places:

1. under Walt Whitman entries in the main index of the book.
2. in the index under the first line of the quote.
3. under the subject heading of America.

Whatever your recollection or your need for a quotation on a particular subject, *Bartlett's Familiar Quotations* is an excellent source.

Book Review Digest. Arranged alphabetically by author of the book reviewed, this digest gives short quotations from selected reviews from many popular American and English periodicals. If a work of fiction has had four or more reviews or a work of non-fiction has had two or more reviews, and if the book is hard-bound and has been published in the United States, it will appear in this digest. It is published monthly and accumulated annually.

You will find this to be a good source in finding both unfavorable and favorable reviews of particular books.

Granger's Index to Poetry and Recitations. This source includes an index of first lines as well as an index of authors to assist you in finding a poem if its title is unknown to you. By using this reference book, you will also be able to locate not only a quotation but also an entire short work. For example, suppose you need to find an anthology or book containing the poem "The Love Song of J. Alfred Prufrock" by T. S. Eliot. You would look up this title in the *Index* and under the title of the poem you will find listed a number of books containing this poem. The titles, however, are coded, and you will find the code explained in the front of the book.

Granger's Index to Poetry and Recitations is a standard, worthwhile source for any student of literature.

Magazines

The *Readers' Guide to Periodical Literature* lists the titles of articles, stories, and poems published during the preceding month in more than 100 leading magazines. It is issued twice a month from September through June and once a month in July and August. An entire year's issues are bound in one hard-cover volume at the end of the year. Articles are listed alphabetically under *subject* and *author* (and *titles* when necessary). You will find the *Readers' Guide* invaluable when looking for articles on a subject for a composition.

The excerpt from the *Readers' Guide* on the following page illustrates how articles are listed.

Exercises Using Reference Materials

A. Dictionaries and Encyclopedias. Using the dictionaries and encyclopedias listed on pages 316–321, indicate the best source for answers to these questions. Include the page reference.

1. Where did the phrase "ugly duckling" originate?
2. Find a short article on cryogenics.
3. In what epic is Hector an important character?
4. How did Currier and Ives become famous?
5. What are the basic steps in computer data processing?
6. What were the "Jim Crow" laws?
7. Compare the form of the Miltonic sonnet with the Shakespearean sonnet.
8. Describe "op art."
9. What are the four main blood groups?
10. What was the original meaning of the word *flivver?*
11. Who wrote the ballet "Slaughter on Tenth Avenue"?
12. Was Robin Hood a real or legendary character?
13. What is existentialism?
14. Find an illustration and description of a lute.
15. What is the story of Scylla and Charybdis?

Excerpt from the *Readers' Guide*

LEADERSHIP
Leadership [address, November 2, 1979] N. D. Potter. Vital Speeches 46:103-8 Ja 1 '80
Where have all the leaders gone? [Canada: with editorial comment by P.C. Newman] R. MacGregor. il Macleans 93:3, 16-19 Ja 28 '80 — title of article; name of magazine
LEADERSHIP (periodical)
Message from the publisher. H. L. Myra. il Chr Today 24:3 Ja 25 '80 — volume number
LEAFLETS. See Pamphlets
LEARNING, Psychology of
Degree of success while learning and academic achievement. E. J. Schneider. Educ Digest 45:21-3 Ja '80
LEARNING and scholarship — subject entry
See also
Education
Student achievements
LEARNING theory. See Learning, Psychology of
LE CARRE, John, pseud. See Cornwell, David John Moore
LECKEY, Delores R.
Mixed & ambigous. Commonweal 107:49:50 F 1 '80 — page reference
LEDERER, Esther Pauline (Friedman) See Landers, Ann, pseud
LEDFORD, Cawood
Wildcats come in loud and clear. W. F. Reed. il por Sports Illus 52:46 F 18 '80 — date of magazine
LEE, M. Owen
More than an opera. il Opera News 44:14+ F 2 '80
Lee, Milton L. and others
Dimethyl and monomethyl sulfate: presence in coal fly ash and airborne particulate matter. bibl f il Science 207:186-8 Ja 11 '80
LEE, Robert, and Mar, Frank — author entry
Reopening church doors in China. il Chr Cent 97:105-7 Ja 30 '80
LEEHRSEN, Charles
Jump: anatomy of the top Olympic spectacle. il Pop Mech 153:91-5+ F '80
LEEWARD Islands
See also
British Virgin Islands — "see also" cross reference
LEFEVER, Ernest W.
Nuclear arms in the third world: options for the future. il Futurist 14:68-70 F '80 — illustrated article
LEFOURNIER, Phillippe
France: where consumers will suffer the most. il Bus W p70-1 F 4 '80
LEG exercises. See Exercise — "see" cross reference
LEGAL fees. See Lawyers—Salaries, fees, etc.
LEGGETT, William
Horse racing [cont] Sports Illus 52:56+ Ja 28 '80

B. Almanacs, Yearbooks and Atlases. Using the almanacs, yearbooks and atlases listed in this chapter, indicate the best source for answers to these questions. Include the page reference.

1. Find a list of the major North American turnpikes.
2. How is a patent issued?
3. What are the major land uses in the United States?
4. Who is the mayor of Los Angeles?
5. What are the warning signs of a heart attack?
6. What is the law on succession to the presidency?
7. Whose portrait is on the $20 bill?
8. Compare the number of American participants in World War II and the Vietnam War.
9. How many times has the United States won the Olympic Games since 1900?
10. Find a map showing climates of the world.
11. What is the National Guard?
12. Find a list of the state compulsory school attendance laws.
13. What play has had the longest Broadway run?
14. Which states have a sales tax?
15. What are some of the endangered species of birds in North America?

C. Biographical References. Using the biographical references listed in this chapter, give the best source for answers to these questions. Include the page reference where you found the information.

1. What series of novels did Upton Sinclair write?
2. Find a list of Isaac Bashevis Singer's works in English translation.
3. What is the setting of Joseph Heller's novel *Catch-22*?
4. What made Bill Mauldin, the cartoonist, famous?
5. What part did Charlotte Corday play in the French Revolution?
6. Which novel of Jessamyn West's became a popular movie?
7. How has Jacques Cousteau graphically shared his experiences as a marine explorer?
8. What were some of Clarence Darrow's most famous cases?

9. Where can you find a picture of Geoffrey Chaucer?

10. What is the background of most of J. P. Marquand's novels?

11. What was Henrik Ibsen's contribution to drama?

12. What story influenced William Golding in the development of his novel *Lord of the Flies?*

13. What honor was Gwendolyn Brooks given by the state of Illinois?

14. What was the ultimate success of Clarence Day's family sketches?

15. What physical handicaps made drawing difficult for James Thurber?

D. Literary Reference Books. Use the literary reference books listed in this chapter to answer the following questions. After each answer write the name of the reference book you used.

1. What is a morality play?

2. What influence did the McGuffey readers have on American education?

3. Find a poem on freedom.

4. On what occasion did John F. Kennedy say, "Let us never negotiate out of fear, but let us never fear to negotiate"?

5. In what century was the Tower of London built?

6. What is the "theater of the absurd"?

7. What are some of the treasures housed in the British Museum?

8. Who wrote the poem "Renascence"?

9. What was meant by Manifest Destiny?

10. What forced the magazine *Literary Digest* to cease publication?

11. Who are the main characters in the musical comedy *Of Thee I Sing?*

12. What are the Leatherstocking Tales?

13. How favorable were the reviews of John Steinbeck's *The Grapes of Wrath?*

14. Where was Tin Pan Alley?

15. What is the plot of Frank Norris' novel *The Pit?*

E. Reader's Guide to Periodical Literature. Use the excerpt from the *Readers' Guide* on page 328 to answer the following questions.

1. On what page in *Christianity Today* will you find a message from the publisher on leadership?

2. Give the complete magazine title of the following abbreviations.

Educ Digest	NY
Sports Illus	Bus W
Chr Cent	Pop Mech

3. What is Ann Landers' real name?
4. Who has delivered an address on leadership?
5. Who has written a continuing article on horseracing?

F. Using Reference Materials for a Research Paper. The American novelist, Sinclair Lewis, is best known as a satirist of the American middle class. In a study of his major novels, *Main Street* and *Babbitt,* some background study of his life and writings would be valuable. From the reference sources listed in this chapter, find the specific books that will answer these questions. Include the page references.

1. Locate comprehensive biographical information.
2. Find reviews of *Babbitt* and *Main Street.*
3. What Minnesota town is the locale for *Main Street?*
4. What was Lewis' reason for declining the Pulitzer Prize in 1926?
5. Compare Sinclair Lewis with Willa Cather as an interpreter of small town life in America.
6. What is the entry under "babbitt" in the unabridged dictionaries?
7. On what occasion did he say, "Our American professors like their literature clear and cold and pure and very dead"?
8. What is the plot of *Arrowsmith?*
9. What was the title of his address in Stockholm on receiving the Nobel Prize for Literature?
10. Were the critics justified in accusing him of romanticism?

Handbook

A detailed Table of Contents of the Handbook appears in the front of this book.

How To Use the Handbook

This Handbook is your reference book. In it the concepts of grammar and usage are organized so that you can study them efficiently and refer to them quickly.

To use the Handbook well, you should first leaf through it to become familiar with its organization and contents. Note especially the following:

Organization of the Handbook

Grammar (Sections 1–4) Sections 1–4 provide a comprehensive treatment of English grammar. They give the rules and explanations for grammatical questions you want answered.

Usage (Sections 5–9) Sections 5–9 are a guide to English usage. When you are puzzled about which form of a word to use in your writing, turn to the appropriate part of these sections.

Forms and constructions marked STANDARD are accepted as standard usage—the kind of usage that is appropriate at all times and in all places. Forms and constructions marked NONSTANDARD are not accepted everywhere. While they may go unnoticed on the playing field or in the locker room, in many other situations they mark the user as careless or untrained in the English language.

Capitalization (Section 10)

Punctuation (Sections 11–14)

Spelling (Sections 15–16)

Good Form (Sections 17–18)

Throughout the Handbook are many exercises that test your understanding of the concepts explained. These exercises are the first steps in putting what you learn here to practical use. The next steps are in your own writing and speaking.

1.0 The Classification of Words

The words in our language have been classified into eight large groups according to the jobs they perform in a sentence. These eight groups are called the eight **parts of speech.**

nouns	adjectives	conjunctions
pronouns	adverbs	interjections
verbs	prepositions	

In addition to the parts of speech, there are three kinds of words, formed from verbs, that do many different jobs. These words are called **verbals.** Verbals are all formed from verbs and have several of the characteristics of verbs. They are unlike verbs, however, in that no verbal can stand by itself as a complete verb. The verbals are the *infinitive,* the *participle,* and the *gerund.*

This section provides a comprehensive treatment of the parts of speech and the verbals.

1.1 The Noun

Certain words in the language are used as labels with which we identify people and things.

A noun is the name of a person, place, or thing.

Things named by nouns may be visible, such as *hats, buildings,* and *magazines.* Things may be items that we perceive with our other senses: *odors, sounds, tastes.* Other things are abstract and not observed through the five senses: *morals, knowledge, wishes,* and so on.

PERSONS	PLACES	THINGS
Thomas Jefferson	Salem	desk
architect	library	courage
salesperson	continent	morality

A **common noun** is the name of a whole group of persons, places, or things. It is a name that is common to the whole group: *coat, road, picture, newspaper.*

A **proper noun** is the name of an individual person, place, or thing.

A proper noun always begins with a capital letter.

COMMON NOUNS	PROPER NOUNS
singer	Beverly Sills
tunnel	Lincoln Tunnel
river	Columbia River
cemetery	Arlington National Cemetery
building	John Hancock Building

As the above list shows, a noun may consist of more than one word. Each word in a proper noun is capitalized.

Any word that can be immediately preceded by *the* is a noun: *the* cake, *the* river, *the* language. Many proper nouns, but not all of them, can also be preceded by *the: the* Black Hills, *the* San Diego Zoo, but not *the* Robert Goddard or *the* Canada.

Exercise A: Find all the nouns in the following sentences.

1. Glass is made of melted sand mixed with soda and lime.
2. Grasshoppers and crickets "sing" by rubbing their legs together.
3. Frogs lay eggs that look like a mass of dark-centered tapioca.

4. The raccoon has a sharp nose, dainty feet, and a long, ringed tail.
5. Snakes move by a wavelike motion along the body.
6. Geckos are lizards that can cling to smooth surfaces.
7. Our thermostat keeps the heat at a constant temperature.
8. Dr. Alexander Fleming discovered penicillin while working as an obscure researcher in a hospital.
9. The anthropologist studies people—their physical structure, their social customs, and their artifacts.
10. The atmosphere is not a calm ocean of air, but a tossing sea laced with swift currents.

Exercise B: Decide which of the following are common nouns and which are proper nouns. Write the proper nouns, beginning each with a capital letter.

1. town, philadelphia, woodhaven, state
2. eskimo, fur, walrus, bering sea
3. airport, midway airport, airplane, hangar
4. magazine, *newsweek*, newspaper, calendar
5. river, hudson river, harbor, bay of fundy
6. gulf, gulf of mexico, lake, lake erie
7. pupil, national honor society, teacher, scholarship
8. spanish, dialect, french, language
9. alabama, state, country, government
10. citizen, neighbor, mayor aldrich, governor

1.2 The Pronoun

Since it would be awkward and cumbersome to repeat the name of a person or thing every time we wish to refer to it, we use other words in place of names. These words are pronouns. They may be used in a sentence in any way that a noun is used.

A pronoun is a word used in place of a noun.

The noun for which the pronoun stands and to which it refers is its **antecedent.**

Kim was satisfied with *her* grades. (*Kim* is antecedent of *her.*)

The *artists* displayed *their* skill. (*artists* is antecedent of *their.*)

Mr. Carter is the *counselor* with *whom* I discussed my plans for college. (*counselor* is antecedent of *whom.*)

The antecedent of a pronoun may appear in a preceding sentence.

The *candidate* was asked about *foreign aid. She* said *it* was necessary for the security of the United States. (*She* refers to the antecedent *candidate; it* refers to *foreign aid.*)

There are six kinds of pronouns:

personal pronouns
compound personal pronouns
indefinite pronouns
demonstrative pronouns
interrogative pronouns
relative pronouns

Personal Pronouns

Pronouns used in place of persons' names are called **personal pronouns.** They permit us to identify the person speaking, the person spoken to, and the person spoken about. Personal pronouns are also used to refer to things.

FIRST PERSON (the person speaking)
I, me, my, mine, we, us, our, ours

SECOND PERSON (the person spoken to)
you, your, yours

THIRD PERSON (the person or thing spoken about)
he, she, it, they
his, hers, its, their, theirs
him, her, them

Personal pronouns change their form for different uses in sentences. This change of form is called the **case** of pronouns. There are three cases: *nominative, possessive,* and *objective.* Personal pronouns also change their form to show the difference between singular (one) and plural (more than one). This change of form is called the **number** of pronouns.

The following table shows the forms for the three *persons,* for the three *cases,* and for the *number* of all of the personal pronouns.

Personal Pronouns

Singular

	NOMINATIVE	POSSESSIVE	OBJECTIVE
First Person:	I	my, mine	me
Second Person:	you	your, yours	you
Third Person:	he, she, it	his, her, hers, its	him, her, it

Plural

	NOMINATIVE	POSSESSIVE	OBJECTIVE
First Person:	we	our, ours	us
Second Person:	you	your, yours	you
Third Person:	they	their, theirs	them

Third person pronouns that refer to male persons are in the **masculine gender.** Those that refer to female persons are in the **feminine gender.** Pronouns that refer to things are in the **neuter gender.**

Here are some important things to remember about pronouns:

The pronoun *it* is called a personal pronoun even though it refers to things more often than to persons.

Countries, ships, and airplanes are sometimes referred to by the feminine pronouns, *she, her, hers.* Animals may be referred to by *it* and *its* or by *he, his, him, she, her, hers,* depending on the sex of the animal.

The words *mine, yours, hers, ours,* and *theirs* are always used as pronouns. The words *my, your, its, our,* and *their* are always used as modifiers before nouns. They are **possessive pronouns.** *His* may be used either as a pronoun or as a modifier.

This transistor radio is *mine.* (pronoun)
Here is *your* license. (modifier)
I agree that *his* is better. (pronoun)
We were proud of *his* record. (modifier)

Exercise: In the following sentences find the personal pronouns. Find the antecedent of each pronoun.

1. Leona did her shopping. Then she went to a museum.
2. Barb and Jim had their lunch. Then they went skiing.
3. Claire has two careers, and she says they are compatible.
4. Her friends in Madison are giving Janet a shower.
5. Elliot said, "I lost my umbrella on the bus."
6. Beth, have you made your decision yet?
7. The salesperson gave Bob her card, but he lost it.
8. Armand bought a sweater. As it didn't fit, he returned it.
9. After Sarah had sanded the chairs, she painted them.
10. Brian has a key, but he didn't bring it with him.

Compound Personal Pronouns

A **compound personal pronoun** is formed by adding *-self* or *-selves* to certain of the personal pronouns, as follows:

FIRST PERSON:	myself, ourselves
SECOND PERSON:	yourself, yourselves
THIRD PERSON:	himself, herself, itself, oneself, themselves

There are no other acceptable compound personal pronouns. Never say *hisself* or *theirselves.*

Compound personal pronouns are used *intensively* for emphasis or *reflexively* to refer to a preceding noun or pronoun.

The mayor *herself* inspected the slum buildings. (intensive)

Mary hurt *herself* when she fell. (reflexive)

Exercise: Supply the correct compound personal pronoun needed in each of these sentences. Find the antecedent for each compound personal pronoun.

1. Roy injured ______ on the band saw.
2. Darlene taught ______ how to play the guitar.
3. You ______ should have delivered the message.
4. Robert hurt ______ by diving in shallow water.
5. The cheerleaders exhausted ______.
6. By abusing his rivals, Ed defeated ______ in the election.
7. Lincoln ______ heard the woman's complaint.
8. They took the responsibility upon ______.
9. Brace ______ for the next announcement.
10. I found ______ in a predicament.

Indefinite Pronouns

Some pronouns, such as *anyone* and *anything,* do not refer to a definite person or thing. They are called **indefinite pronouns.** Normally, indefinite pronouns do not have antecedents. However, the indefinite pronoun itself may be the antecedent of a personal pronoun.

Everyone made *his* own costume.
(The antecedent of *his* is the indefinite pronoun *Everyone.*)

Both of the girls finished *their* sculptures.
(The antecedent of *their* is the indefinite pronoun *Both.*)

SINGULAR INDEFINITE PRONOUNS

another	anything	either	everything	no one
anybody	one	everyone	neither	someone
anyone	each	everybody	nobody	somebody

PLURAL INDEFINITE PRONOUNS

both many few several

The pronouns *all, some, none,* and *any* may be singular or plural, depending upon their meaning in the sentence.

All of the research *was* completed. (singular)
All of the supplies *were* donated. (plural)

Some of the butter *was* rancid. (singular)
Some of the stories *were* published. (plural)

None of the corn *has* been harvested. (singular)
None of the officers *have* resigned. (plural)

Has any of the publicity helped? (singular)
Have any of the risks been considered? (plural)

Demonstrative Pronouns

The words *this, that, these,* and *those* are used to point out which one or which ones are meant. Since they point to, or demonstrate, what is meant, they are called **demonstrative pronouns.** They always refer to a definite person or thing, but the words they refer to may come later in the sentence, or in another sentence altogether.

This is the *poem* I wrote. (*poem* is the word referred to.)

On the ship were two Bengal *tigers. These* were headed for the St. Louis Zoo. (*tigers* is the word referred to by *These.*)

Note: The demonstrative pronouns *this, that, these,* and *those* may be used as adjectives: *this hat, those curtains.*

Interrogative Pronouns

The pronouns *who, whose, whom, what,* and *which* can be used to ask questions. When used in this way, they are **interrogative pronouns.**

Who won the game? *What* did he say?

Whom did she vote for? *Which* should I choose?

Those skis are John's. *Whose* are these?

Relative Pronouns

The words *who, whose, whom, which,* and *that* are sometimes used to introduce an adjective clause. They relate the clause to some other words in the sentence. When used in this way, they are called **relative pronouns.** The clause is called a *relative clause.* (See Section 3.6.)

Exercise A: List the pronouns in these sentences. Tell what kind each pronoun is.

1. Are those hermit crabs? They don't look like whelks.
2. This is my bike. Is that yours?
3. Everyone took the test except him.
4. Which of the Frisbees is yours?
5. Someone with an appreciation of fine food is a gourmet.
6. All of Lou's friends love pistachio ice cream.
7. Several of the rabbits ate everything in the garden.
8. None of my classmates heard me.
9. You should have delivered the message yourself.
10. Is this the book you asked for?

Exercise B: Follow the same directions as for Exercise A.

1. Those are your gym shorts, and these are mine.
2. Few are better educated than she.

3. "That is the Fonz!" someone exclaimed.
4. A few of the short stories are long ones.
5. She asked me to give the book to him.
6. I wish you had given them a more definite answer.
7. Her twin looks older than she.
8. Everybody went out of his way to be nice to Rob.
9. Emily Dickinson's poem begins, "I'm nobody. Who are you?"
10. Who told everyone to wear costumes?

1.3 The Verb

Every sentence must contain a word that tells what is happening. This word is the verb.

A verb is a word that tells of an action or state of being.

Grammatically, the verb is the most important word in the sentence. If you can find the verb and manage it properly, many of your grammar and usage problems will be solved.

Most verbs change their form (their sound or spelling) to show past time and present time. They are the only words to do so. This fact can help you decide which word in the sentence is the verb.

Summer jobs *were* very scarce this year. (past)
Summer jobs *are* very scarce this year. (present)

The rank and file *demanded* a voice in government. (past)
The rank and file *demand* a voice in government. (present)

Most verbs also change their form to show the difference between singular and plural in the third person.

The President *meets* many people in his travels. (third person singular)
Travelers *meet* many interesting people. (third person plural)

Action Verbs

The action asserted by an action verb may be visible, physical action, or it may be invisible action.

Ken *dropped* the test tube. (visible)
The cars *collided.* (visible)
Monica *shoveled* snow. (visible)
We *enjoyed* the comic effects. (not visible)
Eileen *decided* to wait. (not visible)
Her speech *impressed* me. (not visible)

Linking Verbs

A few verbs, such as *be*, link the subject to a noun or adjective. Hence they are called **linking verbs.**

Pat *became* the editor. Helen *seemed* confused.

The most common linking verb is *be* with its forms *be, am, are, is, was, were, been, being.*

Other linking verbs are *appear, become, seem, look, sound, grow, feel, smell, taste, remain, stay.*

The substance *appeared* transparent.
Al *grew* mellower with age.
No one *seems* satisfied.
His father *became* angry.
He *sounds* bored.
Ann *looks* strong.
I *feel* contented.
The grapes *taste* sour.
The room *smells* musty.
We *remained* standing throughout the performance.
The sign *stayed* upright till the storm began.

Many linking verbs may also be used as action verbs.

Jack *felt* a sharp blow.
The farmers *grow* wheat.
The city *sounded* the curfew.
She *looked* under the bleachers.
We *smelled* the hamburgers.
José *tasted* the lobster.
Emma *stayed* until dusk.

Main Verbs and Auxiliaries

Many verbs consist of more than one word. They consist of a **main verb** and one or more **auxiliaries,** or helping verbs. The last word in the phrase is the main verb.

There are three verbs that can be used either as main verbs or as auxiliaries. Here are their forms.

DO	HAVE	BE		
do	has	is	was	be
does	have	am	were	been
did	had	are		being

AS MAIN VERB	AS AUXILIARY
He will *do* his duty.	I *do* need a new dress.
Have they a reason?	We *have* been chosen.
The hinges *are* rusty.	Some customers *are* arriving.
The rockets *were* powerful.	The crops *were* exported.

The most frequently used auxiliaries are the forms of *be* and *have.* The most common of the other auxiliaries are the following:

must	may	shall	could	
might	can	will	should	would

VERB	AUXILIARY	MAIN VERB
has had	has	had
had been	had	been
was doing	was	doing
had done	had	done
could have gone	could have	gone
might have been seen	might have been	seen
is being improved	is being	improved
shall have finished	shall have	finished

Often the parts of a verb are separated by a modifier or modifiers that are not part of the verb.

> The clerk *was* unjustly *accused.*
> Don *had* quietly *assumed* control.

Exercise A: Find each verb and tell whether it is an action verb or a linking verb.

1. Both Anita and Jerry are outstanding athletes.
2. Just leave your boots outside the door.
3. The child looked hungry.
4. The child looked hungrily at the cake.
5. The freshly baked bread smelled delicious.
6. The steak tasted tender and juicy.
7. The audience grew tense with excitement.
8. Bob Summers, a cousin of mine, is a champion bowler.
9. The committee has been meeting at the home of the chairperson.
10. This rope bridge seems relatively safe.
11. Carefully, the guide led the way.
12. That stunt on one ski was stupendous.
13 Her expression betrayed her lack of attention.
14. Laurie tasted the icing on the cupcake.
15. The cupcakes smelled tantalizing.

Exercise B: Find the verb in each of these sentences. Include the auxiliaries. Do not include any word that separates an auxiliary from a main verb.

1. Several candidates are being considered for the job.
2. The thief may still be lurking in this house.
3. I could meet you at the Guggenheim Museum.
4. I have just read some facts about solar energy.
5. Dr. Ferrera will return from her vacation next week.
6. *Moby Dick* is now regarded as a classic.
7. Heather will probably be appointed editor-in-chief.
8. Our old Buick has just been painted.

9. Is anyone using the Volkswagen?
10. New sources of fuel are being developed every year.
11. *Romeo and Juliet,* one of the most famous of romances, will always be a favorite.
12. Everything was being readied for the President's inaugural speech.
13. We probably should have taken the train.
14. Termites have practically consumed the beams on our porch.
15. The mayor would undoubtedly have been defeated anyway.

The Principal Parts

The principal parts of a verb are those from which all forms of the verb are made. They are (1) the *present infinitive* (usually called simply the *present*); (2) the *past;* and (3) the *past participle.*

A **regular verb** is one that forms its past and past participle by adding *-ed* or *-d* to the present.

PRESENT	PAST	PAST PARTICIPLE
need	need*ed*	need*ed*
bake	bake*d*	bake*d*
hear	hear*d*	hear*d*

An **irregular verb** is one that does not form its past and past participle by adding *-ed* or *-d* to the present. (See Section 8.1 for usage of irregular verbs.)

PRESENT	PAST	PAST PARTICIPLE
begin	began	begun
rise	rose	risen
lie	lay	lain

The **present participle** of a verb is formed by adding *-ing* to the present form: *eat—eating; save—saving; put—putting.*

The Progressive Forms

The **progressive forms** of the verb are used to show ongoing action. They are formed by using the forms of *be* with the present participle:

They *are talking.*
The clock *is working.*
The actors *were rehearsing.*
Joe *will be presiding.*
Maria *has been driving.*
The teacher *had been explaining.*
I *must be dreaming.*
Louis *might have been sleeping.*

The Emphatic Forms

Special emphasis is given to a statement by using *do, does,* or *did* with the present form of the verb. These are examples of **emphatic forms.**

She *did stop* the car.
We *do want* world peace.
Mike *does play* a good game.

Transitive and Intransitive Verbs

A **transitive verb** carries over the action from the subject to the object of the verb. An **intransitive verb** expresses an action that is complete in itself; it does not carry action over to an object.

TRANSITIVE	INTRANSITIVE
Cindy *liked* the **novel.**	The experiment *succeeded.*
The debaters *argued* the **point.**	The non-thinkers *conformed.*
The country *faced* a **crisis.**	The game *started* late.
Everyone *expressed* **regret.**	The battle *ended* at dusk.
Diane *bought* the **radio.**	We *walked* to the lake.

Many verbs may be transitive in one sentence and intransitive in another.

TRANSITIVE	INTRANSITIVE
Chico *moved* the **car.**	No one *moved.*
Did they *pass* the **law?**	*Did* they *pass?*
The pilot *could* not *see* the **runway.**	The pilot *could* not *see.*

The Active and the Passive Voice

When the subject performs the action expressed in the verb, the verb is in the **active voice.** When the subject receives the action of the verb, the verb is in the **passive voice.** The passive voice is formed by using some form of *be* with the past participle of the verb.

ACTIVE: The voters *studied* the *issues* carefully.
PASSIVE: The issues *were studied* carefully by the voters.

ACTIVE: The increase in vandalism *angered* the *citizens.*
PASSIVE: The citizens *were angered* by the increase in vandalism.

A transitive verb can be put into the passive voice because it has an object that receives the action of the verb. The object of the active verb becomes the subject in the passive form.

A sentence containing an intransitive verb has no word that receives the action of the verb. Therefore, the sentence cannot be put into the passive voice because there is no word to become the subject.

The class *discussed* Swift's satire. (active)
Swift's satire *was discussed* by the class. (passive)
The alumni *built* a trophy room for the teams. (active)
A trophy room for the teams *was built* by the alumni. (passive)

Exercise A: Identify each verb as transitive or intransitive.

1. Tara breathlessly rushed to basketball practice.
2. Beatrix Potter wrote children's books.

3. Porpoises can communicate through sounds.
4. Polo players on horseback drive a wooden ball with mallets.
5. An investigative reporter will speak to our journalism class next week.
6. Even ancient Egyptians and Romans wore make-up and perfumes.
7. Some students receive programmed instruction from computers.
8. Shirley Temple Black served as ambassador to Ghana.
9. In recent decades, photography has developed into a highly respected art form.
10. Man-made satellites transmit radio and television broadcasts between points on earth.

Exercise B: Find the verb and tell whether it is active or passive.

1. Larger contributions are needed by the National Kidney Foundation.
2. Washington buzzed with politicians and representatives of foreign governments.
3. In 1912, Arizona was admitted to the Union.
4. The trees were pruned by the owner of the nursery.
5. My sister's class elected her president.
6. A package of sunflower seeds will be mailed to you.
7. The great pyramid of Cheops covers thirteen acres.
8. The amendment was passed by a two-thirds vote.
9. The window has been broken by every storm.
10. Basketball was invented in 1891 by James A. Naismith, a Y.M.C.A. instructor.

Exercise C: Change the active verbs to passive and the passive verbs to active.

1. The first ball was thrown out by the mayor.
2. The driver of the red car hit the fire hydrant.
3. Dr. Ramsey operated on my father.
4. Lee was chosen by the group to represent them.
5. The ordinance was finally passed by the City Council.

6. The Sixth Regiment took the city.
7. The maid was dusting the pictures.
8. The photographs have been retouched by the engraver.
9. The parade was reviewed by the governor and the mayor.
10. The famished students quickly devoured the sandwiches.

Tense

Most verbs change their forms to tell present, past, and future time. **Tense** means "time." There are three simple tenses and three perfect tenses for each verb. They are formed as follows:

1. **Present tense.** The **present tense** is formed from the present or simple form of the verb.

The present forms of verbs usually tell of something that exists at the present moment.

The swimmers *stay* near the shore. (right now)
The news *sounds* good. (at this moment)

We do not always use the simple or present forms of verbs to tell of actions that are going on at the moment. We do not say, "I listen." We are more likely to use the **progressive form** "I am listening" or the **emphatic form** "I do listen." An exception is the use of the present to describe ongoing sports events:

McAdoo *intercepts* the pass and New York *wins.*

The present forms of verbs are used to tell of repeated or regular and habitual action.

They *go* to camp every summer.
My father *parks* the car in front of the house.

The present forms of verbs are also used to tell of something that is generally true at all times.

He learned yesterday that water *is* hydrogen and oxygen.
Water *freezes* at 0° Celsius.

The **historical present tense** is used to tell of some action or condition in the past as though it were occurring in the present:

James Bond *enters* the hall silently, *approaches* the door, and carefully *turns* the knob.

2. **Past tense.** Past time is usually told by the past tense, which is the second principal part of the verb: *We talked, they ran, nobody stirred.* Continuing past action is shown by the **past progressive:** We *were having* a good time.

3. **Future tense.** Future time is shown by using *shall* or *will* with the present form of the verb: *We shall arrive, you will hear, I will listen.* (For usage of *shall* and *will*, see Section 8.7.)

Future time may be shown by the present tense together with an adverb or phrase that tells time. Future time may also be shown by the use of a form of *be* with *going to.*

We *get* our polio shots *tomorrow.* (*tomorrow* is an adverb telling time.)
Linda *plays* center field *from now on.* (*from now on* is an adverb phrase telling time.)
The Parks Department *is going to* build new tennis courts.
The Cubs *are going to* win the pennant someday.

4. **Present perfect tense.** The present perfect tense is formed by using *has* or *have* with the past participle (third principal part) of the verb. This tense is used to refer to some indefinite time in the past.

Thousands of Americans *have viewed* the *Mona Lisa.*
Walter *has* already *auditioned* for the show.

The present perfect is also used to show action that began in the past and continues into the present.

She *has worked* here for thirty years. (She is still working here.)
He *has been waiting* for a permit. (present perfect progressive)

5. **Past perfect tense.** The past perfect tense is formed by using *had* with the past participle (third principal part) of the verb. The past perfect tense tells of an action completed in the past before some other action.

EARLIER	LATER
I *had admired* her	before I *met* her.
He *had praised* revolution	until he *realized* its dangers.
We *had been planning* the trip	before Jim *lost* his job.

6. **Future perfect tense.** The future perfect tense is formed by using *will have* or *shall have* with the past participle of the verb (third principal part). This tense is used to tell of one action completed in the future *before* some other action in the future.

Before the musical *closes,* it *will have played* five years.

By the time Bill *arrives,* the race *will have started.*

Note: The verb in the present tense indicates far future action. The second verb, in the future perfect tense, indicates future action *before* the action of the first verb.

Exercise: Find each verb and tell its tense.

1. Somebody finally heard our cries for help.
2. The rehearsal will start promptly at eight.
3. Has the bell rung yet?
4. Melinda will undoubtedly be the next class president.
5. Philip is playing a Strauss waltz.
6. Who will be at the game?
7. Shall we watch a comedian or a play?
8. The Todds had already sold their house.
9. In May, Leon will have been in the Navy two years.
10. By four o'clock the snow plows were clearing the roads.
11. Have you ever forgotten your homework?
12. The juniors arrange a class trip every year.
13. Donna will become an engineer.
14. By that time, Bob will have spent two years in college.
15. Why weren't you at the meeting last night?

Conjugation of *Need*

Conjugation is a presentation of the various forms of a verb. Usually, verbs are conjugated in the order shown here.

Principal Parts: need, needed, needed
Present Participle: needing
Present Infinitive: to need
Perfect Infinitive: to have needed

Present Tense

FIRST PERSON:	I need	we need
SECOND PERSON:	you need	you need
THIRD PERSON:	he, she, it needs	they need

PRESENT PROGRESSIVE: I am needing, you are needing, etc.
PRESENT EMPHATIC: I do need, you do need, he does need, etc.

Past Tense

FIRST PERSON:	I needed	we needed
SECOND PERSON:	you needed	you needed
THIRD PERSON:	he, she, it needed	they needed

PAST PROGRESSIVE: I was needing, you were needing, etc.
PAST EMPHATIC: I did need, you did need, etc.

Future Tense

FIRST PERSON:	I shall (will) need	we shall (will) need
SECOND PERSON:	you will need	you will need
THIRD PERSON:	he, she, it will need	they will need

FUTURE PROGRESSIVE: I shall be needing, you will be needing, etc.

Present Perfect Tense

FIRST PERSON:	I have needed	we have needed
SECOND PERSON:	you have needed	you have needed
THIRD PERSON:	he, she, it has needed	they have needed

PRESENT PERFECT PROGRESSIVE: I have been needing, you have been needing, he has been needing, etc.

Past Perfect Tense

FIRST PERSON:	I had needed	we had needed
SECOND PERSON:	you had needed	you had needed
THIRD PERSON:	he, she, it had needed	they had needed

PAST PERFECT PROGRESSIVE: I had been needing, you had been needing, he had been needing, etc.

Future Perfect Tense

FIRST PERSON:	I shall have needed	we shall have needed
SECOND PERSON:	you will have needed	you will have needed
THIRD PERSON:	he, she, it will have needed	they will have needed

FUTURE PERFECT PROGRESSIVE: I shall have been needing, etc.

Mood

The mood of a verb shows the writer's attitude about the actuality of a happening. The **indicative mood,** which we use most of the time, indicates that we are talking or writing about a fact. That is, we are speaking of something that has happened, is happening, or definitely will happen.

The **subjunctive mood** is used to express only wishes, commands, and conditions that are doubtful or contrary to fact. The forms of the subjunctive mood are like those of the indicative mood except in the third person singular of the present tense where the *s* ending is omitted.

INDICATIVE: He obeys the training rules.
SUBJUNCTIVE: The coach demands that he *obey* the training rules.

The subjunctive form of the verb *be* is a special case. With this verb, the form in the present tense for all persons and numbers is *be*.

PRESENT TENSE: I recommended that they *be* suspended.
If this *be* treason, then I am guilty.

The past subjunctive form of the verb *to be* is *were*.

PAST TENSE: I wish I *were* a musician.
If the witness *were* honest, the accused would be acquitted.
Do you wish he *were* your friend?

The **imperative mood** is used to express a command, a directive, or a request. The imperative mood has only one tense—the present—and only one person—the second.

Adjust your safety belts.
Read the directions carefully.
Please *clear* the aisles.

1.4 The Adjective

To express our point of view fully or to make our meaning clear and definite, we do not rely on nouns and verbs alone. We use other kinds of words to describe or limit or qualify the meaning. We call these words modifiers.

An adjective is a word that modifies a noun or pronoun.

Adjectives are used to tell *which one, what kind, how many,* or *how much* about nouns and pronouns.

WHICH ONE: this, that, these, those
WHAT KIND: large, sweet, dull, anxious
HOW MANY: some, all, several, six, eleven
HOW MUCH: little, much, abundant

The Articles

The word *the* is called a **definite article** because it is usually, though not always, used to refer to a definite or specific thing or person.

The words *a* and *an* are called **indefinite articles** because they refer to no particular thing or person. A is used before words be-beginning with consonant sounds. *An* is used before words beginning with vowel sounds. The sound, not the spelling, makes the difference.

I read *an* editorial on the subject.
Rita made *a* hasty decision.
An honorary degree was conferred on the President.
The council discussed *a* new expressway.

Proper Adjectives

A **proper adjective** is one formed from a proper noun. The proper adjective is always capitalized.

NOUN	ADJECTIVE	NOUN	ADJECTIVE
Italy	Italian	North	Northern
Germany	German	Democrats	Democratic
Africa	African	Israel	Israeli
Egypt	Egyptian	Hawaii	Hawaiian

Predicate Adjectives

An adjective is frequently separated from the noun or pronoun it modifies by a linking verb.

The cat seems *hungry*. The boys were *angry*.

An adjective in the predicate that modifies the subject is a predicate adjective.

Exercise A: Find each adjective and tell which word it modifies. Ignore the articles.

1. The acoustics in the new auditorium are excellent.
2. The irate skunk sent off a pungent odor.
3. Fifty governors met to discuss critical urban problems.
4. Police conducted a thorough investigation of the brutal crime.
5. She was frank with Congressional investigators but uncooperative with the press.
6. The first electric light burned for forty hours.
7. The northern part of Canada is a vast Arctic waste.
8. In a full orchestra there are four families of instruments.
9. Jellyfish are boneless animals with long, stringy tentacles.
10. The traffic was terrible during the late afternoon and early evening.

Exercise B: Follow the same directions as for Exercise A.

1. There were only twenty people in the huge auditorium.
2. Amy gave the dog fresh water and some food.
3. The dance, colorful and sprightly, delighted the large audience.
4. Picasso was one of the major artists of modern times.
5. Some people have a strange antipathy for cats.
6. Aunt Carol is both musical and artistic.
7. The weary hikers tried to ignore their intense hunger.
8. There are several books on architecture on the second shelf.
9. Editorial cartoons are often humorous as well as persuasive.
10. The vehicular intersection by the bridge is dangerous.

Adjectives in Comparisons

Persons and things are compared as to various qualities. The comparison is made by use of two different forms of adjectives.

The **comparative** form of the adjective is formed in two ways:

1. All adjectives of one syllable and a few adjectives with two syllables add *-er*.

young—younger   tall—taller   funny—funnier

2. Most adjectives with two syllables and all adjectives with more than two syllables use *more* to form the comparative.

harmful—more harmful	capable—more capable
careful—more careful	efficient—more efficient

The **superlative** form of the adjective is formed by adding *-est* or by using *most*. Adjectives that form the comparative with *-er* form the superlative with *-est*. Those that form the comparative with *more* form the superlative with *most*.

COMPARATIVE	SUPERLATIVE
younger	youngest
funnier	funniest
more likely	most likely
more cautious	most cautious

Irregular Comparisons

We form the comparative and superlative of some adjectives by changing the words themselves.

	COMPARATIVE	SUPERLATIVE
good	better	best
well	better	best
bad	worse	worst
ill	worse	worst
little	less *or* lesser	least
much	more	most
many	more	most
far	farther *or* further	farthest *or* furthest

Exercise: Find the adjectives and tell whether they are in comparative form or superlative form.

1. I find biography more interesting than fiction.
2. Who is our most likely candidate?
3. The lowest point in the United States is Death Valley.

4. The Sears Tower is taller than the Empire State Building.
5. Chris is the most ambitious person in the class.
6. Dogs have a keener sense of smell than cats.
7. Laura is the fastest runner on the team.
8. The driver chose the route that seemed least dangerous.
9. The amoeba is the lowest of all animal forms.
10. Who is older, Lynn or Randy?
11. Flying in an airplane is less dangerous than driving a car.
12. Which has fewer calories, yogurt or cottage cheese?
13. The worst snowstorm in years has paralyzed Minneapolis.
14. Madlock's batting average is higher than Rose's.
15. Joyce is the person most qualified for the job.

1.5 The Adverb

Nouns and pronouns are modified by adjectives. Other parts of speech are modified by adverbs.

An adverb modifies a verb, an adjective, or another adverb.

MODIFYING A VERB: She voted *wisely*.

MODIFYING AN ADJECTIVE: Information is *readily* available.

MODIFYING AN ADVERB: He felt criticism *very* keenly.

Adverbs tell *where, when, how,* or *to what extent:*

WHERE: They lingered *outside.*
WHEN: The team left *early.*
HOW: The story ended *happily.*
TO WHAT EXTENT: The writing was *totally* illegible.

Many adverbs are formed by adding *-ly* to an adjective: *cautious—cautiously, quick—quickly, soft—softly, thoughtful—thoughtfully*. However, not all modifiers ending in *-ly* are adverbs. The following, for example, are adjectives: *lively, homely, friendly, lovely, kindly*.

Some words may be either adjectives or adverbs.

ADJECTIVE	ADVERB
a *hard* task	Study *hard.*
a *long* journey	Don't be *long.*
a *late* program	We arrived *late.*

Many adverbs do not end in *-ly*. The negatives *no, not*, and *never* are almost always adverbs. Many time-words, such as *now, ever, almost, soon*, are always adverbs.

Directive Adverbs

Adverbs that tell *where* (place or direction) about the verb are called **directive adverbs.** They normally follow the verb they modify.

They tiptoed *in.*	Stack the supplies *inside.*
The box slid *down.*	No one ventured *near.*
The elevator went *up.*	The workers walked *out.*

Many of these directive adverbs are combined with verbs to make idioms: *give out, give up, give in, give off*. An idiom is a group of words with a meaning different from the literal meanings of the words taken individually.

Position of Adverbs

A directive adverb normally follows the verb it modifies. An adverb modifying an adjective or another adverb usually comes immediately before the word it modifies. Other adverbs may be shifted from one place in the sentence to another.

DIRECTIVE: The ship sailed *away.*

ADVERB MODIFYING MODIFIER: It was a *very* tense moment.

He left *rather* unexpectedly.

OTHER ADVERBS: *Quickly*, she opened the letter.

She *quickly* opened the letter.

She opened the letter *quickly*.

Adverbs in Comparisons

Like adjectives, adverbs are used in comparisons. The comparative and the superlative are formed as follows:

1. Adverbs of one syllable add *-er*.

Classes seemed to *go faster* today.
Draw the line *straighter*.

2. Most adverbs ending in *-ly* form the comparative with *more*.

He slammed the door *more violently* the second time.
When I heard a twig snap, I moved *more cautiously*.

3. The superlative form of the adverb is formed with *-est* or *most*. Adverbs that form the comparative with *-er* form the superlative with *-est*. Those using *more* for the comparative use *most* for the superlative.

COMPARATIVE	SUPERLATIVE
sooner	soonest
harder	hardest
more happily	most happily
more willingly	most willingly

Note: See Section 1.4 for irregular comparisons of adjectives. Some of the words listed there as adjectives may also be used as adverbs and are compared in the same way.

Exercise A: Find each adverb and the word or words it modifies.

1. You drive too fast for safety.
2. The supposedly unsinkable *Titanic* had actually sunk.
3. Suddenly a loud shot rang out.
4. The paint is not quite dry yet.
5. The story is only moderately interesting.
6. We rose early, breakfasted quickly, and drove to Memphis.
7. I have already made my decision.
8. Have you ever been to New England before?
9. Unfortunately, I still could not find the key.
10. You will undoubtedly hear from her soon.
11. Hemingway's *A Farewell to Arms* was first published serially.
12. The door will probably open if you press harder.
13. When will you repay the debt?
14. The food was too spicy.
15. The weather satellite sent back clear pictures.

Exercise B: Follow the same directions as for Exercise A.

1. The old man spoke slowly and deliberately.
2. You should check the information again.
3. Yesterday my mother took us there in the car.
4. I did the job very hastily.
5. We arrived too late.
6. Finally he put the menu aside and glanced around.
7. Beverly Sills always sings this piece brilliantly.
8. The mail usually comes very late in the morning.
9. I had never been so angry.
10. The little boy could hardly stay awake.

1.6 The Preposition

The words in an English sentence do not occur in haphazard order. They are arranged in precise patterns in order to convey meaning. The words that go together are joined or linked in a variety of ways. One means of linking words is the **preposition.**

There are seventeen one-syllable prepositions in English.* They are used to show the following relationships.

LOCATION:	at, by, in, on, near
DIRECTION:	to, from, down, off, through, out, past, up
ASSOCIATION:	of, for, with, like

There are also certain two-syllable prepositions.

about	along	below	during
above	among	beneath	except
across	around	beside	inside
after	before	between	outside
against	behind	beyond	over
			under

A number of prepositions have been formed by combining some of the one-syllable prepositions:

into	upon	without
onto	within	throughout

Compound prepositions have been formed by combining a modifier with a preposition or by grouping prepositions, as follows:

according to	out of	on account of	aside from
prior to	owing to	inside of	by means of
in front of	subsequent to	because of	as to

Objects of Prepositions. A preposition never appears alone. It is always used with a word or group of words that is called its **object.**

A preposition relates its object to some other word in the sentence.

The object of a preposition usually follows the preposition. The only exception occurs in a sentence or clause introduced by an interrogative pronoun or a relative pronoun.

* The word *but* may be used as a preposition with the meaning of *except*.

Light filtered *through* the damp subterranean *passage.*
Light filtered *into* the damp subterranean *passage.*
The motorcade moved slowly *through* the crowded *streets.*
Whom did you offer the job *to?*
Jack asked *whom* the telephone call was *for.*
What *hotel* will they have the dance *in?*

The object of a preposition may be a single word or a group of words.

WORD:	The doctor hurried into the *house.*
WORD:	I went with *them* willingly.
WORD:	Upon *arriving,* Joan asked for an interview.
WORD GROUP:	After *testing the equipment,* I found it defective.
WORD GROUP:	Before *recommending the book,* read it carefully.
WORD GROUP:	Explain the problem to *whoever is in charge.*

Exercise: Find the prepositions. Tell the object of each one.

1. Everyone contributed to the success of the party.
2. There are several books with blue bindings on that shelf.
3. Heart disease is one of the chief causes of death.
4. Most accidents in boating happen to amateurs.
5. My first drive on the golf course sliced into the lake.
6. The armistice went into effect on November 11, 1918.
7. The grizzly bear gazed into my camera with all the composure of a professional model.
8. Traffic on Main Street was rerouted because of the accident.
9. The game was postponed on account of rain.
10. Whom are you going with?
11. The meteor blazed through the earth's atmosphere.
12. Give the book to whoever wants it.
13. Inside the cozy cabin, a roaring fire crackled in the fireplace.
14. The rain pelted the roof throughout the night.
15. Prior to accepting the nomination, Aileen discussed the election with her advisors.

1.7 The Conjunction

Another kind of word used to tie the parts of a sentence together is the conjunction.

A conjunction is a word which connects words, phrases, or clauses.

There are three kinds of conjunctions: coordinating conjunctions, correlative conjunctions, and subordinating conjunctions.

Coordinating Conjunctions

There are three conjunctions used only to connect like sentence parts. They are called **coordinating conjunctions** because they tie together things of the same kind or order. These coordinating conjunctions are *and, but, or.*

His chief interests are backgammon *and* ceramics.
(connects nouns)

A camp counselor must be patient *and* resourceful.
(connects adjectives)

The marlin fought savagely *and* cunningly.
(connects adverbs)

Steve Martin got off the plane *and* into a limousine.
(connects prepositional phrases)

We could camp out *or* stay in motels. (connects predicates)

The ship sank, *but* all the passengers were saved.
(connects clauses)

For is used as a coordinating conjunction only between clauses. *Nor* is used as a coordinating conjunction only when it is preceded by another negative word.

Voter apathy is dangerous, *for* it can undermine democracy.
The fellow has *no* education, *nor* is he eager to learn.
The rookie *cannot* field, *nor* can she hit well.

Correlative Conjunctions

A few conjunctions are used in pairs: *not only . . . but (also)*; *either . . . or*; *neither . . . nor*; *both . . . and*; *whether . . . or*. Such conjunctions are called **correlative conjunctions.**

Motocross racing requires *not only* skill *but* great daring as well.
Either chemistry *or* physics is required.
Neither the book *nor* the movie was historically accurate.
Both the organization *and* content of the composition were excellent.
We must consider *whether* he will act responsibly *or* impulsively.

Subordinating Conjunctions

Words used to introduce adverb clauses are called **subordinating conjunctions.** These words not only introduce the subordinate clause but link it to the main clause. Their main function is to make the relation between the two clauses clear. The chief relations they show are *time, place, cause, result, exception, condition,* and *alternative*. The most common subordinating conjunctions are these:

after	as though	provided	till	whenever
although	because	since	unless	where
as	before	so that	until	wherever
as if	if	than	whatever	while
as long as	in order that	though	when	

Conjunctive Adverbs

Certain adverbs are used to join main clauses. When so used, they are called **conjunctive adverbs.** A conjunctive adverb is preceded by a semicolon and followed by a comma. The most common conjunctive adverbs are these:

accordingly	futhermore	moreover	therefore
also	hence	nevertheless	yet
consequently	however	otherwise	

Exercise A: Find the conjunctions and conjunctive adverbs. Tell what kind each joining word is.

1. We tried to hurry, but the crowd delayed us.
2. This is where we live.
3. He trembled as he spoke.
4. Korea has been called "The Land of the Morning Calm"; however, it has seen turbulent days.
5. I felt as if I were drowning.
6. I usually order chicken or fish.
7. Act as if nothing were wrong.
8. I telephoned Sheila while I was in Cleveland.
9. I will not go unless she goes.
10. The crowd cheered as the mayor waved.
11. They live where the weather is always warm.
12. Come for a visit whenever you can.
13. The roads were partly flooded; nevertheless, we kept driving.
14. A paralyzing snowfall hit Buffalo; consequently, all transportation was halted.
15. We put on our skates while we were waiting.

Exercise B: Find the conjunctions. Show what words or word groups they join.

1. Either he or I must go.
2. He has a stern manner but a good heart.
3. I walked across the highway and along the tracks.
4. Tanya tried to ask the librarian, but he was busy.
5. Elaine has written the report and has revised it.
6. William Jennings Bryan ran three times for the Presidency,but he was never elected.
7. She knew when to talk and when to listen.
8. The question was whether to stop here or to drive on to Atlanta.

1.8 The Interjection

An interjection is a word or group of words interjected, or thrown, into the sentence. It is usually followed by an exclamation point.

An interjection is a word or word group used to express surprise or other emotion. It has no grammatical relation to other words in the sentence.

Ouch! Oh! Ah! For heaven's sake! Great! Congratulations!

1.9 Words Used as Different Parts of Speech

Some words, such as *are, think, see,* are always verbs. The personal pronouns, such as *I* and *me,* are always personal pronouns. Many words, however, may be used in a sentence in different ways.

The treaty was signed, *but* we still had misgivings. (conjunction)
Everyone *but* the speaker noticed the incident. (preposition)

Will you turn on the *light?* (noun)
It needs a new *light* bulb. (adjective)
Light the birthday candles. (verb)

Noun or Adjective?

A word used to name a person, place, or thing is a noun. The same word may be used before another noun to tell "what kind." When so used, it is an adjective.

The teacher viewed *history* as a story of the human quest for freedom. (noun)
The *history* book was tattered and out of date. (adjective)

The world's tallest building is in *Chicago.* (noun)
The *Chicago* skyline is changing remarkably. (adjective)

Adjective or Pronoun?

A demonstrative pronoun—*this, that, these,* and *those*—may also be used as an adjective. If the word is used alone in place of a noun, it is a pronoun. If it is used before a noun to tell "which one," it is an adjective.

> *This* is a Polaroid camera. (pronoun)
> *These* are more practical shoes for you. (pronoun)
> *That* experience is hard to forget. (adjective modifying *experience*)
> *Those* aspects of the case are clear. (adjective modifying *aspects*)

In a similar way the words *what, which,* and *whose* may be used alone as pronouns or before nouns as adjectives.

> *What* will your salary be? (pronoun)
> *What* grade did you get? (adjective modifying *grade*)
> *Which* is the best route to take? (pronoun)
> *Which* play should I read? (adjective modifying *play*)
> *Whose* did you want? (pronoun)
> *Whose* skateboard is this? (adjective modifying *skateboard*)

The words *your, my, our, his, her, their* are forms of the personal pronouns used to show possession. Used in this way, they perform the job of adjectives. The words *mine, yours, hers, ours,* and *theirs* are always pronouns. The word *his* may be used either as a pronoun or an adjective. (See Section 1.2.)

> That hat of *hers* is colorful. (pronoun)
> The fingerprints are definitely *his*. (pronoun)
> *His* autobiography is rich in anecdotes. (adjective use)

Adjective or Adverb?

Several words have the same form whether used as adjectives or adverbs. To tell whether a word is used as an adjective or as an adverb, determine what other word in the sentence it goes with, or modifies. This is a matter of sense, which you can get from reading the sentence. If the word modifies a verb, it is used as an adverb. If it modifies a noun or pronoun, it is used as an adjective. If it tells *where, when, how*, or *to what extent*, it is an adverb. If it tells *what kind*, it is an adjective.

> Jets travel *fast*. (adverb telling *how* about *travel*)
> Drive in the *fast* lane. (adjective telling *what kind* about *lane*)

Adverb or Preposition?

A number of words may be used either as prepositions or as adverbs. If the word is followed by a noun or pronoun, it is probably a preposition. The noun or pronoun is its object. If the word in question is not followed by a noun or pronoun, it is probably an adverb. If the word can be moved to another position, it is an adverb.

> The coach sent *in* a substitute.
> The coach sent a substitute *in*.
> (*In* is an adverb. It can be moved without affecting the sense of the sentence.)
> Everyone danced *at* the disco.
> (*at* cannot be moved; it is a preposition.)
> The bulb finally burned *out*. (adverb)
> The cold drove the cattle *inside*. (adverb)
> We were talking *about* the music festival. (preposition)

Exercise A: Determine how the italicized word is used in each sentence.

1. The orchestra warmed up *before* the concert.
2. Neither candidate had held public office *before*.
3. Look *before* you leap.
4. We were just having a *friendly* argument.
5. Sound thinking is *essential* to good writing.

6. The moderator kept the discussion on the *main* topic.
7. A water *main* has burst.
8. The people who *frequent* this place are actors.
9. The woman from the nursery *pruned* the trees.
10. Roy is finding *college* algebra extremely difficult.
11. Whole-wheat bread contains greater *food* value than white.
12. The Acropolis *towers* over the city of Athens.
13. Can a hummingbird really fly so *fast?*
14. *Which* is your raincoat?
15. *Which* raincoat is yours?

Exercise B: Determine how the italicized word is used in each sentence.

1. Flames from the *oil* refinery illuminated the sky.
2. We admired Mr. Leonard's *rose* garden.
3. I *rose* at six this morning.
4. The crocodile sheds *no* tears.
5. The lightning had knocked *down* the flagpole.
6. We took the *through* train to Chicago.
7. Larry's education was *haphazard.*
8. Expect progress, *but* don't expect miracles.
9. They had subsisted on nothing *but* berries and water.
10. The mayor said she would not *countenance* any such proposal.
11. The Senate was faced with a *procedural* deadlock.
12. He looks ridiculous as a *would-be* professor.
13. The party is looking for a *gubernatorial* candidate.
14. *This* Pontiac belongs to the Hatfields.
15. *This* is the car I was telling you about.

1.10 Verbals

There are a number of highly useful words in English that are difficult to classify. These are **infinitives, participles,** and **gerunds.** They are called **verbals** because all of them are formed from verbs.

1.11 The Infinitive

Usually, but not always, the infinitive is preceded by *to*, which is called the "sign of the infinitive." The kinds of infinitives are as follows:

Active Present: to invite
Passive Present: to be invited
Active Perfect: to have invited
Passive Perfect: to have been invited

The infinitive may be used as a noun. It may be subject or object of the verb. It may be a predicate noun or an appositive.

To explain the phenomenon was impossible. (subject of *was*)
The author wants *to write* a trilogy. (object of *wants*)
The aim of the bill is *to reduce* taxes. (predicate noun)
Leo's job, *to barbecue* the meat, took almost two hours. (appositive)

The infinitive may also be used as a modifier. Used as an adjective, it may modify nouns and pronouns.

This is the book *to read.* She is someone *to emulate.*

As an adverb, the infinitive may modify adverbs, adjectives, or verbs.

Laughter is good *to hear.* (modifying the adjective *good*)

Courtney tried too hard *to succeed.* (modifies the adverb *hard*)

They dived *to get* pearls. (modifies the verb *dived*)

The infinitive may appear without the word *to:*

Let him *give* his opinion.
Please *register* for the election.
Helpless, I watched my hat *float* away.

The Infinitive Phrase. An infinitive itself may have modifiers. It may also have a subject, an object, or a predicate word. An **infinitive phrase** consists of the infinitive together with its modifiers, subject, object, or predicate word.

The infinitive may be modified by adverbs, phrases, or clauses. These modifiers are part of the infinitive phrase.

> *To think* logically is necessary in most situations.
> (The adverb *logically* modifies *To think.*)
>
> *To finish* in time, I cannot waste a minute.
> (The phrase *in time* modifies *To finish.*)
>
> I decided *to go* home after I delivered the package.
> (The clause *after I delivered the package* modifies *to go.*)

The infinitive may have a direct object, an indirect object, or a predicate word. These words, completing the meaning of the infinitive, are part of the infinitive phrase.

> *To get* the best *results,* follow directions carefully.
> (*results* is the direct object of *To get.*)
>
> The board voted *to grant her* a posthumous *award.*
> (*her* is the indirect object and *award* is the direct object of *to grant.*)
>
> Pat's sister has decided *to be* a *biochemist.*
> (*biochemist* is a predicate noun after *to be.*)
>
> He intended the soft music *to be soothing.*
> (*soothing* is a predicate adjective after *to be.*)

The infinitive may have a subject. The subject always follows the main verb and comes directly before the infinitive. Since it follows the main verb and is in the objective case, it is sometimes mistaken for an object of the main verb. The subject of the infinitive is part of the infinitive phrase. In the following examples, the entire phrase is the direct object of the verb.

> Both Dan and Ed invited *her to go to the party.*
> The committee persuaded *us to sell the tickets.*
> Frank urged *his parents to reconsider the decision.*

Note: If the main verb is a linking verb (a form of *be, appear, seem,* etc.), the noun following it is a predicate noun. If a predicate noun is followed by an infinitive, the infinitive modifies the noun.

> She is the person *to see.* They are the team *to beat.*

Exercise: Find the infinitive or infinitive phrase in each sentence that follows.

1. The writer attempts to simplify everything.
2. Which is the best course to follow?
3. Jess has finally decided to get a haircut.
4. To pilot a boat skillfully requires practice.
5. We could take a jet from O'Hare to save time.
6. Would you like to have lived in Caesar's time?
7. Everyone in the room heard you say it.
8. Janine's instructions were to whistle three times.
9. I am sorry to have interrupted your conversation.
10. The nurse came periodically to check the sick woman's condition.
11. The citizens voted for a pageant to be held on Washington's Birthday.
12. My advice to you is to buy new skates.
13. My friend Elena is learning to make pottery.
14. To study some instrument is a tradition for everyone in our family.
15. Grover Cleveland was the only President to serve two nonconsecutive terms.

1.12 The Gerund

The gerund is a verbal noun that ends in *-ing*. It is used in a sentence as a noun and in almost every way that a noun can be used.

> *Training* for the Olympics is hard work. (subject of the verb)
> Juanita enjoys *camping*. (object of the verb)
> Before *applying*, check your qualifications. (object of the preposition)

The Gerund Phrase. A gerund may be modified by adjectives or adverbs. It may be completed by objects or predicate words. A **gerund phrase** consists of the gerund together with its modifiers, objects, or predicate words.

The gerund may be modified by single adjectives and adverbs or by phrases and by clauses.

> *Rapid reading* has become a national interest.
> (*Rapid* is an adjective modifying *reading*.)
> Robin tried *walking quickly* to avoid Charles.
> (*quickly* is an adverb modifying *walking*.)
> *Experimenting without adequate equipment* is difficult.
> (*without adequate equipment* is a phrase modifying *Experimenting*.)
> *Persevering after you have failed* is a test of character.
> (*after you have failed* is a clause modifying *Persevering*.)

Gerunds may be completed by objects or predicate words. These words are part of the gerund phrase.

> *Being stage manager* is hard work.
> (*stage manager* is a predicate noun completing *Being*.)
> *Conceding him the victory* was very difficult.
> (*him* is the indirect object and *victory* is the direct object of *Conceding*.)

Exercise: Find the complete gerund phrases in these sentences.

1. He left without asking my permission.
2. Hearing that music always makes me sad.
3. I am interested in reading *The Contender* by Robert Lipsyte.
4. An important skill in oratory is knowing when to stop.
5. Before leaving the house, we locked all the windows.
6. Try singing the tenor part.
7. Eating pizza is a mania with Janice.
8. Shari is clever at imitating others.
9. The screaming of the seagulls came from that cove.
10. Lorraine is skillful at navigating in rough waters.
11. I have finally mastered the art of skimming a newspaper.
12. Let's practice swimming ten laps.
13. The islanders' chief occupations are weaving straw hats and raising cacao.
14. Cleaning up after a party is often harder work than getting ready for a party.
15. This is asking too much.

1.13 The Participle

There are several forms of the participle, all widely used.

PRESENT PARTICIPLE:	instructing
PAST PARTICIPLE:	instructed
PERFECT PARTICIPLE:	having instructed
PASSIVE PERFECT PARTICIPLE:	having been instructed

The present participle always ends in *-ing*. The past particple is the third principal part of the verb, and its endings are various. (See Section 1.3)

The participle is always used as an adjective to modify a noun or a pronoun. In the following examples, the arrow indicates the word modified by the participle.

Hesitating, Art questioned the wisdom of discussing the incident.

Surrounded, the guerrilla forces capitulated.

Having been forewarned, the pilot prepared for an emergency.

The Participial Phrase. A participle may be modified by single adverbs or by phrases and clauses. The participle may also be completed by objects or predicate words. A **participial phrase** consists of the participle together with its modifiers, objects, or predicate words.

When a participle is modified by an adverb, a phrase, or a clause, these modifiers are part of the participial phrase.

Listening attentively, we heard the plane approaching.
(*attentively* is an adverb modifying *Listening.*)

Driving without a license, Jim got into trouble.
(*without a license* is a phrase modifying *Driving.*)

Fiddling while Rome burned, Nero assured himself of a place in history.
(*while Rome burned* is a clause modifying *Fiddling.*)

When a participle is completed by objects or predicate words, these words are part of the participial phrase. In the examples below, the arrow indicates the word modified by the participial phrase.

Having found our way, we continued the hike.
(*way* is the direct object of *Having found.*)

The children sat on the front steps, *looking forlorn.*
(*forlorn* is a predicate adjective completing *looking.*)

Giving her horse a pep talk, the jockey rode toward the starting gate.
(*horse* is the indirect object and *pep talk* is the direct object of *Giving*)

Exercise: Find the complete participial phrase and show which word it modifies.

1. Being an aviator, Ms. Luft enjoyed *Wind, Sand, and Stars.*
2. She stood at the window, anticipating the arrival of the first guests.
3. The player, having accepted a bribe, was expelled.
4. The letter, written hurriedly, contained many errors.
5. The street, crowded with cars, looked impassable.
6. Swinging his tennis racket, Jordan approached the court confidently.
7. Built over a hundred years ago, the house is still sturdy.
8. Tracy is the player now passing the ball.
9. Struck by lightning, the barn caught fire.
10. Neatly dressed, the children set out for school.
11. The White House, first occupied by John Adams in 1800, has been enlarged several times in recent years.
12. Watering his zinnias, Fred noticed that holes were appearing in the leaves.
13. Puzzled about the cause, he wondered whether insects might be responsible.
14. Seeking advice at a seed store, he was told of a useful spray.
15. Responding to his care, the plants began to flourish.

Review Exercise: Find the verbals in these sentences. Identify each verbal as an infinitive, infinitive phrase, gerund, gerund phrase, participle, or participial phrase.

1. From the beginning, the Raiders dominated the game.
2. The horseback riders prepared to ford the clear, cold stream.
3. Paddling a canoe builds shoulder muscles.
4. Dazed by the blow, the boxer fell to the mat.
5. Chicago has a restaurant called Jonathan Livingston Seafood.
6. Albert learned to weave fibers on a hand loom.
7. That banana cream pie certainly looks appealing.
8. Many ships have been lost in the area known as the Bermuda Triangle.

9. Jerry needs tutoring in math and chemistry.

10. A new program encourages students to analyze the architecture around them.

11. Does living on the moon seem likely in the twenty-first century?

12. Paramedics, carrying a stretcher, raced into the house.

13. Scientists hope to explore the ocean as a major food source.

14. Lisa set the timer to take a picture of the whole group.

15. After fielding several questions, the President brought the press conference to a close.

16. The governor plans to hold a state-wide conference on women's issues.

17. Recently computerized, the scheduling of classes is no longer a problem.

18. After trading insults, the two boys got into a fight.

19. The publishers want *Working Woman* to appeal to that large category of consumers.

20. Perennially frozen, the ground in Greenland is covered with permafrost.

REVIEW: THE CLASSIFICATION OF WORDS Identify the italicized words in these sentences as noun, pronoun, verb, adjective, adverb, preposition, conjunction, interjection, infinitive, gerund, or participle.

1. Denise applied *for* a patent on her *new* invention.

2. The audience gave the *veteran* actress a standing *ovation.*

3. *Although she* enjoys Scrabble, Maria prefers *playing* Master Mind.

4. *Aha!* The thief entered *through* this *rear* window.

5. The Electoral College *chooses* the *President* and Vice-President of the United States.

6. *When* Ramona whistled, the horse turned and *galloped* to her side.

7. *With flawless* grace, the pianist played a concerto by *Mozart.*

8. Frannie *routinely* deposits her *weekly* paycheck into a savings account.

9. Al's Restaurant, *which* is *often open* all night, serves pancakes and waffles.

10. The centerfielder *and* the shortstop collided *as they* raced for the ball.

11. The control tower *soon gave* the pilot clearance to land.

12. Brian *created* a unique animated cartoon by *photographing* clay figures.

13. *Anyone who* wants *to work* during the summer should apply in the spring.

14. The ski slopes *near* Aspen *have accumulated* a forty-inch snow base.

15. The curator *bluntly declared* that the painting was a *fake*.

16. Deborah made a *family* tree *showing* all of her ancestors for *five* generations.

17. Graves *vehemently* denied the *charges* of espionage against *him*.

18. *Oh*, those cars are *very* sleek, *but* they gobble fuel!

19. *Exhausted*, *Mark* limped *painfully* toward the finish line.

20. *Some* areas, such as the Greenland ice cap and northwest Siberia, are *still* virtually *inaccessible*.

2.0 The Parts of a Sentence

Words can be used singly or in groups to convey meaning. The words *stop, danger, poison,* for example, express full meaning to the reader. In general, however, meaning is expressed in English by groups of words acting together: *during the game, singing a song, Doug ran.*

These groups of words are neither spoken nor written in haphazard order. In the English sentence there are fixed patterns into which words are arranged to express meaning. These patterns are learned in childhood. They are learned because they are the chief means by which a child can communicate his or her feelings.

Knowing what these sentence patterns are and how they work is essential for effective communication in adult life.

2.1 The Sentence

Sentences are used to make statements and to ask questions. To be understood, they must express a complete thought, a complete idea, or a complete question. Now, a complete thought can be expressed by a word or a phrase:

Great! Not at home Grocery Store

On the other hand, words and phrases may *not* express a complete idea:

Having been nominated   The person in the three-piece suit

You know that these expressions are incomplete because they leave you asking *what? what about it? what happened?*

A group of words must express a complete thought, or it is not a sentence. We begin studying the sentence with this partial definition:

A sentence is a group of words that expresses a complete thought.

INCOMPLETE	The player on the sidelines (What about her?)
COMPLETE	The player on the sidelines was injured.
INCOMPLETE	Jack Allen, a sophomore (Did what?)
COMPLETE	Jack Allen, a sophomore, placed first in public speaking.
INCOMPLETE	Building a boat (Who did what?)
COMPLETE	Building a boat, they were happily occupied.

Exercise: Which of the following groups of words are sentences?

1. Easily the best dancer in the troupe
2. Sleek, high-stepping horses parading around the track
3. A book about the history of Chicago
4. Eugene O'Neill, possibly the greatest playwright of the century
5. Representing the United States in the Olympic Games
6. An expert performer on the parallel bars
7. An interesting article about exchange students
8. Two men on base and Ken Griffey at bat
9. Speleologists explore caves
10. Has the yearbook gone to press
11. The heron, a large water fowl with long, thin legs
12. The Appalachian Mountains, much older than the Alps
13. Lorraine Hansberry's *A Raisin in the Sun,* my favorite play
14. The Red Cross, important in peace time as well as in war
15. Administers help during floods and other natural catastrophes

2.2 Kinds of Sentences

Sentences may be classified as to structure* or as to the purpose of the speaker or writer. There are four principal purposes served by sentences:

1. The **declarative sentence** is used to make a statement. The statement may be one of fact, wish, intent, or feeling.

> Plans for the Bicentennial were begun years before 1976.
> I wanted to read *Victory Over Myself* by Floyd Patterson.

2. The **imperative sentence** is used to state a command, request, or direction. The subject is always *You*. When the subject is not expressed, as is usually the case, it is "understood" to be *You*.

> (You) Follow the directions carefully.
> (You) Take Route 88 for nine miles.
> (You) Call the clinic sometime after six o'clock.

3. The **interrogative sentence** is used to ask a question. It is always followed by a question mark.

> Who wrote *Billy Budd?*
> Do you realize what you are saying?
> What is the temperature of the earth's interior?

4. An **exclamatory sentence** is used to express strong feeling. It is always followed by an exclamation point.

> What a tale that was!   How hungry we were!

Exercise: What kind of sentence is each of the following?

1. Poe's life was short and tragic.
2. Go to the next corner and turn right.
3. Was the speed-reading course effective?
4. Help yourself to some pretzels.

* For classification of sentences by form or structure, see Section 3.0.

5. How small these calculators are!
6. The first tourists to arrive will receive souvenirs.
7. Do exactly as I tell you.
8. It can't be midnight already!
9. This is a book you would enjoy.
10. What events are included in the decathlon?
11. Please explain your answer.
12. Good things often come in large packages.
13. How tired we were!
14. Step this way, please.
15. Is the high school visible from the highway?

2.3 Subject and Predicate

There are two parts in every complete sentence. (1) The **subject** is the person, thing, or idea about which something is said. (2) The **predicate** is the idea expressed about the subject.

Every sentence contains a subject and a predicate.

The subject of the sentence is the person or thing about which something is said.

The predicate tells something or asks something about the subject of the sentence.

The word *predicate* means "to proclaim, declare, preach, or affirm." The predicate of a sentence therefore "proclaims, declares, preaches, or affirms" something about the subject.

We may say that a sentence is a group of words that tells something (*predicate*) about a person or thing (*subject*). Our definition of a sentence may now be expanded:

A sentence is a group of words expressing a complete thought by means of a subject and a predicate.

SUBJECT	PREDICATE
Water	evaporates.
Water	evaporates quickly in the hot sun.

2.4 The Simple Predicate

In every predicate, however long, the most important word—the key word—is the **verb.*** In fact, the verb is the key word of the entire sentence. Sentences may be constructed without nouns, pronouns, or other parts of speech; without a verb, however, there can be no sentence.

The simple predicate of the sentence is the verb.

The simple predicate, which we shall hereafter call the *verb,* may be a phrase consisting of more than one word: *have noticed, might have noticed, is running, had been running.* The words making up the verb may be interrupted by a modifier. Such a modifier is not part of the verb.

have probably *gone*   *had* just *eaten*
was never *questioned*   *had* almost *finished*

The verb may also be compound. The word *compound* means "having more than one part of the same kind." The parts of a compound verb are joined together by a conjunction (*and, or, neither-nor,* etc.).

They **stood** up *and* **cheered** spontaneously.
The union members **may** *either* **accept** *or* **reject** the contract.

2.5 The Simple Subject

Every verb has a subject. It is the word or words that answer *who? or what?* before the verb.

The sled crashed.
Verb: crashed
What crashed?: sled
Subject: sled

Scientists use nuclear energy.
Verb: use
Who uses?: scientists
Subject: scientists

* The **complete predicate** consists of the verb, its modifiers, and complements. The **complete subject** consists of the simple subject and its modifiers.

The **simple subject** is the subject of the verb. The subject of the verb may be a word, a phrase, or a clause.

To want peace is the first requisite. (phrase as subject)
That food shortages will continue seems certain.
(clause as subject)

The subject of a verb may be an entire phrase, but it is never one word within a phrase.

One *of the glasses* was cracked.
(Only one was cracked. *One* is the subject. The word *glasses* lies within the prepositional phrase and is the object of the preposition *of*.)

Fighting sharks is not my idea of fun.
(The gerund phrase *Fighting sharks* is the subject of *is*.)

Marion, *together with her cousins,* is at the lake.
(*Marion* is the subject of *is*; *cousins* is the object of the preposition *together with*.)

The subject of the verb may be compound. The parts of a compound subject are normally joined by a conjunction.

Mood, rhythm, *and* **harmony** are aspects of music.

Television *and* **radio** are mass communication media.

Both **meaning** *and* **form** should be considered in analyzing a poem.

Exercise A: Find the verb and its subject. Watch for compound parts.

1. Our school will soon be celebrating its centennial.
2. Aunt Ethel always tells that old joke about the electric grape.
3. Both Jan and Bob work on the fourth floor.
4. Newsstands and bookstores throughout the country sell the book.
5. A good newspaper reporter checks all the facts of a story.
6. You can either come along or stay here.

7. Neither the young nor the old should have too much idle time.
8. Catching trout is my favorite sport.
9. Many of my friends have part-time jobs.
10. The east wing of the high school building contains the auditorium.

Exercise B: Follow the same directions as for Exercise A.

1. Both philodendrons and palms need indirect sunlight.
2. Putting good ideas into circulation is everybody's job.
3. The old Model-A Ford sputtered, wheezed, and finally came to a halt.
4. A huge crowd and fair weather turned the first track meet into a rousing success.
5. A drop of swamp water is alive with animals.
6. This television and that radio can be adapted for use with a nine-volt battery.
7. A professor of physics at the state university lives next door.
8. A fast camera setting produces slow-motion film.
9. The make-up crew supplied the cast members with cleansing tissue.
10. Dick fell and hurt his knee during last night's game.

2.6 Subjects in Unusual Positions

The subject appears before the verb in most sentences. This subject-verb order is the normal pattern of English sentences. In many sentences, however, this order is reversed.

Questions. In most questions the subject appears between the words making up the verb phrase.

VERB	SUBJECT	VERB
Did	he	forget?
Has	she	returned?
Will	they	understand?
Could	we	have gone?

In most questions beginning with interrogative words such as *where, when, why, how, how much,* the subject falls between the parts of the verb. In questions beginning with *who* or *what,* the verb may follow the subject in normal order:

Who won? What caused the fire?

Sentences Beginning with *There* and *Here*. Many sentences begin with *There* or *Here* followed by some form of *be*: *There is, There was, There will be, Here is, Here were,* and so on. In these sentences *Here* and *There* are introductory words used to get the sentence started. They are never the subject of the verb. In this kind of sentence, the subject follows the verb.

Here is my idea. (*idea* is the subject.)
There are complex issues involved. (*issues* is the subject.)
There will be a flower show this spring. (*show* is the subject.)

Note: Not all sentences beginning with *Here* and *There* follow the above pattern: *Here we can build a campfire. Here he is. There he goes.* In these sentences, *Here* and *There* are adverbs modifying the verb.

Sentences in Inverted Order. For emphasis or for variety of style, the subject is sometimes placed after the verb.

Through the woods strolled a strange *figure.*
Toward the cliff ran the frightened *boy.*
From his mistakes emerged my *victory.*

Finding the Subject of the Verb. To find the subject of the verb in any sentence, find the verb first. Then ask *who?* or *what?* before it. If the sentence is not in normal word order, change it to normal order, and the subject will become clear.

INVERTED: Up from the field flew a family of pheasants.
NORMAL: A family of pheasants flew up from the field.

Exercise A: Find the verb and its subject.

1. There is an urgent need for library books.
2. Where is the school greenhouse located?
3. High into the air leaped the shortstop.
4. Here the embattled farmers stood.
5. Did Dorothy Hamill win an Olympic gold medal?
6. At 10 Downing Street lives the Prime Minister of England.
7. How do you make this dessert, Frank?
8. From all over the world came congratulatory telegrams.
9. There in front of us was an impassable ravine.
10. High above the valley moved a cable car.

Exercise B: Find the verb and its subject.

1. Directly behind me was the mayor.
2. Where are you going after the play?
3. Along the streets of Bern were tempting pastry shops.
4. Here are the books.
5. Straight between the goalie's skates shot the puck.
6. In the back of the theater were several dozen standees.
7. There have been several rumors about the President's plans.
8. Mingling with the crowd were several Secret Service agents.
9. Why have you done this to me?
10. Overhead, in triangular formation, roared the Air Force jets.

2.7 The Direct Object

In many sentences the action verb carries action over from the subject to some other word. It serves to tie these words together. The word to which the action is carried from the subject is the **direct object.**

Sometimes the direct object tells what receives the action of the verb. Sometimes it tells the result of the action.

RECEIVER OF ACTION:	The naturalist set a *trap*. (set what?)
RESULT OF ACTION:	The naturalist captured the *bird*. (captured what?)

RECEIVER OF ACTION: Art carved the *ham*. (carved what?)
RESULT OF ACTION: Art enjoyed the *ham*. (enjoyed what?)

Action verbs that carry over the action from subject to object are called **transitive verbs.** Action verbs that are not followed by direct objects are called **intransitive.** Some verbs may be transitive in one sentence and intransitive in another.

The hikers *whistled*. (intransitive)
The hikers *whistled* a merry *tune*. (transitive)

With some so-called action verbs, the action is not visible, nor otherwise evident. However, the verb does carry the thought from subject to object, tying them together.

I *understand* your position. (understand what?)
The stranger *appreciates* your help. (appreciates what?)
Joanne *honored* my request. (honored what?)

The direct object is a word or group of words to which the verb carries over the action from the subject.

The direct object may be a word, a phrase, or a clause.

Lauren said, "*Uh-oh*." (word)
Carlos wants *to prepare dinner*. (phrase)
He tried *interpreting the poem*. (phrase)
Wilma meant *what she said*. (clause)

The direct object may be compound.

Winter campers need insulated *boots* and nylon *jackets*. (need what?)
I like *to play the piano* and *to compose for it*. (like what?)

A word that completes the meaning of the verb is called a **complement.** The direct object is one kind of complement.

Direct Object or Adverb? To find the direct object, ask *what?* after the verb. An adverb following an action verb tells *where*, *when, how,* or *to what extent* about the verb. A direct object tells *what* after the verb.

> The guerrillas crept *forward.* (where)
> Craig walked *stiffly* to the front of the room. (how)
> The elderly lady dropped the *letter* in the slot. (what)

Exercise: Find the direct objects in these sentences.

1. Controllers tracked the aircraft with radar.
2. Trish liked the ending of the TV movie.
3. With five seconds left in the game, Dallas scored a touchdown.
4. This candy machine did not return my change.
5. For his term paper, Carl researched the life of Golda Meir.
6. At the beginning of each semester, students buy their books.
7. Cars of all makes filled the lot.
8. Lynne gulped her milkshake and raced to class.
9. The local newspaper publicized our student talent show.
10. Ozone may have a damaging effect on the atmosphere.
11. Our canoe brigade followed the route of early explorers.
12. Several debaters captured top honors in the state tournament.
13. Harry Chapin sang his hit songs and a few ballads.
14. Andrea will study politics during a seminar in Washington.
15. Radio station WBEZ broadcasts programs about Hispanic culture.

2.8 The Indirect Object

The indirect object of the verb tells *to or for whom,* or *to or for what,* something is done.

> The manager promised *them* higher wages. (*to* them)
> Dad bought *me* a new AM/FM radio. (*for* me)

A verb has an indirect object only if it also has a direct object. Find the direct objects in the examples above.

The indirect object may be compound: I told *Jim* and *Carlotta* the truth.

The words *to* and *for* are never placed before the indirect object. When followed by a noun or pronoun, *to* and *for* are prepositions. The noun or pronoun following the preposition is its object.

Lend *Bert* your compass. (*Bert* is the indirect object.)
Ed lent his compass *to Bert*. (*Bert* is the object of the preposition.)

The company offered *me* a job. (*me* is the indirect object.)
The company offered a job *to me*. (*me* is the object of the preposition.)

Exercise: Find both the direct and indirect objects.

1. I loaned Alice a book about India.
2. My friend in Atlantic City sent me some salt-water taffy.
3. The committee allowed me five dollars for expenses.
4. I'll give you a lift to the train station.
5. Roy wrote Ann Landers a question.
6. Will the store give you a refund for the sweater?
7. The survivor told the reporters the story of her ordeal.
8. We offered Pat cash for his jeep.
9. Does Santa Claus give bad children ashes?
10. We mailed her pictures of our new house.
11. Sing us a song, Jean.
12. Gail Sheehy handed the reviewer a copy of her new book.
13. Mr. Briggs left his college a million dollars.
14. The coach gave us excellent training in hockey.
15. Barbara Walters asked Anwar Sadat very pointed questions.

2.9 Predicate Words

The linking verb links its subject to a word in the predicate. The word in the predicate, so linked, is called a **predicate word.** The subject may be linked to a **predicate noun,** a **predicate pronoun,** or a **predicate adjective.**

Shakespeare was perhaps the world's greatest *dramatist.* (predicate noun)

The winner could have been *you.* (predicate pronoun)

The chemistry experiment seemed *easy.* (predicate adjective)

A word that completes the meaning of a verb is called a **complement.** Predicate words complete the meaning of linking verbs, and since they refer to the subject, they are called **subject complements.**

Diagraming. The simple sentence with an action verb is diagramed as follows:

Eskimos hunt.

Eskimos hunt walrus.

Eskimos hunt walrus skillfully.

Note: The single-word modifier goes on a slant line below the word it modifies.

The simple sentence with a linking verb is diagramed as follows:

Dad looks grim.

Pam is president.

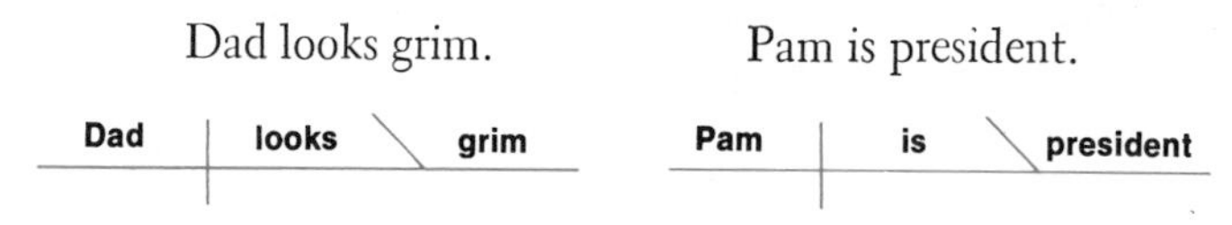

Note: The line following the linking verb slants toward the subject.

The action verb with an indirect object is diagramed as follows:

The President awarded Wyeth the Freedom Medal.

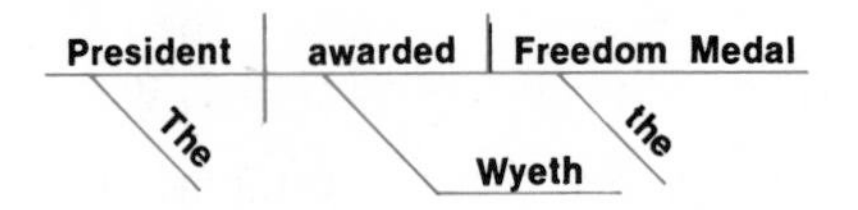

Exercise A: Find the predicate words.

1. The Governor looked tired after her trip.
2. The juniors were quite successful in the drive.
3. These funnels are handy for pouring liquids.
4. The snow was deep in the driveway.
5. Bob will probably be an excellent rancher.
6. The Republicans' chances seemed promising.
7. Her wisdom became apparent.
8. Should this cream cheese taste so sour?
9. The Rocky Mountain bighorn is a wild sheep.
10. The best writer in our class is Barbara Brady.

Exercise B: Make five columns. Head them *Subject, Verb, Direct Object, Indirect Object*, and *Predicate Word*. Place those parts of the following sentences in the proper columns.

1. In the fog, the car hit a post.
2. She is a firm, but fair disciplinarian.
3. Charles Dickens paid his first visit to the United States in 1842.
4. The pizza smelled tantalizing in the oven.
5. The attendant gave us a new ping-pong ball.
6. Devora sent me a telegram from Los Angeles.
7. Dave's steer won a blue ribbon at the 4-H fair.
8. Many people regard autumn as their favorite season.
9. The pugilist dealt his opponent a savage blow.
10. Mr. Quinn paid Roseann three dollars for mowing the lawn.

2.10 Compound Parts of Sentences

Subjects, verbs, objects, predicate words, and predicates may all be compound. That is, they may consist of more than one part *of the same kind*. The parts are joined by a conjunction.

COMPOUND SUBJECT:	Old *cars* and rusted *parts* clutter the junkyard.
COMPOUND VERB:	The sea *whirls* and *eddies*.
COMPOUND DIRECT OBJECT:	Volcanoes eject *lava* and *rocks*.
COMPOUND INDIRECT OBJECT:	The officer told *Tom* and *me* the news.
COMPOUND OBJECT OF PREPOSITION:	We talked about our *careers* and our *hopes*.
COMPOUND PREDICATE WORD:	He was *restless* and *fearful*.
COMPOUND PREDICATE:	Clare *turned off the television set* and *began her homework*.

Diagraming. Compound sentence parts are diagramed as follows:

Ed and Judy (*compound subject*) stayed and worked (*compound verb*).

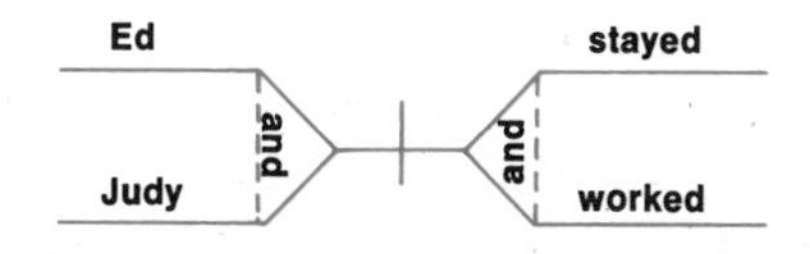

The director gave Joseph and Susan (*compound indirect object*) their scripts and costumes (*compound direct object*).

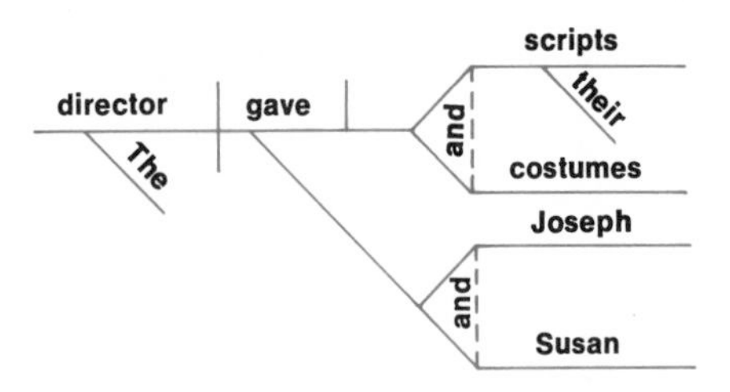

The opinions of the reporters and candidates (*compound object of preposition*) were diverse but pertinent (*compound predicate adjective*).

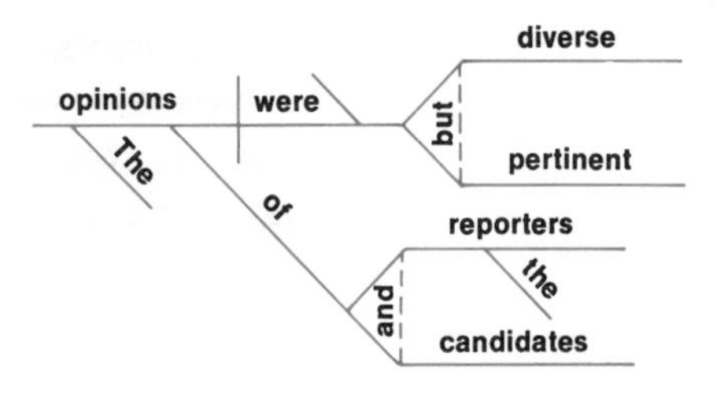

The class read the novel and evaluated the plot (*compound predicate*).

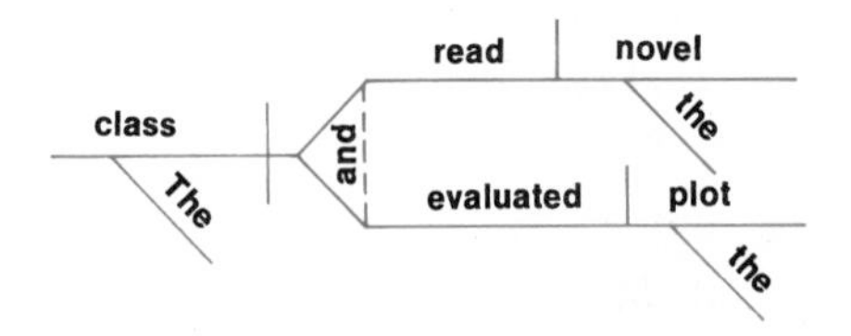

Exercise: Make five columns. Head them *Subject, Verb, Direct Object, Predicate Word,* and *Predicate*. Find the compound parts of the following sentences, and write these parts in the proper columns.

1. Down at the other end of the pool were Julie and Debby.
2. The lecturer discussed India and China.

3. A third-string halfback made the interception and scored the touchdown.
4. Our cheering section seemed listless and completely indifferent.
5. We were not only hungry but extremely tired.
6. Mitch tries but seldom succeeds.
7. Helping underdeveloped countries seems both charitable and practical.
8. Lee is a homemaker and a dietitian.
9. Marilyn loves golf but cannot make a living at it.
10. On the table are two batteries and a new bulb.
11. Joe took the snowshoes, skis, and skates from the closet.
12. Walking toward us were the mayor and his assistant.
13. Bach, Mozart, and Beethoven are Ann's favorite composers.
14. A helicopter rushed food and supplies to the stranded mountain climbers.
15. The book and the pamphlets will give you information about fields of specialization.

2.11 The Phrase

A phrase is a group of words without a subject and a verb, used as one part of speech.

A phrase is used as one part of speech. A **verb phrase** is two or more words used as a verb: *would have been, will drive.* A **noun phrase** is two or more words used as a noun: *Yosemite National Park, Ohio Turnpike.*

2.12 The Prepositional Phrase

The prepositional phrase consists of the preposition, its object, and modifiers of the object.

> Macbeth yielded to temptation *at his wife's persuasion.*
> *In our first football game,* Carl played first-string quarterback.

The object of a preposition is always a noun, a pronoun, or a group of words used as a noun.

The cottage is *near* the ocean. (*ocean* is the object of *near.*)
We lent our books *to* them. (*them* is the object of *to.*)
Law is a career *for* which I am qualified. (*which* is the object of *for.*)
By raising Mike's salary, Mr. Cook persuaded him to stay. (*raising Mike's salary* is a gerund phrase. It is the object of *By.*)
The merchants promised the plaque *to* whoever won three times. (*whoever won three times* is a noun clause, the object of *to.*)

The prepositional phrase is a modifier. It is used either as an adjective or as an adverb. A prepositional phrase that modifies a noun or pronoun is an **adjective phrase;** that is, it is a phrase used as an adjective.

Her car is the one *with the sun roof.* (*with the sun roof* modifies the pronoun *one.*)

The sound *of music* filled the corridors. (*of music* modifies *sound.*)

Distrust *among nations* threatens peace. (*among nations* modifies *distrust.*)

An adjective phrase always comes immediately after the noun or pronoun it modifies.

A prepositional phrase that modifies a verb, an adjective, or an adverb is an **adverb phrase.** That is, it is a phrase used as an adverb to tell *where, when, how,* or *to what extent* about the words it modifies.

The letter was hidden *under some books.* (*under some books* tells *where* about the verb *was hidden.*)

The baby cries early *in the morning* to awaken her parents. (*in the morning* tells *when* about the adverb *early*.)

The project was successful *beyond everyone's expectations*. (*beyond everyone's expectations* tells *to what extent* about the adjective *successful*.)

When two or more prepositional phrases follow each other in succession, they may modify the same word, or one phrase may modify the object in the preceding phrase.

We *ate* *at a diner* *after the show*. (Both phrases modify *ate; at a diner* tells *where* and *after the show* tells *when* about the verb.)

Joan put the music *on the chair* *near the piano*. (*on the chair* modifies *put; near the piano* modifies *chair*.)

They analyzed the symbolism *in a novel* *about court intrigue* *in sixteenth-century England*. (*in a novel* modifies the verb *analyzed; about court intrigue* modifies *novel; in sixteenth-century England* modifies *intrigue*.)

Diagraming. Prepositional phrases are diagramed as follows:

Dom ordered a copy *of the book*. (adjective phrase)

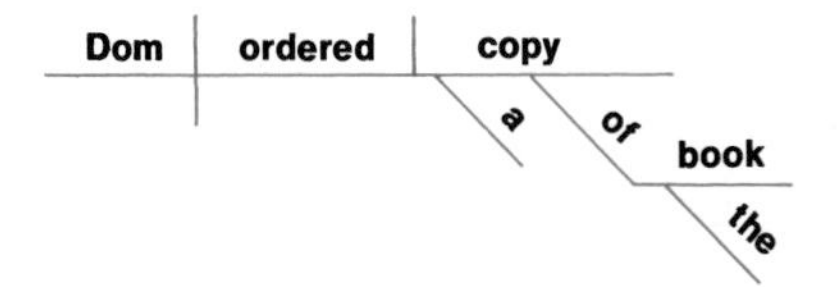

The season opens *early in the month*. (adverb phrase)

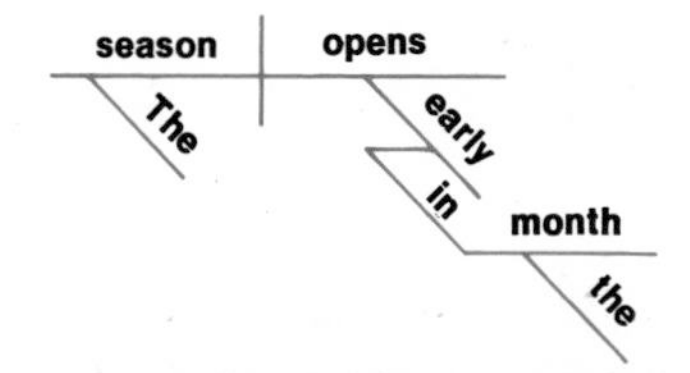

The ball went *over the fence.* (adverb phrase)

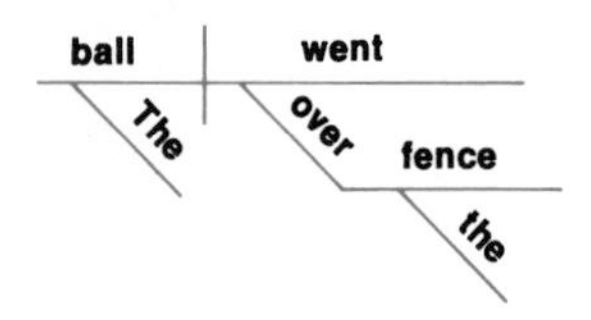

The stack *of books on the porch* got soaked. (adjective phrase)

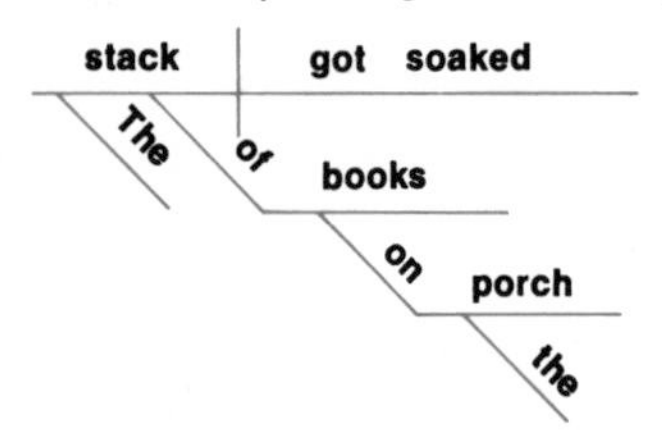

Exercise A: Write each prepositional phrase and the word or words it modifies.

1. There were newspaper clippings between the pages of the book.
2. I went to the counselor's office and asked advice about my courses.
3. The book with the green cover is mine.
4. Some forms of cancer have been checked by radioactive materials.
5. Unbridled power in the hands of one person is always dangerous.
6. The china on the shelf of the cupboard is very rare.
7. There was a feeling of unrest among the players.
8. All but one of these sentences are easy.
9. Cerebral palsy is high on the list of unsolved medical problems.
10. Each year, in our country, ten thousand children are born with injuries to the brain cells.

Exercise B: Write each prepositional phrase and the word or words it modifies.

1. Guatemala is located near Mexico.
2. Excavations at a prehistoric Mayan site began recently.
3. The excavations are in the Mayan jungle in Guatemala.

4. The area was occupied about 500 B.C.
5. Hieroglyphic writings of the Mayas were found on stone slabs.
6. Most of the pottery was made between A.D. 200 and 900.
7. The Mayas excelled in astronomy and in mathematics.
8. Their pyramids tower over a cluster of smaller mounds.
9. The pyramids were used for the worship of a number of nature gods.
10. Excavating for relics in Guatemala must be very exciting.

2.13 The Infinitive Phrase*

Usually, but not always, the **infinitive phrase** begins with *to*. The phrase consists of *to*, the infinitive, its complements and its modifiers. If the infinitive has a subject, that is also part of the phrase.

Yolanda likes *to read widely*. (The infinitive phrase is object of the verb *likes*.)

Tony is able *to take dictation well*. (The infinitive phrase modifies the adjective *able*.)

I watched *him dive*. (The infinitive phrase is object of *watched*. The infinitive is *dive* without the usual *to*. *Him* is subject of the infinitive.)

Ponce de Léon was trying *to find the Fountain of Youth*. (The infinitive phrase is object of the verb *was trying*.)

Diagraming. The infinitive phrase is diagramed as follows:

Hal hoped to see a good play soon.

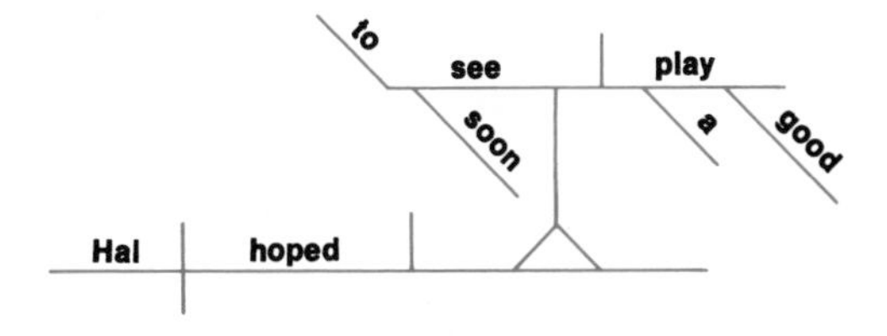

* See also Section 1.11.

To resolve the controversial issue was very difficult.

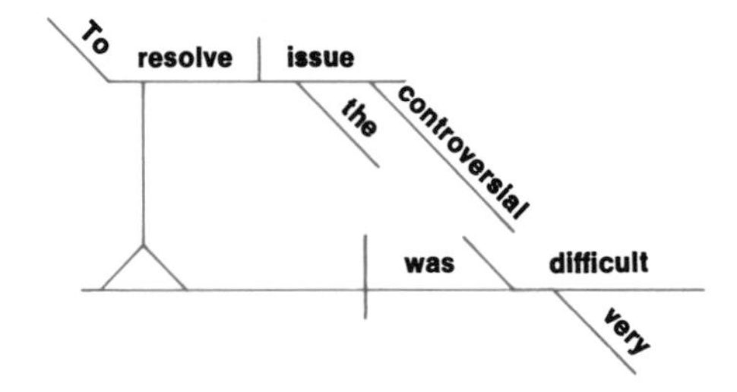

Exercise: Find the infinitive phrases in the sentences below.

1. The man wanted to cash a check.
2. We went to see the African exhibit at the museum.
3. She visited the library to find out about her ancestors.
4. The librarian displayed magazines to attract readers.
5. To work hard is to be happy.
6. I am happy to accept your invitation.
7. I have work to do.
8. It is too late to start now.
9. The doctor started to leave.
10. The team went to Clinton to debate on foreign relations.
11. I asked permission to work in the library.
12. The dramatic club has decided to present *Our Town*.
13. I wish I had time to spend on my carpentry project.
14. To be a good conversationalist is to be a good listener.
15. We saw Henry play.

2.14 The Participial Phrase*

The **participial phrase** usually begins with the participle. The phrase consists of the participle, its modifiers, and its complements. The modifiers and complements may themselves be phrases and clauses.

* See also Section 1.13.

Mary reread the instructions, *trying to salvage the dress.* (The participial phrase modifies *Mary*. The infinitive phrase *to salvage the dress* is the object of the participle *trying*.)

Having heard the signal, the runners pounced off the starting mark. (The participial phrase modifies *runners*.)

Stopped at the border, the travelers had to show their visas. (The participial phrase modifies *travelers*.)

Explaining how the problem could be solved, the teacher began to work it out. (The participial phrase modifies *teacher*. The noun clause *how the problem could be solved* is the object of *Explaining*.)

Diagraming. The participle and the participial phrase are diagramed as follows:

Chuckling quietly, the stranger walked away.

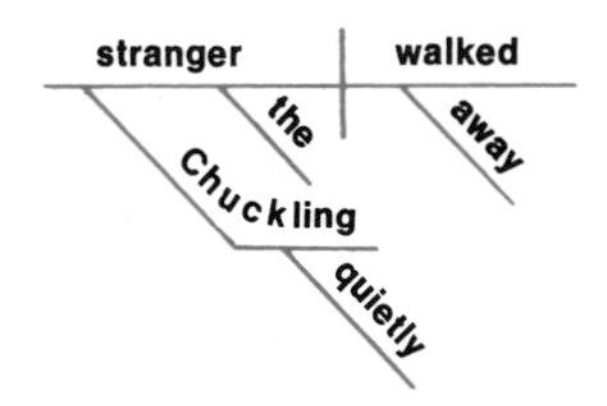

Quickly calculating the risk, he scaled the wall.

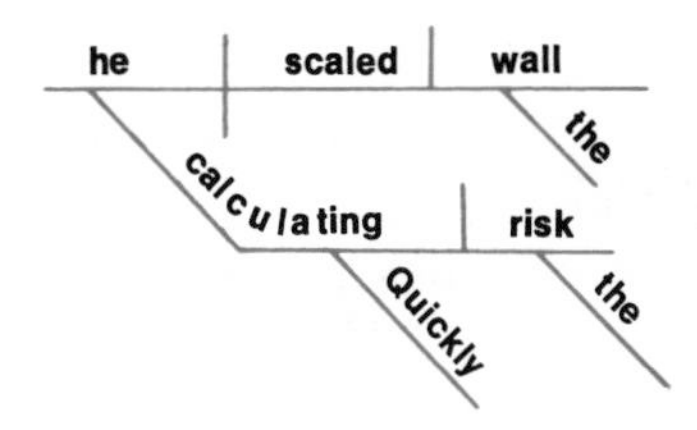

Exercise: Find the participial phrases. Tell the word each phrase modifies. Do not overlook phrases made from past participles and present participles.

1. Pushing hard, he managed to move the trunk an inch.
2. The boy wearing the red jacket is Larry.
3. Living in Chevy Chase, she was within easy reach of the Capital.
4. Guided by radar, the pilot kept in her lane.
5. Convinced of her client's innocence, the defense attorney worked harder than ever.
6. A film well liked by people of all ages is Disney's *Fantasia.*
7. Seen through a microscope, a drop of swamp water teems with animals.
8. Every night we could hear the waves lapping on the beach.
9. Never having eaten spumoni before, I didn't know what to expect.
10. Having conquered the world's highest peak, Edmund Hillary was knighted by Queen Elizabeth.
11. Exhausted from the climb, the hikers lay down to rest.
12. Fast becoming an American uniform, blue jeans are made to fit everyone.
13. Shut off from navigation, Africa had been difficult to explore.
14. Called "the man of the century," Albert Schweitzer gave unselfishly of himself to Africa.
15. Enriched by words from ancient and modern tongues, the English language is extraordinarily expressive.

2.15 The Gerund Phrase*

The **gerund phrase** consists of the gerund, which always ends in *-ing,* and the modifiers and complements of the gerund. The modifiers themselves may be phrases. The gerund phrase is always used as a noun.

* See also Section 1.12.

Planning for a career requires foresight. (The gerund phrase is the subject of the verb *requires.*)
He finished *assembling the amplifier.* (The gerund phrase is the object of the verb *finished.*)
By *concentrating doggedly,* he grasped the idea. (The gerund phrase is the object of the preposition *By.*)
Studying all night when you have an exam is self-defeating. (The gerund phrase is the subject of the verb *is.* The adverb clause *when you have an exam* modifies the gerund.)

Diagraming. The gerund and the gerund phrase are diagramed as follows:

Sailing is great fun.

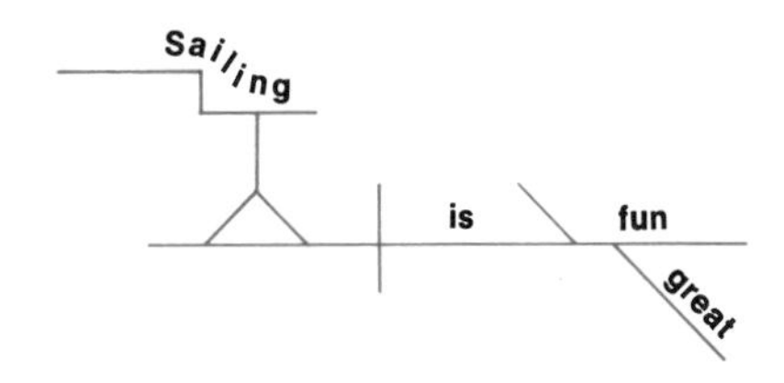

Careful checking revealed the mistake.

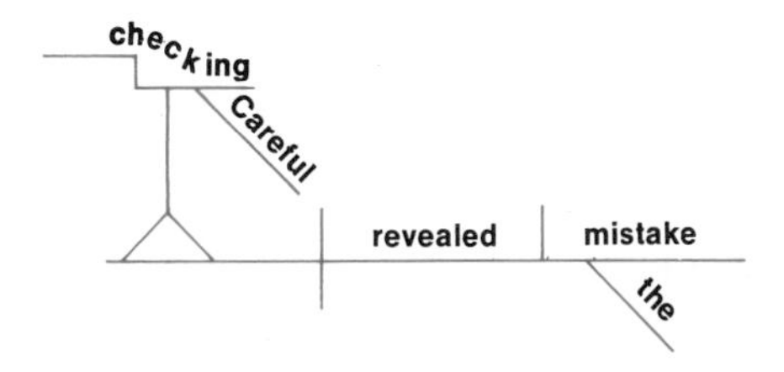

They began sorting the shells.

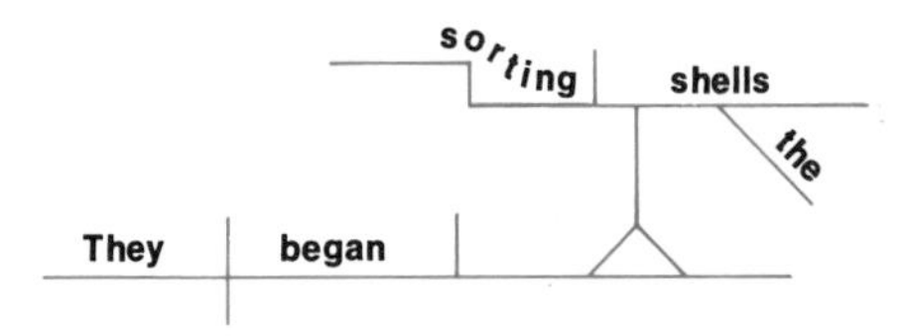

After returning from the swim, we feasted.

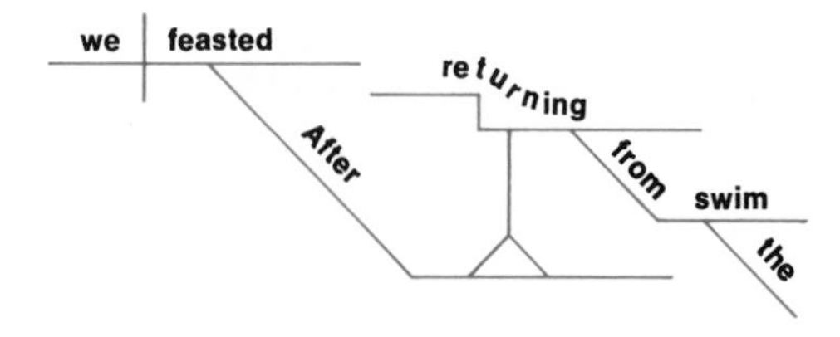

Exercise A: Find the gerund phrases. Tell how each is used.

1. Her father was delighted at Kate's winning the athletic scholarship.
2. Directing a play is a complex job.
3. The course requires the reading of many plays.
4. Working all summer for a lawyer gave Kathy an advantage.
5. He found excitement in using a powerful telescope.
6. Driving to the top of Mt. Palomar was a memorable experience.
7. I enjoyed watching the sunset at Palm Springs.
8. Competing as a speaker gave Charles confidence.
9. Knowing where to look for information saves time.
10. Rehearsing the play occupies Janet's time after school.
11. Before writing a composition, you should prepare an outline.
12. I enjoy walking my dog Pretzel.
13. Running a summer camp is a heavy responsibility.
14. Watching television can be both entertaining and educational.
15. The law forbids smoking in the theater.

Exercise B: Find the infinitive, gerund, and participial phrases.

1. Spectators admired the speedboat cutting through the water.
2. In college Beth decided to specialize in nuclear physics.
3. Riding a moped is faster and easier than riding a bicycle.
4. Reading science fiction consumed many hours of his time.
5. Several people claim to have seen the Loch Ness monster.

6. Having studied bookplates, Katy was able to design one for the school library.

7. The drama portrayed a person hardened by power.

8. The German dirigible *Hindenburg* exploded in mid-air, killing thirty-six people.

9. The Secretary of State hopes to negotiate a Middle East peace settlement.

10. By having been alert to a previous court decision, the lawyer won the case.

11. *Cohere* means "to stick together."

12. We want to see the sunrise at Bryce Canyon.

13. By paying interest at 6½ percent, the bank increased its number of depositors.

14. This old house, defying wind and weather, has stood here for two hundred years.

15. For serving as manager of the team, Leslie received a special award.

2.16 The Appositive Phrase

An appositive is a word placed after another word to explain or identify it.

The novel, a mystery story, appealed to me.
Pat, an honor student, earned a gold pin.

The appositive always appears after the word it explains or identifies. It is always a noun or pronoun, and the word that it explains is also always a noun or pronoun.

An **appositive phrase** consists of the appositive and its modifiers, which themselves may be phrases or clauses.

The fair, *an annual event that attracts thousands*, opens next week. (The appositive phrase identifies *fair*. The adjective *annual* and the adjective clause *that attracts thousands* modify the appositive *event*.)

The principal presented the trophy, *a tall silver cup with handles*. (The italicized words are the appositive phrase, identifying *trophy*. The adjectives *tall* and *silver* modify the appositive *cup*, as does the adjective phrase *with handles*.)

Note: The compound personal pronoun used intensively is not regarded as an appositive. It is used for emphasis and does not explain or identify the word to which it refers: The superintendent *herself* was not sure of the answer.

Diagraming. The appositive is diagramed as follows:

The author, a dynamic speaker, lectured about UFOs.

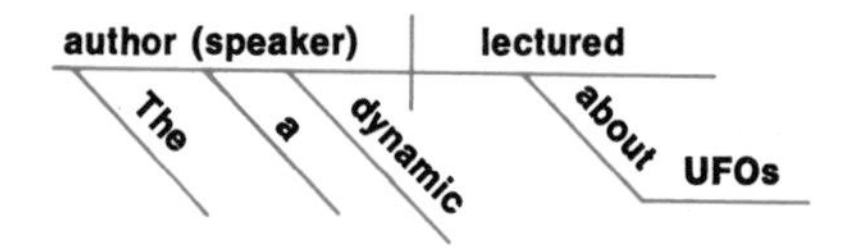

2.17 Diagraming the Simple Sentence

Meaning is conveyed in English by word-groups arranged in definite order in the sentence. Diagraming has helped you see which words go together and how they are arranged.

The base of the simple sentence is composed of subject-verb-complement. These words are placed on the base line of the diagram. The indirect object is placed below the verb.

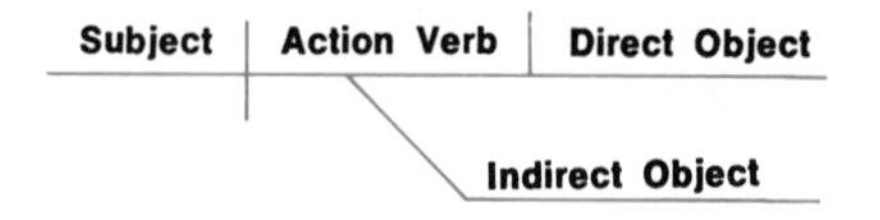

The introductory word *There* or *Here* is placed above the base line, as in the following diagram. Note the slant line after the linking verb.

The subject of an imperative sentence, *you* (understood), is placed in parentheses, as follows:

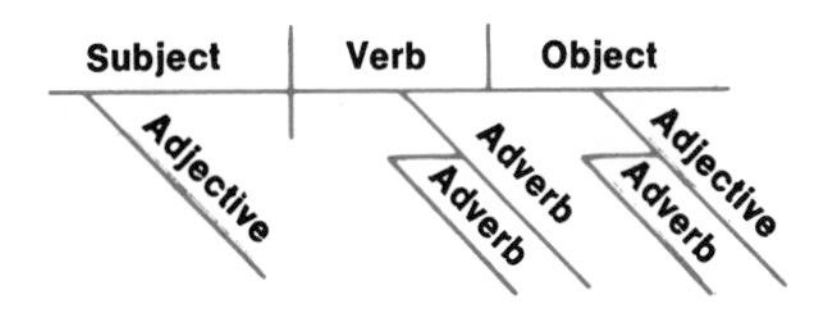

A single-word modifier is placed on a slant line below the word it modifies. An adverb modifying an adjective or adverb is placed as shown below.

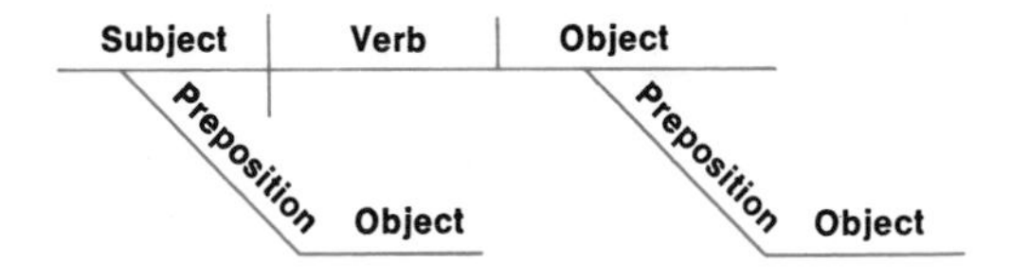

The prepositional phrase is attached to the word it modifies, as follows:

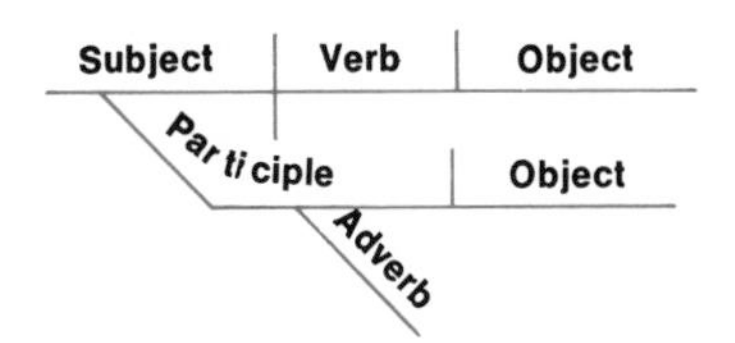

The participial phrase is shown as follows:

The gerund phrase is placed above the base line unless it is the object of a preposition.

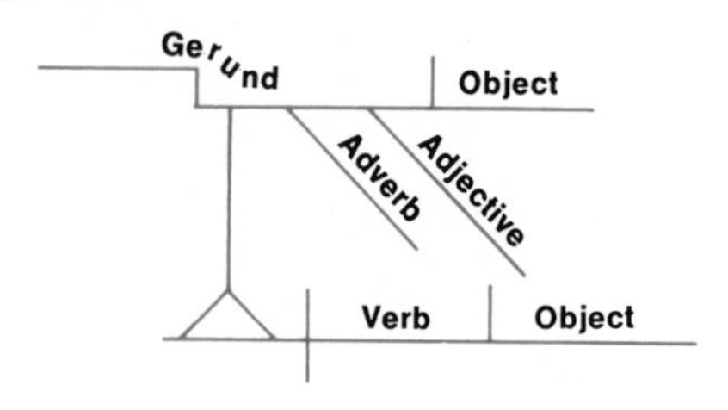

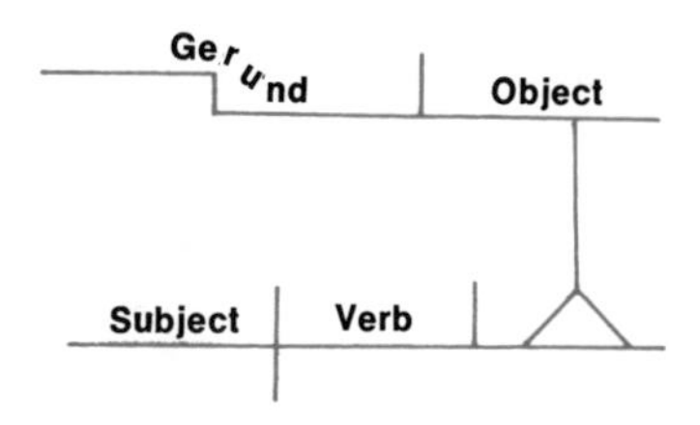

The infinitive phrase is shown in this way:

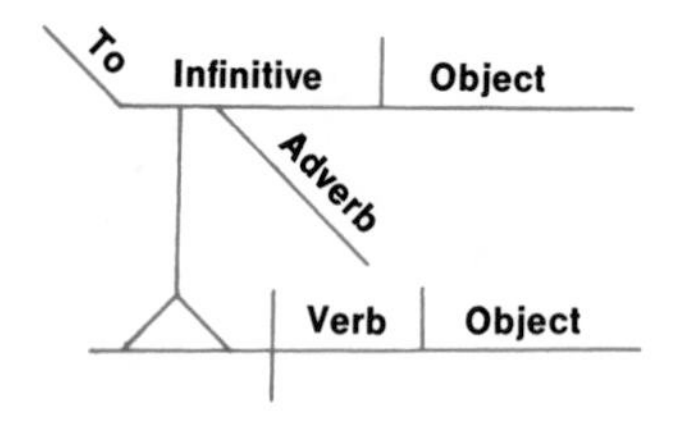

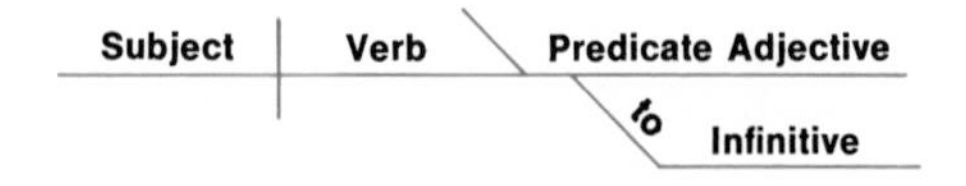

REVIEW: THE PARTS OF A SENTENCE Make six columns. Head them *Subject, Verb, Direct Object, Indirect Object, Predicate Word,* and *Prepositional Phrase.* Place those parts of the following sentences in the proper columns. Not every sentence will contain all six parts. Watch for compound parts.

1. Jed loaned me his car for the evening.
2. The psychic predicted an end to war.
3. Cuba is the largest island in the West Indies.
4. Three valuable Cézanne paintings were stolen from the Art Institute.
5. Penny grooms and rides horses at the local stable.
6. The tourists wanted to linger in Toronto.
7. Christy and her two brothers arranged a surprise party for their parents' anniversary.
8. Measuring with metrics is quite easy.
9. Noah leaves school early to work at the skating rink.
10. Some indoor plants are not very hardy.
11. Different kinds of music can create different moods.
12. Photographers use dramatic lighting and unusual angles for special effects.
13. George Carlin told the audience a hilarious story.
14. Snorkeling is a popular sport in warm climates.
15. Barbara and Dee studied the chapters and their notes.
16. Ms. Charles read the class excerpts from *Walden.*
17. The school cafeteria uses texturized vegetable protein occasionally.
18. United States citizens may own gold but may not use it as currency.
19. Copyrights guarantee artists and authors control over the reproduction of their works.
20. The campaigning governor promised his constituents lower taxes and a balanced budget.

3.0 Sentence and Clause

We have seen (Section 2.2) that sentences can be classified according to the purpose of the speaker: *declarative, imperative, interrogative*, and *exclamatory*. This classification is helpful in problems of punctuation.

For help in writing better sentences, there is another, more useful classification. This is the classification by form. There are three basic forms of sentences: the *simple sentence*, the *compound sentence*, and the *complex sentence*. A fourth kind, the *compound-complex sentence*, is a combination of other forms.

3.1 The Simple Sentence

A simple sentence contains only one subject and predicate. Both the subject and the predicate may be compound.

You will recall that *compound* means having two or more similar parts.

COMPOUND SUBJECT The *designer* of the car and the *consultant* worked together for many months. (The designer worked; the consultant worked.)

COMPOUND VERB The audience *cheered* and *applauded* the actor. (The audience cheered; the audience applauded.)

COMPOUND PREDICATE I *located the leak* and *called the plumber.* (I located; I called.)

COMPOUND SUBJECT AND PREDICATE Faculty *advisers* and student *officers* of the various organizations *discussed the problem* and *arrived at a solution.* (Advisers and officers discussed; advisers and officers arrived.)

All of the preceding sentences are simple sentences. In these sentences both parts of a compound subject go with the same verb, or both parts of a compound verb have the same subject. In all of these sentences there is only one subject-verb connection.

For contrast, note that in the following sentence the first subject goes with the first verb while the second subject goes with the second verb. There are two subject-verb connections. This is not a simple sentence:

The *boys prepared* lunch; the *girls played* soccer.

The Compound Predicate. The compound predicate is worth special attention because it is most useful in writing clear, smooth sentences.

The compound predicate consists of two verbs having the same subject. At least one of the verbs has a complement.

The earthquake *destroyed* the *city* and *left thousands* homeless.
Both of his children *studied* hard and *won scholarships.*

Exercise A: Identify the compound parts in the following sentences. Look for compound subjects, compound verbs, and compound predicates.

1. The roses and the carnations were in the same vase.
2. For five hours I read and wrote.
3. Lightning and thunder preceded the thunderstorm.
4. The young performer sang and danced his way to fame.
5. After takeoff, the airplane faltered and dove.
6. The turtle lays eggs and never gives the next generation a backward glance.

7. The lake and the mountain behind it were covered with snow.
8. Scott brought his permission slip but forgot his money.
9. Car pools always save fuel and often promote friendships.
10. Is Nick Carraway or Jay Gatsby the hero of *The Great Gatsby*?

Exercise B: Follow the same directions as for Exercise A.

1. In her campaign speech, Jennifer promised, pleaded, coaxed, and cajoled.
2. Killer whales hunt in packs and are the worst threat to other creatures of the sea.
3. Ostrich eggs are as big as grapefruit and weigh two to three pounds.
4. Decaying leaves and animal matter make the richest soil.
5. Many environmentalists and animal-lovers object to using animal skins for fur coats.
6. The Sierra Club protects wildlife and promotes ecological concerns.
7. The roller coaster swooped, soared, and screeched around its twisting tracks.
8. The anteater rips anthills open with its powerful claws and then removes the ants with its long tongue.
9. Koala bears always smell sweetly of eucalyptus and constantly wear an expression of hurt dignity.
10. All birds, reptiles, fishes, amphibians, and mammals have backbones and are called vertebrates.

3.2 The Compound Sentence

The compound sentence consists of two or more simple sentences put together.

The parts of a compound sentence are put together: (1) with a comma and a coordinating conjunction (*and, but, or, for, nor*); (2) with a semicolon.

The plan seemed feasible, *but* I still felt unsure.
The plane made a forced landing, *and* a crowd gathered quickly.
You can drive slowly and survive, *or* you can drive fast and become a statistic.

I understood his problem, *for* I had once faced it myself.

Mary could not remember where she had left her music, *nor* could her friends help her.

I understood his problem; I had once faced it myself.

José joined the drama club; Sheila preferred the debating club.

Conjunctive adverbs (*then, however, moreover, hence, consequently,* etc.) are also used to join the parts of a compound sentence. The conjunctive adverb is preceded by a semicolon.

All the polls predicted a Dewey victory in 1948; *however,* Truman won.

Read the directions carefully; *then* begin the examination.

The majority voted against it; *therefore,* the picnic was canceled.

Diagraming. The compound sentence is diagramed on two parallel base lines as follows:

The car was nearly full, but we piled in.

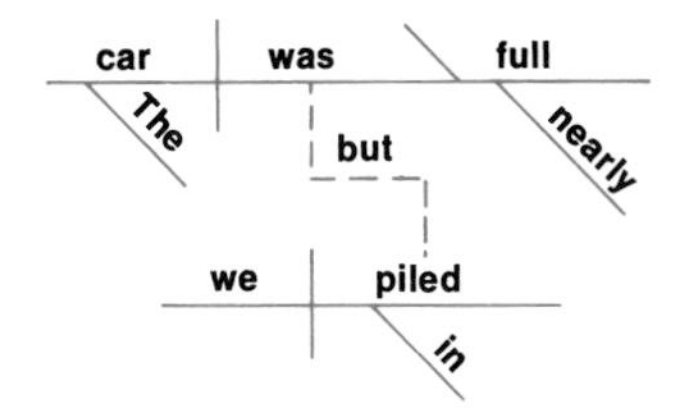

The announcer repeated the news; the tragedy completely unnerved us.

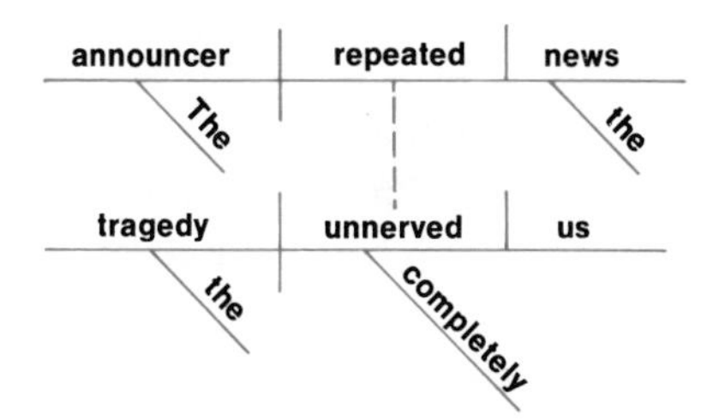

Compound Sentences and Compound Predicates. In the compound predicate every verb has the same subject. In the compound sentence, each verb has a different subject. This difference can be seen readily in diagrams.

SIMPLE SENTENCE WITH COMPOUND PREDICATE:

They accepted my story and published it.

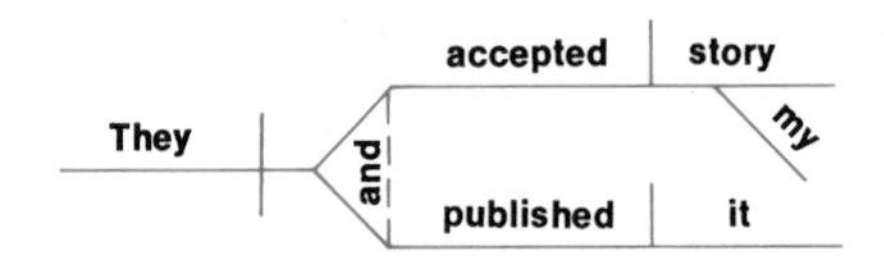

COMPOUND SENTENCE:

They accepted my story, but the editor delayed publication.

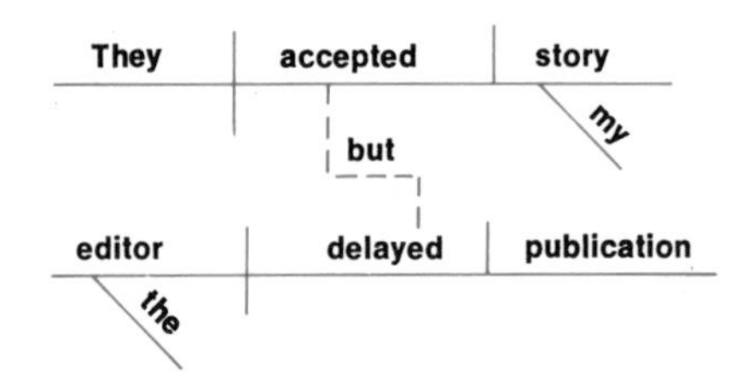

Exercise A: Decide which of these sentences are compound and which are simple. In the simple sentences identify all compound predicates.

1. Laura learned German and got a job as an interpreter.
2. Canada covers almost half of North America and is as large as all Europe.
3. Jeff commutes by train, but Vicky walks to work.
4. Lulu asked for a sundae, but she got a malt.
5. Lacrosse is fun, but it can be dangerous.
6. Peg and Jill played expertly and saved the game.
7. This car needs a muffler and new brakes, but its engine is sound.
8. Mike has played all positions on the team and is now a top-ranking player.

9. Skin diving is exciting, but it can be hazardous for beginners.

10. After winning the game, the team lifted their coach and tossed her into the shower.

Exercise B: Follow the same directions as for Exercise A.

1. The Voice of America broadcasts radio programs to 120 countries and uses thirty-six different languages.

2. I missed the overture but saw the rest of the play.

3. Thomas Jefferson founded the University of Virginia in 1819 and designed some of the buildings.

4. Poe wove a quality of music into his poems and became the father of the short story.

5. Your first problem is correct, but you have made an error in the second.

6. Pocahontas was the daughter of Powhatan, the most powerful chieftain in Virginia.

7. Shall we take a jet from JFK Airport, or shall we take a ship from New York?

8. The Irish potato is not a native of Ireland, nor has the Jerusalem artichoke any connection with Jerusalem.

9. Robert E. Lee not only won the devotion of his men but also commanded the respect of his enemies.

10. In 1943 a cornfield in Mexico cracked open, and a new volcano, Paricutin, erupted.

3.3 The Clause

A clause is a group of words containing a verb and its subject.

According to this definition, a simple sentence is a clause. Indeed, the simple sentence is sometimes defined as consisting of one main clause. However, we shall find it simpler to use the word *clause* to name a *part* of a sentence.

Each part of a compound sentence has its own verb and subject. These parts of the compound sentence are therefore clauses.

Each clause in a compound sentence can be lifted out and written separately as a simple sentence.

A clause that can stand by itself as a sentence is a main clause.

We have defined a compound sentence as consisting of two or more simple sentences put together. We can now also define it as consisting of two main clauses.

A clause that cannot stand by itself as a sentence is a subordinate clause.

s. v.
While you were talking . . . (What happened?)

s. v.
Unless she improves her spelling . . . (What?)

s. v.
If you have the strength . . . (Then what?)

Phrase or Clause? A clause has a subject and a verb. A phrase does not.

I heard them *rehearsing for the concert.* (phrase)

s. v.
I heard them *when they were rehearsing for the concert.* (clause)

Students *in the caucus* did admirable work. (phrase)

s. v.
Students who were in the caucus did admirable work. (clause)

Exercise A: Are the italicized words in each sentence a phrase or a clause?

1. Jim scowls *when Jamie tells him his faults.*
2. *Because she worked nights,* she was sleepy in school.
3. The jury recessed *to eat their dinner.*
4. Kristin licked her lips *as she savoured the banana split.*
5. *According to John Mason Brown,* television is chewing gum for the eyes.
6. *Unless more tickets are sold,* the dance will be canceled.
7. Some schools have classes *to prepare students for parenthood.*
8. *In conferences with college representatives,* students get information and ask questions.

9. Interesting animals *found in South America* are the llama, the vicuña, and the tapir.

10. *Stuffed with books, coats, and old gym socks,* my locker popped open.

Exercise B: Follow the same directions as for Exercise A.

1. Advertisers use music, repetition, slogans, and humor *to make people remember their products.*
2. They proposed a contract *that was more remunerative.*
3. The giant panda is much more closely related to the raccoon than to the bear, *which it resembles.*
4. Gerald Ford was the first Vice-President *who was not elected.*
5. The red wolf and the Eastern timber wolf are endangered species *that are native to North America.*
6. Jules Verne had an extremely vivid imagination *coupled with a rare scientific knowledge.*
7. The toboggan is eight feet long, and *a foot and a half wide.*
8. Indian hunters were the first *to build toboggans.*
9. Usually a wolf does not attack *unless it is cornered or threatened.*
10. *How migrating birds find their way* is a great mystery.

3.4 The Complex Sentence

The complex sentence consists of one main clause and one or more subordinate clauses.

In a complex sentence, the subordinate clause is always used as a noun or a modifier. If it is used as a modifier, the subordinate clause modifies a word in the main clause.

Although he did not know the answer, he raised his hand. (clause modifies *raised*)

Read the paper *while you are waiting.* (clause modifies *Read*)

This is the music *that I like.* (clause modifies *music*)

In each example above, the main clause can stand as a sentence by itself: *he did not raise his hand, Read the paper, This is the music.*

The subordinate clauses, however, cannot stand alone because their meaning is incomplete.

> Although he knew the answer . . . (what happened?)
> while you are waiting . . . (What is to be done?)
> that I like . . . (What is it?)

Complex sentences containing noun clauses are somewhat different. The noun clause may be used as a noun *within the main clause*. The noun clause, in other words, is part of the main clause.

> *That he voted for the Equal Rights Amendment* is certain. (Noun clause is subject of *is.*)
>
> *What you read* influences your thinking. (Noun clause is subject of *influences.*)
>
> The teachers felt responsible for *what the students did.* (Noun clause is object of the preposition *for.*)
>
> No one understood *what she was saying.* (Noun clause is object of *understood.*)

In these sentences, neither the main clause nor the noun clause can stand by itself. Nonetheless, a sentence containing one main clause and a noun clause is regarded as a complex sentence.

Exercise A: Indicate whether each of the following sentences is simple, compound, or complex.

1. The rear tire needed no air, but the front tire did.
2. The ball circled the rim of the basket and finally slipped in.
3. Unless Julia can obtain a scholarship, she may not go to college next fall.
4. Dad is unhappy about his golf score, which has not been improving lately.
5. Did you know that the onion is a lily?

6. At the end of the season, the team was given a banquet and presented with trophies.

7. The campers said good-bye with regret; they would not meet again for a long time.

8. The motor sputtered and then stalled.

9. The motor sputtered before it stalled.

10. On this tour, you can take a side trip to Disney World at no extra cost.

Exercise B: Find the subordinate clause in each sentence below.

1. Bill Cosby has a humor that wears well.

2. Because she excels in math, Kelly plans to become an engineer.

3. Bridal Veil Falls is at its best in late afternoon, when it forms beautiful rainbows.

4. South American monkeys have tails that are prehensile, or grasping.

5. James Madison is the person who drafted the Bill of Rights.

6. The candidate's mistakes in grammar show that he is too illiterate for the office.

7. The bald eagle looks bald only because it has white feathers on its head.

8. This is the meadow where I saw the deer.

9. The car she drives is an old Ford.

10. The trapdoor spider lives in a silk-lined room with a door that fits exactly.

11. Mary Harris Jones, who was known as "Mother Jones," organized labor unions and crusaded for workers' rights in the late 1800's.

12. Before child labor laws were passed, children were exploited in the work force.

13. We were in the train station when we heard the election results.

14. The Bronz Zoo, which is the largest in the world, covers 252 acres.

15. *Macbeth* is the story of a man who suffered disaster through too much ambition.

3.5 The Compound-Complex Sentence

A compound-complex sentence consists of two or more main clauses and one or more subordinate clauses.

The main clauses are joined by a coordinating conjunction (preceded by a comma), a conjunctive adverb (preceded by a semicolon), or by a semicolon alone. The subordinate clause modifies a word in one of the main clauses or acts as a noun within one of them.

MAIN CLAUSE | MAIN CLAUSE | SUBORDINATE CLAUSE

Carol entered the meet, and she won the medal that was donated by her uncle.

MAIN CLAUSE | MAIN CLAUSE | SUBORDINATE CLAUSE

We missed the bus; however, we arrived home before the others did.

3.6 The Adjective Clause

The single-word adjective, the adjective phrase, and the adjective clause are used in the same way. They modify a noun or pronoun.

An adjective clause is a subordinate clause used to modify a noun or pronoun in the main clause.

Introductory Words. A majority of the adjective clauses in modern writing begin with an introductory word. There is a growing tendency, however, to use adjective clauses with no introductory word.

That is the spot *where I fell.* (*Where* is an introductory word.)
This is the time *when we must attack.* (*When* is an introductory word.)
Legends *I read* told of his origin. (no introductory word)
Legends *that I read* told of his origin. (*that* is an introductory word.)

It's a program *I enjoy.* (no introductory word)
It's a program *that I enjoy.* (*that* is an introductory word.)

In the first two examples, the introductory words *where* and *when* are both used within the subordinate clause as modifiers of the verb: *fell* **where;** *attack* **when.**

Relative Pronouns. The pronouns *who, whose, whom, which,* and *that* are used to introduce adjective clauses. Used in this way they refer to a word in the main clause and are used in place of that word. That word is the antecedent of the pronoun. It is also the word modified by the adjective clause.

Tom Dooley was the doctor *who inspired him.*
(*doctor* is antecedent of *who* and is modified by the adjective clause.)

She is a writer *whose works deserve acclaim.*
(*writer* is antecedent of *whose* and is modified by the adjective clause.)

The trout season, *which opens in April,* is welcomed by anglers.
(*season* is antecedent of *which* and is modified by the adjective clause.)

An adjective clause introduced by a relative pronoun is sometimes called a relative clause.

The relative pronoun has two functions. It introduces the clause, and it is used as a sentence part within the clause.

The explanation *that she gave* was lucid.
(*that* is the direct object of *gave.*)

That teacher is the one *whom I respect highly.*
(*whom* is the direct object of *respect.*)

The letter *to which you refer* has been lost.
(*which* is the object of the preposition *to.*)

My mother is a person *who likes hard work.*
(*who* is the subject of *likes.*)

Diagraming. The adjective clause is joined to the word it modifies in the main clause. A dotted line leads from this word to the introductory word. Note that the relative pronoun is placed to show its use in the sentence.

The car that I borrowed belongs to Tammy.

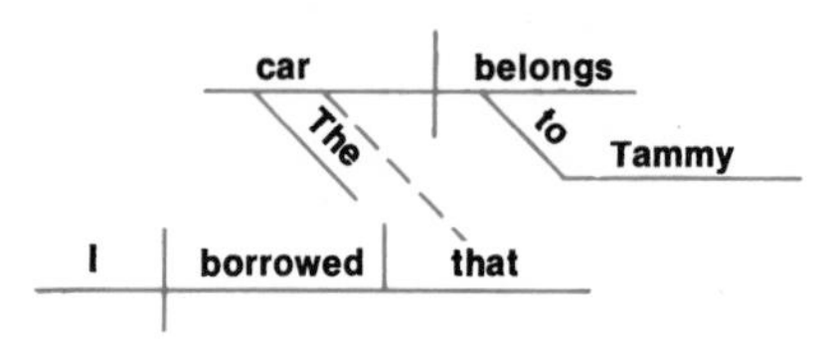

This is the building where my father works.

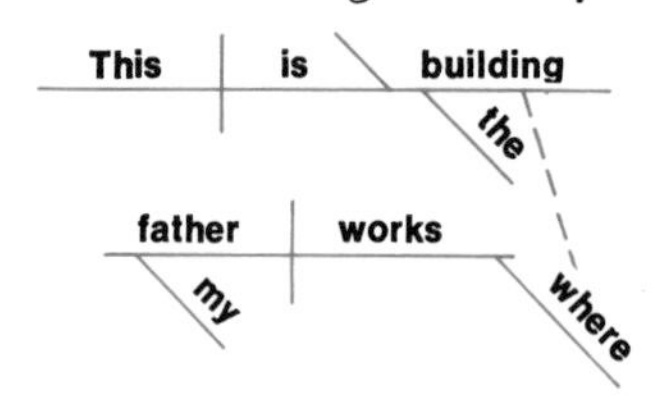

Exercise: Find each adjective clause and the word it modifies.

1. This is the room that I decorated.
2. Springs are fed by rain, which seeps through the soil.
3. I couldn't find the place where you bought the bulbs.
4. A sharp tool was the first utensil that human beings needed.
5. Germany is the country where Beethoven was born.
6. I have seen the house in which Betsy Ross lived.
7. You can buy dwarf lemon trees that will grow in your room.
8. The dog that barks the loudest usually bites the least.
9. How can we choose a play that everyone will like?
10. His father, whom he introduced as a captain, was not wearing a uniform.
11. Her conviction that taxes need to be raised kept her from winning the election.
12. Surely the story you are telling me is not true.
13. All that glitters is not gold.
14. A diver who gets panicky may rise to the surface too rapidly.
15. He or she may get the "bends," which is a dangerous condition.

3.7 The Adverb Clause

The single-word adverb, the adverb phrase, and the adverb clause are all used in the same way. They are used to modify verbs, adjectives, and adverbs.

An adverb clause is a subordinate clause used to modify a verb, adjective, or adverb in the main clause.*

Adverb clauses tell *where, when, why, how, to what extent,* and *how much* about the word they modify.

ADVERB CLAUSES MODIFYING VERBS

We **put** the *key where we could locate it easily.* (where)
When you go to New York, **see** the Guggenheim Museum. (when)
The candidate **canceled** her speech *because she had a cold.* (why)
The dog **looked** *as if he would attack us.* (how)

ADVERB CLAUSES MODIFYING ADJECTIVES

This test is as **hard** *as the first one was.* (to what extent)
The school days are **longer** *than they used to be.* (how much)

ADVERB CLAUSE MODIFYING AN ADVERB

The dog ran **quicker** *than the sheep did.* (how much)

Subordinating Conjunctions. Every adverb clause is introduced by a subordinating conjunction. The function of this word is to show how two clauses are related. By use of the subordinating conjunction, one clause is made to tell *where, when, why, how, to what extent,* or *how much* about another.

When a subordinating conjunction is placed before a clause, the clause can no longer stand alone.

The cheerleader is losing her voice. (complete)
If the cheerleader loses her voice . . . (incomplete)
Since the cheerleader is losing her voice . . . (incomplete)

* Some authorities suggest that an introductory adverb clause may modify an entire main clause rather than a single word in it.

A new building has been erected. (complete)
When a new building is erected . . . (incomplete)
Until a new building is erected . . . (incomplete)

A subordinating conjunction may be placed before either of two main clauses to tie it to the other. Which clause is subordinate depends upon the meaning the writer wants to express.

Although Mark Twain was a great humorist, he was pessimistic.
Although Mark Twain was pessimistic, he was a great humorist.
Because he was a victim of persecution, his fame grew.
Because his fame grew, he was a victim of persecution.

Subordinating conjunctions can be used to show a great variety of relationships between main ideas. The careful choice of conjunctions will enable you to express your ideas clearly and exactly.

TIME:	as, after, before, since, until, when, whenever, while
CAUSE OR REASON:	because, since
COMPARISON:	as, as much as, than
CONDITION:	if, although, though, unless, provided, provided that
PURPOSE:	so that, in order that

Note how different conjunctions create a change in meaning.

Before the schedule was changed, I was upset.
Because the schedule was changed, I was upset.
Until the schedule was changed, I was upset.

Elliptical Clauses. The word *elliptical* comes from *ellipsis*, which means "omission of a word." An **elliptical clause** is one from which words have been omitted.

While he was playing chess, he was contented.
While playing chess, he was contented.
When she is driving, she listens to the radio.
When driving, she listens to the radio.

Diagraming. The adverb clause is diagramed on a separate line:

When his friend whistled, he dashed outside.

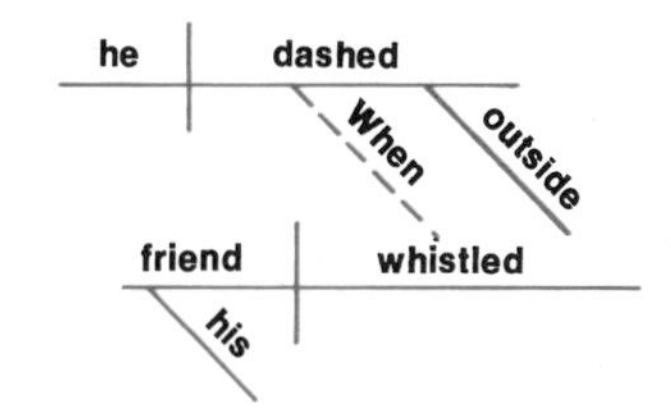

Exercise: Find each adverb clause and the word it modifies.

1. The parade was postponed because the floats were not finished.
2. If we win this game, the trophy will be ours.
3. They arrived after you left.
4. When she saw the rain, she ran to close the windows.
5. Class begins promptly when the bell rings.
6. They will buy the house provided they can get a mortgage.
7. The horse ate as if it had been without food for days.
8. The children followed the kitten wherever it went.
9. Robin felt invigorated after she had swum six lengths of the pool.
10. Although the film got bad reviews, it attracted huge crowds.
11. Many citizens were irate when their taxes were increased.
12. When studying, Mother must not be disturbed.
13. The student newspaper is more controversial than it ever was.
14. Park the car wherever you can find a place.
15. I pulled to the side of the road so that the trailer truck could pass.

3.8 The Noun Clause

A noun clause is a subordinate clause used as a noun.

The noun clause may be used as subject or direct object of the verb, as a predicate noun, as object of a preposition, or as an appositive.

I understand *what the law requires.* (direct object)
He was wondering about *where she had gone.* (object of preposition)
The fact *that I am his son* makes no difference. (appositive)
Whoever told you that was wrong. (subject)
The exciting part is *how Linda got the autograph.* (predicate noun)

Introductory Words. As the examples above clearly show, noun clauses may be introduced by some of the same words that introduce adverb clauses: *when, where.* Used with noun clauses, these words are not regarded as subordinating conjunctions. They are merely introductory words, used as adverbs within the noun clause.

Similarly, noun clauses may be introduced by the same words used to introduce relative clauses: *who, whose, whom, which, that, when, where.* Used in noun clauses, these words are not regarded as relative pronouns, but they may serve as subjects or objects within the noun clause.

Larry explained **where** *Ann was.* (noun clause as the object of *explained*)
Luke went **where** *the fish were biting.* (adverb clause modifying *went*)
Holly is the one **who** *broke the record.* (adjective clause modifying *one*)
Who *won the election* is uncertain. (noun clause as the subject of *is*)

Many noun clauses are written without any introductory word. Every direct quotation preceded by words such as *I said, she asked, Eva replied* is a noun clause without the introductory word. Every indirect quotation is a noun clause preceded by the introductory word.

She said *that the road was treacherous.* (noun clause as the object of *said*)
She said, "*The road was treacherous.*" (noun clause as the object of *said*)

Diagraming. The noun clause is diagramed as shown below. Note that the use of the noun clause determines its position in the diagram.

I think that you are improving.

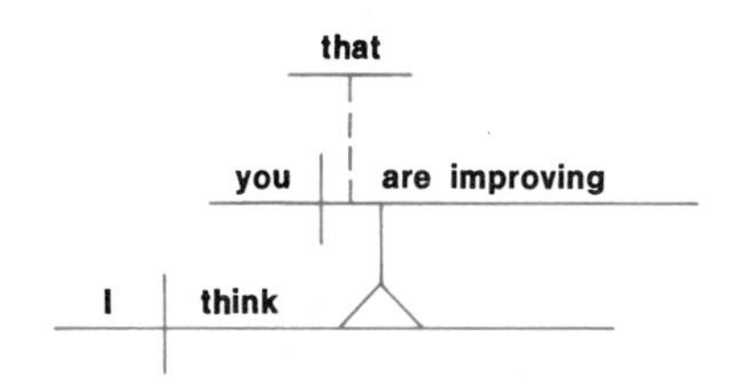

He gave help to whoever was needy.

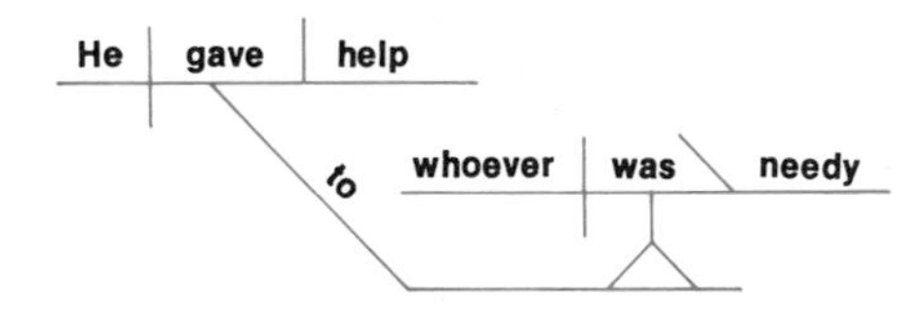

Exercise A: Identify each noun clause. Tell how each is used.

1. Lee asked what I was doing.
2. The fact that he had read about neutrons helped him.
3. What the players will do next is anyone's guess.
4. I inquired where she lived.
5. Please tell me why you did it.
6. I wonder who wrote the letter.
7. I know that you had hoped for a place on the program.
8. The fact that she attended the meeting is significant.
9. We gave the book lists to whoever asked for them.
10. The photographer claimed that photography is the most truthful art.
11. Please tell him what he wants to know.
12. That it is a beautiful work of art is plain to see.
13. The instructor told us that we were improving.
14. Whether the governor will veto the law is the big question.
15. What the future holds for us remains a challenging mystery.

Exercise B: Find the subordinate clauses in these sentences. Label them as adjective, adverb, or noun clauses.

1. The marathon swimmer feared that a shark was near.
2. Although the ice is thin, it is safe for skating.
3. Kendra discovered that her locker had been ransacked.
4. When a boat sails "before the wind," it follows the wind's course.
5. Mauna Loa in Hawaii is the largest volcano that is still active.
6. Dr. Albert Sabin developed an oral vaccine that prevents polio.
7. Many secretaries use shorthand whenever they take dictation.
8. Sonia threw the Frisbee to a spot where Ramon couldn't reach it.
9. Ms. Forrest asked the class who wrote the book *Jubilee*.
10. Illinois is named after the Indians who settled the state.
11. The administration finally decided where the student lounge would be located.
12. Whoever is arrested is informed of her or his rights.
13. Evaluating the truth of advertisements is difficult because most use vague terms.
14. Alexander Solzhenitsyn is a writer whom the Soviets exiled.
15. A short story is not as complex as a novel is.

3.9 The Sentence Redefined

We are now ready to complete the definition of a sentence that we started in Sections 2.1 and 2.3. We may begin by noting once again the differences between phrases, clauses, and sentences.

A **phrase** is a group of words used within a sentence as a single part of speech. A phrase may be used as a noun, a verb, an adjective, or an adverb. It does *not* contain a subject and verb.

A **clause** is a group of words which contains a subject and its verb. It may be used within the sentence as a noun, an adjective, or an adverb.

PHRASE: Working on our project . . .

s. v.
CLAUSE: While *we were working* on our project . . .

A main clause can stand by itself as a sentence. A subordinate clause cannot stand by itself.

MAIN CLAUSE MAIN CLAUSE
The camera was new, but the shutter did not work.

The camera was new. (*complete*)
The shutter did not work. (*complete*)

SUBORDINATE CLAUSE MAIN CLAUSE
Although the camera was new, the shutter did not work.

The shutter did not work. (*complete*)
Although the camera was new . . . (*incomplete*)

Clauses and phrases are sentence parts. The sentence itself is not part of any other grammatical construction. (The paragraph is not a grammatical construction.) Our complete definition of a sentence, then, is in three parts:

A sentence is a group of words that

1. **expresses a complete thought,**
2. **contains a subject and verb,**
3. **is not part of any other grammatical construction.**

REVIEW: SENTENCE AND CLAUSE Indicate whether each of the following sentences is simple, compound, or complex. In addition, find any subordinate clauses and label them as noun, adverb, or adjective clause.

1. Bonita learned about medical careers by volunteering as a hospital aide.
2. Mr. Forbes explained how the cast was chosen.
3. Nanci expected her friends to notice her new haircut, but no one did.

4. When the divers surfaced, they showed us the recovered jewels.

5. We must hurry, or the tickets will be sold out.

6. Chuck likes Corvettes, but they are very expensive to maintain.

7. Was Daylight Savings Time instituted to save fuel?

8. Ann asked, "Who writes to 'Dear Abby'?"

9. A story that I wrote was published in *Scholastic* magazine.

10. Spoken Spanish varies because there are many regional dialects.

11. Many classes at our school are taught bilingually.

12. The canoe overturned at the spot where the rapids begin.

13. The police officer issued Ellen a ticket for driving too fast for conditions.

14. Although most houseplants look harmless, some are poisonous.

15. Jeff found an expanse of land that is perfect for cross-country skiing.

16. Gina not only plays in the school band, but she also performs in the city orchestra.

17. For the last forty years the United States and Australia have dominated the Davis Cup matches.

18. Scientists are studying which planets can sustain life.

19. Some people own microwave ovens, which cook with electromagnetic waves.

20. The person to whom Shakespeare wrote his sonnets is called "the dark lady."

4.0 Complete Sentences

Uncompleted sentences are more often a problem in writing than in speaking. If you use an uncompleted sentence in speaking with someone face-to-face, he or she can interrupt and ask you what you mean. In writing, you usually do not have a second chance.

The sentence is the best means you have for getting your meaning across to someone else in writing. Through study and practice, you can learn to write effective and forceful sentences. To write effectively, however, you must learn to avoid two kinds of sentence errors: (1) the sentence fragment, and (2) the run-on sentence. Both of these errors cause confusion for the reader.

4.1 Fragments Resulting from Incomplete Thought

An uncompleted sentence is called a **sentence fragment.** It is only a part, or fragment, of a sentence.

You can think much faster than you can write. Many of your sentence errors, if you make them, happen because your mind has raced on ahead of your hand. You have started to write a second thought before you have finished writing the first. Or, perhaps in haste, you have left out a key word necessary for a complete sentence. Suppose you intended to say something like this:

> Ted and Miriam had a loud quarrel. After the quarrel, they wondered why they had been angry. They talked about their differences the next day.

In the hurry to get on with your writing, however, what you put down was something like this:

> Ted and Miriam had a loud quarrel. After they wondered why they had been angry. They talked about their differences the next day.

The second group of words is not a sentence. It causes confusion. The reader may suppose that you meant to say, "Ted and Miriam had a loud quarrel after they wondered why they had been angry."

Exercise A: Find the sentence fragments. Add the words needed to make each fragment a sentence.

1. As a child, I always made decisions slowly. Especially when choosing candy in the candy store.
2. My ten cents for candy. Always seemed like ten dollars.
3. The candy store had lots of candy on display. Most of it penny candy.
4. I always stood in front of the glassed-in shelves. Just looked and looked.
5. Some animals are nocturnal. For example, owls and bats.
6. After we went to a snack shop.
7. They tried every door in the house. But could not get in until the windows.
8. Lynn advanced toward Sam. Offered him a lemon pie.
9. The missing suitcase in the cupboard under the stairs.
10. Easton, where I was born. Just across the river from Phillipsburg.

Exercise B: Three of the following groups of words are sentences. The rest are fragments. Find the fragments and add words needed to make them sentences.

1. Heart disease, one of the chief causes of death
2. How the leopard managed to escape from its cage
3. *The Taming of the Shrew*, one of Shakespeare's wittier comedies
4. James Madison was one of the most scholarly of our Presidents
5. The pink camellia, which was especially beautiful
6. If Martin weren't so unpredictable
7. The many billboards along the highway
8. The winding road, bordered by beautiful trees and the ocean
9. Carter Lake in Oregon rests in the cone of a dead volcano
10. Deborah Sampson, disguised as a man, fought in the American Revolution

4.2 Phrases as Fragments

You know that a phrase is a group of words that does not contain a verb and its subject. A phrase, therefore, cannot be a sentence by itself. It is a *part* of a sentence.

You are not likely to mistake a prepositional phrase for a complete sentence. If you write a long prepositional phrase or a series of phrases as a sentence, it is probably because you have punctuated incorrectly.

FRAGMENT Nina studied advanced English. *In summer school.*

SENTENCE Nina studied advanced English in summer school.

You are more likely to mistake a verbal phrase for a complete sentence. This error occurs because verbals look like verbs and function somewhat like verbs. Like verbs, they may be modified by adverbs. They can be followed by objects or predicate words. They are not complete verbs, however, and they cannot be used as the main verb of a sentence.

The most troublesome verbals are those that end in *-ing*. All gerunds and present participles end in *-ing*. You will avoid many sentence errors if you will remember this fact:

No word ending in *-ing* can be a verb unless it is a one-syllable word like *sing, ring,* or *bring.*

If an *-ing* word is preceded by *is, are, was,* or some other form of *be*, the two words together are a verb.

PARTICIPLE	COMPLETE VERB
reading	is reading
holding	had been holding
breaking	were breaking

A long infinitive phrase may sometimes be mistaken for a complete sentence. Such a phrase sounds like a sentence since it often has everything that a sentence requires except a subject.

INCORRECT	This is my aim. To establish a trust fund for you.
CORRECT	This is my aim. I plan to establish a trust fund for you.
INCORRECT	Dr. Kane was very eager. To encourage my interest in becoming a surgeon.
CORRECT	Dr. Kane was very eager to encourage my interest in becoming a surgeon.

A noun and an appositive phrase are sometimes written incorrectly as a complete sentence. Although the combination may seem like a sentence, it always lacks a verb.

FRAGMENT	This biography, *the only definitive account.*
SENTENCE	This biography is the only definitive account.
SENTENCE	This biography, the only definitive account, is a masterpiece.
FRAGMENT	My sax, *a new alto.*
SENTENCE	My sax, a new alto, was very expensive.

Exercise A: Rewrite the groups of words beside each number below to make a complete sentence. You may need to add words in some instances.

1. The loon is a gray and brown bird. Very clumsy on the shore.
2. You can hold this microphone in your hand or mount it on a stand. Either way.
3. Buying a headphone and testing it instead of doing his homework.
4. Patricia went to see her counselor. To discuss her problems.
5. Our sociology class invited speakers from the community. Such as police officers, social workers, doctors, and members of the clergy.
6. I found it exciting. To see Andrea McArdle perform in *Annie.*
7. Vesuvius, the most famous volcano in the world.
8. Greece is still an extremely poor country. A warehouse of rocks and ruins.
9. Mike Anderson, the photographer for the school newspaper.
10. He was in a great hurry. To get to Richmond by six o'clock.

Exercise B: Follow the same directions as for Exercise A.

1. Owning a car involves a number of responsibilities. Paying for gas, insurance, and upkeep.
2. The speaker, a foreign correspondent for *The New York Times.*
3. The color red conveys certain meanings. Associated with danger.
4. Maple trees border the avenue. Bright orange, flaming red, and gold.
5. Diana Nyad, a well-known marathon swimmer.
6. Scientists hope to explore Venus. To determine whether life exists on that planet.
7. Kutztown is in the Pennsylvania Dutch country. The scene of an annual folk festival.
8. Mr. Ludwig's car was delivered today. Canary yellow and white.
9. Be there on Friday, March 12. At three o'clock.
10. The Declaration of Independence, one of the important documents in the struggle for human freedom.

4.3 Clauses as Fragments

A subordinate clause cannot stand alone as a sentence. (See Section 3.3.) A sentence may be changed into a subordinate clause by having a subordinating conjunction placed before it.

SENTENCE: I was trying to think of an excuse.
SUBORDINATE CLAUSE: *As* I was trying to think of an excuse . . .

Writers sometimes mistakenly place a period before or after a subordinate clause as though it were a sentence.

INCORRECT: When the landlord came. He broke up our stickball game.
CORRECT: When the landlord came, he broke up our stickball game.

INCORRECT: Jan sold her car. Because it used too much gas.
CORRECT: Jan sold her car because it used too much gas.

Exercise: Rewrite the word groups below to eliminate the fragments.

1. Few students borrow books from the school library. Although it has a wide selection.
2. We rushed to the scene at once. When we heard the news.
3. Jenny found time for chess, music, and debating. While she was editor of the school paper.
4. This is the old house. Where Aunt Trish was born.
5. Jody was decorating the school gym for the dance. When she should have been writing her term paper.
6. The pilot could not communicate with the airport. Because the radio was out.
7. The two pieces of wood must be quickly clamped together. Before the glue dries.
8. The letter arrived in the morning mail. Just after Dad had left.
9. Many people discover fascinating information. As they research their family's roots.
10. There was no fire-fighting company in Philadelphia. Until Ben Franklin formed one in 1746.

Review Exercise: In this exercise you will find examples of many kinds of fragments. Change them into sentences.

1. Leslie tried to buy glue. To mend the red dish.
2. They coasted down the hill. Thinking they could control the sled.
3. The game was over. The score 7–2 in our favor.
4. To get the car on Saturday night. Jennifer promised that she would mow the lawn.
5. Finding a summer job. It's difficult because of the competition.
6. Talking about life at sea. Joe made his listeners feel excitement and adventure.
7. The students presented Thornton Wilder's *Our Town*. After only three weeks' rehearsal.
8. Noel won an award in photography. At the art festival.
9. There is an organization for left-handed people. Called Lefthanders International.
10. The table next to the wall. It should be moved.
11. Outlining can improve learning and test scores. A good study technique.
12. America is adopting international standards of weights and measures. By converting to the metric system.
13. The Orientals have an exciting history. Going back thousands of years.
14. Dr. Power came for dinner last night. An excellent conversationalist.
15. I plan to buy a Seiko watch. Which will replace my Timex.

4.4 Run-on Sentences

A **run-on sentence** is two or more sentences written as though they were one sentence. That is, the writer fails to use a period or other end mark at the end of each sentence.

RUN-ON: Years ago, driving was a pleasure there was less traffic.

CORRECT: Years ago, driving was a pleasure. There was less traffic.

RUN-ON: All watched the launching excitedly it was spectacular.
CORRECT: All watched the launching excitedly. It was spectacular.

The most common run-on sentence error is the joining of two sentences by a comma. This error is called the **comma fault.**

COMMA FAULT: Shari decided not to go tobogganing, she was too cold.
CORRECT: Shari decided not to go tobogganing. She was too cold.

COMMA FAULT: The huge crane collapsed, it crushed a car below.
CORRECT: The huge crane collapsed. It crushed a car below.

In the foregoing examples, notice that the two sentences are closely related and that the second sentence begins with a personal pronoun: *she, it.* Watch for situations like these in your own writing and avoid the comma fault.

4.5 Avoiding the Run-on Sentence

There is no objection to joining two or more closely related statements into one sentence. In fact, it is often better to join them than to write them separately. There are three ways in which closely related sentences can be joined to make a compound sentence: (1) with a comma and a coordinating conjunction; (2) with a semicolon; (3) with a semicolon and a conjunctive adverb.

RUN-ON: Pat has two hobbies. He collects old coins, he saves match covers.
CORRECT: Pat has two hobbies. He collects old coins, and he saves match covers.

RUN-ON: Sandra did not choose her courses wisely, consequently her credits for college admission were inadequate.
CORRECT: Sandra did not choose her courses wisely; consequently, her credits for college admission were inadequate.

RUN-ON: We stayed up late watching television, then we could not get up in the morning.
CORRECT: We stayed up late watching television; then we could not get up in the morning.

Note: When a conjunctive adverb such as *consequently, however, moreover, therefore,* or *nevertheless* introduces a second main clause, it is preceded by a semicolon. Usually, it is followed by a comma.

Exercise A: Correct each of the following run-on sentences in one of these ways: (1) by using a period and a capital letter; (2) by using a semicolon; or (3) by using a comma and *and, but,* or *or.*

1. Only one paddle-wheel steamboat still operates on the Mississippi, she's the *Delta Queen.*
2. Something went wrong with the party, it just wasn't a success.
3. I overslept again, nobody woke me.
4. There must be a mistake, I didn't order any linoleum.
5. Don't be discouraged, Kerry, try to look at the bright side.
6. Some of the guests sat on the patio, others sat on the lawn.
7. I've been trying to close this suitcase, it's impossible.
8. I didn't finish the test, neither did Louise.
9. Mike tried to get up, he was simply unable to stand.
10. Laura and Lee were both being considered, Laura got the job.
11. The Peter Zenger case was a famous colonial trial, it established freedom of the press.
12. First we went to Sequoia, then we visited King's Canyon.
13. Tom's jokes delighted Nan, they annoyed me.
14. Laughs drowned out the speaker, we could hardly hear him.
15. Hamilton wrote the Federalist Papers, he got help from Madison and Jay.

Exercise B: The first part of a sentence is given on each line below. Add a second main clause, beginning it with the word in parentheses at the end of the line. If the word is a conjunctive adverb, place a semicolon before it and a comma after it. If the word is a personal pronoun, use a semicolon or use a comma with a coordinating conjunction.

1. Some of the steak was burned (nevertheless)
2. Not only did they come for dinner (they)
3. That nail should be bent back (it)
4. I know Jacques Cousteau (in fact)
5. He was advised not to use colored stationery (he)
6. In high school she learned how to take notes (therefore)
7. My boss wants dependable workers (she)
8. I was amazed to learn that he played in a band (moreover)
9. The blizzard lasted all day (consequently)
10. Often people believe what they want to believe (they)
11. We had planned an all-day picnic (however)
12. No sign of the crew has been found (nevertheless)
13. Playing high school sports teaches teamwork (moreover)
14. Television programs can be educational (for example)
15. The concert began with a medley of songs (then)

REVIEW: COMPLETE SENTENCES Rewrite the following fragments and run-ons as complete sentences.

1. The American crocodile once existed in great numbers, it is now an endangered species.
2. Joyce learned how to develop film. Assisting a photographer.
3. Sometimes twins are the best of friends. And sometimes not.
4. *Jaws* was a box-office hit, it grossed eighty million dollars.
5. My brother and I often play backgammon. After we have finished our homework.
6. This restaurant has twenty toppings for hamburgers, I chose avocado.
7. Citrus crops in Florida were damaged. During unseasonably cold weather.

8. Members of the Dance Club performed several dance numbers. Ranging from baroque to disco.

9. Does meditation work, is it restful and refreshing?

10. The U. S. Weather Bureau predicted a major blizzard. Worse than last year's.

11. Yolanda exhibited her pictures in the library. Also several etchings and one woodprint.

12. Some people are extroverts, others are introverts.

13. Marcel Marceau, who revived the ancient art of pantomime.

14. The FBI traced the ransom note. Which demanded a million dollars.

15. The magazine has many regular features, one is called "Feedback."

16. Ancient medical practices, relying chiefly on magic.

17. The Three Stooges used slapstick comedy, they relied on visual humor and horseplay.

18. Acrophobia is fear of heights, claustrophobia is fear of closed spaces.

19. The radio theater program presented a Woody Allen play. That parodied Greek tragedies.

20. Margaret Mead conducted anthropological research in New Guinea, Samoa, and Bali. Studying child-rearing practices.

5.0 Agreement of Subject and Verb

A common error in American speech is the failure to make subject and verb agree in number (*you was, we was, he don't*). Errors of agreement in speaking are sometimes difficult to avoid. In writing, however, these errors should be easier to avoid because the writer always has the time and the opportunity to revise his or her work before presenting it to a reader.

5.1 Subject-Verb Agreement in Number

There are two numbers in grammar: **singular** and **plural.** A word is singular in number if it refers to one person or thing. A word is plural if it refers to more than one person or thing.

Except for *be*, English verbs show a difference between singular and plural only in the third person and only in the present tense. The third person singular present form ends in *s*.

I, you, we, they	walk	he, she, it	walks

The verb *be* presents several special problems in agreement. First, the second person pronoun *you* is always used with the plural form of the verb: *you are, you were*. Second, the difference between singular and plural is shown in the past tense as well as in the present tense.

Present Tense		Past Tense	
SINGULAR	PLURAL	SINGULAR	PLURAL
I *am*	we *are*	I *was*	we *were*
you *are*	you *are*	you *were*	you *were*
he, she, it *is*	they *are*	he, she, it *was*	they *were*

Common errors with *be* are *you was, we was, they was*.

A singular verb is used with a singular subject.

A plural verb is used with a plural subject.

The subject determines whether the verb is singular or plural. The verb does not agree with any other part of the sentence.

The theorem (singular) *is* clear.
The theorems (plural) *are* clear.

The coach (singular) *works* hard.
The coaches (plural) *work* hard.

Note: A verb also agrees with its subject in *person*. When there are two or more subjects that differ in person, the verb agrees with the subject nearest to it.

Neither Kent nor I *am* prepared.
Either Mr. Walder or the Kellys *are* moving.

5.2 Words Between Subject and Verb

The verb agrees only with its subject. Occasionally a word with a different number from that of the subject occurs between the subject and the verb. This word usually has no effect upon the number of the verb even though it is closer to the verb than the subject is.

The *plane,* carrying fifty passengers, *is* landing.
(*plane* is the subject)
One of the cars *needs* a battery.
(*One* is the subject.)
The *candidates* for the Presidency *are* stumping the country.
(*candidates* is the subject.)
The *uprisings* in small countries often *involve* violence.
(*uprisings* is the subject.)

The words *with, together with, along with, as well as* are prepositions. The objects of these prepositions have no effect upon the number of the verb.

The trapped *miner,* together with the rescue squad, *is* safe.
(*miner* is the subject.)
His facial *expression,* as well as his tone of voice, *gives* him away.
(*expression* is the subject.)
The *defendant,* with her lawyer, *enters* the courtroom.
(*defendant* is the subject.)

Exercise: Choose the right verb from those given in parentheses.

1. Our choir with its sixty voices (is, are) very popular.
2. A bunch of grapes often (makes, make) an attractive centerpiece for a dining table.
3. The bride, with her attendants, (is, are) coming down the aisle.
4. Jack, as well as Jean, (plays, play) in the All-State Orchestra.
5. The rugs in our house (has, have) been tacked down to prevent slipping.
6. This book of poems (is, are) illustrated with photographs.
7. Bicycling trips through the countryside (makes, make) me appreciate nature.
8. My towel, together with my sunglasses, (was, were) washed away by the waves.
9. Several sticks of dynamite (makes, make) a large explosion.
10. One of the most daring feats (is, are) the fifty-foot dive into five feet of water.

11. They (was, were) relieved that I had decided to stay home.
12. The noise of so many typewriters (was, were) deafening.
13. The teacher, not the pupils, (was, were) doing most of the work.
14. Frank's knowledge of the Old Masters (is, are) remarkable.
15. Her choice of words (is, are) incredible for a ten-year-old.
16. The code of ethics for our school (is, are) posted in the hall.
17. At birthday parties there (is, are) always cake, along with ice cream.
18. Nobody except members and their guests (is, are) allowed to attend the ceremony.
19. Art, with some of his friends, (has, have) gone to band practice.
20. The bandleader, together with two arrangers, (is, are) preparing a disco version of the tune.

5.3 Indefinite Pronouns

Some indefinite pronouns are always singular. Others are always plural. Some may be either singular or plural.

SINGULAR			PLURAL
each	everyone	anybody	several
either	everybody	anyone	few
neither	no one	someone	both
one	nobody	somebody	many

Each of the tests *is* challenging.
Neither of your parents *is* disappointed.
Everybody in the cast *was* applauded.
Several of the books *are* lost.
Few of the crowd *have* left.
Both of the contestants *were* congratulated.

SINGULAR OR PLURAL

some	all	most
none	any	

Some, all, most, none, and *any* are singular when they refer to a quantity. They are plural when they refer to a number of individual items.

> *Some* of the money *was* stolen. (quantity)
> *Some* of their answers *were* wrong. (number)
>
> *Most* of the sugar *is* gone. (quantity)
> *Most* of the survivors *were* dazed. (number)
>
> *All* of the food *was* donated. (quantity)
> *All* of the tools *were* expensive. (number)

None and *any* may be either singular or plural depending on whether the writer is referring to one thing or to several.

> None of the stories *was* true. (not one)
> None of the stories *were* true. (no stories)
>
> Any of these careers *is* rewarding. (any one)
> Any of these careers *are* rewarding. (any careers)

Exercise: Choose the right word from the two given.

1. Every one of the runners (was, were) given an award.
2. Most of the cabins in the camp (was, were) repainted.
3. Not one of my shipmates (was, were) able to swim.
4. Neither of these books (interests, interest) me.
5. One of the most timid of animals (is, are) the giraffe.
6. (Does, Do) either of you play a guitar?
7. Neither of the physics experiments (has, have) been completed.
8. Several of the roads (was, were) washed away by the flood.
9. Not one of the officers (was, were) at the meeting.
10. Few of the jokes (was, were) amusing.
11. One of the best clarinetists (is, are) Benny Goodman.
12. Either of the motorboats (is, are) available.
13. Not one of the bulbs (was, were) working.
14. Everyone in the regiment (seems, seem) courageous.
15. Several of our best players (has, have) the flu.

16. Each of us (has, have) a perfect attendance record.
17. All of my research on runaways (was, were) fascinating.
18. One of Arthur Miller's best plays (is, are) *The Crucible.*
19. Nobody in those communities (wants, want) a sales tax.
20. Anyone who wants to help collect funds (is, are) welcome.

5.4 Compound Subjects

Compound subjects joined by *and* are plural.*

Physical fitness and mental agility *are* necessary for athletes.

Singular words joined by *or, nor, either-or, neither-nor* to form a compound subject are singular.

Neither his sincerity nor his reliability *is* questioned.
Either their team or our team *has* a chance to win.
Ellen or Gordon *deserves* the scholarship.

When a singular word and a plural word are joined by *or* or *nor* to form a compound subject, the verb agrees with the subject that is nearer to it.

Neither the folk singers nor their agent *likes* the program.
(*agent* is closer to the verb than *folk singers.*)
The management or the unions *are* making concessions.
Neither the actors nor the play *appeals* to anyone.

Exercise: Find the errors in subject-verb agreement in these sentences. Write the sentences correctly. Two of the sentences are correct.

1. The engine and one car was derailed.
2. Chuck or his brother are usually at the meetings.
3. Are your mother or your father going to the school play?
4. Neither the driver nor her passengers was expecting a bump.
5. The captain or the lieutenant is always on duty.
6. Neither the children nor the baby sitter were happy.

* If the words making up the compound subject are habitually used together to refer to a single thing, the subject may be used with a singular verb: *bread and butter, macaroni and cheese,* etc.

7. Swimming and ice skating calls for good judgment.
8. Were either Josie or Emily there?
9. Either Joe or Henry are going to save a seat for you.
10. Neither illness nor financial loss seem to lessen her spirit.
11. Neither the Wilmington squad nor the Plainfield team were invited to the tournament.
12. Either the meat or the potatoes are burning.
13. To travel and to write a novel is Judy's ambitions.
14. A basketball court and an indoor track is in the gymnasium.
15. Neither the Wayside Inn nor the House of the Seven Gables are in Boston.

5.5 Subject Following Verb

The most difficult agreement problem in speech arises when the subject follows the verb. The speaker must think ahead to the subject in order to decide whether the verb is to be singular or plural.

This problem arises in sentences beginning with *There* and *Here*. It also arises in questions beginning with *who, why, where, what, how*.

NONSTANDARD: Here'*s* the tickets for the game.
STANDARD: Here *are* the tickets for the game.

NONSTANDARD: There'*s* only two possible answers.
STANDARD: There *are* only two possible answers.

NONSTANDARD: Who'*s* the officers in the debating club?
STANDARD: Who *are* the officers in the debating club?

NONSTANDARD: What'*s* your reasons for refusing?
STANDARD: What *are* your reasons for refusing?

NONSTANDARD: Down the avenue *comes* the band and the color guard.
STANDARD: Down the avenue *come* the band and the color guard.

5.6 Predicate Words

The linking verb agrees with its subject, *not* with the predicate word.

NONSTANDARD:	New theories *is* not the answer.
STANDARD:	New theories *are* not the answer.
NONSTANDARD:	Joe's first love *are* sailboats.
STANDARD:	Joe's first love *is* sailboats.
NONSTANDARD:	Being accepted and registering *is* only the beginning.
STANDARD:	Being accepted and registering *are* only the beginning.

5.7 *Don't* and *Doesn't*

The word *does* and the contraction *doesn't* are used with singular nouns and with the pronouns *he, she,* and *it*. The word *do* and the contraction *don't* are used with plural nouns and with the pronouns *I, we, you,* and *they*.

DOES, DOESN'T	DO, DON'T
the boat does	the boats do
he doesn't	we don't
she doesn't	you don't
it doesn't	they don't

Exercise: Choose the right word from the two given in parentheses.

1. After the thaw (comes, come) the floods.
2. There (is, are) oranges in the refrigerator.
3. The fruit I like best (is, are) seedless grapes.
4. Why (doesn't, don't) he take the back road?
5. On the Fourth of July (comes, come) our annual picnic.
6. There (was, were) fifty people present at the meeting.
7. (Where's, Where are) the instructions for this game?
8. There (is, are) many ways to cook a lobster.
9. If she (doesn't, don't) agree, Stephanie will say so.

10. Inside the cave (was, were) many stalactites.

11. For the person who wants to advance, (there's, there are) numerous evening courses.

12. There (was, were) four students on the team.

13. On the bulletin board (was, were) a list of ten names.

14. (There's, There are) many details involved in the plan.

15. Why (is, are) the environmentalists protesting the new power plant?

16. The gift I like best (is, are) books.

17. From a single plant (comes, come) dozens of flowers.

18. My only regret (is, are) the days wasted.

19. A glass of lemonade and a comfortable chair on the back lawn (is, are) all I want.

20. There (seems, seem) to be a pile of letters in the box.

5.8 Collective Nouns

A collective noun names a group of people or things: *committee, flock, team, herd, crowd.*

When the writer refers to a group acting together as one unit, the collective noun is used with a singular verb. When the writer refers to the individuals in the group acting separately, one by one, the collective noun is used with a plural verb.

The herd *heads* for the barn. (united action)
The herd *were* running in all directions. (separate action)

The team *was* the winner of the play-off. (united action)
The team *were* voting for a captain. (separate action)

Once the writer decides whether the collective noun is a unit or a group of individuals, he or she must abide by that choice. Later in the same sentence the writer may not use a verb or pronoun of different number.

NONSTANDARD The panel *has* (singular) submitted *their* (plural) findings.
STANDARD The panel *has* submitted *its* findings.

5.9 Nouns Plural in Form

Some nouns are plural in form but are regarded as singular in meaning. That is, they end in *s* as most plural nouns do, but they do not stand for more than one thing: *news, mumps, measles*. Therefore, they are used with a singular verb.

There are many words ending in *-ics* that may be either singular or plural: *economics, athletics, civics, politics*. These words are singular when they are used to refer to a school subject, a science, or a general practice. When singular in meaning, they are not usually preceded by *the, his, her, some, all* and singular modifiers.

Politics *is* a field for serious study. (singular)
Her politics *are* in no way suspect. (plural)

Economics *appeals* to many college students. (singular)
Our economics *are* endangered by right- and left-wing extremists. (plural)

Hysterics *are* sometimes halted by a slap in the face. (plural)

News *is* a major attraction on television. (singular)

Not all athletics *are* recommended for every student. (plural)

5.10 Titles and Groups of Words

The title of a book, play, story, film, musical composition, or other work of art is used with a singular verb. The name of a country is used with a singular verb. Such words, even though they may be plural in form, refer to a single thing.

The Netherlands *has* a colorful history.
Leaves of Grass is Walt Whitman's greatest achievement.
The United States *is* a relatively young nation.
Amahl and the Night Visitors is an opera in English.
The Potato-Eaters is a famous painting by Van Gogh.

Any group of words referring to a single thing or thought is used with a singular verb.

> What our country needs *is* dedicated men and women.
> "Haste makes waste" *is* sound advice.

5.11 Words of Amount and Time

Words or phrases that express periods of time, fractions, weights, measurements, and amounts of money are usually regarded as singular.

> Two-thirds of the town's housing *has* been renovated.
> Two yards of wire *is* enough to buy.
> Three dollars *seems* like a fortune to him.
> Fifty tons *is* the capacity of the freight train.
> Two hours *has* sometimes seemed like eternity.

If a prepositional phrase with a plural object falls between the subject and the verb, the verb is singular if its subject is considered as a single thing or thought. The verb is plural if its subject is felt to be plural.

> Ten pounds of potatoes *is* what we ordered.
> (singular meaning)
> Ten crates of oranges *were* piled on the floor.
> (plural meaning)

Exercise: Choose the right words from those given in the parentheses.

1. The man's ethics (was, were) questionable.
2. What our magazine needs (is, are) more contributors.
3. Mathematics (is, are) Martina's favorite subject.
4. What this theater needs (is, are) two new projectors.
5. Three-fourths of our lawn (has, have) been reseeded.
6. About three-quarters of the oranges (was, were) moldy.
7. The jury (was, were) arguing heatedly.

8. Over one-half of the employees in this town (commutes, commute).
9. Two or three feet of twine (is, are) probably enough.
10. Five dollars (is, are) too much to pay for a parking place.
11. Measles (is, are) a contagious disease.
12. Three hundred miles (is, are) a good day's trip.
13. The team (is, are) getting into their new uniforms.
14. Politics (has, have) always been my sister's main interest.
15. Two thousand pounds of paper (was, were) collected.
16. Ten weeks (is, are) the length of time required for the course.
17. *The Six Wives of Henry VIII* (was, were) shown on public television.
18. The Netherlands (has, have) just issued some interesting stamps.
19. Only one-half of the eligible voters (has, have) registered.
20. Ten cartons of canned goods (was, were) piled outside the store.

5.12 Relative Pronouns

A relative pronoun stands in place of its antecedent (the word to which it refers). If that antecedent is plural, the relative pronoun is plural. If the antecedent is singular, the relative pronoun is singular.

A relative pronoun agrees with its antecedent in number.

When a relative pronoun is used as subject of the verb in the relative clause, the number of the verb depends upon the number of the pronoun's antecedent.

These are the *researchers* (plural) who (plural) *are* testing our new products.

Chagall is the *artist* (singular) who (singular) has made a free-form mosaic in downtown Chicago.

Katie is one of those *members* who always *volunteer*.
(*members* always volunteer.)

He was the only *one* of the skin divers who *was* attacked by a shark. (only *one* was attacked.)

The problem of agreement arises in the last two sentences above because there are two words, either of which *might* be the antecedent of the relative pronoun. Usually the meaning of the sentence shows which word *is* the antecedent.

Exercise A: Choose the right word for those given in parentheses.

1. Debby is the only one of the girls who (has, have) practiced.
2. This is one of the motorhomes that (is, are) fully equipped.
3. The eagle is one species which (nests, nest) in a high tree.
4. This is the first of several meetings that (is, are) to be held.
5. Lisa was the one among all her classmates who (was, were) chosen to head student government.
6. Which of the students who (takes, take) math use calculators?
7. Of all the novels that (is, are) on the shelf, Pearl Buck's is the most intriguing.
8. With a bag full of books that (was, were) due at the library, Nicole trudged through the snow.
9. Ruffin is the only one of the dogs that (does, do) somersaults.
10. He is one of those teachers who (expects, expect) the best from each student.

Exercise B: Follow the same directions as for Exercise A.

1. We found one of the kittens that (was, were) lost.
2. Which of the counselors who (advises, advise) juniors would you recommend?
3. Carrie is one of those golfers who always (gets, get) a good score.
4. A clarinet is one of those instruments that (needs, need) a reed.
5. Public documents are one of the sources that (reveals, reveal) one's ancestors.

6. *The Canterbury Tales* is one of those books that (defies, defy) translation into modern English.

7. Binet is one of the researchers who (has, have) studied intelligence.

8. Of all the diseases that (attacks, attack) elderly persons, hardening of the arteries is the most common.

9. Art Buchwald is one of those columnists who (uses, use) humor to make a point.

10. Peter is the only one of the boys who (has, have) a scholarship.

REVIEW: AGREEMENT OF SUBJECT AND VERB In the following sentences, choose the right verb from those given in parentheses.

1. The bunch of ripe red grapes (is, are) delicious.
2. Gary's attitude, as well as his study habits, (is, are) improving
3. Some of the planes (is, are) landing in the fog.
4. Everybody in the drama class (performs, perform) in one play.
5. Either the elevator or the escalator (goes, go) to the top floor.
6. Neither the coach nor the fans (approves, approve) of the referee's call.
7. There (is, are) several reasons for my decision.
8. In my locker (sits, sit) my tennis shoes and racket.
9. That skier (doesn't, don't) use ski poles.
10. Extracurricular activities (is, are) a way to meet people.
11. Jackie's favorite dessert (is, are) fudge brownies.
12. The band (marches, march) onto the field in a V formation.
13. The jury (has, have) declared its verdict.
14. Athletics for girls (is, are) expanding at most schools.
15. The British Isles (has, have) had a succession of monarchs.
16. *The Martian Chronicles* (describes, describe) life on Mars.
17. Three-fourths of these diamonds (comes, come) from Africa.
18. Eighteen ounces of water (fills, fill) this canteen.
19. Iceland is one of those countries that (has, have) little pollution.
20. Leslie Stahl is the only one of those reporters who (is, are) based in Washington.

6.0 Pronoun Usage

In grammar, the term *inflection* has a special meaning. It means "a change in form to show how a word is used in a sentence." Prepositions, conjunctions, and interjections do not change their form. All other parts of speech do. Usually, the change in form is just a change in spelling:

NOUN:	boy	— boy's	— boys	— boys'
VERB:	walk	— walks	— walked	— walking
ADJECTIVE:	big	— bigger	— biggest	
ADVERB:	hard	— harder	— hardest	

Often, however, the change involves the use of a completely new word:

VERB:	go	— went	— gone
PRONOUN:	I	— me	— mine

Pronouns change their form in both ways. The changes in pronouns correspond to their use in sentences. These changes are called the **cases** of pronouns. The cases are the **nominative, possessive,** and **objective.**

You will recall that pronouns can be used in sentences in the following ways:

subject of the verb	predicate pronoun	appositive
object of the verb	object of a preposition	modifier

Nearly all pronouns change their form for different uses in the sentence. The indefinite pronouns have the least change. They change only when used as modifiers. As modifiers, they are in the possessive case:

		POSSESSIVE
everyone	—	everyone's
nobody	—	nobody's
anyone	—	anyone's

The pronouns *this, that, these, those, which,* and *what* do not change their forms to indicate case. None of these has a possessive form.

The pronoun inflections are as follows:

NOMINATIVE	POSSESSIVE	OBJECTIVE
I	my, mine	me
we	our, ours,	us
you	your, yours	you
he	his	him
she	her, hers	her
it	its	it
they	their, theirs	them
who	whose	whom
whoever	whosever	whomever

6.1 The Pronoun as Subject of a Verb

The nominative form of the pronoun is used as subject of a verb.

The problem of which pronoun form to use as subject arises chiefly when the subject is compound. The compound subject may be made up of pronouns or of both nouns and pronouns.

To decide which pronoun form to use in a compound subject, *try each part of the subject by itself with the verb.*

Dan and (I, me) bought the used car.
(Dan bought; I bought, *not* me bought.)

My parents and (they, them) are going to Florida.
(My parents are going; they are going, *not* them are going.)

Sally and (he, him) went fishing.
(Sally went; he went, *not* him went.)

We and (they, them) worked at the lodge.
(We worked; they worked, *not* them worked.)

The plural forms *we* and *they* sound awkward in many compounds. They can be avoided by recasting the sentence.

AWKWARD: The referees and we have agreed.
BETTER: We and the referees have agreed.

AWKWARD: We and they prefer camping.
BETTER: We all prefer camping.

6.2 The Predicate Pronoun

The verb *be* is a linking verb. It links the noun, pronoun, or adjective following it to the subject. A pronoun so linked is called a **predicate pronoun.**

The nominative pronoun form is used as a predicate pronoun.*

The problem of which form to use in a predicate pronoun occurs primarily after the verb *be*. The rule applies to all verb phrases built around forms of *be: could have been, can be*, etc.

It *was* **I** who refused to go.
Could it *have been* **she** who won?
It *must have been* **they** who gave the signal.

Sometimes the nominative form sounds awkward. The awkwardness can be avoided by recasting the sentence.

AWKWARD: The co-editors are she and Toby.
BETTER: She and Toby are the co-editors.

AWKWARD: It was we who made the suggestion.
BETTER: We are the people who made the suggestion.

* Standard usage permits the exception in both speech and writing of *It is me.*

6.3 The Pronoun as Object of a Verb

The objective pronoun form is used as direct or indirect object.

The problem of which pronoun form to use as object of the verb arises chiefly when the object is compound. The compound object may consist of pronouns or of both nouns and pronouns.

To decide which pronoun form to use in a compound object, *try each part of the object by itself with the verb.*

Phil showed Tad and (I, me) how to complete the experiment.
(showed Tad; showed me, *not* showed I)
The problem puzzled Yolande and (he, him).
(puzzled Yolande; puzzled him, *not* puzzled he)
Mrs. O'Leary told (they, them) and (we, us) about the potato famine.
(told them, *not* told they; told us, *not* told we)
Do you want (she, her) and (I, me) to read the part?
(want her, *not* want she; want me, *not* want I)

Exercise A: Choose the right form from those given in parentheses.

1. The Ford Foundation gave (she, her) and her assistant a grant.
2. I invited Theresa and (he, him) to the party.
3. Show Larry and (I, me) the map of Long Island.
4. The only returning staff members are Terry and (he, him).
5. (She, Her) and Tim will design the posters.
6. Are you implying that it was (he, him)?
7. If I were (she, her), I'd take a foreign language.
8. Wasn't it (he, him) who gave the nominating speech?
9. The workers rescued (she, her) and the other miners.
10. Lil and (he, him) have been studying the classical guitar.
11. The Rotary Club gave Wendy and (I, me) partial scholarships.
12. The orthodontist examined Margaret and (he, him).
13. Mary and Carlotta taught Dave and (I, me) several new folk dances.
14. What reason did (she, her) and the architect give?
15. Will you lend Marty and (I, me) your field glasses?

Exercise B: Choose the right form from those given in parentheses.

1. We saw Michelle and (she, her) at the science fair.
2. How many hamburgers did you and (he, him) eat?
3. If I were (she, her), I would apply for the job.
4. Why don't you meet Vinny and (I, me) on the first tee?
5. We suspect that it was (she, her) who played the practical joke.
6. They spotted (he, him) and his accomplice in the getaway car.
7. Will you help Bernie and (I, me) shovel the snow?
8. Neither the Gibsons nor (we, us) have been to Sea Island.
9. I couldn't believe that it was (they, them).
10. Wasn't it (she, her) who became a famous court reporter?
11. The tallest boys in the class are Sandy and (I, me).
12. It was either Olivia or (he, him) who saw the eclipse.
13. Randy and (she, her) have been accepted at Gettysburg College.
14. The co-captains of the baseball team are Cliff and (he, him).
15. It was (they, them) who discovered the theft.

6.4 The Pronoun as Object of a Preposition

The objective pronoun form is used as object of a preposition.

The problem of which pronoun form to use as object of a preposition arises only when the object is compound. The compound object may consist of pronouns or of both nouns and pronouns.

To decide which pronoun to use in a compound object of a preposition, *try each part of the object by itself with the preposition.*

The librarian is reserving a book for him and (I, me).
(for him; for me, *not* for I)
The news came as a surprise to Sheila and (we, us).
(to Sheila; to us, *not* to we)
I received letters from (they, them) and Nancy.
(from them, *not* from they)

The preposition *between* causes especially noticeable errors in pronoun usage. Use only the objective pronoun forms after *between*.

between you and him, *not* between you and he
between him and me, *not* between he and I

6.5 The Pronoun Used with a Noun

In a construction such as *we girls* or *us boys*, the use of the noun determines the case form of the pronoun.

We Republocrats are a united party.
(*Republocrats* is the subject of *are*; the nominative pronoun is therefore required.)

The lifeguard drove us surfers from the beach.
(*surfers* is direct object of *drove*; the objective pronoun is therefore required.)

To decide which pronoun form to use in a construction such as *we boys*, try the pronoun by itself with the verb or preposition.

The warning was directed mainly to (we, us) boys.
(to us, *not* to we)
They allowed (we, us) amateur photographers to compete.
(allowed us, *not* allowed we)
(We, Us) flag bearers will lead the line of march.
(We will lead, *not* Us will lead)

Exercise A: Choose the right form from those given in parentheses.

1. (We, Us) students in the Film Club elected officers.
2. Did you hear the news about (he, him) and his brother?
3. Between you and (I, me), I regret my hasty answer.
4. Why should there be a misunderstanding between Ed and (I, me)?
5. Nobody went to the bowling alley except Denise and (I, me).
6. I wrote letters to Amelia and (he, him).

7. Dad has packed lunches for you and (I, me).
8. No one was there but Leonard and (he, him).
9. (We, Us) varsity players hope to get athletic scholarships.
10. The guidance counselor's reminders were intended for Diane and (I, me).
11. The snow sculptures were done by Meg, Tim, and (I, me).
12. None of (we, us) juniors was put on the team.
13. These plans must be kept a secret among (we, us) four.
14. Several of (we, us) sophomores were asked to attend.
15. The first ones to board the plane were (we, us) reporters.

Exercise B: Choose the right form from those given in parentheses.

1. The coach praised (we, us) players for our teamwork.
2. Wait for Gus and (I, me) in the stationery store.
3. The gym was decorated by Don, Sandra, and (I, me).
4. The prize money will be divided between you and (I, me).
5. Directly below Pat and (I, me) sat the corps of cadets.
6. Who marches between you and (he, him) in the parade?
7. The florist talked to Peggy and (I, me) about the corsages.
8. Everyone was interested except Grace and (I, me).
9. This matter concerns no one but you and (I, me).
10. To (we, us) substitutes, the regulars looked helpless.
11. A trust fund is being established for Kevin and (he, him).
12. The reprimand was intended for (we, us) girls.
13. There was not a scholarship winner among (we, us) applicants.
14. The screen version was written by the author and (she, her).
15. The guide showed (we, us) tourists an unusual formation.

6.6 *Who* and *Whom* in Questions

The pronouns *who* and *whom* are used as interrogative pronouns in questions. Within the question, the pronoun may be the subject of the verb, object of the verb, or object of a preposition.

In standard usage, the nominative form *who* is used as the subject of the verb. The objective form *whom* is used as the object of the verb or of a preposition. (In informal usage there is a growing tendency to use *who* at the beginning of a sentence, whether subject or object.)

The pronouns *whoever* and *whomever* follow the same rules as *who* and *whom.*

To decide which form to use, determine how the pronoun is used within the question.

> To (who, whom) were you writing?
> (*whom* is correct as the object of the preposition *To.*)
>
> (Who, Whom) gave you the information?
> (*Who* is correct as the subject of the verb *gave.*)
>
> (Who, Whom) are you talking about?
> (*Whom* is correct as the object of the preposition *about.*)
>
> (Who, Whom) was the teacher praising?
> (*Whom* is correct as the object of the verb *was praising.*)
>
> (Who, Whom) found the missing child?
> (*Who* is correct as the subject of the verb *found.*)

Do not be misled by parenthetical expressions like *do you think, can you imagine, do you suppose, do you believe.* They do not determine the case of the interrogative pronoun.

> Who do you think will win the championship?
> (*Who* is the subject of *will win.*)
>
> Whom do you suppose he recommended?
> (*Whom* is the object of *recommended.*)
>
> Who do you believe is the stronger leader?
> (*Who* is the subject of *is.*)

6.7 *Who* and *Whom* in Clauses

The pronouns *who* and *whom* may be used as relative pronouns to introduce adjective clauses or as introductory words in noun clauses. These pronouns also perform a job within the clause they introduce.

Whoever and *whomever* follow the same rules as *who* and *whom* when used as introductory words.

The use of the pronoun within the clause determines whether the nominative or objective form is used.

I did not see *whom Jed met.*
(Noun clause; *whom* is the object of the verb *met* within the clause.)

Our teachers are those *whom we should remember with gratitude.*
(*whom* is the object of *should remember* within the clause.)

He is the candidate *who was not elected to office.*
(*who* is the subject of the verb *was elected* within the clause.)

I wonder *who received the Nobel Prize.*
(Noun clause; *who* is the subject of the verb *received* within the clause.)

She is the person *to whom you should write.*
(*whom* is the object of the preposition *to* within the clause.)

Whoever writes the best essay will win a trip to Washington.
(*Whoever* is the subject of the verb *writes* within the noun clause.)

Victory comes to *whoever stands for high principles.*
(The noun clause is the object of the preposition *to; whoever* is the subject of the verb *stands* within the clause.)

It is important to cooperate with *whomever you elect.*
(The noun clause is the object of the preposition *with; whomever* is the object of the verb *elect* within the clause.)

Exercise: Choose the right form from those given in parentheses.

1. (Who, Whom) do you think will get the leading part?
2. (Who, Whom) are those people touring the building?
3. Robert Redford is the actor to (who, whom) Sid was referring.
4. (Who, Whom) are they sending to meet the train?
5. Ms. Voss is the person from (who, whom) you must get permission.
6. (Who, Whom) do you believe is telling the truth?
7. (Whoever, Whomever) applies must fill out an application blank.
8. (Who, Whom) do you suppose gave him the key to the room?
9. She is the lawyer for (who, whom) I work.
10. Ms. Chan motivates all the students (who, whom) she teaches.
11. He is a person (who, whom) I trust implicitly.
12. (Who, Whom) did you say was elected vice-president?
13. The lecturer varied his talk depending on (who, whom) was in the audience.
14. We must support (whoever, whomever) is elected.
15. The case will come up before (whoever, whomever) is presiding at this session.
16. I'll vote for (whoever, whomever) has the proper qualifications.
17. You may go with (whoever, whomever) you choose.
18. Give the message to (whoever, whomever) answers the telephone.
19. There is the counselor about (who, whom) you were asking.
20. (Who, Whom) does the new baby look like?

6.8 Pronouns in Comparisons

Sometimes a comparison is made by using a clause that begins with *than* or *as*.

> Marie is more musical *than Lillian is.*
> I have as much will power *as anyone else has.*
> George trusts you more *than he trusts her.*

Sometimes the final clause in the comparison is left incomplete.

Marie is more musical than Lillian (is).
I have as much will power as anyone else (has).

To decide which pronoun form to use in an incomplete comparison, complete the comparison.

Harry earned more credits than (I, me).
(Harry earned more credits than *I earned.*)
The noise scared Phyllis more than (I, me).
(The noise scared Phyllis more than *it scared me.*)

6.9 Possessive Case with Gerunds

The possessive form of the pronoun is used when the pronoun immediately precedes a gerund.

All gerunds end in *-ing,* and they are all formed from verbs. The present participle also ends in *-ing,* and it, too, is formed from a verb. If the *-ing* word is used as a modifier, it is a participle. If it is used as a noun, it is a gerund.

The possessive form of the pronoun is used before a gerund. The nominative and objective forms are used before a participle.

The teacher discouraged *his daydreaming.*
(*daydreaming* is a gerund, the object of the verb discouraged.)

I saw *him browsing* in the library.
(*browsing* is a participle modifying *him.*)

Their driving was terrifying to others.
(*driving* is a gerund, the subject of the verb *was.*)

We watched *them driving* down the street.
(*driving* is a participle modifying *them.*)

6.10 The Pronoun with Infinitives

The objective form of the pronoun is used as the subject, object, or predicate pronoun of an infinitive.

The clerk asked *me to complete* the form. (*me* is the subject of *to complete.*)
Ray urged *her to keep* the cat. (*her* is the subject of *to keep.*)
They took *him* to be *me.* (*him* is the subject of *to be,* and *me* is the predicate pronoun following *to be.*)
His boss decided *to reward him.* (*him* is object of *to reward.*)
We expected the winner *to be her.* (*her* is the predicate pronoun following *to be.*)

6.11 The Pronoun as an Appositive

The form of a pronoun used as an appositive is determined by the use of the noun to which it is in apposition.

Your representatives, *Hugh* and *I*, need your help.
(*Hugh* and *I* are in apposition to *representatives,* which is the the subject of *need.* Therefore, the nominative form of the pronoun is required.)

For both of us, *Pam* and *me*, the victory was sweet.
(*Pam* and *me* are in apposition to *us,* which is the object of the preposition *for.* Therefore, the objective form of the pronoun is required.)

Uncle Gino offered the newcomers, *Sophia* and *him*, good jobs.
(*Sophia* and *him* are in apposition to *newcomers,* which is the indirect object of *offered.* Therefore, the objective form of the pronoun is required.)

To determine which form of the pronoun to use in apposition, try the appositive by itself with the verb or preposition.

The victims, Jerry and (her, she), had been riding in the back.
(She had been riding; *not* her had been riding.)

The awards were given to the juniors, Willy and (she, her).
(The awards were given to her, *not* to she.)

6.12 Compound Personal Pronouns

Compound personal pronouns are used only when their antecedents appear in the same sentence.

STANDARD: Jean bruised herself when she fell.
STANDARD: It is said that history often repeats itself.

NONSTANDARD: The decision is up to yourself.
STANDARD: The decision is up to you.

NONSTANDARD: The presents were for ourselves.
STANDARD: The presents were for us.

Exercise: Choose the standard form from those given in parentheses.

1. Dan and (I, myself) are in charge of the barbecue.
2. Essie is taller than (he, him).
3. Few girls are better dancers than (she, her).
4. Irene or (I, myself) will be glad to introduce you.
5. The baby sitter must have thought Linda to be (I, me).
6. My twin Jane is a few minutes older than (I, me).
7. (Our, Us) missing the bus caused us to miss the opening number.
8. Mr. Horn didn't like (our, us) playing catch on his front lawn.
9. I taught Mike and (she, her) how to ski.
10. We worried about (their, them) driving home in the storm.
11. The measuring stick proved that I was taller than (she, her).
12. Ginny and (I, me, myself) designed and built a rock garden.
13. Another girl and (I, myself) served as co-chairpersons for the homecoming dance.
14. The final decision must be made by you and (I, me).
15. The losers, Gerald and (she, her), were good sports.
16. We praised the losers, Gerald and (she, her).
17. Anyone as young as (she, her) cannot be admitted.
18. The prize was awarded jointly to Steve and (me, myself).
19. No one can make the decision but (him, himself).
20. Mr. Moss seemed even more frightened than (we, us).

6.13 Pronouns and Antecedents

A pronoun agrees with its antecedent in number, gender, and person.

Agreement in Number. If the antecedent of a pronoun is singular, a singular pronoun is required. If the antecedent is plural, a plural pronoun is required.

The indefinite pronouns that are singular in meaning cause the greatest difficulty. The following are referred to by singular pronouns.

anybody	either	neither	somebody
anyone	everybody	nobody	someone
each	everyone	one	

Each of the waiters wore *his* uniform.
Everyone indicated *his or her* preference.

Note: The general rule does not always apply to *everyone* and *everybody*. In certain sentences these words must be referred to by plural pronouns to make good sense.

POOR: *Everyone* stood when *he* or *she* saluted the flag.
BETTER: *Everyone* stood when *they* saluted the flag.

POOR: *Everybody* cheered when *she* or *he* saw the President.
BETTER: *Everybody* cheered when *they* saw the President.

In the sentences above, the verbs are all in the past tense. Verbs in the past tense do not change form to show singular and plural. If the verbs were in the present tense, the singular verb would be required and the singular personal pronouns (she, her, he, his) would also be required.

Everyone stands when *he or she* salutes the flag.
Everybody cheers when *she or he* sees the President.

Two or more singular antecedents joined by *or* or *nor* are referred to by a singular pronoun.

Either Joni or Rita will bring *her* guitar.
Neither Sal nor Ed has paid *his* fees.

Collective nouns may be referred to by either a singular or plural pronoun, depending upon the meaning intended.

The committee *has* announced *its* plans.
The committee *have* offered *their* services.

The indefinite pronouns *all, some, any, most,* and *none* may be referred to by either a singular or plural pronoun, depending upon the meaning intended.

Some of the workers *have* lost *their* jobs.

Some of the cider *has* lost *its* tang.

All of the networks *are* holding over *their* best shows.

Note: In all of the foregoing examples, the collective nouns and indefinite pronouns are used as subjects. The number of the verb and the number of the pronoun referring to them must be the same.

NONSTANDARD: Some of the jury *are* giving *its* opinions.
STANDARD: Some of the jury *are* giving *their* opinions.

NONSTANDARD: None of the debaters *was* convincing *their* audience.
STANDARD: None of the debaters *were* convincing *their* audience.
STANDARD: None of the debaters *was* convincing *her* audience.

Agreement in Gender. Masculine gender is indicated by *he, his, him.* Feminine gender is indicated by *she, her, hers.* Neuter gender is indicated by *it* and *its.* These pronouns must be the same in gender as the word to which they refer.

The dog tried to slip out of *its* collar. (neuter)
The investigator submitted *his* report. (masculine)
The realtor was proud of *her* sales record. (feminine)

When a singular pronoun must refer to both feminine and masculine antecedents, the phrase "his or her" is acceptable. It is, in fact, preferred by some people who wish to avoid what they consider to be sexist language.

STANDARD: No parent wants to deny *his* child an education.
STANDARD: No parent wants to deny *his or her* child an education.

Agreement in Person. A personal pronoun must be in the same person as its antecedent. The words *one, everyone,* and *everybody* are in the third person. They are referred to by *he, his, him, she, her, hers.*

NONSTANDARD: *One* should consider *your* hobbies an investment.
STANDARD: *One* should consider *his or her* hobbies an investment.

NONSTANDARD: *I* am convinced that the noise affects *your* work.
STANDARD: *I* am convinced that the noise affects *my* work.

Exercise A: Find and correct the errors in agreement in these sentences. Make sure that both verb and pronoun are correct.

1. Neither Lori nor Bernadette have been in a play before.
2. Everyone plans to bring their lunch.
3. One should try to learn from your mistakes.
4. Each of the caricatures were cleverly drawn.
5. No one likes to feel that they are being left out.
6. Does everyone have their art supplies?
7. Has any of the teachers dismissed their students?
8. Every citizen should exercise their right to vote.
9. Each of them hope to get a summer job.
10. I find that my geometry homework is easier to do if you do it early.

Exercise B: Follow the same directions as for Exercise A.

1. The soccer team ride on its own special bus.
2. No one should give up until you have tried.
3. Either Linda Ronstadt or Olivia Newton-John write their own songs.
4. Each of the thirty pupils raised their hand.
5. No one should try to be their own lawyer.
6. Everyone with a scientific mind should develop their potential.
7. Every player must provide their own shoes.
8. Has everyone done their homework?
9. If one doesn't know the road, you are apt to miss the cutoff.
10. We discovered that you couldn't hear a thing in the back row.

6.14 Indefinite Reference

To avoid any confusion for the reader, every personal pronoun should refer clearly to a definite antecedent.

INDEFINITE: A statement was issued, but *they* refused to comment on its significance.
BETTER: A statement was issued, but Pentagon officials refused to comment on its significance.

INDEFINITE: *It* says in the paper that Senator Nancy Kassebaum will run for reelection.
BETTER: The *Times* announced that Senator Nancy Kassebaum will run for reelection.

INDEFINITE: I want to be a doctor because *it* is rewarding.
BETTER: I want to be a doctor because helping the sick is rewarding.

INDEFINITE: Be sure to see Rome if *they* include it in the itinerary.
BETTER: Be sure to see Rome if the agency includes it in the itinerary.

The pronoun *you* is sometimes used when it is not meant to refer to the person spoken to. The effect is usually confusing.

INDEFINITE: History shows that *you* must respect the dignity of the individual if *you* want *your* nation to survive.

BETTER: History shows that a nation's survival depends upon respect for the dignity of the individual.

INDEFINITE: In every contest *you* have specific rules to follow.

BETTER: In every contest there are specific rules to follow.

Exercise A: Revise the sentences below to remove all indefinite references of pronouns.

1. It says on the radio that a hurricane is coming this way.
2. When the President appeared, they played "Hail to the Chief."
3. Daydreaming can help you to relax.
4. In this exercise it says we are to eliminate indefinite references.
5. I studied hard, and I'm very confident about it.
6. In the armed services they train you for a special skill.
7. Steve Martin makes you laugh whenever he performs.
8. At our school they don't have a golf team.
9. In pioneer days you had to make the trip on horseback.
10. On that program they satirize television talk shows.

Exercise B: Follow the same directions as for Exercise A.

1. It says on the monument that the soldier is unknown.
2. Many people become very well educated without learning it just in school.
3. In the pocket calculators, it takes little power to operate them.
4. At the Coast Guard station they patrol the waters.
5. More and more married couples are choosing to be childless or are postponing them.
6. In the future they predict that you'll shop by computer.
7. Graduating seniors have to choose between work and school, and it is very difficult.
8. With flextime jobs, you choose your own hours.
9. In the "Help Wanted" section they tell you accountants and bookkeepers are needed.
10. Gerri likes to farm because it keeps you close to the land.

6.15 Ambiguous Reference

The word *ambiguous* means "having two or more possible meanings." The reference of a pronoun is ambiguous if the pronoun may refer to more than one word. This situation arises whenever a noun or pronoun falls between the pronoun and its true antecedent.

AMBIGUOUS: Take the cap off the bottle and give *it* to me.
BETTER: After you take off the cap, give the bottle to me.

AMBIGUOUS: The Red Sox and Yanks were scoreless until *their* pitcher tired.
BETTER: The Red Sox and Yanks were scoreless until the Yankees' pitcher tired.

AMBIGUOUS: Mary told Kim that *she* was going to be a great movie star.
BETTER: Mary told Kim, "I am going to be a great movie star."

AMBIGUOUS: Bob told Harry that *his* dog was found.
BETTER: Bob told Harry, "Your dog was found."

Exercise A: Revise the sentences below to remove all ambiguous pronoun references.

1. Before putting the car in the garage, Mom cleaned it out.
2. The librarian took the books off the shelves and labeled them.
3. Bert told Ernie that he needed a haircut.
4. When the reporter interviewed the consumer expert, she was unfriendly.
5. Replace the gears on both engines and lubricate them.
6. Eleanor asked Kay if her cousin had arrived.
7. Mary gave Andrea a math problem she could not solve.
8. We took the screens from the windows and ran the hose over them.
9. Kelly told his father that he had been worrying too much.
10. After Ms. Nardi took the newspaper out of her briefcase, she set it on the desk.

Exercise B: Follow the same directions as for Exercise A.

1. Nancy told Zora that her painting had received the award.
2. Take the gloves off your hands and wash them.
3. The hockey player told the rugby player that he played rough.
4. As the lifeguard approached the swimmer, he shouted loudly.
5. Barry told Kevin that his camera was defective.
6. The trucker sat in the cab of the eighteen-wheeler and surveyed it with pride.
7. Kim practiced ballet with Suzi until she had to leave.
8. As Jan planted bushes between the trees, she pruned them.
9. Skyscrapers are sometimes constructed with marble on a steel frame because it is durable.
10. Ms. Olson told Ms. Maki that the account was hers.

6.16 Vague Reference

The words *this*, *which*, *that*, and *it* are sometimes used to refer to a preceding idea or chain of ideas. The reader is confused by this vague reference.

VAGUE: The organ accompaniment was very loud. *This* made the singer's voice almost inaudible.

BETTER: The singer's voice was almost inaudible because the organ accompaniment was very loud.

VAGUE: Computers are being used to help farmers get data on crop qualities and selling prices. *This* helps them to know which of their operations are profitable.

BETTER: The use of computers to get data on crop qualities and selling prices is helping farmers to know which of their operations are profitable.

VAGUE: Long summer vacations becoming boring for city high high school students who are unemployed and cannot afford trips, *which* is one of the major causes of juvenile delinquency.

BETTER: One of the major causes of juvenile delinquency is the boredom of city high school students who are unemployed and cannot afford trips.

VAGUE: The weather was humid, and not a leaf was stirring on the few trees in the neighborhod. *It* made everyone irritable.

BETTER: Everyone was irritable because the weather was humid and not a leaf was stirring on the few trees in the neighborhood.

Exercise A: Revise the sentences below to remove all vague references of pronouns.

1. They sailed constantly. It was their favorite pastime.
2. The mayor promised to pave the road out our way. It sounded good to us.
3. Tanya reads widely and enjoys it very much.
4. Don bought a 1970 Plymouth, which was a mistake.
5. We sat through the movie twice, which made us very late for supper.
6. Early the next morning we left Canada, and that made us sad.
7. My aunt pays me to babysit, and it has been good experience.
8. Linda studies on the stairs because she says it is comfortable.
9. Many factories and autos pollute the environment. This affects people's health.
10. We bought a house in Arizona. It was more than we had expected to pay.

Exercise B: Follow the same directions as for Exercise A.

1. Some people heat their homes with solar energy, which is sensible.
2. The average person watches twenty-nine hours of television per week. This means that fewer books are being read.
3. College tuition is rising, which is a good reason to get a summer job.
4. Skilled labor is expensive, which makes Mr. Betts afraid to expand his business.
5. The school orchestra played each piece very well, and everyone liked it.
6. Trigonometry is a hard subject. This makes students take snap courses.

7. Computers can run businesses, do housework, and diagnose diseases, which allows humans to do other things.

8. The average life expectancy has increased. This should encourage awareness of the problems of the elderly.

9. The candidate says she wants to reform the prison system, and she seems sincere about it.

10. We took a left turn, which was a mistake.

Review Exercise: Revise the sentences below to remove vague, indefinite, or ambiguous reference of pronouns.

1. Linda and Lauri took turns playing her guitar.
2. At camp they expect you to eat in the lodge.
3. Jim told his brother that he was in the musical.
4. The permanent-press shirt looked smooth, which pleased me.
5. Mix the gravel with the cement when it is wet.
6. Motocross is Erica's favorite pastime, and she goes to them on weekends.
7. Mr. Cross talks haltingly, which makes him hard to understand sometimes.
8. The child hit the lamp with a bottle, breaking it.
9. We arrived at the theater early, which meant we had time to read the program.
10. They tell us that the fiords of Norway are majestic.
11. The stocker took the cans from the cartons and set them aside.
12. People nowadays have plenty of leisure time, and that means learning to use it well.
13. Poison ivy and poison oak can ruin your vacation, and it is a shame that everyone isn't immune to it.
14. Special tablets can give you immunity to such plants, and that is clinically safe.
15. Claire reminded her mother that she had wanted to stop at the bookstore.
16. Our timetable was outdated, which made us miss the train.
17. I was hypnotized once, and it seemed very eerie after I came out of it.
18. They say that you should try barbecued fish fillets.

19. Spelunkers like to explore Southern caves, which has been done since the fourteenth century by Native Americans in Kentucky.

20. Crossword puzzles increase our knowledge of words, for this is one way we become familiar with unusual words.

REVIEW: PRONOUN USAGE Choose the correct form from those in parentheses.

1. Did you and (he, him) go to Val's party?
2. It was (they, them) who advocated the bottle bill.
3. Sean showed Megan and (I, me) the best bike routes.
4. Gwen saved seats for you and (I, me).
5. (We, Us) consumers have begun to demand safer products.
6. The negotiator arranged a pact between the union leaders and (they, them).
7. (Who, Whom) do you think she will hire?
8. Pollsters interviewed (whoever, whomever) answered the door.
9. Dr. Esteban is the physician (who, whom) our family trusts.
10. Johnson has worked as a stunt driver longer than (he, him).
11. The audience applauded (him, his) conducting.
12. Our teacher expected (we, us) to dissect white rats.
13. Most reporters get their assignments from the editors, Ms. Ryan and (she, her).
14. Some of the ballplayers would not sign (his, their) contracts.
15. Bob asked for advice from (I, me, myself).
16. Everybody has forgotten (her, their) lines.
17. The crew have taken (its, their) places.
18. Each of the divers polished (his, their) dives.
19. Anyone with schedule problems should see (your, his or her) counselor.
20. In modern times (they, astronomers) have been able to determine the size of comets.

7.0 Adjective and Adverb Usage

Certain adverbs are formed by adding *-ly* to adjectives, as *deliberate—deliberately*. The problem then is whether to use the modifier with or without the *-ly* ending after a verb.

7.1 Adverbs with Action Verbs

When a modifier comes just before an action verb, it is always an adverb, and no problem arises. When the modifier follows the action verb, there is a temptation to use an adjective rather than an adverb.

The problem is made more difficult by the fact that many adverbs have two forms, one with and the other without the *-ly* ending.

Shut the door *tight*.   Drive *slow*.   Don't play so *loud*.

All of the words used above as adverbs are also used as adjectives: *tight* collar, a *slow* stream, a *loud* noise, and so on.

Most of the words that may be either adjectives or adverbs are words of one syllable. Adjectives of two or more syllables almost never have the same form for the adverb.

The *angry* mob shouted defiantly. (adjective)
He swung the bag *angrily*. (adverb)

Careful inquiries were made. (adjective)
We proceeded *carefully*. (adverb)

After an action verb use the *-ly* form of the modifier if the modifier has two or more syllables.

7.2 Adjectives with Linking Verbs

Linking verbs are usually followed by adjectives rather than adverbs. The adjective is a predicate adjective and modifies the subject.

There is no problem with modifiers following the form of *be*, the most common linking verb. Most of the other linking verbs, however, may also be used as action verbs. As action verbs, they may be followed by adverbs.

The ship *appeared suddenly* out of the fog.
(*appeared* is an action verb modified by an adverb.)

The parents *appeared worried*.
(*appeared* is a linking verb followed by a predicate adjective.)

He *looked suspiciously* at my driver's license.
(*looked* is an action verb modified by an adverb.)

Sean *looked ridiculous*.
(*looked* is a linking verb followed by a predicate adjective.)

The following verbs are linking verbs. Most of them may also be used as action verbs.

look	appear	smell	stay	grow	seem
sound	feel	taste	remain	become	

To decide whether a verb is used to link or to show action, try substituting a form of *be*. If the sentence still makes sense, the verb is a linking verb.

The salesperson *seemed* (confident, confidently).
(*The salesperson was confidently* does not make sense. *The salesperson was confident* makes sense; *seemed* is a linking verb here.)

The salesperson *looked* (inquiring, inquiringly) at the customer.
(*was* does not make sense with either modifier; *looked* is an action verb here.)

Exercise A: Choose the standard form from those given in parentheses.

1. The young actor appeared quite (nervous, nervously).
2. Matt plays too (rough, roughly) with the little children.
3. I worked (steadily, steady) for five hours.
4. The child looked (envious, enviously) at her brother's candy.
5. The hikers grew (uneasy, uneasily) as nightfall approached.
6. Be sure to measure the ingredients very (careful, carefully).
7. The cherry pie smelled (delicious, deliciously) in the oven.
8. His voice sounded (harshly, harsh) on the telephone.
9. Margie's marks have improved (considerable, considerably).
10. The speaker approached the platform (nervous, nervously).

Exercise B: Decide whether the italicized modifier is standard or nonstandard. If it is nonstandard, substitute the standard form.

1. Ted has been feeling *strange* all afternoon.
2. The lemonade tasted *sour*.
3. The whole story sounds *peculiar*.
4. Be sure to put the paint on *even*.
5. Pick the baby up as *gentle* as you can.
6. This hot chocolate tastes too *sweet*.
7. I couldn't hear the signals *clear* enough.
8. The children remained *silent* throughout the concert.
9. Anna cleared the hurdle *easy*.
10. Mr. Hale sounds *abrupt* when he meets people.

7.3 *This—These; That—Those*

This and *that* modify singular words. *These* and *those* modify plural words. The words *kind, sort,* and *type* require a singular modifier.

NONSTANDARD: *These* kind sold immediately.
STANDARD: *This* kind sold immediately.

NONSTANDARD: *These* sort of games are tiring.
STANDARD: *This* sort of game is tiring.

7.4 *Them—Those*

Those may be either a pronoun or an adjective. *Them* is always a pronoun and never an adjective.

NONSTANDARD: Did you enjoy *them* stories?
STANDARD: Did you enjoy *those* stories? (adjective)

7.5 *Bad—Badly*

In standard usage, *bad* is always used after linking verbs.

He felt bad. (*not* he felt badly)
He looked bad.
The water tastes bad.
The news sounds bad.

7.6 *Good—Well*

Good is used only as an adjective to modify nouns and pronouns.

Well is an adjective when it means "in good health." *Well* is used as an adverb to modify an action verb when it means that the action was performed properly or expertly.

The patient looks *well* today. (adjective)
The lawn mower is working *well* now. (adverb)

7.7 *Fewer—Less*

Fewer is used to describe things that can be counted. *Less* refers to quantity or degree.

Careful driving results in *fewer* accidents.
Use *less* heat for that dish.
I have *less* respect for him now.

Exercise: Decide whether the italicized words are standard or nonstandard usage. Substitute a standard form for each nonstandard usage.

1. Jeff feels *good* about winning the essay contest.
2. I did *well* in the history test.
3. The injured skier needed help *bad*.
4. If you check your answers, you will have *less* errors.
5. I don't like *that* sort of hat.
6. *These* kind is much more practical.
7. This recipe requires *less* milk and *less* eggs.
8. Did you eat *well* at camp?
9. I'd like to have one of *them* pocket calculators.
10. Mindy felt *badly* about quitting the team.
11. The bass guitar sounds *well* in that arrangement.
12. I don't play chess very *good*.
13. Nowadays there are *fewer* circuses than there used to be.
14. *Those* kinds of remarks never help.
15. *Those* kind of camera is very expensive.
16. The reviewer commented that the book ended *badly*.
17. Where did you get *them* kittens?
18. Our car runs *well* since we had the engine overhauled.
19. *These* kind of exercise is easy to do.
20. *Them* four-cylinder cars are economical to operate.

7.8 Comparative and Superlative

The comparative form is used to compare two things; the superlative is used in comparing more than two.

STANDARD: We tried both lobsters and fried clams, but we liked lobsters *better*. (*not* best)

STANDARD: Of her five major subjects, Penny likes history *best*. (*not* better)

STANDARD: I could have gone by plane or by ship, but I decided that flying was *more exciting*. (*not* most)

7.9 The Double Comparison

The comparative form of a modifier is made either by adding *-er* or by using *more*. It is nonstandard to use both.

The superlative form of a modifier is made either by adding *-est* or by using *most*. It is nonstandard to use both.

NONSTANDARD: We had a more easier time with that test.
STANDARD: We had an easier time with that test.

NONSTANDARD: Speak in a more softer tone.
STANDARD: Speak in a softer tone.

NONSTANDARD: It was the most funniest movie I ever saw.
STANDARD: It was the funniest movie I ever saw.

7.10 Illogical Comparisons

The word *other*, or the word *else*, is required in comparisons of an individual member with the rest of the group.

ILLOGICAL: Our school won more scholarships than any school in the city. (Our school is also in the city.)
CLEAR: Our school won more scholarships than any *other* school in the city.

ILLOGICAL: Angela is as bright as anyone on the debating team.
CLEAR: Angela is as bright as anyone *else* on the debating team.

The words *than* or *as* are required in a compound comparison.

ILLOGICAL: The begonia is as healthy if not healthier than the cactus.

CLEAR BUT AWKWARD: The begonia is as healthy as, if not healthier than, the cactus.

BETTER: The begonia is as healthy as the cactus, if not healthier.

ILLOGICAL: This cake is as good if not better than the one I baked for the County Fair.

CLEAR: This cake is as good *as*, if not better than, the one I baked for the County Fair.

ILLOGICAL: We had as many errors if not more than our opponents.

CLEAR: We had as many errors *as*, if not more than, our opponents.

Both parts of a comparison must be stated completely if there is any chance of its being misunderstood.

CONFUSING: I admire her more than Joan.

CLEAR: I admire her more than Joan *does*.

CLEAR: I admire her more than I *admire* Joan.

CONFUSING: Central defeated Southern worse than Northeast.

CLEAR: Central defeated Southern worse than Northeast *did*.

CLEAR: Central defeated Southern worse than it *defeated* Northeast.

ILLOGICAL: The training of a nurse is longer than a technician.

CLEAR: The training of a nurse is longer than *that* of a technician.

BETTER: A nurse's training is longer than a technician's *is*.

Exercise A: Revise the following illogical comparisons.

1. You should try to make your explanation more clearer.
2. Vicki beat me in tennis worse than Chuck.

3. Who is the oldest, you or Frank?
4. Ms. Gerardi likes picnics more than her husband.
5. This model is probably as expensive if not more expensive than that one.
6. Of the two candidates, Leslie seems the most likely to win.
7. This dessert is more tastier.
8. I like Susan better than Charlotte.
9. Pat thinks *Seventeen* has better articles than any magazine.
10. The gas mileage of a compact car is much better than a full-size.

Exercise B: Follow the same directions as for Exercise A.

1. W. Somerset Maugham's *Of Human Bondage* is as good or better than any of his other books.
2. It was the most saddest movie I had ever seen.
3. Which of the two hats do you think is the most appropriate?
4. Transferring schools was much more easier than Steve had expected.
5. Of the two exercises, the second is easiest.
6. I like professional hockey better than Harry.
7. The United States is bigger than any country in the Americas.
8. Which of these two trees do you think is healthiest?
9. Strawberries are much more cheaper this week than last.
10. Diamonds are harder than any substance.

7.11 The Double Negative

A double negative occurs when a negative word is added to a statement that is already negative. The double negative is nonstandard usage.

NONSTANDARD: He did*n't* ask me *nothing*.
STANDARD: He did*n't* ask me *anything*.

NONSTANDARD: Clerks do*n't* have *no* homework.
STANDARD: Clerks do*n't* have *any* homework.

Hardly, scarcely, or *barely,* used with a negative word, is nonstandard.

NONSTANDARD:	There was*n't hardly* any rain in May.
STANDARD:	There was *hardly* any rain in May.
NONSTANDARD:	The award did*n't scarcely* cover her expenses.
STANDARD:	The award *scarcely* covered her expenses.

REVIEW: ADJECTIVE AND ADVERB USAGE These sentences cover all of the problems of adjective and adverb usage in this section. Choose the standard form from those in parentheses.

1. Morris (can, can't) hardly keep up with his work.
2. (Fewer, Less) people shop on Monday than on any other day.
3. You (will, won't) get hardly any bad effects from this medicine.
4. The inland route is longer, but it is (safer, more safer).
5. I (can't, can) scarcely believe that such a terrible thing has happened.
6. Please talk as (quiet, quietly) as possible.
7. You'll stay in good condition if you exercise (regular, regularly).
8. We haven't had (any, no) warm weather since August.
9. Do you feel (confident, confidently) about today's game?
10. He (didn't have, had) hardly any money with him.
11. The river has risen (considerable, considerably) tonight.
12. Little Timmy (could, couldn't) scarcely keep his eyes open.
13. Are (them, those) portable typewriters heavy?
14. The air hole in the box should be a little (wider, more wider).
15. Instant oatmeal tastes surprisingly (well, good).
16. She ran down the hill as (quick, quickly) as she could.
17. I enjoy (those, that) kind of movie because it is good entertainment.
18. This coat material feels (rough, roughly).
19. The team was not (real, really) interested in finishing the game.
20. Of all the members of the glee club, Ben has the (better, best) voice.

8.0 Verb Usage

Most verbs in English cause no problems of usage at all. They are **regular verbs.** That is, the past tense is formed by adding *-ed* or *-d* to the present, and the past participle is the same as the past tense form:

PRESENT	PAST	PAST PARTICIPLE
appear	appear*ed*	appear*ed*
listen	listen*ed*	listen*ed*
use	use*d*	use*d*
excuse	excuse*d*	excuse*d*
print	print*ed*	print*ed*
crawl	crawl*ed*	crawl*ed*

There are about sixty commonly used verbs, however, whose past forms do not follow this pattern. They are **irregular verbs.** The most commonly used verbs, *be* and *have*, not only form the past tenses irregularly but change from person to person in the present tense: *I am, you are, she is; I have, she has.*

8.1 The Past Forms

The main problem with irregular verbs is the choice between the past form and the past participle form. These are two of the **principal parts** of every verb. (See Section 1.3.) All forms of any verb are made from the principal parts. Since they are always given in the same order in dictionaries and reference books, learning them in that order will make usage choices easier.

The past tense form is used alone. The past participle form is used with forms of *be* or *have*.

The hunter *shot* the bear. (past)
The stores *were* all *closed.* (past participle with form of *be*)
My father *had* already *written.* (past participle with form of *have*)

Jennifer *jammed* the gears on her bicycle. (past)
The soldier *was awarded* a medal for heroism (past participle with form of *be*)
He *has* not yet *decided* on a career. (past participle with form of *have*).

There are five groups of irregular verbs.

Group 1. The easiest of the irregular verbs are those that have the same form in all principal parts.

PRESENT	PAST	PAST PARTICIPLE
burst	burst	burst
cast	cast	cast
cost	cost	cost
fit	fit	fit
hurt	hurt	hurt
put	put	put
read	read	read
set	set	set
shed	shed	shed

Group 2. A second group that causes little difficulty contains verbs that have the same form for the past and the past participle.

PRESENT	PAST	PAST PARTICIPLE
bring	brought	brought
catch	caught	caught
dive	dived *or* dove*	dived
fight	fought	fought
flee	fled	fled
fling	flung	flung
get	got	got *or* gotten
lead	led	led
lend	lent	lent
lose	lost	lost
say	said	said
seek	sought	sought
shine	shone	shone
sit	sat	sat
sling	slung	slung
sting	stung	stung
sweep	swept	swept
swing	swung	swung

Exercise A: In the sentences below, the present form of the verb is given in parentheses. Substitute either past or past participle, whichever the sentence requires.

1. The mayor was (sting) by the unexpected criticism.
2. Charles Evans Hughes (lose) the Presidency by only 23 electoral votes.
3. As the curtain rose, the audience (burst) into applause.
4. Unexpected frosts have (cost) farmers millions of dollars.
5. No one was (hurt) in the collision.
6. The epidemic has already (spread) to neighboring towns.
7. The election of 1860 (bring) Lincoln to the White House.
8. The villagers (flee) before the rising waters.

* Where two forms are given, both are standard usage, but the first is more common.

9. The shortstop (catch) the ball and tagged the runner.
10. The hurricane had (fling) street signs to the pavement.
11. Bernstein (lead) the orchestra in an all-Beethoven program.
12. The bank (lend) Mom some money to remodel the house.
13. The old farmer's wrinkled face (shine) with pride as he surveyed his harvest.
14. The large urban vote (swing) the election.
15. Annette (bring) me an Italian newspaper.
16. The powerful waves had (sweep) the dinghy ashore.
17. Elyse (seek) the advice of her counselor.
18. The peddler (sling) his bag of wares over his shoulder.
19. Curtis (say) he would pick us up after the game.
20. One swimmer had (dive) in before the gun sounded.

Exercise B: Choose the standard form from those in parentheses.

1. Ronnie blew up the balloon until it (bust, busted, burst).
2. Paula has already (caught, catched) the legal limit of trout.
3. The quarterback (hurt, hurted) his weak knee.
4. Eleanor Roosevelt once (sayed, said), "No one can make you feel inferior without your consent."
5. Alex (lent, lended) me his power saw.
6. The speedboat (swang, swinged, swung) around the buoy.
7. Dad has (losed, lost) his automobile insurance policy.
8. The cadets (flung, flinged, flang) their caps into the air.
9. The hornet (stang, stung) Dorothy on the elbow.
10. Rescuers (led, leaded) the dazed miners out of the shaft.
11. Aunt Marion (brang, brought) back slides of her trip.
12. As usual, Suzanne had (dived, dove) flawlessly.
13. The sun has not (shined, shone) for over a week.
14. The campers (fleed, fled) as the river began to rise.
15. Our trip (cost, costed) more than we had anticipated.
16. The maintenance crew (sweeped, swept) the gym floor.
17. Just as the bell rang, I realized I had (brang, brung, brought) the wrong book to class.
18. The deckhand (slang, slung, slinged) the anchor overboard.
19. The batter (swinged, swang, swung) at the ball but missed.
20. The weightlifter raised the barbell then (setted, set) it down.

Group 3. Another group of irregular verbs adds ***n*** or ***en*** to the past form to make the past participle.

PRESENT	PAST	PAST PARTICIPLE
bear	bore	borne*
beat	beat	beaten
bite	bit	bitten
break	broke	broken
choose	chose	chosen
freeze	froze	frozen
speak	spoke	spoken
steal	stole	stolen
swear	swore	sworn
tear	tore	torn
wear	wore	worn

Exercise A: Choose the standard form from those in parentheses.

1. Somebody has (broke, broken) Steve's toy pickup truck.
2. Jamie's dump truck was (broke, broken) also.
3. The company (beared, bore) all of the expenses of her trip.
4. Has the team (chose, chosen) its captain yet?
5. The Supreme Court justices (wore, weared) their black robes.
6. The eggs were (beat, beaten) separately to make a fluffy omelet.
7. Meat that has been thawed should not be (froze, frozen) again.
8. I could have (sweared, swore, sworn) that there were two people in that car.
9. Have you (broken, broke) your appointment with the eye doctor again?
10. Allen has (chose, chosen) *The Bermuda Triangle* for his report.
11. The patient (bore, beared) traces of deep suffering.
12. Uncle Ben wishes he had (chose, chosen) a different profession.

* Note that *borne* retains the final ***e***.

13. Several diamond rings have been (stole, stolen) from Ms. Van Hoot's apartment.
14. I have just (tore, torn) my new jacket on a nail.
15. The witness was promptly (swore, sworn) in.
16. The insect repellent kept us from being (bit, bitten) by mosquitoes.
17. Sue has hardly (spoke, spoken) to me since my arrival.
18. We have (beat, beaten) Dover only once in the last ten years.
19. Marsha (teared, torn, tore) the letter up and threw it away.
20. Have you ever (spoke, spoken) at an assembly?

Exercise B: The present form of the verb is given. Substitute past or past participle, whichever the sentence requires.

1. Thousands panicked when the stock market (break).
2. What book have you (choose) for your report?
3. You should have (wear) your woolen mittens.
4. Phil has (steal) more bases than any other player on the team.
5. Felice has (break) the school record for the high jump.
6. The Red Sox have finally (beat) the Yankees.
7. The rock (tear) a hole in the bottom of the canoe.
8. The tribe (swear) to avenge the death of their chief.
9. The milk on the porch has (freeze) solid.
10. The carpet on the stairs was (wear) out.
11. The committee has not yet (choose) a date for the annual dinner dance.
12. The candidate (speak) earnestly and persuasively.
13. The campers were badly (bite) by mosquitoes.
14. Leslie was (beat) badly in the quarter-finals.
15. The doctor thinks Andy's wrist is (break).
16. Have you ever (speak) in public?
17. The steak in the refrigerator was (freeze) solid.
18. Even our greatest Presidents have (bear) constant criticism of their programs.
19. Our mail carrier has never been (bite) by a dog.
20. We have already (beat) Springfield once this year.

Group 4. Another group of irregular verbs is alike in changing the middle vowel from ***i*** in the present, to ***a*** in the past, and to ***u*** in the past participle. Memorize these seven verbs as a unit. They are the only verbs to follow this pattern.

PRESENT	PAST	PAST PARTICIPLE
begin	began	begun
drink	drank	drunk
ring	rang	rung
sing	sang	sung
sink	sank *or* sunk	sunk
spring	sprang *or* sprung	sprung
swim	swam	swum

Exercise: The present form is given in parentheses. Substitute past or past participle, whichever the sentence requires.

1. I (ring) for the nurse.
2. I (drink) the cocoa even though it was stone cold.
3. Andrew Carnegie (begin) his career as a bobbin boy in a factory.
4. She had (sing) at La Scala before coming to the Metropolitan.
5. The fisherman (sink) a line through the hole in the ice.
6. They turned back after their rowboat had (spring) a leak.
7. We (drink) cool spring water while camping in Colorado.
8. When Claire arrived, the examination had already (begin).
9. Have you ever (drink) papaya juice?
10. All over the yard, dandelions had (spring) up.
11. The *Graf Spee* was (sink) by her own crew.
12. The telephone (ring) once and then stopped.
13. The role of Carmen has been (sing) by many famous opera stars.
14. Skin divers (swim) down to inspect the sunken ship.
15. The *Edmond Fitzgerald* (sink) in the tumultuous waters of Lake Superior.
16. When Johnson missed the field goal, our hearts (sink).
17. The men (spring) out of their bunks when the captain entered.

18. We must have (drink) a whole case of Pepsi.

19. At the three-quarter mark, the Navy crew had (begin) to tire.

20. Cheryl (swim) in the 50-yard free-style event.

21. Cheers (ring) out when the Penn quarterback fumbled the ball.

22. Have you ever (drink) goat's milk?

23. While the crowd held its breath, Jack Nicklaus (sink) the winning putt.

24. A mouse had taken the cheese and (spring) the trap.

25. The players (drink) a toast to the winning pitcher.

Group 5. Another group of irregular verbs is alike in making the past participle from the present form rather than from the past form.

PRESENT	PAST	PAST PARTICIPLE
blow	blew	blown
come	came	come
do	did	done
draw	drew	drawn
drive	drove	driven
eat	ate	eaten
fall	fell	fallen
give	gave	given
go	went	gone
grow	grew	grown
know	knew	known
ride	rode	ridden
rise	rose	risen
run	ran	run
see	saw	seen
shake	shook	shaken
slay	slew	slain
take	took	taken
throw	threw	thrown
write	wrote	written

Exercise A: Choose the standard form from those in parentheses.

1. Most of the icicles have (fell, fallen) to the ground.
2. Alan has (gone, went) to the basement for the brace and bit.
3. You should have (gave, given) the matter more thought.
4. I wonder who has (took, taken) my scarf.
5. The officials have always (run, ran) this town efficiently.
6. I (seen, saw) an unusual television play last night.
7. This letter must have been (wrote, written) on a moving bus.
8. Many celebrities had (came, come) for the opening night performance.
9. The catcher (throwed, threw) the ball into center field.
10. The wind had (shaken, shook) all the apples from the tree.
11. The students (took, taken) their lunches with them.
12. I had never (ate, eaten) fried clams before.
13. The wind (blew, blowed) down several trees last night.
14. This year all the birthdays in our family have (fell, fallen) on weekends.
15. The teller was badly (shook, shaken) by the attempted robbery.
16. Sally must have (knowed, knew, known) where we were going.
17. The President must have (shook, shaken) hands with a thousand people.
18. Who (did, done) the illustrations for this book?
19. Stocks have (rose, risen) for the tenth consecutive day.
20. Have you ever (ridden, rode) in a helicopter?

Exercise B: The present form is given in parentheses. Substitute the past or past participle, whichever the sentence requires.

1. I (see) the new high school yesterday.
2. The soldiers stood at attention while taps was (blow).
3. Amy and Fran have (drive) across the continent in six days.
4. I (do) the sanding job in two hours.
5. Mr. Cross (give) me his entire coin collection.
6. We have (grow) our own vegetables for years.
7. The judge (throw) the case out of court.
8. Archie (shake) the mop vigorously.

9. The next census will be (take) in 1980.
10. The price of butter has (rise) sharply.
11. Have you ever (eat) Philadelphia scrapple?
12. The new Broadway musical (draw) capacity audiences.
13. Betty has (write) a letter to *The Chicago Tribune*.
14. A stranger (come) up to us and asked for directions.
15. I should have (know) the stores would be closed.
16. Angrily the catcher (throw) her mask to the ground.
17. Bart would have (go) if he had had a coat and tie.
18. The salesperson (do) his best to sell Dad some insurance.
19. Cindy lectured while Chuck (run) the projector.
20. The tide has already (rise) two feet.

Exercise C: The present form is given. Substitute the past or past participle as the sentence may require.

1. The Yale goal post was (take) down by the happy Harvard rooters.
2. You must have (know) I was coming.
3. These orchids were (grow) in Hawaii.
4. The pitcher quickly (throw) the ball to first base.
5. Mrs. Wharton has (go) to Michigan on business.
6. A heavy blanket of snow had (fall) during the night.
7. I had never (eat) fried shrimp before.
8. It had (take) all morning to pack the car for the trip.
9. The ink had (run) down the length of the paper.
10. The mayor was (shake) by the news of his defeat.
11. Have you (ride) in Fred's new Chevette?
12. The referee (blow) the whistle when I stepped out of bounds.
13. I (do) the best job I could with that old lawn mower.
14. Over 100,000 people (come) to see the game.
15. Six fire engines were (draw) up in a neat row.
16. One of the guards was (slay) in the prison riot.
17. The firefighters scrambled when the siren (blow).
18. Who (draw) this sketch?
19. Some of the girls have (go) to the Museum of Natural History.
20. In five minutes she had (draw) a sketch of Ann's profile.

8.2 Problem Pairs of Verbs

Three pairs of verbs are often confused because the meanings of each pair are closely related. They are related, but they are not identical. To use these verbs correctly, it is important to keep their meanings distinct.

Lie and lay. The verb *lay* means "to put or place something." The verb *lie* has many meanings, all of them having in common the idea of "being in a horizontal position, or to remain, or to be situated."*

Lie is always an intransitive verb. It never has an object. *Lay* is a transitive verb. It almost always has an object. The principal parts of these verbs are as follows:

PRESENT	PAST	PAST PARTICIPLE
lay	laid	laid
lie	lay	lain

Rise and raise. The verb *rise* means "to go to a higher position." The verb *raise* means "to lift to a higher position."

Rise is intransitive; it never has an object. *Raise* is transitive; it almost always has an object. Things *rise* by themselves; they are *raised* by something else. The principal parts of these verbs are as follows:

PRESENT	PAST	PAST PARTICIPLE
rise	rose	risen
raise	raised	raised

Sit and set. The verb *sit* usually means "to rest with the legs bent and the back upright," but there are many other related meanings. The verb *set* means "to put or place something."

Sit is an intransitive verb; it never has an object. *Set* is a transitive verb; it almost always has an object. The principal parts of the verbs are as follows:

* There is a homonym meaning "to tell an untruth." The principal parts of that verb are *lie, lied, lied.*

PRESENT	PAST	PAST PARTICIPLE
sit	sat	sat
set	set	set

Note: It is very difficult to make any general statements about English usage that will hold without exception. There are exceptions to the statements given above about the three pairs of verbs:

The sun *sets* early in the winter. (intransitive)
The mixture will *set* in an hour. (intransitive)

Sit the patient in the chair. (transitive)
The hens are *laying* well. (intransitive)

Exercise A: Choose the standard form from those in parentheses.

1. New London (lies, lays) between New York and Boston.
2. Alonzo told the dog to (lie, lay) down.
3. The customer (lay, laid) two quarters on the counter.
4. Pat (lay, laid) on the beach and sipped lemonade.
5. The deserted bus was (lying, laying) in the ditch.
6. The foreign ministers (lay, laid) the groundwork for the summit conference.
7. Charlie is (lying, laying) in the hammock.
8. The baby was (lain, laid) on the bassinet.
9. The book that I (lay, laid) on the table has disappeared.
10. Your wallet is (lying, laying) on the floor.
11. Garrett (lay, laid) the silverware on the table.
12. Grandmother has gone upstairs to (lie, lay) down.
13. The pup is (lying, laying) the bone under the table.
14. The pup is (lying, laying) under the table.
15. Have the foundations been (lain, laid) for the new school?
16. I was (lying, laying) down when the Russells came.
17. The group (lay, laid) their plan before the City Council.
18. My purse had (lain, laid) in the breezeway all night.
19. The injured worker (lay, laid) unconscious on the ground.
20. At the foot of Mt. Vesuvius (lies, lays) Naples.

Exercise B: Choose the standard form from those in parentheses.

1. Peggy (rose, raised) quickly and answered the door.
2. The curtain was (rising, raising) as we reached our seats.
3. What time did the sun (rise, raise) this morning?
4. The elderly man (rose, raised) from his chair with difficulty.
5. The nurse (rose, raised) the patient's pillow.
6. Has the water (risen, raised) at all since last night?
7. The sun had not yet (risen, raised) above the horizon.
8. Gales of laughter (rose, raised) from the audience.
9. I am glad that these questions have been (risen, raised).
10. The supermarket will (rise, raise) the price of dairy products next week.
11. Commuter fares have (risen, raised) substantially in recent years.
12. Will everyone in favor please (rise, raise)?
13. Will everyone in favor please (rise, raise) his or her hand?
14. A heavy cloud of black smoke was (rising, raising) from the oil refinery.
15. The officers saluted as the flag was (risen, raised).
16. Our spirits (rose, raised) when our team tied the score.
17. The price of lumber has (risen, raised) sharply again.
18. Everyone (rose, raised) when the team trotted onto the field.
19. The rent cannot be (rose, raised) more than five percent.
20. Jeff's cake failed to (rise, raise).

Exercise C: Choose the standard form from those given in parentheses.

1. (Sit, Set) in the armchair if you wish.
2. I'll (sit, set) the tray on your lap.
3. Come and (sit, set) by the fire.
4. Please (sit, set) this vase on the desk.
5. We have (sat, set) in the sun for over an hour.
6. Just (sat, set) your glass on the table.
7. May I (sit, set) this wet umbrella in the kitchen?
8. From where I was (sitting, setting), it looked like a touchdown.

9. Sean was too nervous to (sit, set) still.
10. Barbara (sat, set) the lantern inside the tent.
11. My nephew scrambled over and (sat, set) on my lap.
12. Motionless, the model (sat, set) in front of the art class.
13. Did Elena (sit, set) her ticket on the mantel?
14. Antique dealers are (sitting, setting) high prices on their wares.
15. The four-year-old (sat, set) her popsicle on the bench.
16. The actress was (sitting, setting) her deck chair in the sun.
17. The actress was (sitting, setting) in the sun.
18. Everyone (sat, set) quietly during Marie's talk.
19. Just (sit, set) the trunk in the hall.
20. How long have these cartons of milk been (sitting, setting) on the step?

8.3 Distinguishing Two Actions in the Past

In telling of things that have happened in the past, it is sometimes necessary to tell of one thing that happened before another.

The past perfect tense is used to tell about the earlier of two past happenings.

	EARLIER / LATER
STANDARD:	I *had swum* to shore before the storm broke.

	LATER / EARLIER
STANDARD:	I understood that you *had eaten* earlier.

NONSTANDARD: I told the printer last week that I *have canceled* the order.
STANDARD: I told the printer last week that I *had canceled* the order.

NONSTANDARD: The paper stated that the candidate already *conceded*.
STANDARD: The paper stated that the candidate *had* already *conceded*.

8.4 The Tense of Infinitives

The perfect infinitive (see Section 1.11) is used to show an action earlier than that of the main verb. The present infinitive is used to show action at the same time as that of the main verb, or later.

I am sorry *to have offended* you. (earlier time)
I was sorry *to have offended* you. (The perfect infinitive shows the earlier of the two past times.)
We are happy *to welcome* you. (same time)
We were happy *to welcome* you. (same time)
Mom plans *to leave tonight.* (later time)

The present infinitive is used if the main verb contains the word *have.*

NONSTANDARD: She would have preferred *to have gone* alone.
STANDARD: She would have preferred *to go alone.* (same time)
STANDARD: She would prefer (now) *to have gone* alone. (earlier)

NONSTANDARD: Joel intended *to have invited* you. (The intention preceded the inviting.)
STANDARD: Joel had intended *to invite* you.
STANDARD: Joel intended *to invite* you.

8.5 The Split Infinitive

When a modifier appears between *to* and the verb in an infinitive phrase, the infinitive is said to be split. It is wise to avoid splitting the infinitive. Usually, the modifier can be placed before or after. There are some sentences, however, in which a split infinitive is the only means of avoiding clumsy expression.

NEEDLESSLY SPLIT: Nick was urged to immediately register.
IMPROVED: Nick was urged to register immediately.

NEEDLESSLY SPLIT: They agreed to voluntarily participate.
IMPROVED: They voluntarily agreed to participate.

AWKWARD: The plan is intended substantially to increase sales.
PERMISSIBLE: The plan is intended to substantially increase sales.

8.6 The Tense of Participles

The present participle and the past participle show an action or state of being at the same time as that of the main verb.

Shaken by the experience, he went home immediately.
(past participle; same time as main verb)
Knowing her way around San Francisco, Jill always has a good time there.
(present participle; same time as main verb)

The perfect participle shows an action or state of being earlier than that of the main verb.

STANDARD: *Having helped* in the rescue, Davina received a citation.
(The helping occurred before the receiving.)
STANDARD: *Having explored* the cave, the scientists returned to camp.
(The exploration took place before they returned.)

NONSTANDARD: *Approving* the program, we set up research centers.
STANDARD: *Having approved* the program, we set up research centers.

NONSTANDARD: *Buying* a ticket, Jack went into the stadium.
STANDARD: *Having bought* a ticket, Jack went into the stadium.

NONSTANDARD: *Reaching* the wall, we climbed it and jumped to safety.
STANDARD: *Having reached* the wall, we climbed it and jumped to safety.

Exercise: Change the nonstandard usage to standard usage in the following sentences.

1. The Dickinsons are hoping to some day build a garage.
2. I felt I answered the questions correctly.
3. I'm not going to ever make that mistake again.
4. Lisa would have been delighted to have won a door prize.
5. Missing the first act, Mary did not enjoy the play.
6. The play started before we entered the theater.
7. We served ice cream that we made ourselves.
8. The band would have preferred to have toured only six weeks.
9. We were warned to carefully obey the camp rules.
10. Some of the students admitted that they were misled by the glib sales talk.
11. I would have liked to have seen the expression on his face.
12. Making the best of the ingredients, Pat turned out a good meal.
13. I hoped to have finished the job last night.
14. Curtis is determined to somehow get to Europe.
15. Polly planned to have prepared an authentic Hawaiian luau.
16. Grandparents seem to instinctively adore their grandchildren.
17. Completing his quota of calls, the canvasser went home.
18. I was thrilled that the magazine decided to publish my story.
19. The club members voted on all the questions they discussed at the meeting.
20. Saving the little girl from the fire, the rescue squad was given a steak dinner.

8.7 *Shall* and *Will*

Earlier practice, which some people still insist upon, is as follows:

Future time is shown in the first person by *shall* with the verb. Future time is shown in the second and third person by *will* with the verb.

Emphasis or determination about future action is shown in the first person by *will* and by *shall* in the second and third persons.

	FUTURE TIME	EMPHASIS
FIRST PERSON:	We shall tell you.	We will do our best.
SECOND PERSON:	You will see the pictures	You shall win the game.
THIRD PERSON:	They will cooperate.	They shall not leave the house.

Today, however, the usage of *shall* and *will* is undergoing rapid change. In speech, the general custom is to use the contractions *I'll, he'll, you'll,* which suit either *shall* or *will*. In good writing today, the tendency is to use *will* for all three persons.

8.8 The Subjunctive

The subjunctive form of the verb is used to express (1) a statement contrary to fact; (2) a request or command; (3) a wish, hope, or prayer.

If you were there now, would you be happy? (contrary to fact)
The customer demanded *that the store refund his money.* (*command*)
The blessing of God *descend* upon you. (prayer)

The subjunctive forms of the verb *be* are as follows: *be* with all persons in the present tense except for clauses contrary to fact, which take *were*.

If this *be* a dream, let me sleep.
If he *were* dependable, I would not worry.

For all other verbs, the only difference between regular forms and the subjunctive is that the *s* is dropped in the third person singular.

The teacher suggested that he *buy* more books.
The manager requested that no one *leave* the theater.

The words *would have* are not used in a clause beginning with *if* or *even though.*

NONSTANDARD: If he *would have* apologized, I would have overlooked it.
STANDARD: If he *had* apologized, I would have overlooked it.

NONSTANDARD: If you *would have* gone, you would have seen the Pope.
STANDARD: If you *had gone,* you would have seen the Pope.

Exercise A: Find the nonstandard usage in each of the following sentences. Supply the standard form.

1. I suggest that Carrie brings the tape recorder.
2. If I was you, Gary, I would apply for that job.
3. If the snow would have stopped, we would have walked.
4. I move that the meeting is adjourned.
5. The sports shop owner asked that the newspaper prints an advertisement for her store.
6. If Caroline was one year older, she wouldn't have a curfew.
7. The principal requested that the crosswalks are policed.
8. Rob kept wishing he was working in the research division.
9. If I would have known about the dinner, I would have planned to come earlier.
10. Jean never would have agreed to that plan, even if you would have been the one to suggest it.

Exercise B: Follow the same directions as for Exercise A.

1. If Judy was here, we could begin the meeting.
2. The lawyer demands that her client is given his freedom.
3. If I was a millionaire, I wouldn't want a better house than the one I now live in.
4. The fire department requests that these doors are kept closed.
5. If you would have kept your eyes on the road, this would not have happened.
6. If I wasn't related to my brother, I'd like him a lot.
7. The bill proposed that capital punishment is abolished.

8. We would be there by now if we would have taken the plane.
9. I know what I would do if I was coach.
10. The management asks that each person without a ticket lines up on the left.

REVIEW: VERB USAGE Choose the correct verb form from those in parentheses.

1. The gymnast (swang, swung) in an arc on the parallel bars.
2. Thieves have (stole, stolen) several art treasures recently.
3. Julia has never (sang, sung) a solo.
4. *National Lampoon* (did, done) a parody of a daily newspaper.
5. Bart has (took, taken) the snowmobile to town for supplies.
6. Carefully, they (swam, swum) past the coral reef.
7. Construction workers (lay, laid) the foundation for the new office building.
8. Exhausted, the winning miler (lay, laid) down on the grass.
9. Spectators at the chess tournament (sat, set) quietly.
10. The reporter (raised, rose) his binoculars to look at the UFO.
11. The hot-air balloon (raised, rose) quickly.
12. Of the thirty guests Lars (invited, had invited), only six came to the party.
13. In this golf tournament, Nancy Lopez is favored to (easily win, win easily).
14. The student president would have liked to (have met, meet) with the school board.
15. (Having changed, Changing) its menu, the cafeteria became more popular.
16. If this country (was, were) a true democracy, it would not have a Congress.
17. If her car (wouldn't have, hadn't) skidded, Janet Guthrie would have won the race.
18. (Receiving, Having received) much publicity, the new restaurant was crowded.
19. Carmen hopes to (master, have mastered) surfing soon.
20. After Anita (stretched, had stretched) the canvas, she began to paint.

9.0 The Right Word

The preceding pages of this Handbook have been concerned with problems of usage. They have presented choices of words and constructions that are accepted as **standard usage**—the kind of usage that is appropriate at all times and in all places.

Some forms and constructions have been marked **nonstandard usage.** While these may go unchallenged or unnoticed in casual conversations with friends, they are nonstandard because they are not acceptable everywhere. In many situations they mark the user as careless or untrained in the English language.

American English is not composed of just *standard* and *nonstandard usages*. Every good dictionary makes other distinctions such as *colloquial, slang, dialectal, archaic, poetic*. These labels limit the areas in which a word or expression is accepted. Thus, some words are acceptable in poetry but nowhere else. Slang expressions are acceptable only in everyday speech, not in writing.

A special note should be made of the term **colloquial.** Colloquial language is the informal language of everyday speech and writing. You would not expect to find it in a government document or in a formal speech, but there is no objection to colloquial usage in school, in business, or in ordinary everyday situations.

The glossary that follows lists alphabetically (a) usage items not covered in the preceding pages, and (b) words commonly confused as to meaning.

This glossary is too short to cover all the problems and questions that may arise. It is intended only as a first resort; if it fails, consult a good dictionary.

Distinctions of Meanings and Items of Usage

accept, except *To accept* is to agree to something or to re-receive something willingly. *To except* is to exclude or omit. As a preposition, *except* means "but" or "excluding."

> Carol *accepted* the offer at once.
> We will *except* the seniors who are going to college. (verb)
> Everyone *except* the driver was laughing. (preposition)

advice, advise You *advise* someone. What you give that person is *advice.*

affect, effect *Affect* is a verb meaning either to influence or to pretend. *Effect* as a verb means to accomplish or to produce as a result. As a noun, *effect* means "result."

agree to, with, on You agree *to* something such as a plan of action. You agree *with* someone else. Or, something such as spinach does not agree *with* you. You agree with others *on* a course of action.

allusion, illusion, delusion An *allusion* is a reference to something. An *illusion* is a false idea or a faulty interpretation of the facts. A *delusion* is a belief in something that is contrary to fact.

> The newspaper story made an *allusion* to our poor football record.
> Betty had the *illusion* that her work was satisfactory.
> Hitler suffered from the *delusion* that he could make no mistakes.

alumna, alumnus An *alumna* is a female graduate; the plural is *alumnae*. An *alumnus* is a male graduate; the plural is *alumni*.

all right The misspelling *alright* is nonstandard usage. The two words are separate.

all the Clumsy and nonstandard in such expressions as "all the longer," "all the farther," and so on.

NONSTANDARD: Is that all the louder you can yell?
STANDARD: Can't you yell any louder than that?

altogether, all together *Altogether* means "entirely" or "on the whole." *All together* means that all parts of a group are considered.

The report of the accident is *altogether* wrong. (entirely)
The crew pulled on the rope *all together*.

among, between *Between* expresses the joining or separation of *two* people or things. *Among* refers to a group of three or more.

NONSTANDARD: Let's divide the money *between* the three of us.
STANDARD: Let's divide the money *among* the three of us.

amount, number *Amount* is used to indicate a total sum of things. It is usually used to refer to items that cannot be counted. *Number* is used to refer to items that can be counted.

The *amount* of food consumed is amazing. (*food* cannot be counted.)
The *number* of hamburgers consumed is amazing. (*hamburgers* can be counted.)

angry at, with You are angry *with* a person and angry *at* a thing.

anywheres, nowheres, somewheres The final *s* is nonstandard. The words are *anywhere, nowhere, somewhere*.

apt, likely, liable These three words have in common the meaning of *probable*. However, they cannot be substituted for each other at random. With respect to probability, *apt* means "naturally inclined to." *Likely* means "something that can reasonably be expected." *Liable* means "subject to something, usually something unpleasant."

Most people are *apt* to worry when the airplane suddenly drops in a downdraft.
It is *likely* to rain before nightfall.
If you speed on this road, you are *liable* to be arrested.

bad, badly See Section 7.5.

being This completely acceptable present participle is most safely used as part of a main verb. Used as a modifier it creates extremely awkward sentences. *Being as* and *being that* are not satisfactory substitutes for *since* or *because*.

AWKWARD: Being on the jury, she could not talk about the case.
BETTER: Since she was on the jury, she could not talk about the case.

NONSTANDARD: Being that he is the boss, we do what he says.
STANDARD: Because he is the boss, we do what he says.

beside, besides *Beside* means "at the side of." *Besides* means "in addition to."

Larry's dog rode *beside* him in the front seat.
There are other rewards *besides* the money.

between each *Between* is not followed by a singular noun.

NONSTANDARD: Between each bite, he sipped his cocoa.
STANDARD: Between *bites*, he sipped his cocoa.

NONSTANDARD: Between every page, Jack inserted a paper.
STANDARD: Between *the pages*, Jack inserted papers.

borrow, lend *Borrow* and *lend* are verbs. You *borrow from* someone. You *lend to* someone.

NONSTANDARD: Will you *borrow* me your atlas?
STANDARD: Will you *lend* me your atlas?
STANDARD: May I *borrow* your atlas?

bring, take *Bring* means "motion toward" someone or some place; *take* means "motion away from" someone or some place.

I will *take* this book to school. (*away* from here)
He will *bring* us some milk. (*toward* us)
Sarah will *take* me home. (*away* from here.)

but that, but what The word *but* has a negative meaning. If it is preceded by another negative, it creates a double negative situation.

NONSTANDARD: I have *no* doubt *but that* Terri will win.
STANDARD: I have *no* doubt that Terri will win.

can, may *Can* means "able or having the power to do something." *May* is used to ask or to grant permission. It also expresses the probability of something happening.

Can you solve the first problem? (ability)
May we go to the library? (permission)
It *may* snow tomorrow. (probability)

Could is the past tense of *can; might* is the past tense of *may.*

compliment, complement A *compliment* is a remark spoken in praise. A *complement* is something needed to complete a whole.

continual, continuous *Continual* means "occurring repeatedly or at intervals over a long period." *Continuous* means "extending without interruption in space or time."

There were *continual* sounds of hammering.
There is a *continuous* stretch of desert across North Africa.

differ from, with One thing or person differs *from* another in characteristics. You differ *with* someone when you disagree with him or her.

different from In most situations *different from* is better usage than *different than*. However, there are some situations in which *than* must be used to avoid awkward expression.

Gil's book is different *from* ours.
The school is much different *than* it used to be.

emigrate, immigrate To *emigrate* is to leave one's homeland. To *immigrate* is to enter a country for the purpose of settling there. An *emigrant* is one who is on his or her way from a former home. An *immigrant* is one who has arrived in a new country.

etc. The abbreviation *et cetera* means "and so forth," or "and others." The abbreviation is avoided in most writing. If it is used, it must not be preceded by *and*, because the *et* means "and."

fewer, less See Section 7.7.

formally, formerly *Formally* means in a formal manner. *Formerly* means previously.

She was *formerly* Ambassador to Belgium.
We have never been introduced *formally*.

good, well See Section 7.6.

had of, off of The *of* is both unnecessary and undesirable.

NONSTANDARD: I wish you *had of* come.
STANDARD: I wish you *had* come.

NONSTANDARD: Dick jumped *off of* the stage.
STANDARD: Dick jumped *off* the stage.

hanged, hung Criminals are *hanged*. Things are *hung* on walls, hooks, or elsewhere.

> The mob *hanged* the horse thief.
> The doctor's diplomas *hung* on the office wall.

imply, infer A speaker or writer suggests or *implies* something. The reader, listener, or observer comes to a conclusion or *infers* something on the basis of what she or he sees and hears.

> The speaker *implied* that we are lazy.
> I *infer* that you disagree with the speaker.

in, into *In* means inside something. *Into* tells of motion from the outside to the inside of something.

NONSTANDARD: The books fell *in* the mud.
STANDARD: The books fell *into* the mud.

NONSTANDARD: Jane ran *in* the house.
STANDARD: Jane ran *into* the house.

ingenious, ingenuous *Ingenious* means "clever and resourceful." *Ingenuous* means "frank and honest."

kind, sort, type See Section 7.3.

kind of a, sort of a The *a* is unnecessary.

NONSTANDARD: What *kind of a* car did you buy?
STANDARD: What *kind of* car did you buy?

lay, lie See Section 8.2.

leave, let *Leave* means "to go away from." *Let* means "permit." The principal parts are *leave, left, left*, and *let, let, let*.

NONSTANDARD: Please *leave* the boy go on with his story.
STANDARD: Please *let* the boy go on with his story.

NONSTANDARD: We should have *left* Sue go.
STANDARD: We should have *let* Sue go.

STANDARD: *Leave* me alone with my work. (Depart.)
STANDARD: *Let* me alone. (Don't interfere.)

like, as, as if While the use of *like* as a conjunction is common in speaking, its use as a conjunction is not fully established in writing. *Like* is better used as a preposition.

NOT ACCEPTED: I feel *like* Sally does about swimming.
BETTER: I feel *as* Sally does about swimming.

NOT ACCEPTED: Jeff acted *like* he had already heard the story.
BETTER: Jeff acted *as if* he had already heard the story.

majority This word can be used only with items that can be counted. It is incorrectly used in speaking of time or distance.

NONSTANDARD: The *majority* of the milk did not sour.
STANDARD: *Most* of the milk did not sour.

NONSTANDARD: The *majority* of the time was spent in sleeping.
STANDARD: *Most* of the time was spent in sleeping.

NONSTANDARD: The *majority* of the decoration is amateurish.
STANDARD: *Most* of the decoration is amateurish.

of When *could have, might have, must have,* and similar phrases are spoken, they usually come out as contractions: *could've, might've, must've,* and so on. Because the contracted form *'ve* sounds like *of*, some persons write mistakenly *could of, might of, must of*.

NONSTANDARD: Someone *might of* seen you.
STANDARD: Someone *might have* seen you.

percent, percentage *Percent* is correctly used only when preceded by a number. When there is no preceding number, *percentage* is correct.

About 70 *percent* of the pictures turned out well.
A large *percentage* of our students go to college.

raise, rise See Section 8.2.

seldom ever The *ever* is unnecessary. You can say instead *seldom, very seldom*, or *hardly ever*.

AWKWARD: We *seldom ever* saw the owner of the house.
BETTER: We *very seldom* saw the owner of the house.

so There is a good deal of objection to this completely acceptable conjunction on the grounds that it is overused. If you overuse it, try some other connective. *So* as a conjunction usually indicates result. The clause it introduces states the result; the main clause states the cause. You can eliminate the *so* entirely by changing the main clause to a subordinate clause introduced by *since* or *because*.

CAUSE RESULT
The house was dark, *so* we turned around and came home.

CAUSE RESULT
Since the house was dark, we turned around and came home.

So is correctly used in place of *so that* to indicate result.

Judy did her homework on Friday night *so that* she could go out on Saturday.

Judy did her homework on Friday night *so* she could go out on Saturday.

So should never be used for emphasis unless it is followed by a clause beginning with *that*.

NONSTANDARD: He was so busy.
STANDARD: He was so busy that he could not go.

way, ways *Ways* is misused when it refers to distance.

NONSTANDARD: We went a little *ways* into the forest.
STANDARD: We went a little *way* into the forest.

REVIEW: THE RIGHT WORD Rewrite the following sentences, making them conform to standard usage.

1. I would of borrowed you this calculator if it hadn't of broken.
2. Can we please plan the career conference for a day beside Saturday?
3. One alumnus acted like she owned the school.
4. Is that all the longer the anesthetic will have an affect?
5. The passenger got angry at the cab driver, who wouldn't drive anywheres near the concert hall.
6. It is difficult to except a complement graciously.
7. Our chaperone left us travel a short ways on our own.
8. One continual line of fans poured in the Astrodome.
9. Between each act, we took refreshments back here to our seats.
10. This kind of a sports car differs with Italian models.
11. The shops, parking lots, and etc., had seldom ever been so crowded.
12. I don't doubt but that the swindler is too ingenuous to get caught.
13. Most of the crash survivors were alright, but two were apt to be in the hospital for weeks.
14. Being that the club officers meet altogether on a regular basis, they can plan club activities in advance.
15. The corporation divided its profits between its large amount of stockholders.
16. The President made an illusion to the Premier's advise.
17. I imply from the evidence that the candidate excepted illegal contributions.
18. A large percent of accused witches were jailed instead of hung.
19. The majority of e. e. cummings's poems are different than conventional poems.
20. Formally, the United States had quotas for emigrants from certain countries.

10.0 Capitalization

10.1 *A.D., B.C., I, O*

Capitalize the abbreviations *A.D.* and *B.C.*, the pronoun *I*, and the interjection *O*.

The abbreviations *B.C.* and *A.D.* occur only with the number of a year: 1001 B.C., A.D. 1492. The interjection O occurs in poetry, in the Bible, or in prayers or petitions: O Lord, O King.

O is quite different from the explosive interjection *oh*, which is capitalized only at the beginning of a sentence.

10.2 First Words

Capitalize the first word of a sentence, a direct quotation, and a line of poetry.

What brought the man to our hideout?

"I have come," he said, "to repay a debt."

Whenever Richard Cory went down town,
We people on the pavement looked at him:
He was a gentleman from sole to crown,
Clean favored, and imperially slim.*

Note: The second example is a divided quotation. The second part of a divided quotation does not begin with a capital letter unless it starts a new sentence. (See Section 14.2.)

* From *Richard Cory* by E. A. Robinson, quoted by permission of the Macmillan Company.

10.3 Proper Nouns and Adjectives

A **common noun** is the name of a whole group of persons, places, or things. A **proper noun** is the name of an individual person, place, or thing. A **proper adjective** is an adjective formed from a proper noun.

COMMON NOUN	PROPER NOUN	PROPER ADJECTIVE
king	Edward	Edwardian
state	Texas	Texan
plane	Concorde	
car	Corvette	

Proper nouns and adjectives occur in many compound words. Capitalize only the parts of these words that are capitalized when they stand alone. Do not capitalize prefixes such as *pro-*, *un-*, *anti-* attached to proper nouns and adjectives.

un-American   pro-French   Spanish-speaking people

Proper nouns occur in great variety. The following rules with their illustrations will help you solve the capitalization problems that proper nouns present.

10.4 Geographical Names

In a geographical name, capitalize the first letter of each word except articles and prepositions.

The article *the* appearing before a geographical name is not part of the geographical name and is therefore not capitalized.

CONTINENTS: Australia, Africa, Europe

BODIES OF WATER: the Atlantic Ocean, San Francisco Bay, the Mississippi River, the Great Lakes, the Strait of Magellan, the Firth of Forth, Cape Cod, Dismal Swamp

LAND FORMS: the Gobi Desert, the Rocky Mountains, Crystal Cave, Mount Hood, Shenandoah Valley

POLITICAL UNITS: the United States of America, the Republic of Texas, the Commonwealth of Massachusetts, the Province of Quebec, St. Louis County, Newcastle Township, Stratford-on-Avon, the Fields of Dan, the Department of Health, Education, and Welfare

PUBLIC AREAS: Glacier National Park, Mammoth Cave, Big Hole Battlefield, Fort Laramie, Joshua Tree Monument

ROADS AND HIGHWAYS: Fifth Avenue, New Jersey Turnpike, U.S. Highway 1, Kennedy Expressway, Twelfth Street, Michigan Boulevard, London Road

10.5 Common Nouns in Names

A common noun that is part of a name is capitalized. A common noun used to define or refer to a proper noun is not capitalized.

PART OF THE NAME	REFERENCE OR DEFINITION
New York State	the state of Minnesota*
New York City	the city of Buffalo
the Western Plains	plains in the West
Hudson Valley	the valley of the Hudson

10.6 Words Modified by Proper Adjectives

The word modified by a proper adjective is not capitalized unless adjective and noun together are a geographical name.

the Indian Ocean	the Indian nation
the Swiss Alps	a Swiss watch
the English Channel	the English language
the Irish Sea	Irish songs

* In official documents, words like *city, state,* and *county* are capitalized when they are part of the name of a political unit: *The County of Westchester, the State of Mississippi, the City of Los Angeles.*

Exercise: Copy the following sentences, supplying any necessary capitals.

1. A chief crop of hawaii is pineapples.
2. The british frigate bowed to the american ship.
3. Yellowstone national park is in the state of wyoming.
4. Thousands of people of irish descent marched down fifth avenue in the St. Patrick's Day parade.
5. At the mouth of the mississippi lies the city of new orleans.
6. Have you visited mt. rushmore in the black hills?
7. Saul was made the first king of the hebrew nation in 1095 b.c.
8. About one-third of the canadian people are french-speaking.
9. The largest state, alaska, contains the largest national monument, glacier bay.
10. The u.s. bureau of the mint manufactures coins in denver and philadelphia.
11. The canadians were neither pro-russian nor pro-american in the hockey play-offs.
12. The suez canal links the mediterranean sea and the red sea.
13. The shenandoah river in virginia flows into the potomac river.
14. Malone is a town in new york near the canadian border.
15. Not far from pike's peak lies the city of colorado springs.
16. I want french toast, canadian bacon, and english muffins.
17. The st. lawrence seaway is the largest waterway built since the panama canal.
18. The american continents were named for an italian sailor, amerigo vespucci.
19. In the gobi desert of asia, nomadic mongols live in felt tents.
20. After the spaniards had conquered the aztec capital, they rebuilt the city and called it mexico city.

10.7 Directions and Sections

Capitalize names of sections of the country but not of directions of the compass.

The climate attracts settlers to the West.
The South is now heavily industrialized.

To the north is Sacramento.
We are going south this winter.
St. Louis is east of Kansas City.
The shopping center is west of here.
The East is more densely populated than the Southwest.

Capitalize proper adjectives derived from names of sections of the country. Do not capitalize adjectives derived from words indicating direction.

a westerly breeze	a Midwestern university
a northbound flight	a Southern state

Exercise: Copy the following sentences, supplying any necessary capitals. If a sentence is correct, write C next to the number.

1. Anne has applied to three colleges in the midwest.
2. The Appalachian Mountains extend down the eastern side of North America.
3. It is doubtful that the cold front now in the middle west will reach the eastern states.
4. Read the timetable upward for eastbound trains.
5. The southernmost point of the United States is Key West, Florida.
6. Lars went to a vocational school in the southwest.
7. After touring the near east, we flew west to Rome.
8. Our oldest university, Harvard, is an eastern school.
9. The nearest ranger station is a mile south of here.
10. The street on the west side of our school is Mills Street.
11. Our doctor was born and raised in the south.
12. Stratford-on-Avon is a small town eighty miles northwest of London, England.
13. The middle east is well represented at the United Nations.
14. Alison traveled westward through four southern states.
15. The mystique of the far east lures some travelers to the Orient.
16. Are the Watsons going south for the winter?
17. The path of the hurricane changed from a northwesterly to a northeasterly direction.

18. Do midwestern teams play better football than eastern teams?

19. The Joshua tree wages its life battle in the scorching aridity of the southwest.

20. The north central states are one of our country's chief farming, mining, and manufacturing areas.

10.8 Languages, Races, Nationalities, and Religions

Capitalize the names of languages, races, nationalities, and religions and the adjectives formed from them.

the Caucasian race	Buddhism	Jew
the Spanish language	Catholic	Brazilian
Mexican history	Protestant	Dutch

Do not capitalize names of school subjects unless they are specific course names. Names of languages, however, are always capitalized.

history	American History III
English	German
algebra	Advanced Algebra and Trigonometry II
science	Chemistry 1B

10.9 Organizations and Institutions

Capitalize important words in the names of organizations, buildings, firms, schools, churches and other institutions. Do not capitalize *and* or prepositions. Capitalize an article (*a, an,* or *the*) only if it appears as the first word in a name.

Chicago Symphony Orchestra	Evanston Chamber of Commerce
College of William and Mary	Standard Gas, Incorporated
St. Luke's Hospital	Library of Congress
Book-of-the-Month Club	Hadley School for the Blind
the Empire State Building	Metropolitan Museum of Art

Note: In brand names, only proper nouns and adjectives are capitalized: *Chevy van, Chevy Monza; Post cereals, Post Toasties.*

Exercise: Copy the following sentences, supplying any necessary capitals.

1. All science students must take biology I and II before they take a chemistry course.
2. There is a sale on california oranges and chiquita bananas at tony's market.
3. Copies of all new books go to the library of congress.
4. Ship the latin and english books to morris hills regional high school.
5. Ms. hovis works for the department of agriculture in a laboratory at beltsville, maryland.
6. Dr. quinn has belonged to the american dental association for the past five years.
7. The new york public library has an exhibit of japanese woodcuts.
8. The guest speaker is a physicist who used to work for the national aeronautics and space administration.
9. Professor saville of oberlin college addressed the league of women voters.
10. The rockefeller institute for medical research is located on york avenue.
11. A graduate of beloit college, elise is going to continue her studies at the university of illinois school of veterinary medicine.
12. You can get hunt's tomato sauce at hoffman's fine foods.
13. The masterwork chorus will give a concert in the morristown high school auditorium.
14. Have you seen mr. case's new pontiac sunbird?
15. Two new speech electives are oral interpretation I and creative dramatics III.
16. The ajax printing company is next to the first national bank.
17. Wisconsin will play northwestern in dyche stadium.
18. The american petroleum company sponsors a number of excellent programs.
19. The ford foundation supports many important educational research projects.
20. The home economics department just purchased two litton microwave ovens and an amana freezer.

10.10 Titles of Persons

Capitalize words that show rank, office, or profession, when they are used with a person's name.

Doctor Walsh | Sister Mary | Father Flynn
Lieutenant Flagg | Rabbi Jacobs | Judge Wright
Chief Joseph | Controller Bucklin | Dean Smith

The titles of high officials are capitalized even when they are used without the official's name.

the President of the United States | the Governor
the Secretary of State | the Pope
the Vice-President | the Bishop

The prefix *ex-* and the suffix *-elect* are not capitalized when attached to titles: *ex-President Nixon,* the *Senator-elect.*

10.11 Family Relationships

Capitalize the name of a family relationship when it is used with a person's name.

Aunt Faye Uncle Abe Grandma Rial

When words like *mother, father, dad,* and *mom* are used alone in place of a particular person's name, they are capitalized. When modified by a possessive pronoun, as in *your mother,* they are not capitalized. When these and other words of family relationship do not stand for a particular person, they are not capitalized.

Uncle Phil will be here tomorrow.
We have a letter from Cousin Sue.
Bob asked Dad for the car yesterday.
I saw your mother at the airport.
Does Alice have a sister?

10.12 Titles of Books and Works of Art

Capitalize the first word and every important word in the titles of books, stories, articles, poems, films, works of art, and musical compositions.

The only words considered not important are conjunctions, articles (*a, an,* and *the*), and prepositions containing fewer than five letters. But even these are capitalized when used as the first word in a title.

Under Milkwood	"I Like To See It Lap the Miles"
Go Tell It on the Mountain	*Out of the Silent Planet*
the *Mona Lisa*	*One Flew over the Cuckoo's Nest*

Exercise: Copy each word that requires a capital in these sentences.

1. Is mom going to drive judge fuller to the airport?
2. My sister played "tales from the vienna woods" and "voices of spring."
3. Have dad and mom met lieutenant wickham?
4. My sister saw *annie hall* four times and *bananas* twice.
5. I think aunt dorothy or my mother will drive.
6. At the banquet the governor praised the secretary of state and the vice-president.
7. My aunt ruth's daughter is my cousin, and my mother's aunt is my great-aunt.
8. My favorite overture is beethoven's "egmont."
9. The chief speaker at the meeting will be fire chief schwenker.
10. Amy asked aunt lois to lend her *rockets, missiles, and space travel.*
11. Have you ever read hemingway's *a farewell to arms,* mother?
12. Alec's father drove us out to see grandmother stone, who is dad's grandmother.
13. I have read "to a skylark" in shelley's *complete poems.*
14. The mayor introduced senator sitwell as the next president of the united states.

15. Two biographies of ex-president kennedy are *a thousand days* and *kennedy.*

16. When he was formulating his energy program, president carter was advised by secretary of energy schlesinger.

17. I would like you to meet ms. gavin, who is senator-elect.

18. The matter of your suspension is to be taken up with dean wood tomorrow.

19. The secretary of housing and urban development is flying to meet the president-elect.

20. Assistant attorney-general robertson may be the next chief justice of the supreme court.

10.13 The Deity

Capitalize all words referring to the Deity, the Holy Family, and to religious scriptures.

God	the Almighty	the Gospel
the Father	the Lord	the Torah
the Son	Jehovah	the Talmud
the Holy Ghost	Allah	the Koran
the Virgin Mary	the Bible	

Capitalize personal pronouns but not relative pronouns that refer to the Deity.

May God make His light to shine down upon you.
Praise God from whom all blessings flow.

10.14 Days, Months, Holidays

Capitalize the names of days of the week, of months, and of holidays. Do not capitalize the names of seasons.

Monday	the Fourth of July	autumn
January	Washington's Birthday	Veterans Day

10.15 Historical Names

Capitalize the names of historical events, documents, and periods.

Declaration of Independence	the Middle Ages
Battle of the Bulge	the Jacksonian Period

Exercise A: Copy the words that require capitals in these sentences.

1. Margaret's favorite period in history is the age of enlightenment.
2. The boston tea party took place in 1773.
3. The second continental congress lasted for five years.
4. The first shots of the american revolution were fired at the battle of lexington.
5. The nun asked the lord for his guidance.
6. Our town has a parade every spring on memorial day.
7. The bible study group meets thursday evenings in january and february.
8. The school year usually starts on the tuesday after labor day.
9. Columbus day is now celebrated on the monday closest to october 12.
10. The victorian era is usually thought of as an age of gentleness and propriety.
11. The period in which shelley, keats, and byron wrote is known as the romantic age.
12. We celebrated new year's eve at sue murphy's house.
13. Some renaissance artists were inspired by the classic works of the ancient greeks and romans.
14. The united states senate rejected the treaty of versailles.
15. Chief sitting bull defeated general custer in the battle of little big horn.

Exercise B: Copy the words that need capital letters.

1. My aunt's interests are music, archery, golf, english literature, and american history.
2. I think millet's best painting is "the man with a hoe."

3. The language of the brazilian people is portuguese.
4. The magna carta of england was imposed upon king john.
5. Lucas served us french toast with vermont maple syrup.
6. My mother plays the violin with the boston symphony orchestra.
7. In 1890, the battle of wounded knee was the last major conflict between indians and u.s. troops.
8. The president of the langston literary guild called the meeting to order.
9. Why did the young indian woman save captain john smith's life?
10. On the first friday in april, the american legion will hold its annual convention in detroit.
11. Confucius, the chinese philosopher, was born in 551 b.c.
12. One of the late margaret mead's cultural studies was *coming of age in samoa.*
13. Originally, the southern states of south carolina, georgia, alabama, mississippi, and florida formed the confederate states of america.
14. Seldom is there an equal balance of power between republicans and democrats in the united states congress.
15. The poem "the charge of the light brigade" tells of a heroic event in the crimean war.

REVIEW: CAPITALIZATION Copy the words that require capital letters in these sentences.

1. The spring dance is scheduled for the saturday after st. patrick's day.
2. Evan likes polish sausage on french bread with green peppers.
3. The red cross has local offices on tenth street.
4. Our english class read *the grapes of wrath, moby dick,* and *the jungle.*
5. My mother and father took a first aid course at evansville hospital.
6. The pipeline transports oil south from alaskan oilfields.
7. The environmental protection agency has banned certain pesticides.

8. The name *susan* comes from the hebrew word for lily.

9. Last week aunt stephanie directed a performance of *madame butterfly* at the lyric opera house.

10. Every sunday father cunningham reads several bible verses.

11. In july grandma grant opened her restaurant, called grandma's gastronomy.

12. The parade on memorial day will come south down central avenue.

13. Students in advanced biology IIB examined the aquatic life in glen lake.

14. The league of nations held its first meeting at geneva, switzerland, in 1920.

15. We took route 66 west across the mississippi river and into the flatlands of the west.

16. In northern ireland, protestants and catholics have been engaged in a vicious struggle.

17. The only one of the great lakes that is entirely in the united states is lake michigan.

18. In 1184 b. c., the city of troy fell to the greeks.

19. In capetown, south africa, dr. christiaan barnard pioneered heart transplants.

20. During the civil war, brigadier general b. e. bee said, "there is jackson standing like a stone wall."

11.0 End Marks and Commas

11.1 Periods at the Close of Sentences

Place a period at the close of every declarative sentence and of most imperative sentences.

A period is also used at the close of groups of words that are used as sentences even though they are not complete sentences.

Please hand me the broom.
Oh, no. We were not near the fire.

11.2 Periods in Abbreviations

Place a period after every part of an abbreviation.

E. A. Robinson	Edwin Arlington Robinson
A.D.	Anno Domini
U.S.A.	United States of America

Since the 1930's it has become the custom not to use periods in abbreviations of certain government agencies and of international organizations.

FHA	Federal Housing Authority
FBI	Federal Bureau of Investigation
UN	United Nations
HEW	Department of Health, Education, and Welfare

11.3 Exclamation Points

Place an exclamation point after an exclamatory sentence and after an exclamation set off from a sentence.

Great! We can't lose now.
What a pass!
Hold that line!
Wow! I don't believe it!
We want Jackson!
Wilson for Senator!

11.4 Question Marks

Place a question mark after an interrogative sentence or after a question that is not a complete sentence.

The word order in questions is sometimes the same as in declarative sentences. In speech, the speaker raises his or her voice at the end of the sentence to show that it is a question. In writing, the question mark performs the same function.

Have they changed premiers?
Do you call this a composition?
The date? January 21.
They have changed premiers?
This is a composition?

Exercise: Copy these sentences, using end marks and punctuation as required for sentences and abbreviations. Use question marks only for sentences in normal interrogative form.

1. Just hand me that pair of pliers
2. What a close call that was
3. Lt Marks asked to be sent overseas
4. Please notify the YWCA of your change of address
5. You could have taken a later flight, couldn't you
6. You can reach me at 208 So King St, Mt Arlington, N J
7. Down, Rover The idea of your jumping up like that
8. Please send the package C O D to Nashville, Tenn
9. Marcus Aurelius died in A D 180
10. Does the FCC ever censor television programs
11. How kind you are

12. Could I get you a cup of coffee or tea
13. Jessica received her B S degree from N Y U
14. Has Charlie a driver's license
15. The principal asked whether Charlie had a driver's license

Uses of the Comma

11.5 Introductory Words

Introductory words such as *yes, no, well, why,* and *oh* are followed by a comma.

Oh, no, not another detour.
Well, there we were, drifting with the current.
Why, nobody with any sense would do that.

Adverbs such as *besides, however, anyhow, nonetheless* at the beginning of a sentence are followed by a comma.

11.6 Introductory Phrases and Clauses

A participial phrase at the beginning of a sentence is followed by a comma.

A long adverbial clause at the beginning of a sentence is followed by a comma.

A succession of prepositional phrases at the beginning of a sentence is followed by a comma.

Watching the trail, we saw the wagon train approach. (participial phrase)
On the ledge at the top of the tower, the princess brushed her long blond tresses. (succession of prepositional phrases)
When the prince arrived, he scratched his bald head and looked up at the tower. (adverbial clause)

11.7 Transposed Words and Phrases

Words and phrases moved to the beginning of a sentence from their normal position are usually set off by a comma.

He naturally checked the address in the directory. (normal order)
Naturally, he checked the address in the directory. (transposed order)

It was obviously a case of mistaken identity. (normal order)
Obviously, it was a case of mistaken identity. (transposed order)

You need a guide book to get the most out of the fair. (normal order)
To get the most out of the fair, you need a guide book.

Exercise: Copy the following sentences, inserting commas where necessary. Two of the sentences are correct.

1. When the lightning struck our terrier pup dashed under the dining room table.
2. Driving on Dad began to sing.
3. For the best view sit here.
4. If I had moved an inch the boat would have turned over.
5. Well you do seem a little heavier.
6. If your answers are incorrect change them.
7. When Leila has finished the house will look like new.
8. Down at the bottom of the valley people were walking about.
9. Now we know your secret!
10. While the fire was burning Otto had to keep getting more and more firewood.
11. Yes I thought Arlene's speech was the best.
12. From the stage people looked as if they were enjoying the show immensely.
13. Why every picture in my roll of film was spoiled!
14. Speaking in public was a skill he had exhibited since grade-school days.
15. While Roger watched Dora played two sets of tennis with Mom.

11.8 Appositives

An appositive is set off from the rest of the sentence by commas.

Ms. Clark, *an authority on Dutch elm disease,* thinks our tree can be saved.
The collector, *Mr. Lisle,* bought the chair at an auction.

11.9 Words of Direct Address

Words of direct address are set off by commas.

Ray, did you buy a season ticket?
My fellow citizens, I ask you to vote—not for me alone—but for a greater America.

11.10 Parenthetical Expressions

Words and phrases used to explain or qualify a statement are called **parenthetical expressions.** These same words and phrases may also be used as basic parts of the sentence. It is only when they are parenthetical that they are set off by commas.

I understand that her theory is sound.
Her theory, *I understand,* is sound.

Of course Mort knows where it is.
Mort, *of course,* knows where it is.

Parenthetical expressions are set off by commas.

Some expressions often used parenthetically are:

of course	as a matter of fact	for example
in fact	I believe (hope, think)	on the other hand
indeed	I suppose	

Conjunctive adverbs (see Section 1.7) used parenthetically within the sentence are set off by commas: *therefore, moreover, nevertheless, however, consequently,* and so on.

> You realize, *therefore,* that you run a risk.
> The coat, *moreover,* does not fit properly.
> The carnival, *however,* was a tremendous success.

Occasionally, words like *however, therefore,* and *consequently* are used to modify a word in the sentence. As modifiers they are an essential part of the meaning of a sentence. Since they are essential they are not set off by commas.

> My friends insisted that I could not succeed. I was *therefore* determined not to give up.
> The procedure for screening security risks was *consequently* changed.
> My father cannot stop smoking *however* hard he tries.

11.11 Dates, Addresses, Geographical Names

In dates and addresses of more than one part, set off every part after the first from the rest of the sentence.

> We visited the baseball museum in Cooperstown. (one part)

> In Cooperstown, New York, we visited the museum.
> (two parts, the second set off by commas)

> The package arrived on June 6. (one part)

> Wisconsin entered the Union on May 29, 1848.
> (two parts with a comma after the first)

> The letter was addressed to 280 East End Avenue, Pleasantville, Ohio 43148, where he formerly lived.
> (three parts, the second and third set off by commas)

Note: The day of the month and the month are one item. The name of the street and the house number are one item. The name of the state and the zip code are one item.

> June 6 240 East Thirty-first Street Illniois 60610

Exercise A: Copy these sentences, inserting the necessary commas.

1. Write to me at 110 North Spooner Street Madison Wisconsin 53705.
2. Would you consider July 4 1776 a more important date than March 4 1789?
3. The affair on the whole came off very successfully.
4. Both athletes and actors it is said are highly superstitious.
5. You bad dog you have chewed my slipper.
6. Ladies and gentlemen of the jury I wish to present Exhibit A.
7. That was as I shall explain the narrowest escape of my life.
8. Hans after all is a foreign exchange student and needs time to adjust.
9. Mother have you met Ms. Connors my history teacher?
10. On June 1 1980 the play opened in Chicago Illinois and Los Angeles California.

Exercise B: Follow the same directions as for Exercise A.

1. Lucky the beagle next door barks twice when the bell rings.
2. If you move the picture to the right Nancy it will look better.
3. Julia Ward Howe writer of "The Battle Hymn of the Republic" was a prominent worker for world peace.
4. His strange laugh a high-pitched cackle could be heard above the audience.
5. Let me remind you my friends that we simply must sell more tickets for the dance.
6. If you really want to watch this program Lynn stop reading that magazine.
7. George Washington retired from the army at Annapolis Maryland on December 23 1783.
8. The record states that he was born on February 2 1944 at 1091 San Pasqual Street Pasadena California.
9. Send your contributions to Mr. Frank Quinn 1851 West 107th Street Chicago Illinois 60643.
10. I shall be at the Beach Hotel 11 South Kentucky Avenue Atlantic City New Jersey.

11.12 Nonrestrictive Modifiers

A clause that identifies or points out the person or thing it modifies is a **restrictive clause.** It is essential to the meaning of the sentence. It cannot be dropped out without confusing the meaning or making the meaning incomplete.

Restrictive clauses are *not* set off from the rest of the sentence by commas.

The biography *that I mean* is the new one about Conan Doyle.
(The clause tells *which* biography.)

Young people need heroes *whom they can admire and imitate.*
(The clause describes essential characteristics of heroes.)

The person *who has a pleasant disposition* attracts friends.
(Without the clause the sentence has no specific meaning.)

A **nonrestrictive clause** does not contain information essential to the meaning of the sentence. It presents merely added information. It can be dropped without confusing the meaning of the sentence.

Nonrestrictive clauses are set off by commas from the rest of the sentence.

The speed limit, *which is rigidly enforced,* helps decrease traffic accidents.

Teachers, *who spend their lives educating young people,* are rarely remembered when their students attain success as adults.

Participial phrases that identify or point out the thing or person they modify are restrictive.

The jet *making a forced landing* has mechanical trouble.
(Without the phrase, the sentence loses its specific meaning.)

The bird *perched on the tree outside the window* awakened me with its chirping. (The phrase identifies the bird.)

Nonrestrictive participial phrases merely add meaning. They are not essential and can be dropped without making the sentence meaning incomplete.

Looking back, we could see the undulating hills.
The boys, approaching the clearing, saw the campfire.

Nonrestrictive participial phrases *are* set off from the rest of the sentence by commas. Restrictive phrases are *not* set off by commas.

Exercise: Number your paper 1–20. Decide whether the adjective clause or the participial phrase is restrictive or nonrestrictive. After each number write *restrictive* or *nonrestrictive*. Copy and insert commas in the sentences in which commas are needed.

1. The train that goes to Philadelphia is on Track 3.
2. Ms. Moss who teaches industrial arts has just bought a car.
3. Robyn who is a jockey must keep her weight down.
4. Harold Leach is the boy wearing the green sweater.
5. My ice skates which had been packed in a carton were lost in the move to our new home.
6. Buy the paper that is least expensive.
7. The little girl smiling shyly is my sister.
8. The plane that left Honolulu at noon carried two hundred passengers.
9. Enclosed is forty dollars which is the amount you asked for.
10. This bank established by my grandmother many years ago has grown into a thriving institution.
11. The vacation seemed unreal coming after months of anticipation.
12. Chris's cheesecake of which I eat more than my share is our family favorite.
13. The person receiving the package must sign for it.
14. Michele who is my closest friend would not even talk to me.
15. Players who are over six feet tall have an advantage in basketball.
16. Cora's application handed in two weeks ago has not been acted on as yet.
17. All people dream nightly often having several dreams.

18. Renoir is the Impressionist who painted *Luncheon of the Boating Party*.
19. Carolyn who was the first speaker introduced the subject.
20. The girl who was the first speaker is Carolyn Davis.

11.13 Compound Sentences

Place a comma before the conjunction that joins two main clauses in a compound sentence.

You must get your work done on time, *or* you will be fired.
Thomas More hoped to die peacefully, *but* one day he became certain that he would die at the executioner's hand.
Suddenly the thunder rolled, *and* the picnickers scattered.
I could not remember the title of the book, *nor* could I remember the author.

When the clauses are quite short, the comma may be omitted.

She invited me to dinner and I accepted.
I ate shrimp and Jim had clams.

11.14 Series

A **series** is a group of three or more items of the same kind.

SERIES OF NOUNS: *Typewriters*, *calculators*, and *dictaphones* were ordered for the business education rooms.

SERIES OF VERBS: The human rights committee *met*, *discussed* specific proposals, and *adopted* a new constitution.

SERIES OF ADJECTIVES: Blamed for the loss of the game, Paul felt *embarrassed*, *bewildered*, and *lonely*.

SERIES OF PHRASES: Lorna piled the luggage *on the counters*, *in the corners*, and *outside the doors of the waiting room*.

Commas are used to separate the parts of a series.

No comma is required after the last item in a series. When the last two items of a series are joined by *and* or *or*, the comma is sometimes omitted. To avoid all possibility of misunderstanding, it is wise to use a comma before the conjunction.

Do not use a comma if all parts of the series are joined by *and*, *or*, or *nor*.

The electric fan whirred and buzzed and oscillated.
A book or a newspaper or a magazine will satisfy me.

11.15 Coordinate Adjectives

Commas are placed between coordinate adjectives that modify the same noun.

The soaring, majestic spire seemed to reach for the sky.
The flashing, blinding, zigzag lightning terrified us.

To determine whether adjectives are coordinate, try placing an *and* between them. If it sounds natural, they are coordinate, and a comma is needed.

PROBLEM: The soft soothing music relaxed him.
NATURAL: The soft *and* soothing music relaxed him.
SOLUTION: The soft, soothing music relaxed him.

PROBLEM: The tempting delicious aroma made our mouths water.
NATURAL: The tempting *and* delicious aroma made our mouths water.
SOLUTION: The tempting, delicious aroma made our mouths water.

PROBLEM: The small gray car uses less gasoline.
NOT NATURAL: The small *and* gray car uses less gasoline.
SOLUTION: The small gray car uses less gasoline.

In general, it is safe to omit the comma before numbers and adjectives of size, shape, and age.

CORRECT: The little round jug
CORRECT: A fat old dachshund
CORRECT: Four local bands

Exercise: Copy these sentences, placing commas where they are needed. One sentence is correct.

1. Elections are open to sophomores juniors and seniors.
2. The house is modern but the furniture is old-fashioned.
3. Please get a pound of butter a loaf of bread and a melon.
4. The rain was gentle warm and spring-like.
5. I like vanilla but maple walnut is my favorite.
6. I did not see the hole in the ice nor did I hear the warning cries.
7. We packed some sandwiches and fruit and then we rode our bikes to the fairgrounds.
8. For breakfast we had ham and eggs toast and jam and coffee.
9. Notice your own mistakes or someone else will.
10. The old dilapidated backless book was finally discarded.
11. Our class baked huckleberry pecan and pumpkin pies.
12. I gave up my social life studied hard and managed to pass the examination.
13. The salesperson showed me a tape recorder but it was too expensive.
14. I never saw anyone as inquisitive as persistent or as baffling as Grandpa Larsen.
15. She was a sprightly old woman.
16. That I was weak tired and sick to my stomach made no difference to my boss.
17. It was one of those warm muggy days in early September.
18. Some people prefer traditional names but others favor unusual off-beat names.
19. The legislature passed laws in the areas of education health and welfare.
20. Daniel Boone served well in the American Revolution but we remember even better his courage on the Wilderness Trail.

11.16 Clarity

Use a comma to separate words or phrases that might be mistakenly joined in reading.

There are three common situations in which words may be mistakenly read together. The first occurs when the conjunctions *but* and *for* are mistaken for prepositions.

CONFUSING: No one spoke but Christie looked hopefully at the doctor.
CLEAR: No one spoke, but Christie looked hopefully at the doctor.

CONFUSING: George wrote to the factory for a part was missing.
CLEAR: George wrote to the factory, for a part was missing.

A second source of confusion is a noun following a verbal phrase.

CONFUSING: Before attacking the soldiers checked supply lines.
CLEAR: Before attacking, the soldiers checked supply lines.

CONFUSING: To understand a student must grasp basic principles.
CLEAR: To understand, a student must grasp basic principles.

CONFUSING: After eating the survivors had renewed strength and hope.
CLEAR: After eating, the survivors had renewed strength and hope.

A third source of confusion is the word that may be either adverb, preposition, or conjunction at the beginning of the sentence.

CONFUSING: With Joseph Andrew pitched the tent.
CLEAR: With Joseph, Andrew pitched the tent.

CONFUSING: Below the rocks were sharp and treacherous.
CLEAR: Below, the rocks were sharp and treacherous.

11.17 Words Omitted

Use a comma when words are omitted from parallel word groups.

Pat sewed the seams, and Leroy, the hem.
I prefer languages; my sister, science.
The riper, the tastier.

Exercise A: Copy these sentences, placing commas where necessary to avoid confusion.

1. Inside the fire was burning brightly.
2. The day before he had scarcely spoken.
3. Jeff had to hurry for the clock was wrong.
4. In her Mother has unlimited confidence.
5. To Sally Ray was a faithful friend.
6. Before dressing the little girl ate breakfast.
7. Having ordered Jill studied the faces of the other diners.
8. Joe has read four novels by Charles Dickens; Martha three.
9. Beyond the rainbow glistens with color.
10. Sarah Edmonds served as a soldier for the Union Army in the Civil War; Pauline Cushman as a Union spy.

Exercise B: Follow the same directions as for Exercise A.

1. To prepare each student should review the assigned chapters.
2. Throughout the convention was interrupted by demonstrations.
3. By counting the leaders realized that one camper was missing.
4. Donna is going to the University of Iowa; Star to the Air Force Academy.
5. The swimmer knew all the strokes but the butterfly was her favorite.
6. By criticizing a person often hurts feelings.
7. A copyright is granted for the lifetime of the owner of the copyright plus fifty years; a patent for seventeen years.
8. To Alice Elizabeth sent a handsome gift.
9. *Abraham Lincoln* was written by John Drinkwater; *Abe Lincoln in Illinois* by Robert E. Sherwood.
10. Owen's occupation is carpentry; his hobby fixing old clocks.

REVIEW: END MARKS AND COMMAS Copy the following sentences, inserting end marks, periods, and commas where necessary.

1. Yes we have tickets for the concert Rachel
2. Undoubtedly New York has some of the finest museums in the world
3. Besides the deadline is June 6 1980
4. Wow They beat U S C
5. The U S S R I believe opposed UN recognition of China
6. Well Ms Evans cardio-pulmonary resuscitation classes are held on Tuesdays Thursdays and Saturdays
7. G K Chesterton a British author wrote *The Man Who Was Thursday*
8. Leaning over the balcony Laura spotted the approaching mob
9. Will the Democrats hold their convention in Dallas Texas or Miami Florida
10. On May 10 1979 the judge dismissed the case
11. N O W of course supports the E R A
12. If you need me I can be reached at 6012 Piccadilly Lane London England
13. The student body charmed by Robinson's promises elected him president
14. Some legal cases drag on for years providing employment for many lawyers
15. "Trekkies" admire the cool rational hero of "Star Trek" Mr Spock
16. Alice Rivlin who is a noted economist directed the Congressional Budget Office
17. Fire demolished the structure but no one was hurt
18. Some of the attractions of San Francisco California are streetcars scenery and sourdough bread
19. Wildcat fans will cheer for the trophy is now theirs
20. Christopher Reeve played Superman; Margot Kidder Lois Lane

12.0 The Semicolon, the Colon, the Dash, and Parentheses

12.1 Semicolons Between Main Clauses

A semicolon is placed between the main clauses of a compound sentence when they are not joined by a conjunction.

The clauses of a compound sentence are closely related in thought. That is the reason for joining them into one sentence rather than writing them as separate sentences.

In some sentences the semicolon is more effective in joining main clauses than one of the conjunctions. This is especially true when *and* or *but* add little meaning to the joined clauses.

> You may approve of the measure, *but* we do not.
> You may approve of the measure; we do not.

> Mr. Ames discussed the nature of time, *and* he introduced many new ideas to us.
> Mr. Ames discussed the nature of time; he introduced many new ideas to us.

12.2 Semicolons and Conjunctive Adverbs

A semicolon is used between clauses joined by conjunctive adverbs or by phrases like *for example, in fact, for instance.*

The problem of absences has become acute; in fact, it is first on the agenda for faculty consideration.

Three people had asked me to that movie; however, I had promised Hubert that I would play Monopoly with him that night.

Sir Walter Scott was only a silent partner in the bankrupt firm; nevertheless, he assumed responsibility for the debts.

Jill has a genius for leadership as well as many other talents; for example, she can play three musical instruments.

Note that the conjunctive adverb or phrase is followed by a comma in the examples above.

12.3 Semicolons Between Word Groups Containing Commas

A sentence containing a great many commas is difficult to read. If commas precede the conjunction between main clauses, another comma at this point would lose its value as a guide to the reader.

A semicolon is used between main clauses joined by a conjunction if the clause before the conjunction contains commas.

The train stops at Davis, Foster, and Central Streets; but it does not run at all after midnight.

The camp counselors planned games, races, and a variety show; and everyone agreed that the program was successful.

Her brother won't clean, cook, or do laundry; nor will he do any other chores around the house.

A semicolon is used between a series of phrases if they contain commas.

My ambition is to be a lawyer; Noreen's, a photojournalist; and Jack's, the owner of a chain of stores.

At the carnival Rick won a radio; Sandi, a cassette tape recorder; and Emil, a huge panda bear.

The tickets for Thursday evening cost $3.50; Friday and Saturday evenings, $5.00; and Sunday afternoon, $4.50.

Exercise: Two of the following sentences need no semicolons. For the other sentences, indicate the point at which a semicolon should replace a comma.

1. If you enjoy hunting and fishing, go to Maine, but if you enjoy crowds and excitement, go to Atlantic City.
2. Linda sang and danced in the school musical, and she won the debate tournament.
3. Inside the old house, it was dark, outside, the air was cool and fragrant.
4. In some ways I like geometry, in other ways I don't.
5. Stop in for your papers on Monday or Tuesday, otherwise, you may have to wait a whole week.
6. Mom would not change her mind and let us go, however, she agreed to our having company for dinner.
7. Thoreau was unlike many of his contemporaries, he would not compromise his convictions.
8. Juanita is as excited as a child when it snows, she never saw a snowstorm until she was twenty.
9. On the night before, Bert had gone to bed early, consequently, he was at his best for the examination.
10. The following officers were elected: Elaine Berek, president, Jane Carrolton, vice-president, George Goodson, secretary.
11. Gritting his teeth, he steeled himself for the jab, but when the nurse injected the vaccine, he scarcely felt any pain.
12. A tragedy often ends with a catastrophe, on the other hand, a comedy ends happily.
13. On his short-wave set, Ed has received stations in Pusan, Korea, Anchorage, Alaska, Edmonton, Canada, and Shannon, Ireland.

14. Diane enjoyed the pictures of the Olympic Games, she was a newsphotographer and a track star herself.

15. Every morning he set out to sea, and every evening he returned with a boatload of fish.

12.4 Colons To Introduce Lists

The colon is used to throw the reader's attention forward to what follows. It is in some respects like an equal sign, saying that what follows is the explanation or equivalent of what has gone before.

A colon is used to introduce a list of items.

Usually, a colon is required when a list is preceded by the words *the following* or *as follows*. A colon is not used before a series of modifiers or complements immediately following the verb.

> We camped out at the following places: Lake Tahoe, Nevada; Jackson's Hole, Wyoming; and Yellowstone National Park. (list)
>
> His virtues are patience, wisdom, and understanding of human motives. (series of complements following a verb)
>
> The distinguishing features of the hog-nosed skunk are a hog-like snout, a broad white band across the back, and short, coarse fur. (series of complements following a verb)
>
> Information is available in encyclopedias, in atlases, and in dictionaries. (series of modifiers following a verb)

12.5 Colons with Formal Quotations

A colon is used to introduce a formal quotation.

> The president opened the meeting with these words: "We are beginning a period of expansion in which all of you will play a key role. Many of you will have added responsibilities; others will have entirely new responsibilities."

12.6 Colons Before Explanatory Statements

A colon is used between two sentences when the second explains the first. The second sentence begins with a capital letter.

Now I understand what caused his downfall: His failure to admit his guilt and make a public apology turned away those who might have shown him mercy.
I think I know the cause: I ate six chocolate eclairs and three brownies.

12.7 Other Uses of the Colon

A colon is also used (1) after the formal salutation of a letter, (2) between the hour and minute figures of clock time, (3) in Biblical references, (4) between the title and subtitle of a book, (5) between numbers referring to volume and pages of books and magazines.

Dear Sir or Madam:
Dear Ms. Sims:
6:15 A.M.
Volume II: pages 65–72

Genesis 2:4–7
The Wide World: A High School Geography

12.8 The Dash To Show Break in Thought

A dash is used to show an abrupt break in thought.

In dialogue, the break in thought is often caused by uncertainty or hesitancy as in the first example below.

The trouble is—I suppose he knows it himself—he just can't get along with people.
We are to meet at Mary's for the surprise—oh, have the plans been changed?
I am firmly convinced—but what weight do my opinions carry anymore?

12.9 The Dash with Interrupters

A dash is used to set off a long explanatory statement that interrupts the thought.

Robert Frost—who had to gain his first recognition abroad—is now considered by many to be America's most distinguished poet.

There was a feeling of curious anticipation—a feeling shared throughout the world—when Communist China first invited the President of the United States to visit Peking.

12.10 The Dash Before a Summary

The dash is used after a series to indicate a summarizing statement.

Old prints, faded manuscripts, the yellowed pages of books long out of print—these were his special delights.

Simplicity of operation, low cost, assembly-line production—these were the factors that Henry Ford introduced to revolutionize the manufacture of automobiles and make them available to the masses.

Exercise: Copy the following sentences, inserting semicolons, colons, and dashes where necessary.

1. The plant shop sold only the following varieties English ivy, Swedish ivy, and grape ivy.
2. Jack telephoned to ask that on my way home I buy the following whole wheat bread, Swiss cheese, and dill pickles.
3. The train was due at 5 30, but it was not there by 6 15.
4. The title of the book is *Past to Present A World History*.
5. The newsboy gave poor service he was afraid of the dog.
6. Let me explain how I oh, here comes George!
7. My schedule this year includes the following subjects English III, French III, Algebra II, Physics II, and Physical Education III.
8. Eliza would not want a kitten for a pet she has a canary.
9. We can summarize Emerson's philosophy in these words "Trust thyself; every heart vibrates to that iron string."

10. Tom Saunders was a model student he made all A's he was a talented football player he worked for the good of the school.

11. "He he didn't refuse you, did he?" asked Aunt Jane.

12. We went down the embankment in a hurry slid down, in fact.

13. I know how the accident happened by the way Kate stopped in a few minutes ago and left a message for you.

14. Do we can we send fourteen-year-olds out onto the gridiron to be mauled and maimed?

15. Robert Holt we call him class clown was in the main hall "directing traffic."

16. In the general atmosphere of gaiety the dance was the high point of the holiday festivities Fred soon forgot he was homesick.

17. Here we are, face to face with a difficult and new problem difficult and new, that is, in the sense that we are strangers to it.

18. The campus was beautifully planted with pin oaks, flowering trees, and a variety of gardens all gifts of former graduating classes.

19. To arrive promptly, to concentrate on his work, to organize these were the things he found difficult.

20. Judge Potter she is a friend of my mother's helped me get a summer job.

12.11 Parentheses To Enclose Supplementary or Explanatory Words

Commas, dashes, or parentheses are used to set off words that are supplementary or explanatory. Commas are used when the material set off is fairly close to the main thought of the sentence. Dashes are used to set off material more loosely connected, and parentheses are used to set off material so loosely related to the main thought that it might be made a separate sentence.

There are few occasions in high school writing when parentheses are needed. The safest course for the student is to use commas, or even dashes, to set off parenthetical matter. If the material is so distantly related as to require parentheses, the passage might better be rewritten to place the parenthetical material in a separate sentence.

COMMAS ADEQUATE: Mark's best point, *which he saved for the end,* was that every group needs leadership.

DASHES REQUIRED: Modern science no longer deals directly with the visible world—that is, it deals directly only with ions, atoms, electrons, and other particles that are too small to be seen.

PARENTHESES APPROPRIATE: She speaks French and Arabic (her family has lived in France and the Middle East), but English is her first language.

PARENTHESES AVOIDED: She speaks French and Arabic, since her family has lived in France and the Middle East, but English is her first language.

12.12 Punctuation Within Parentheses

Commas, semicolons, and periods are placed outside the closing parenthesis. The question mark and exclamation point are placed inside if the parenthetical material is itself a question or exclamation; otherwise, outside.

The ballet begins at 8:30 (no seating after the curtain).
Donna has four brothers; Alice, two (counting her stepbrother); Ann, three.
Everyone hoped that Jim would at least offer (as if he ever offered!) to help in the emergency.
I was not interested (why should I be?) in their plans.

12.13 Brackets

Brackets are used to enclose corrections or material inserted by a writer who is quoting someone else's material.

"On the 4th [5th] of March, Hayes took office." (correction)
The letter read: "We have him [Jordahl] at our mercy." (explanatory word inserted by the writer)

12.14 Ellipses

Indicate the omission of unused parts of a quotation by ellipses: three dots (. . .) to indicate an omission within a sentence; four dots (. . . .) to indicate an omission at the end of a sentence.

> With malice toward none; with charity for all . . . let us strive on to finish the work we are in; to bind up the nations wounds. . . . —ABRAHAM LINCOLN

REVIEW: THE SEMICOLON, THE COLON, THE DASH, AND PARENTHESES Copy the following sentences, inserting semicolons, colons, dashes, and parentheses where necessary.

1. School clubs are enjoying great popularity in fact, some have doubled their membership.
2. The ice cream shop has the following new flavors fudge brownie, coconut, huckleberry, and bubble gum.
3. Mr. Jonas had a surprise His car had a flat tire.
4. Katie's appointment was at 3 30 however, she arrived at 4 30.
5. Princess Caroline's story is told in Volume 3 pages 90–99.
6. I'm waiting for oh, here she comes now.
7. Jim, our forward, is injured but his substitute is very capable.
8. Deep-dish pizza oh, it's so delicious! originated in Chicago.
9. Gemologists recognize real diamonds laypeople often do not.
10. Josh read *Thomas Jefferson An Intimate History*.
11. Funny faces, silly props, and a white suit these are Steve Martin's trademarks.
12. Suffragettes crusaded for women's right to vote consequently, the nineteenth amendment was passed.
13. Earth, Wind and Fire toured the following cities Los Angeles, California Boston, Massachusetts and Chicago, Illinois.
14. Glass, steel, concrete modern architects use them freely.
15. George Benson plays guitar Stevie Wonder, piano and Maynard Ferguson, trumpet.

13.0 The Apostrophe

The apostrophe is used with nouns to show possession or ownership: *Ted's uniform, Sylvia's performance, the cat's claws.* The apostrophe is also used to show the following:

CLOSE RELATIONSHIP:	Jane's friend, someone's uncle
SOURCE OR ORIGIN:	Lynn's remarks, Lill's idea
IDENTIFYING CHARACTERISTICS:	Tessie's thoughtfulness, Ron's attitude, the child's lisp

13.1 The Possessive of Singular Nouns

The possessive form of a singular noun is usually made by adding an apostrophe and *s* ('s) to the noun.

boy + 's = boy's   city + 's = city's
Charles + 's = Charles's   Ross + 's = Ross's

Note: A few proper nouns ending in *s* may take the apostrophe only: Jesus', Moses'. In general, however, the correct way to make a singular noun possessive is to add an apostrophe and *s*.

13.2 The Possessive of Plural Nouns

If a plural noun does not end in s, add both apostrophe and s ('s) to form the possessive.

men + 's = men's   children + 's = children's
alumni + 's = alumni's   women + 's = women's

If a plural noun ends in s, add only the apostrophe to form the possessive.

horses + ' = horses'   waiters + ' = waiters'
actors + ' = actors'   editors + ' = editors'

Exercise: Number 1–20 on your paper. Write *correct* for each sentence in which the possessive form is correct. If the form is incorrect, write it correctly.

1. "The Children's Hour" is one of Longfellows best-known poems.
2. The first witness' testimony greatly impressed the jury.
3. Jess's make-up was like an actress's.
4. Brooks's store is having a sale on men's shoes.
5. Charles's father was invited to sit at the captains' table.
6. Our Olympic team did well in women's downhill skiing.
7. The Joneses dog barked all night.
8. The dentists' conversation put her patients at ease.
9. The jewels in the duchess' tiara were diamonds and emeralds.
10. Dad attended the alumnis' annual dinner.
11. Robert Burns's poems are beloved by the Scots.
12. Moses' Ten Commandments are also known as the Decalogue.
13. One canary birds' song could be heard over the mens' voices.
14. The Burnses farm sits on a knoll between two oak trees.
15. Have you read Henry James's *Washington Square?*
16. Les' sister goes to a girl's preparatory school.
17. The womans' estate was administered by her lawyers.
18. For Bess's birthday her mother gave her a watch.
19. Both editor's arguments influenced the author's decision.
20. Squirrel's tails are not bushy in the springtime.

13.3 The Possessive of Compound Nouns

A **compound noun** is a noun composed of more than one word. Some compound nouns are written with hyphens between the parts.

Only the last part of a hyphenated noun shows possession.

father-in-law + 's = father-in-law's
editor-in-chief + 's = editor-in-chief's
attorney-general + 's = attorney-general's

Nouns such as *the Queen of England, the President of the United States, the Secretary of State* form the possessive by adding an apostrophe and *s* to the last word only: the *Secretary of State's name.* However, this awkward construction can be avoided by using an *of* phrase.

the name of the Queen of England
the address of the President of the United States
the duties of the Secretary of State

13.4 Joint Ownership

When the names of two or more persons are used to show joint ownership, only the name of the last person mentioned is given the possessive form. Add an apostrophe or an apostrophe and *s* in accord with the spelling of that name.

Louise and Tom's family
father and sons' banquet
author and critic's correspondence

The rule applies also to names of firms and organizations.

Clarke and Taylor's sale
Brown, Jackson and Company's building
The League of Women Voters' pamphlet

13.5 Separate Ownership or Possession

If the names of two or more persons are used to show separate ownership, each name is given the possessive form.

Madison's and Jefferson's careers
Webster's and Clay's orations

This construction may become awkward. It can be avoided by using an *of* phrase.

the careers of Madison and Jefferson
the orations of Webster and Clay

13.6 Possessive of Indefinite Pronouns

Use an apostrophe and *s* to form the possessive of indefinite pronouns.

someone + 's = someone's   nobody + 's = nobody's
another + 's = another's   anyone + 's = anyone's

The apostrophe and *s* are added to the last word in forms like *someone else, anybody else, no one else:*

no one else's   anybody else's

The apostrophe is not used to form the possessive of personal pronouns.

NONSTANDARD: their's, your's, her's, our's, it's
STANDARD: theirs, yours, hers, ours, its

13.7 Expressions of Time and Amount

When used as adjectives, words expressing time and amount are given the possessive form.

a day's wages   three days' wages
an hour's time   two hours' time

a month's delay	four months' delay
a week's vacation	two weeks' vacation

Exercise: Copy the italicized words, changing them to show ownership or possession correctly.

1. Carrie's *sister-in-law* party was a great success.
2. The weather is *nobody* fault.
3. *Jane and Tim* cousin spent the weekend with them.
4. The red scarf is *your's*; the blue one is *her's*.
5. Herb said, "It's a good fifteen *minutes* walk to the bus stop."
6. The *attorney-general* office is on the tenth floor.
7. The *Senator from Maine* motion was being considered.
8. The *accountant* and *taxpayer* signatures were on the tax return.
9. The *West Side Savings Bank* window was broken.
10. The workers struck for two *week* vacation with pay.
11. I took *someone else* umbrella by mistake.
12. The *Marquess of Queensberry* rules are a code for the boxing ring.
13. The committee heard the *Secretary of Commerce* report.
14. There was a gala opening of *Clayton and Hart* store today.
15. The *catcher* throw cut off the base runner.
16. The Quick Cleaners clean a suit in three *hours* time.
17. If that remark were *anybody else* except yours, I would get mad.
18. *Madison and Jefferson* letters are of great historical interest.
19. The *Governor of Ohio* address was the main speech at the dinner.
20. Those skis are *their's*; these are *our's*.

13.8 Apostrophes To Show Omissions

An apostrophe is used to show the omission of letters or figures.

the Homestead Act of '62	*1862*
the class of '85	*1985*
o'clock	*of the clock*
shouldn't	*should not*

13.9 Plurals of Letters, Words, Numbers, and Signs

An apostrophe is used to show the plurals of letters, words, numbers, and signs used as words.

How many *s*'s are there is Mississippi?
Beware of using too many *and*'s in your themes.
His 7's look like 9's.
Make sure that your +'s look different from your −'s.

Note: The plurals of letters, numbers, signs, and words used as words are always italicized in print. In manuscript and typescript they may be underlined or placed in quotation marks. (See Section 14.7.)

Exercise A: Copy the following sentences, inserting an apostrophe (and *s*) where needed. This exercise reviews all the uses of apostrophes.

1. Shes the best basketball player on the team.
2. Havent you asked for a weeks vacation?
3. I can never distinguish your *i*s from your *e*s.
4. After ten days delay, the publisher answered my letter.
5. Mother belongs to two womens political groups.
6. Alice's speech had too many *and*s and *but*s.
7. White and Judsons store has just installed escalators.
8. In the spring of 76 we visited Washingtons home at Mt. Vernon.
9. We discovered we had bought fifty dollars worth of groceries.
10. My brother-in-laws telephone number is unlisted.
11. Venus orbit is between Mercurys and the Earths.
12. Is that jacket hers? It looks suspiciously like her sisters.
13. Columbus sailors threatened to throw him overboard.
14. A meeting was held in the editor-in-chiefs office.
15. Graces parents are planning to take a three months cruise.
16. We bought a record of one of Strauss waltzes.
17. Dahl and Gross store is having a fashion show today.
18. The bus leaves Harringtons Corner at six oclock.

19. The Brooks dog goes over to Jim and Babs house every day.
20. No one elses singing could compare with hers.

Exercise B: Write the possessive singular and the possessive plural of each of the following words:

1. day	6. salesperson	11. mouse
2. city	7. sister	12. woman
3. class	8. son	13. county
4. principal	9. country	14. Jones
5. baby	10. lady	15. he

REVIEW: THE APOSTROPHE The following sentences contain errors in the use of apostrophes. Copy the sentences correcting all errors.

1. Margaret's and Don's mother, after two year's work in a bookstore, decided to start her own business.
2. Rutherford B. Hayes term of office was in the late 1800s.
3. Didnt Sarah and Diane's home runs tie the score?
4. Alex said he hadnt read any of Keats poems.
5. Joan begins all her sentences with *and sos*.
6. My sister spent the weekend at her mother's-in-law home.
7. Tim's and Kim's parents car is a 76 Volkswagen.
8. Les' sister dots her *is* with a circle.
9. Wasnt the five oclock bus late tonight?
10. Hanks' cake won a prize at the food fair.
11. Theres your jacket; Ive mended the sleeve.
12. Nobody elses violin was out of tune except Charles'.
13. Green's and Company store was closing just as I arrived.
14. I couldnt read Phils' writing because his *es* and *is* look alike.
15. Politician's lives are open to public scrutiny.
16. The dog led it's master to the commander's-in-chief tent.
17. Which came first, Adams's or Jeffersons' administration?
18. The dogs hair was all over the visitors suit.
19. Dad didn't see anything funny in Louis and Steves prank.
20. All the employees at Morgan's and Clark's department store get two week's vacation.

14.0 Quotations

14.1 Direct and Indirect Quotations

In a direct quotation, the words of the speaker are directly quoted exactly as she or he spoke them.

> Montaigne said, "The greatest thing in the world is to know how to be yourself."
> "The horse," Jim said, "is rearing again."

An indirect quotation reports the meaning expressed by the speaker but does not give her or his exact words.

> INDIRECT: The television announcer warned that a hurricane was approaching.
> DIRECT: "A hurricane is approaching," the television announcer warned.

Quotation marks are not used with an indirect quotation.

14.2 Punctuation of Direct Quotations

Punctuation and capitals are used as follows in direct quotations:

1. **In dialogue, the first word of the quotation is capitalized.** The material quoted from another writer may begin in the middle of a sentence. If so, the first word is not capitalized.

Washington considered religion "an indispensable support" of government.

2. **The speaker's words are set off from the rest of the sentence.** Note the placement of commas in these examples:

The reviewer stated, "Doctorow's novel is a masterpiece."
"Doctorow's novel is a masterpiece," the reviewer stated.

When the end of the quotation is also the end of the sentence, the period falls inside the quotation marks.

3. **If the quoted words are a question or an exclamation, the question mark or the exclamation point falls inside the quotation marks.** In this situation no comma is needed.

"How do you like your courses?" Sue asked.
"Don't touch that!" he shouted.

4. **If the entire sentence is a question or an exclamation, the exclamation point or question mark falls outside the quotation marks.**

Wasn't their campaign slogan "Tippecanoe and Tyler too"?
I deny my opponent's charge that I am "avoiding the issues"!

5. **The colon and the semicolon at the close of a quotation fall outside the quotation marks.**

The governor told his constituents that the following were on his list as "must legislation": a tax cut, aid to education, and subsidy for city transit.
Read A. E. Van Vogt's "The Enchanted Village"; then compare it with Stanley G. Weinbaum's "Parasite Planet."

6. **Both parts of a divided quotation are enclosed in quotation marks. The first word of the second part is not capitalized unless it begins a new sentence.**

"It was a great shock," Harry said, "to hear of his illness."
"I recommend not telling the patient," the doctor said. "You may alarm him and aggravate his suffering."

7. **In dialogue, a new paragraph and a new set of quotation marks show a change in speaker.**

> "Why do you want to drop out of school?" the counselor asked.
> "I've been in school for ten years," Tony said. "I want to get out and earn some money."
> "If you check the job market for unskilled workers," the counselor replied, "you'll find you have as much chance to get a job as you would to bat clean-up spot for the New York Yankees."

14.3 Quotations Within Quotations

Single quotation marks are used to enclose a quotation within a quotation.

> Gary reported, "When somebody told Churchill not to end sentences with a preposition, Sir Winston replied, 'That is the kind of nonsense up with which I will not put.' "
> Sheila asked, "Was it Roosevelt who said, 'The only thing we have to fear is fear itself'?"

14.4 Long Quotations

A quotation may be several paragraphs in length.

In long quotations, begin each paragraph with quotation marks. Place quotation marks at the end of the last paragraph only.

Exercise: Copy the following sentences, adding the necessary punctuation marks and capital letters.

1. Did you bring all the necessary documents asked the lawyer
2. The prosecuting attorney insisted that the witness answer the question
3. Look out the ranger shouted
4. Return all books by Friday said the librarian or there will be a fine

5. If the groundhog sees his shadow on February 2 said Bonnie there will be six more weeks of winter

6. Why don't you take your vacation in winter she asked there are many Southern cruises

7. Why can't I learn to study for these examinations with more confidence Jim asked

8. Just think said the comedian when Mozart was my age he'd been dead for two years

9. I was speeding the driver admitted but I am sure I did not pass a red light

10. When we get enough signatures she said we will hand the petition to the governor

11. I wish I could attend this school said Steve I like the gymnasium

12. The director yelled stop overacting the actress said

13. Boonesboro Jack reported is the name of the first American settlement west of the Appalachians

14. Did she say yes or yes, if your brother agrees

15. Bill reported that Dick had declared flatly there are no trout in this stream

14.5 Setting Off Titles

The title of a book, magazine, newspaper, long pamphlet, or bulletin is usually italicized in print. In your own writing, you indicate the italics by underlining.

To distinguish the title of a *part* of a book, magazine, or newspaper, quotation marks are used.

Use quotation marks to enclose the titles of chapters and other parts of books, and to enclose the titles of stories, poems, essays, articles, and short musical compositions.

In *Literature of America* I read Shirley Jackson's story "The Lottery."

Isaac Asimov's "Anatomy of a Martian" first appeared in *Esquire*.

14.6 Words Used in Special Ways

Words used in special ways or special senses are enclosed in quotation marks.

A writer may want to show that he is using a word as someone else has used it. The writer can make clear that he himself does not accept this use of the word by enclosing it in quotation marks.

Slang words and phrases are also enclosed in quotation marks to indicate that the writer does not accept them as standard usage.

> The bank teller was immediately called "on the carpet" for a shortage in his accounts.
>
> Social workers now call poor people "the socially disadvantaged."
>
> My brother was once in the habit of calling everything "far out"; the month before that, everything had been "groovy."
>
> The economists talked about making a study of "human resources."
>
> One reviewer actually wrote that her performance was the "definitive Lady Macbeth"!

Note: When a comma or period immediately follows the quoted word, it falls *inside* the quotation marks. The semicolon falls *outside* the quotation marks. See the third example above. If the quoted word appears at the end of a question or exclamation, the question mark or exclamation point falls *outside* the quotation marks. See the last example above.

14.7 Words Used as Words

A word referred to as a word is italicized in print. In writing, the word is underlined.

> In general, avoid using the word *physiognomy* for *face*.
>
> I dislike the words *oriented* and *orientation*.

When a word and its definition appear in the same sentence, the word is italicized, and the definition is placed in quotation marks.

The word *perspicuity* means "clearness of expression."

Exercise: Copy the following sentences. Insert quotation marks where necessary. Indicate italics by underlining.

1. Mary said that she was reading Stephen Leacock's essay My Financial Career.
2. John asked her if that essay is included in Literary Lapses.
3. We asked the candidate what he meant by law and order.
4. Matt uses the word like too much.
5. Did the report say continuously or continually?
6. The Garden Party is my favorite story in Women in Fiction.
7. Letters to the Editor in the May issue of Time is particularly entertaining.
8. Margo ends every sentence with y'know observed Kelly.
9. You will enjoy the chapter called The Long Snowfall in Rachel Carson's interesting volume The Sea Around Us.
10. We will have our first air-raid drill this morning, the voice from the loudspeaker announced.
11. The school I attended last year called them safety drills.
12. Have you read Shelley's poem To a Skylark?
13. The word enjoin means to command or order.
14. She once wrote appitamy for epitome.
15. Clare Boothe Luce once called confused thinking about international affairs globaloney.

REVIEW: QUOTATIONS Copy the following sentences, adding the necessary punctuation marks and capital letters. Indicate italics by underlining.

1. All aboard shouted the conductor.
2. Whose jeans are these Ryan asked.
3. Your deadline is tomorrow the editor announced.

4. We will soon have the equipment the principal noted for a school radio station.
5. Courtney remarked that the curly look is in.
6. Ralph Waldo Emerson defined a friend as the masterpiece of nature.
7. The huge sign said Keep out; we did.
8. How dare you call me a rude dude!
9. Is Coca-Cola's slogan It's the real thing?
10. Soccer is the newest sport at Taft the coach said let's make it the best.
11. Erin asked did that sign say Dangerous curve ahead?
12. Tony said our teacher told us only your best is good enough.
13. Carrie's favorite short story is F. Scott Fitzgerald's Babylon Revisited.
14. W. H. Auden's poem The Unknown Citizen satirizes conformity.
15. The first chapter of The Scarlet Letter, The Prison-door, contrasts the prison with a wild rose bush.
16. Who first recorded the song You Don't Bring Me Flowers Francine asked.
17. The coach asked me to relieve the starting pitcher said Bobbie.
18. The only comment on Judith's test paper was superb.
19. The car salesperson called the 1973 Toyota pre-owned.
20. Nemesis means an avenger or an unbeatable rival.

15.0 Spelling

Do you have trouble with spelling? If so, you may be consoled by the fact that other students for generations back have also had trouble. If you are interested in improving your spelling, you may be encouraged to know that many generations of poor spellers before you have learned to spell.

There is no simple way to teach you to spell. There is no easy way to learn. If you are concerned about the problem, however, there are several helpful suggestions:

1. **Proofread all your writing.** Even the ablest scholar may write "their" for "there" or "here" for "hear" in a first draft. Many apparent errors are not spelling errors at all. They are mistakes caused by carelessness and haste.

2. **Learn to look at the letters in a word.** Most of us have learned to read by recognizing whole words or parts of words. Spelling errors are errors in the letters that compose a word. You will find it helpful to break a word into its parts to see and to memorize the spelling of each part.

3. **Keep a list of your spelling errors.** The point is that you can spell correctly most of the words you use. Your errors fall within a narrow range. If you will concentrate on this range—provided by your list—you may show quick improvement.

4. **Practice on your own spelling problem.** There is no reason why you cannot totally eliminate spelling errors *if you want to.* One recommended procedure is to use a card pack. Print your problem words on cards in large letters. Take a card from the pack. Look at every letter and let the order of the letters sink into your mind. Pronounce each part of the word separately. Turn the card over. Write the word on a piece of paper. Turn the card over again and compare what you have written with the correct spelling.

5. **Memorize and apply the few rules of spelling given below.** Be sure you understand the rules, or your memory work will be wasted. Practice using the rules so that their use becomes automatic and you can write *bragging, reference, occurrence,* and so on, quickly.

Exercise: Divide these words into syllables. Do not be concerned as to whether they conform to the dictionary division. Just make sure that every word part has a vowel sound.

1. occurrence	7. humorous	13. italicize
2. accidentally	8. specifically	14. miniature
3. accommodate	9. necessary	15. extraordinary
4. incredible	10. disappearance	16. secretarial
5. miscellaneous	11. mimeograph	17. athletic
6. maintenance	12. immediately	18. privilege

15.1 The Final Silent *e*

When a suffix beginning with a vowel is added to a word ending in a silent *e*, the *e* is usually dropped.

believe + ing = believing	architecture + al = architectural
invite + ation = invitation	admire + able = admirable
ice + y = icy	fame + ous = famous
create + ive = creative	imagine + ary = imaginary

When the final silent *e* is preceded by *c* or *g*, the *e* is usually retained before a suffix beginning with *a* or *o*.

courage + ous = courageous   peace + able = peaceable
notice + able = noticeable

When a suffix beginning with a consonant is added to a word ending in a silent e, the e is usually retained.

state + ment = statement   safe + ty = safety
same + ness = sameness

The following words are exceptions: *truly*, *argument*, *wholly*, *awful*.

15.2 Words Ending in *y*

When a suffix is added to a word ending in *y* preceded by a consonant, the *y* is usually changed to *i*.

There are two exceptions: (1) When *-ing* is added, the *y* does not change. (2) Some one-syllable words do not change the *y*: *dryness*; *shyness*.

merry + ment = merriment   sixty + eth = sixtieth
city + es = cities   hazy + ness = haziness
hurry + ed = hurried   carry + ing = carrying

When a suffix is added to a word ending in *y* preceded by a vowel, the *y* usually does not change.

delay + ing = delaying   employ + er = employer
enjoy + ed = enjoyed

EXCEPTIONS: day + ly = daily, gay + ly = gaily.

Exercise A: Find the misspelled words in these sentences and spell them correctly.

1. The arriveal of the fameous actress caused quite a stir.
2. The administrateion may soon be forced to take disciplineary action.

3. Brian's argument was truely ridiculous.
4. The cold air was exhilarateing.
5. Their efforts toward a peacable settlement were both createive and couragous.
6. The sofa bed, the heavyest item, could not be moved.
7. The guideance counselor is in her office dayly.
8. Danielle's lazyness is outragous.
9. His motives are not wholely admireable.
10. Believing that the inviteation was meant for her, JoAnn accepted.
11. The host greeted us sincerly and graceiously.
12. Many people have been makeing donateions to the Heart Fund.
13. Some of Frank Lloyd Wright's architectureal achievements are truely exciteing.
14. The Americans easyly overran the Spanish fortifycations.
15. The merryment lasted until an extremly late hour.
16. We are planning a surprise celebrateion for my grandparents' fiftyeth anniversary.
17. We enjoyed drifting lazyly down the stream.
18. Billie staggered clumsyly with the two heavyest suitcases.
19. The defendant's hazyness in recalling certain details was noticeable.
20. Tolkien's characters, though imagineary, are thoroughly believeable.

Exercise B: Add the suffixes as shown and write the new word.

1. mystery + ous
2. relay + ing
3. body + ly
4. frenzy + ed
5. appraise + ed
6. waste + ful
7. amaze + ing
8. insure + ance
9. grease + y
10. situate + ion
11. worry + ing
12. carry + ed
13. enjoy + able
14. create + ive
15. copy + ing
16. educate + ion
17. assemble + age
18. wide + ly
19. constitute + ion
20. like + able
21. move + ment
22. change + able
23. change + ing
24. hurry + ing
25. debate + able
26. hasty + ly
27. merry + ly
28. easy + ly
29. day + ly
30. argue + ment

15.3 The Suffixes *-ness* and *-ly*

When the suffix *-ly* is added to a word ending in *l*, both *l*'s are retained. When *-ness* is added to a word ending in *n*, both *n*'s are retained.

gradual + ly = gradually
actual + ly = actually
even + ness = evenness
thin + ness = thinness

15.4 The Addition of Prefixes

When a prefix is added to a word, the spelling of the word remains the same.

dis + appear = disappear
mis + spell = misspell
im + mobilize = immobilize
il + legal = illegal
dis + similar = dissimilar
re + commend = recommend
trans + ship = transship
re + enter = re-enter

15.5 Words with the "Seed" Sound

Only one English word ends in *sede: supersede.*

Three words end in *ceed: exceed, proceed, succeed.*

All other words ending in the sound of *seed* are spelled *cede: secede, accede, recede, concede, precede.*

Exercise A: Correct the spelling errors in these sentences.

1. This faded old map is virtualy ilegible.
2. Kansas is being penalized fifteen yards for ilegal proceedure.
3. The eveness of the two teams made the game unusualy exciting.
4. A re-examination of our foreign policy was considered unecessary.
5. Rays from iradiated cobalt or gold have successfully attacked cancerous tissue.

6. Breaking a leg normaly imobilizes a person for months.
7. The captain's sterness caused disatisfaction among his crew.
8. The meeting is usualy preceeded by a potluck supper.
9. The SEC investigates iregularities in the stock market.
10. Scientists dissagree as to whether the nose cone actualy re-entered the atmosphere.
11. This exceptionaly brilliant youngster should be unusualy successful.
12. The officer answered civily that driving without a license was ilegal.
13. Nuclear-powered ships will eventually supercede conventionaly powered types.
14. The attorney dissagreed that the statement was irelevant.
15. The judge ruled that the evidence presented was imaterial, and the case proceded.

Exercise B: Add the suffixes and prefixes as indicated. Write the new word.

1. thin + ness
2. mis + take
3. ir + relevant
4. im + moderate
5. dis + satisfied
6. co + operate
7. incidental + ly
8. im + mobilize
9. uneven + ness
10. im + moral
11. confidential + ly
12. re + examine
13. ir + radiate
14. cordial + ly
15. dis + solution

15.6 Words with *ie* and *ei*

When the sound is long e (ē), the word is spelled *ie* except after c.

i before e

relieve	priest	chief
believe	shield	yield
piece	brief	niece

except after c

receive	ceiling	deceit
perceive	conceive	receipt

Exceptions: either, neither, financier, weird, species, seize, leisure. You can remember these words by combining them into such a sentence as: *Neither financier seized either weird species of leisure.*

Exercise A: Correct the spelling errors in these sentences.

1. My neice is here for a breif visit.
2. In her liesure time, she often yeilds to mischief.
3. Niether ex-convict was sentenced for theivery.
4. Martha dropped her handkercheif on the pier.
5. I am releived that I have found the reciept.
6. Across the feild raced the Labrador retreiver.
7. I beleive this is a rare speceis of butterfly.
8. The Vikings siezed the initiative on the first play and never yielded it.
9. We can, I believe, retreive the missing bicycle.
10. Can you peice together these wierd happenings?
11. People who seem concieted are either insecure or insensitive.
12. The survivors greived as they told of the feirce storm.
13. The releif pitcher did not yeild a single hit.
14. The financier had not decieved her best freind.
15. A wierd shreik peirced the stillness of the night.
16. The cheif of police cornered the theif at the end of a peir.
17. The power that Hitler weilded was almost inconcievable.
18. Neither driver would yeild the right of way.
19. This crossbeam should releive the wieght on the ceiling.
20. C. M. Bowra's book *The Greek Experience* sums up the whole acheivement of Greek civilization.

Exercise B: Copy the words below, filling the blank spaces with *ie* or *ei*.

1. perc__ve	6, f__rce	11. gr__vance
2. n__ther	7. n__ce	12. hyg__ne
3. c__ling	8. sh__ld	13. p__r
4. rec__pt	9. s__ze	14. spec__s
5. repr__ve	10. p__ce	15. l__sure

15.7 Doubling the Final Consonant

Words of one syllable, ending in one consonant preceded by one vowel, double the final consonant before adding a suffix beginning with a vowel.

1. The words below are the kind to which the rule applies.

fat big slug brag

These words double the final consonant if the suffix begins with a vowel.

fat + er = fatter slug + er = slugger
big + est = biggest brag + ing = bragging

2. The rules does not apply to the following one-syllable words because two vowels precede the final consonant.

heat sleep near foot

These words do not double the final consonant.

heat + er = heater near + est = nearest
sleep + ing = sleeping foot + ing = footing

3. The final consonant is doubled in words of more than one syllable:

When they end in one consonant preceded by one vowel.
When they are accented on the last syllable.

re·fer′ o·mit′ con·cur′

The same syllable is accented in the new word formed by adding the suffix:

o·mit′ + ed = o·mit′ted
re·fer′ + al = re·fer′ral
con·cur′ + ence = con·cur′rence

If the newly formed word is accented on a different syllable, the final consonant is not doubled.

re·fer′ + al = re·fer′ral
pre·fer′ + ence = pref′er·ence
con·fer′ + ence = con′fer·ence

Exercise A: Copy these words, indicating with an accent mark (′) where each word is accented.

1. control
2. excel
3. limit
4. resist
5. omit
6. regret
7. allot
8. impel
9. travel
10. distill
11. forget
12. murmur
13. defer
14. benefit
15. admit
16. differ
17. infer
18. propel

Exercise B: Add the ending indicated, and write the new word.

1. control + ing
2. bat + ed
3. compel + ed
4. bed + ing
5. differ + ence
6. limit + ed
7. commit + ed
8. book + ed
9. fur +y
10. disappear + ed
11. put + ing
12. get + ing
13. plan + ing
14. prefer + ed
15. sit + ing
16. remit + ance
17. transfer + al
18. nod + ing
19. begin + ing
20. expel + ed
21. admit + ance
22. let + ing
23. pad + ed
24. murmur + ing
25. repel + ed
26. omit + ed
27. commit + ed
28. ton + age
29. allot + ed
30. defer + ed

REVIEW: SPELLING Correct the spelling errors in these sentences.

1. After maping out her course, the pilot enterred the cockpit of her plane.
2. Deena beleives that rideing a raft over rapids was her bigest challenge.

3. The two waring nations finaly declared a truce.
4. The unnusualy mercyless ruler took away all libertys.
5. Who could be funnyer or wittyer than Woody Allen?
6. Many stars give commercial endorsments.
7. Jesse James was an infameous bandit who robed banks.
8. The unatural, glareing flash occured at midnight.
9. Fans shreiked as Owens was carryed from the feild.
10. Lowerring the unnemployment rate is one task for Congress.
11. The quarterback proceded without any noticable injurys.
12. The engine eventualy sputterred and stoped.
13. Niether suspect admited being the theif.
14. Dora praised Ken for the eveness of his kniting.
15. We looked with amazment at the wierd figure.
16. Nutritionists test varyous foods for wholesomness.
17. Some people are worrying about obeseity while others are freting over thiness.
18. Creativeity involves, I beleive, comeing up with off-beat ideas.
19. Rachel's explanation immediatly clearred up the confuseion.
20. A Supreme Court ruleing superceeds lower-court decisions.

16.0 The Plurals of Nouns

16.1 Regular Formation of Plurals

The plural of most nouns is formed by adding *s.*

employee + s = employees	door + s = doors
sense + s = senses	badge + s = badges

16.2 Plurals Formed with *es*

The plural of nouns ending in *s, sh, ch, x,* and *z* is formed by adding *-es.*

fox + es = foxes	church + es = churches
sash + es = sashes	class + es = classes

16.3 Plurals of Nouns Ending in *y*

When a noun ends in *y* preceded by a consonant, the plural is formed by changing the *y to i* and adding *es.*

city	citi + es = cities
beauty	beauti + es = beauties
company	compani + es = companies
worry	worri + es = worries

When a noun ends in *y* preceded by a vowel, a plural is formed by adding *s*.

play + s = plays　　holiday + s = holidays
galley + s = galleys　　alloy +s = alloys
delay + s = delays　　valley + s = valleys

16.4 Plurals of Nouns Ending in *o*

The plural of nouns ending in *o*, preceded by a vowel, is formed by adding *s*.

studio + s = studios　　radio + s = radios
rodeo + s = rodeos　　ratio + s = ratios
folio + s = folios　　duo + s = duos

The plural of most nouns ending in *o*, preceded by a consonant, is formed by adding *s*, but for some nouns of this class the plural is formed by adding *es*.

piano + s = pianos　　auto + s = autos
solo + s = solos　　alto + s = altos
credo + s = credos

tomato + es = tomatoes　　echo + es = echoes
potato + es = potatoes　　hero + es = heroes

There are some words ending in *-o* with a preceding consonant that may form the plural with either *s* or *es*: *motto, mango, mosquito.* The safest thing to do is to memorize the few words that add *-es* and to consult the dictionary when in doubt about others.

16.5 Plurals of Nouns Ending in *f* or *ff*

The plural of most nouns ending in *f* or *ff* is formed regularly by adding *s*.

waif + s = waifs　　proof + s = proofs
chief + s = chiefs　　gulf + s = gulfs
staff + s = staffs　　sheriff + s = sheriffs

The plural of some nouns ending in *f* or *fe* is formed by changing the *f* or *fe* to *ve* and adding *s*.

leaf—leaves	knife—knives	life—lives
wife—wives	loaf—loaves	elf—elves
wolf—wolves	sheaf—sheaves	thief—thieves

Since most of these words with irregular plurals are in common use, careful listening may help you to spell them correctly. If you are doubtful about spelling, however, look up the singular form of the word in a dictionary. If the plural of a word is irregularly formed, the plural will be given immediately after the singular.

16.6 Nouns with Irregular Plurals

The plural of some nouns is formed by a change of spelling.

foot—feet	goose—geese
man—men	mouse—mice
woman—women	ox—oxen
child—children	basis—bases
datum—data	phenomenon—phenomena
index—indices *or* indexes	hypothesis—hypotheses

The plural and singular forms are the same for a few nouns.

sheep	corps	Chinese
deer	quail	Portuguese

16.7 The Plurals of Names

The plural of a name is formed by adding *s* or *es*.

George Wolf—the Wolfs	Joyce Williams—the Williamses
Winifred Perry—the Perrys	Henry Jones—the Joneses

16.8 The Plurals of Compound Nouns

When a compound noun is written without a hyphen, the plural is formed at the end of the word.

handful + s = handfuls   teaspoonful + s = teaspoonfuls
cupful + s = cupfuls   doghouse + s = doghouses

When a compound noun is made up of a noun plus a modifier, the plural is added to the noun.

brothers-in-law (the phrase *in law* is a modifier.)
commanders-in-chief (the phrase *in chief* is a modifier.)
attorneys-general (*general* modifies *attorneys.*)
notaries public (*public* modifies *notaries.*)
hangers-on (*on* modifies *hangers.*)
bills of sale (the phrase *of sale* modifies *bills.*)

The following are exceptions: *smashups, standbys, lean-tos.*

Exercise A: Form the plural of each of the following words.

1. gash
2. life
3. valley
4. belief
5. worry
6. laboratory
7. cupful
8. holiday
9. gulf
10. loaf
11. corps
12. datum
13. cattle
14. church
15. grief
16. wife
17. potato
18. handful
19. hypothesis
20. basis
21. phenomenon
22. sheriff
23. smashup
24. teaspoonful
25. hanger-on
26. bill of sale
27. notary public
28. commander-in-chief
29. chief of police
30. mother-in-law

Exercise B: Find the errors in plural forms in the following sentences.

1. The northern lights are an unusual phenomena.
2. There are several boxs of matches in the cupboard.
3. Passer-bys admired the photoes.
4. For home economics we bought oranges, potatos, and tomatos.

5. Our allys needed our help against their enemys.
6. The picnickers used dull knifes to cut the loafs of bread.
7. The childrens brought handsful of sand from the beach.
8. I have two sister-in-laws living in Milwaukee.
9. Use two cupsful of flour and two tablespoonsful of sugar.
10. None of the studioes is large enough for two grand pianoes.
11. There are too many autoes in our citys.
12. Two sopranoes will sing solos.
13. The watchmens were neglecting their dutys.
14. The thiefs covered their faces with handkerchieves.
15. We saw over a dozen deers in the woods and in the vallies.
16. The wolfs have been attacking the sheeps.
17. Both of my brother-in-laws are fishermans.
18. There are still a few wild turkies in these valleys.
19. We are going on a picnic with the Thomas's and the Barry's.
20. Over one-fourth of all the people on earth are Chineses.
21. You must expect delayes in postal service during the holidays.
22. The opposing commander-in-chiefs met with their staffs.
23. The scientists advanced different hypothesises.
24. Shall we plant lily-of-the-valleys in our window boxs?
25. The editor-in-chiefs of several dailys met with their staffes of reporters.

REVIEW: THE PLURALS OF NOUNS Form the plural of each of the following words.

1. X-ray
2. trolley
3. lady-in-waiting
4. witness
5. newspaperwoman
6. spoonful
7. datum
8. brush
9. trio
10. spoof
11. lasso
12. bill of fare
13. tomato
14. life
15. galaxy
16. tradesperson
17. Williams
18. sergeant-at-arms
19. fox
20. jackknife

17.0 The Forms of Letters

In general, there are two classes of letters: (1) *friendly letters*, and (2) *business letters*. Any letter written for business purposes is a business letter; all other letters—love letters, apologies, invitations, letters written home, etc.—are called friendly letters.

The terms *friendly* and *business* are simply means of designating different forms. They do not refer to the tone in which the letter is written. A business letter may be extremely cordial and friendly. A friendly letter may be most businesslike. A friendly letter may, actually, be cold and unfriendly in tone.

There are two aspects to the forms of letters. The first pertains to the "letter picture," that is, to the arrangement of the content on the page. The second pertains to punctuation, forms of address, and other aspects of content.

17.1 The Friendly Letter

1. It is generally considered that a handwritten letter is more friendly, thoughtful, and considerate than a typed letter. Nonetheless, friendly letters may be typewritten if the circumstances make typing appropriate.

2. Handwritten letters are written on personal stationery, which comes in assorted sizes and colors. Scented papers and papers of unusual color are not considered to be in good taste.

If a friendly letter is typed, plain white typing paper 8½″ by 11″ is appropriate.

3. While there is some choice as to the size, shape, and color of correspondence paper, there is no choice as to the writing instrument. Pen and ink are required; pencil is not appropriate.

The Picture of the Friendly Letter

Indented Style

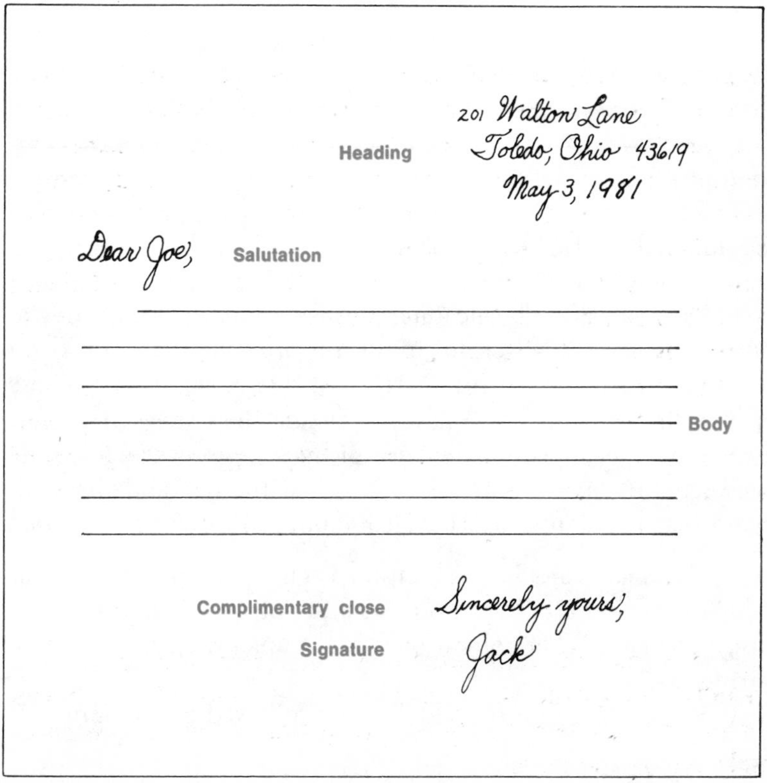

Heading
201 Walton Lane
Toledo, Ohio 43619
May 3, 1981

Dear Joe, Salutation

Body

Complimentary close Sincerely yours,

Signature Jack

Modified Block Form

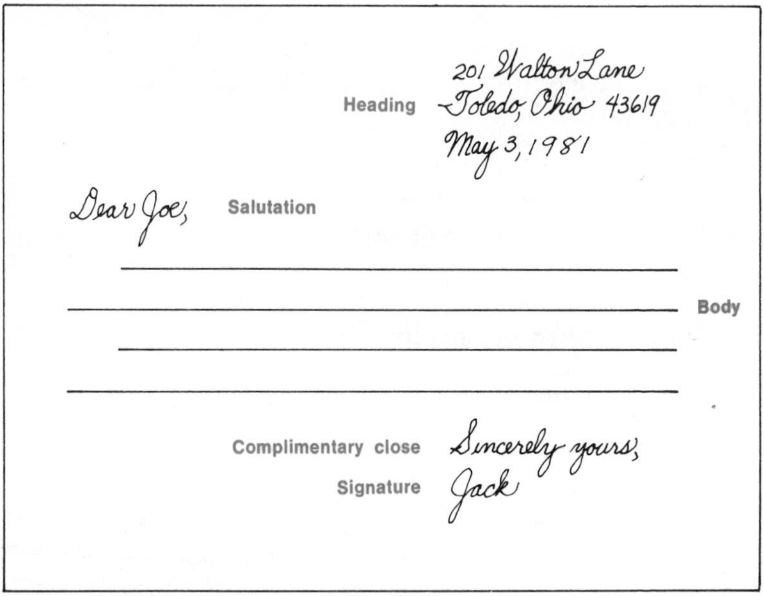

201 Walton Lane
Heading Toledo, Ohio 43619
May 3, 1981

Dear Joe, Salutation

Body

Complimentary close Sincerely yours,
Signature Jack

Style of the Friendly Letter

1. **The Heading.** The heading consists of the writer's address and the date. It is better not to use any abbreviations, but if you abbreviate one item such as Street (St.) or Avenue (Ave.), use abbreviations throughout. Always include the date.

No commas appear at the ends of lines. Commas appear only between the city and state and between the day and the year. Note that the state and ZIP code are not separated by a comma.

2. **The Salutation.** The salutation begins with the word *Dear* which is capitalized. The word *Dear* is not used with a person's last name alone. The salutation, for example, is *Dear Mr. Jones,* not *Dear Jones.*

The salutation of a friendly letter is followed by a comma.

3. **The Body.** The first paragraph begins with a paragraph indention. Each later paragraph begins with the same indention.

The left margin is even, on a vertical line below the first letter of *Dear—*. The right margin should be kept as even as possible. It is better to let a line run short than to hyphenate a word at the end of a line.

4. **The Close.** The close of a friendly letter varies with the situation. The only inappropriate close is *Very truly yours*, which is suitable only in business letters. The close may be *Yours, Love, With love, Sincerely, Cordially, Affectionately*, etc.

The first letter of the first word in the close is capitalized. No other capitals are used. The close is followed by a comma.

The Envelope

The picture of the envelope follows that of the letter itself. If the letter uses the indented style, for example, the envelope uses it, too. The writer's address is placed in the upper left corner as a convenience to postal authorities.

Indented Style

James L. Cawder
1421 Northwood Drive
Pleasantville, New York 10570

Ms. Anne Byers
1401 Seminole Road
Wilmette, Illinois 60091

17.2 The Business Letter

The Picture of the Business Letter

Block Form

Heading
6 Evergreen Terrace
Maplewood, New Jersey 07040
February 6, 1981

Costa Brothers
142 Millburn Avenue
Camden, New Jersey 08107
Inside address

Dear Sir or Madam: Salutation

Body

Complimentary close Sincerely yours,

Signature Kelly O'Shea

Modified Block Form

6 Evergreen Terrace
Heading Maplewood, New Jersey 07040
February 6, 1981

Costa Brothers
142 Millburn Avenue Inside address
Camden, New Jersey 08107

Dear Sir or Madam: Salutation

Body

Complimentary close

Signature

The business letter is generally used to receive or impart specific information. There are three basic types of business letters: the letter of request, the order letter, and the letter of complaint or adjustment.

A good business letter requires a different kind of writing and a different form from the friendly letter. The business letter is usually typed and always concise. The information it contains can then be understood quickly and easily. Handwritten letters are acceptable, but they too should be neat and to the point.

In both typed and handwritten business letters, it is desirable to keep the right margin even. The left margin must also be kept even. In both forms of business letters, a full line space is left between paragraphs.

1. **The Heading.** The heading of a business letter follows the form of that in the friendly letter except that it is always in block form without indented lines. The letterheads of business firms always have the address printed on them. The heading, then, consists only of the date.

2. **The Inside Address.** The inside address is the address of the person or organization to whom the letter is written. If the writer wants the letter to go to a particular person in the organization, this should be indicated. The writer may use either of two forms:

Ms. J. B. Bennett, Vice-President
The Powers Company
421 Main Street
Madison, Wisconsin 53703

The Powers Company
421 Main Street
Madison, Wisconsin 53703
Attention: Ms. J. B. Bennett,
Vice-President

3. **The Salutation.** The salutation of a letter addressed to a business firm or to an organization is *Dear Sir or Madam*. The salutation of a letter addressed to an individual is *Dear* —. If the writer knows intimately the person to whom he or she is writing, the writer may use that person's first name: *Dear Henry*.

The salutation of a business letter is always followed by a colon.

4. **The Close.** The close of a business letter is usually one of the following:

Very truly yours,	Yours truly,
Yours very truly,	Sincerely yours,
Yours sincerely,	

Only the first letter of the first word in the close is capitalized. The close is followed by a comma.

5. **The Signature.** In all typed business letters, the writer's name is typed below the close. The writer then signs his or her name above the typed name. The reason for typing the name is that many signatures are difficult to read.

The Envelope

Ms. Jane Allen
9 Satter Road
Red Oak, Iowa 51566

Payne and Company
1402 Massachusetts Avenue
Boston, Massachusetts 02138

Attention:
Personnel Manager

The writer's name and address appear in the upper left corner. The punctuation is the same as that of the heading. The first line of the address is placed just above the lower half of the envelope.

18.0 Good Manuscript Form

It is well established that readers will grade a paper higher if it is neat and legible than if it is messy in appearance and hard to read. Good manuscript form assures a good reading for what you have to say. Many high schools and colleges have regular forms that students are expected to follow. Others require manuscripts to follow the form described below.

18.1 Legible Writing

Few schools require that student papers be typewritten. A typed paper, however, is easier to read than one written by hand.

If a paper is written by hand, it should be written with pen, in a dark blue or black ink. An ink of any other color is not acceptable. Letters should be formed so that there is no doubt as to what they are: *a*'s and *o*'s should be distinctly different; *e*'s and *i*'s should be distinct; if *i*'s are dotted, there can be no chance of their being mistaken for *e*'s.

18.2 Margins and Spacing

Leave a margin of an inch at the top, the bottom, and the right side of each page. The left margin should be slightly wider. If a paper is typed, the left-hand margin must be carefully maintained. The right-hand margin should be approximately the same, and it should be as even as possible without an excess of hyphens to show the break in a word. It is a good rule not to permit more than two successive lines to end with a hyphen.

All typed copy should be prepared with a double space between lines. Usually five letter spaces are provided for each paragraph indentation. One space separates each word; two spaces follow the end punctuation of a sentence. If material must be deleted, it can be struck out by *x*'s or capital *M*'s.

18.3 Proper Labeling

Your teacher will give you instructions on the heading for your papers. Follow these instructions exactly. Usually, you will be expected to place your name at the upper right-hand corner of the first page. On a line below your name, you will place the name or number of the course, and on a third line, you will place the date.

Number each page beginning with page two. (Do not number the first page.) The number may be placed in the upper right-hand corner. To guard against loss or misplacement, you may place your name under the page number.

18.4 Placement of the Title

The title of a paper appears only on the first page. Place the title two lines below the last line of your heading, and center it. Allow two lines between the title and the first line of your copy.

Capitalize the first word and all important words in the title. (See Section 10.12.) If you are typing, do not capitalize every letter but only the initial letters. Do not underline the title; do not place it in quotation marks unless it is a quotation from some other source.

If a paper is longer than three or four pages, your teacher may ask you to supply a title page. This is a separate page containing the heading in the upper right-hand corner and the title centered on the page.

18.5 Preparation of Final Copy

No one can write a paper exactly as he or she wants it the first time. After you have written your first draft, read it over carefully. Revise and correct it. After you have completed your revision, make a final copy. Then read over this copy.

You may find that you have left out words, or you may find errors. You can insert words neatly by writing them above the line where they should appear and by using a caret ($\wedge$) to show their position. You can make corrections neatly by drawing a line through a word and writing the correction above it. If more than two or three corrections per page are necessary, recopy the page.

18.6 Numbers in Writing

Numbers that can be expressed in fewer than four words are usually spelled out; longer numbers are written in figures.

They made a profit of *thirty-one thousand* dollars.
The new school plant cost *two million* dollars.
Scott sold 124 boxes of candy this week.
There are only *twenty-four* seats left for tonight's show.
Ms. Blackall wrote a check for $5,450 for a new car.

A number beginning a sentence is spelled out.

Twelve students from our school won scholarships.
Forty-six students saw *Othello* at the Playhouse in the Park.

18.7 Figures in Writing

Figures are used to express dates, street and room numbers, telephone numbers, page and chapter numbers, decimals, and percentages.

President Kennedy was assassinated on November 22, 1963.
Send the letter to 5127 Banner Street, Room 492.
Joanne's new telephone number is 786–1905.
The test will cover Chapters 3 and 4, pages 27 through 68.
My temperature was only 98.1 degrees.
Only 20 percent of the students voted against the dance.

Note: Commas are used to separate the figures in sums of money or expressions of large quantities. They are not used in dates, serial numbers, page numbers, addresses, or telephone numbers:

INCORRECT: Thoreau's *Walden* was first published in 1,854.
CORRECT: Thoreau's *Walden* was first published in 1854.
CORRECT: The fare for the tour was $1,150.50.
CORRECT: The world's population increases by 100,000 a day.

Exercise: Copy these sentences, correcting any errors in the writing of figures. Four of the sentences are correct as they stand.

1. The Library of Congress has almost 400 miles of bookshelves.
2. The library contains nearly 16,000,000 books.
3. The population of Los Angeles is now over 3,000,000.
4. The cost of the house is $47,650.
5. Our telephone number here is 251–7,050.
6. The auditorium has a capacity of 700 people.
7. 5 of the students in my class want to join VISTA.
8. About sixty percent of our high school graduates go to college.
9. Over one hundred thousand people worked on the 1980 census.

10. Questionnaires were mailed to nearly 60,000 households.
11. The first census was taken in seventeen hundred and ninety.
12. My new address is three hundred twenty York Boulevard.
13. Over eight hundred people attended the lecture.
14. Helen's room number at the hospital is three twenty-eight.
15. The highest temperature ever recorded in this country is 134 degrees.

18.8 Abbreviations in Writing

Abbreviations may be used for most titles before and after proper names, for names of government agencies, and in dates.

BEFORE PROPER NAMES:	Dr., Mr., Mrs., Ms., Messrs., Rev., Hon., Gov., Capt.
AFTER PROPER NAMES:	Jr., Sr., D.D., Ph.D.
GOVERNMENT AGENCIES:	FBI, FCC, AEC
DATES AND TIME:	A.D., B.C., A.M., P.M.

There are no periods after abbreviations of government agencies.

The abbreviations of titles are acceptable only when used as part of a name. It is not acceptable to write *The secy. of the club is a dr.* The titles *Honorable* and *Reverend* are not abbreviated when preceded by *the: The Honorable John Ross.* They appear with the person's full name, not just the last name. Abbreviations are not appropriate for the President and Vice-President of the United States.

In ordinary writing, abbreviations are not acceptable for names of countries and states, months and days of the week, nor for words that are part of addresses or firm names.

UNACCEPTABLE: A new cultural center was built in N.Y.
BETTER: A new cultural center was built in New York.

UNACCEPTABLE: Forty-six thousand U.S. troops died in battle in Vietnam.
BETTER: Forty-six thousand United States troops died in battle in Vietnam.

UNACCEPTABLE: Bart works for the Spalding Adv. Co.
BETTER: Bart works for the Spalding Advertising Company.

UNACCEPTABLE: School will reopen on Mon., Sept. 3.
BETTER: School will reopen on Monday, September 3.

In ordinary writing, abbreviations are not acceptable for the following: names of school courses, *page, chapter, Christmas,* and words standing for measurements such as *bu., in., hr., min., sec.*

18.9 The Hyphen

A hyphen is used at the end of a line to divide a word between syllables.

Hypnosis is increasingly being used in the medical profession to study the human mind, to reduce tension, and to increase motivation.

Note: At least two letters of the hyphenated word should appear on each line.

A hyphen is used in any compound word that requires one. A good dictionary will indicate standard hyphenation.

coat-of-arms	double-cross	make-believe
great-aunt	twelve-year-old	has-been
run-through	cross-purposes	looker-on

Although practices vary, two or more words used together as an adjective before a noun are usually hyphenated. When the same words appear after the noun, however, they often are not hyphenated.

STANDARD: *Fatuous* is a little-used word that means "foolish."
STANDARD: The word *fatuous* is little used.

seven-year term	slow-acting medicine
well-planned schedule	on-screen personality
deep-rooted fears	light-hearted song
law-abiding citizen	round-the-clock service

Compound numbers between twenty-one and ninety-nine are hyphenated. Fractions, such as *three-eighths* are hyphenated unless either the denominator or the numerator is already a hyphenated word, as in *one forty-eighth* or *twenty-one fiftieths*.

In certain cases, a hyphen is added to a word along with a prefix or suffix. *Co-chairperson* is hyphenated, for example, even though *coauthor* is not. The prefixes *all-*, *self-*, *co-*, and *ex-* often use hyphens. A hyphen is always appropriate when a proper noun takes a prefix or suffix.

self-respect	mid-Victorian	Chaplin-like
de-emphasis	all-embracing	ex-Senator
anti-Marxist	non-Italian	pre-Renaissance

Exercise: Correct the errors in manuscript form in the following sentences.

1. The Arab owned Clarke Chem. Co. is a mfr. of pharmaceutical products.
2. Ms. Hollis and ex Senator Chas. Dutton attended a convention in Evanston, Ill.
3. My appointment with Dr. Walsh is on Thurs. at 3:00 P.M.
4. The vice pres. of the club presides in the absence of the pres.
5. Mom's checking account is at the 1st Nat'l Bank.
6. Isn't your father a vice pres. of his co.?
7. My sister has to read two chaps. a wk. in her psych. course.
8. Look at the double spaced chart on the second p. of Chap. 9.
9. In Mar. of 1977 the FDA banned the use of saccharin in food and drinks.
10. Dr. Cutler said the median ht. of seventeen year old girls is about 5 ft. 4 in.
11. What day of the wk. does Xmas fall on this yr.?
12. A lt. gen. in the U.S. Army wears three silver stars.
13. Is Great aunt Sylvia treas. of the Forbes Mfg. Co.?
14. The Rev. John Barry will speak at the Norton H.S. graduation ceremony.
15. The 747 flew from Los Angeles, Cal., to New York in 5 hr. and 30 min.

18.10 Italics for Titles

The word *italics* is a printer's term. It refers to a kind of type. When a writer wants to indicate that a word is in italic type, he or she underlines it in the manuscript.

Titles of complete books and plays, of newspapers, magazines, works of art, and long musical compositions are printed in italics. The names of ships, trains, and airplanes are also printed in italics.

PRINTED FORM: The orchestra is rehearsing Handel's *Messiah*.
MANUSCRIPT FORM: The orchestra is rehearsing Handel's Messiah.

PRINTED FORM: A *Man for All Seasons* is a provocative play about St. Thomas More.
MANUSCRIPT FORM: A Man for All Seasons is a provocative play about St. Thomas More.

PRINTED FORM: Look in *The New York Times* for the President's arrival in *Air Force One*.
MANUSCRIPT FORM: Look in The New York Times for the President's arrival in Air Force One.

18.11 Italics for Foreign Words and Phrases

Many foreign words have become so widely used that they are now part of the English language: *chauffeur, cul-de-sac, entrepreneur*. These naturalized words are printed in regular type. Foreign words and phrases that have not become naturalized in our language are printed in italics: *cum laude, voilà, mirabile dictu, verboten*.

The only way to be sure whether a word or phrase of foreign origin should be printed in italics (underlined in manuscript) is to consult the dictionary.

18.12 Italics for Words, Letters, or Figures

Italics are used for words, letters, or figures referred to as such.

In printed works, words, letters, or figures referred to as such are in italics. In writing, they are underlined.

PRINTED FORM: The *to* should have been written *too*.
MANUSCRIPT FORM: The to should have been written too.

PRINTED FORM: In Australia, the long *a* is pronounced as long *i*.
MANUSCRIPT FORM: In Australia, the long a is pronounced as long i.

18.13 Italics for Emphasis

Italics (underlining) are used to give special emphasis to words or phrases.

The tendency in modern writing is to avoid the use of italics for emphasis. One reason is that italic type is considered harder to read than regular (roman) type, particularly if there is a great deal of it. Another reason is that modern writers are developing a direct, straightforward style which gives emphasis to important words without use of printing devices.

In high school writing, use italics for emphasis only to make meaning clear.

The writer *implies* a suggested meaning; the reader *infers* it.
The opposite of pure science is *not* impure science, but *applied* science.

18.14 Correction Symbols and Revision

Both in high school and in college your teacher will make marginal notes in your themes and reports before returning them to you. These notes will indicate errors or awkward passages that require rewriting. The correction of errors will make you alert to their recurrence in your later writing. Practice in rephrasing an awkward sentence will give you greater skill in turning out careful, clear writing that means what you want it to mean.

Many schools and colleges have their own system of indicating writing faults briefly. If your school has such a system of abbreviations, it will be made available to you. Your teachers may prefer to use the symbols listed below. These are symbols used by professional copyreaders who work for publishers. The manuscript bearing the marks is returned to the author, no matter how experienced or professional she or he may be, for correction and revision before the manuscript is set in type.

ab *Abbreviation.* Either the abbreviation is not appropriate or the abbreviation is wrong. Consult a dictionary.

agr *Agreement.* You have made an error in agreement of subject and verb or of pronoun and antecedent. Consult Sections 5.1 and 6.13 in your Handbook.

awk *Awkward.* The sentence is clumsy. Rewrite it.

cap *Capital letters.* You have omitted necessary capitals. Consult Section 10 in your Handbook.

cf *Comma fault.* You have joined two sentences together with a comma. Change the punctuation.

dang *Dangling construction.* You have written a verbal phrase in such a way that it does not tie up to another word in the sentence. Rewrite the sentence.

frag *Sentence fragment.* You have placed a period after a group of words that is not a sentence. Join the fragment to an existing sentence or add words to complete the thought.

ital *Italics.* You have omitted italics that are needed.

k *Awkward.* See *awk* above.

lc *Lower case*. You have mistakenly used a capital letter where a small letter is required.

ms *Manuscript form*. You have not followed the proper manuscript form. Consult Section 18 in your Handbook.

no ¶ *No paragraph*. You have started a new paragraph too soon. Join these sentences to the preceding paragraph.

¶ *Paragraph*. Begin a new paragraph at this point.

nc *Not clear*. Your meaning is not clear. Rewrite the passage to say what you mean.

om *Omission*. You have left out words that are needed for clarity or smoothness of style.

p *Punctuation*. You have made an error in punctuation. Consult Sections 11, 12, 13, or 14 in your Handbook for sentences like the one you have improperly punctuated.

ref *Reference*. There is an error or a weakness in the reference of pronoun to antecedent. Consult Section 6 in your Handbook.

rep *Repetition*. You have repeated a word too often, or you have repeated something you wrote in preceding sentences.

shift *Shift*. You have shifted point of view or tense needlessly.

sp *Spelling*. You have misspelled a word. Consult a dictionary.

t *Tense*. You have used the wrong tense form. Consult Section 8 in your Handbook.

tr *Transpose*. You have misplaced a modifier; consult Chapter 10. Or, your meaning would be clearer if a sentence or passage were placed at another point.

wd *Wrong word*. You have confused homonyms, or you have used a word that does not fit the meaning, or you have used a slang word inappropriately. Consult a dictionary or Section 9 in your Handbook.

REVIEW: GOOD MANUSCRIPT FORM Copy the following sentences, correcting errors in abbreviation, the writing of figures, and hyphenation. Use underlining to indicate italics.

1. A Concord, N. H., clockmaker invented the alarm clock in 1,787.
2. The Rialto Theater at 64 N. Ohio St. charges only $2.
3. 1 state, Wash., and 4 state capitals are named after Presidents.
4. The FBI sometimes works with Interpol, an international police organization for over 100 countries.
5. Snow capped Mount Everest is 29,028 ft. high.
6. The self important boxer lost by a K.O. in the 10th round.
7. Only twenty four people entered the contest.
8. The ex Marine single handedly fought the Portuguese man of war.
9. Prof. Hannah Gray was chosen to be the pres. of the U. of Chicago.
10. On Mon., Feb. 16, at 2:00 P. M., our class will visit the Calif. Ct. of Appeals.
11. The highest R.R. speed in the U.S. was 183.85 m. p. h.
12. Dr. Jekyll and Mr. Hyde were the creations of Robt. Louis St-evenson.
13. I think about ten percent of the clues in the book The Adventures of Sherlock Holmes are misleading.
14. The assignment is to read Ch. 2, pp. 23–38, of The Great Gatsby.
15. The story about embezzlement at Crate, Inc. is on p. 2 of The New York Times.
16. Arts magazine featured Grandma Moses, the self taught painter.
17. The Titanic hit an iceberg and sank on Apr. 14, 1912.
18. I counted four and's in that ill organized sentence.
19. Smoking in the theater is strictly verboten.
20. Blums and Co. in St. Paul, Minn., is a fine dept. store.

Acknowledgments

William Collins Publishers, Inc., for entries from *Webster's New World Dictionary of the American Language, Students Edition,* appearing on pages 2 and 3-4. Charles Scribner's Sons, for "By Morning", from *To Mix with Time* by May Swenson; copyright 1954 by May Swenson; this poem first appeared in *The New Yorker.* Charles Scribner's Sons, for "Richard Cory" from *The Children of the Night* by Edwin Arlington Robinson; copyright 1907 by Charles Scribner's Sons. Jonathan Cape, Ltd., for "The Sniper" from *Spring Sewing* by Liam O'Flaherty; copyright by Liam O'Flaherty.

Editor-in-Chief: Joseph F. Littell
Editorial Director, English Programs: Joy Littell
Managing Editor: Kathleen Laya
Assistant Editors: Bonnie Dobkin, Joseph L. Page

Cover design: Sandra Gelak
Art production and handwritten art: Kenneth Izzi
Diagrams: Amy Palmer

Correction Symbols

ab	abbreviation
agr	agreement
awk	awkward
cap	capital letters
cf	comma fault
dang	dangling construction
frag	sentence fragment
ital	italics
k	awkward
lc	lower case
ms	manuscript form
no ¶	no paragraph
¶	paragraph
nc	not clear
om	omission
p	punctuation
par	parallelism
ref	reference
rep	repetition
shift	shift
sp	spelling
t	tense
tr	transpose
wd	wrong word

For a detailed explanation of these correction symbols, see Handbook **Section 18.**

Index

82 83 / 10 9 8 7 6 5 4

Handbook

1.0 The Classification of Words 335

2.0 The Parts of a Sentence 383

3.0 Sentence and Clause 414

4.0 Complete Sentences 435

5.0 Agreement of Subject and Verb 446

6.0 Pronoun Usage 460

7.0 Adjective and Adverb Usage 483

8.0 Verb Usage 492

9.0 The Right Word 512

10.0 Capitalization 522

11.0 End Marks and Commas 535